# THE MAN FROM THE TRAIN

## THE SOLVING OF A CENTURY-OLD SERIAL KILLER MYSTERY

## BILL JAMES

and RACHEL McCARTHY JAMES

SCRIBNER

New York   London   Toronto   Sydney   New Delhi

Scribner
An Imprint of Simon & Schuster, Inc.
1230 Avenue of the Americas
New York, NY 10020

Copyright © 2017 by Bill James

First Scribner hardcover edition September 2017

SCRIBNER and design are registered trademarks of The Gale Group, Inc.,
used under license by Simon & Schuster, Inc., the publisher of this work.

For information about special discounts for bulk purchases,
please contact Simon & Schuster Special Sales at 1-866-506-1949
or business@simonandschuster.com.

The Simon & Schuster Speakers Bureau can bring authors to your live event.
For more information or to book an event, contact the Simon & Schuster Speakers
Bureau at 1-866-248-3049 or visit our website at www.simonspeakers.com.

Interior design by Kyle Kabel

Manufactured in the United States of America

1   3   5   7   9   10   8   6   4   2

Library of Congress Cataloging-in-Publication Data is available.

ISBN 978-1-4767-9625-3
ISBN 978-1-4767-9627-7 (ebook)

This book is dedicated to those who lost their lives to the violence chronicled in the following pages.

# Contents

1    Preface

3    Villisca

### SECTION I
### 1909 *to* 1912

| | | |
|---|---|---|
| CHAPTER I | 7 | The Bloody Penny |
| CHAPTER II | 16 | Logan's Turnpike |
| CHAPTER III | 22 | The Scandalous Schultzes |
| CHAPTER IV | 28 | Marshalltown |
| CHAPTER V | 39 | The New Orleans Axeman |
| CHAPTER VI | 43 | Which Is Not Really a Chapter |
| CHAPTER VII | 44 | Martin City |
| CHAPTER VIII | 56 | The Casaways |
| CHAPTER IX | 66 | Oregon |
| CHAPTER X | 81 | The Double Event |
| CHAPTER XI | 88 | Monmouth |

# CONTENTS

CHAPTER XII    93    Ellsworth

CHAPTER XIII    104    Paola

## SECTION II
### *Summer* 1912

CHAPTER XIV    121    Villisca 2

CHAPTER XV    129    Villisca 3

CHAPTER XVI    144    Villisca 4

CHAPTER XVII    166    Villisca 5

CHAPTER XVIII    182    Dynamite Pfanschmidt

## SECTION III
### 1900 *to* 1906

CHAPTER XIX    199    Stepping Backward

CHAPTER XX    208    Trenton Corners

CHAPTER XXI    217    Standing by Henry

CHAPTER XXII    230    An Uncertain Set of Names

CHAPTER XXIII    233    Just When You Thought This Story Couldn't Possibly Get Any Uglier

CHAPTER XXIV    250    Hughes

CHAPTER XXV    255    The Christmas Day Murders

CHAPTER XXVI    265    West Memphis

CHAPTER XXVII    268    Jacksonville

CHAPTER XXVIII    271    Cottonwood, Alabama

CHAPTER XXIX    276    Murder in the Cold

CHAPTER XXX    284    The Worst One Ever

CHAPTER XXXI    291    The Lyerly Family

# CONTENTS

## SECTION IV

CHAPTER XXXII    309    Hiatus

CHAPTER XXXIII    319    The Crimes of 1908

## SECTION V

CHAPTER XXXIV    333    Conversation with the Reader

CHAPTER XXXV    353    Hurley

CHAPTER XXXVI    364    Beckley and Beyond

CHAPTER XXXVII    373    The Zoos and the Hubbells

CHAPTER XXXVIII    381    Clementine Barnabet

CHAPTER XXXIX    415    Harry Ryan

CHAPTER XL    420    The First Crime

CHAPTER XLI    435    Brookfield and Villisca

CHAPTER XLII    444    Where the Evening Is Spread Out Against the Sky

CHAPTER XLIII    456    Hinterkaifeck

461    *Acknowledgments*

It is a warm night, most often on a weekend. There is a very small town with a railroad track that runs through the town, or sometimes along the edge of it. You can't get more than a few hundred feet away from the railroad track and still be in the town. He is looking for a house with no dog. He would prefer a house on the edge of town, just isolated enough to provide a little bit of cover. A big two-story house would be best, with a family of five. A barn where he can hide out from sundown until the middle of the night, but in that era, before the automobiles came, almost every house had a barn; even the houses in Chicago and Philadelphia had barns. He is looking for a house with a woodpile in the front yard, and an axe sticking up out of the woodpile.

# Preface

I have long been fascinated by the notion that knowledge can be created about the past. Dinosaurs are the easiest example. For tens of thousands of years, humans had no awareness that the world had once been inhabited by gigantic beasts. Now, we know not merely that these animals existed, but we have identified hundreds of species of them. We know what they looked like, generally, and what they ate. We know which type of dinosaur lived where, and in what era. We know what happened to them. We have not merely created this knowledge, we have disseminated it so widely across our culture that the average five-year-old now can name a dozen types of dinosaurs, and has a collection of little plastic models of them.

In my day job I am a baseball writer. We know many, many things now about the baseball players of the 1950s and 1960s, about Willie Mays and Bob Gibson and Stan Musial, that those men themselves did not know and could not possibly have known when they were playing. We have pieced together records of their careers that are far more complete than the records which were kept at the time. Modern historians know things about the Romans that the Romans themselves did not know and could not have known.

A hundred years ago and a little more, there were a series of terrible crimes that took place in the American Midwest (although it actually started in the Northeast and the South, the midwestern portion of the series is the well-known part). The most famous of these crimes are the murders in Villisca, Iowa, but it is apparent to anyone who will take the time to look that the Villisca murders were a part of a series of similar events. I was reading about that series of crimes and I had a thought. "I'll bet there were others," I thought, "that the contemporary authorities never linked to the same criminal."

With modern computers, we can search tens of thousands and hundreds of thousands of small-town newspapers, looking for reports of similar events.

And I found one.

And then I found another one, and another one, and another one. I hired my daughter as a researcher, and she started finding them. We had no idea what we were dealing with. And we never dreamed that we would actually be able to figure out who he was.

By the time he came to Villisca, The Man from the Train had been murdering randomly selected families for a decade and a half. People had been executed for his crimes; people had been lynched for his crimes; and people were rotting away in prison for his crimes.

Skeptical? Of course you're skeptical. You're either skeptical or you're stupid, and you don't look stupid. But hear me out. Have I got a story to tell you.

—Bill James

# Villisca

The Devil came to Villisca on June 9, 1912, and to this day, if you mention "Villisca" to anyone from Iowa, the first thing they will think about is the murders. It was a Sunday night, and the streetlights were out due to a dollars-and-cents dispute between the city and the power company. Without lights the overcast skies had returned Villisca to the choking blackness that was a normal part of human experience until late in the nineteenth century, but which many people now have never experienced.

There was a Children's Day service at the Presbyterian church; Josiah and Sarah Moore and their children attended and participated in the service, which Sarah had helped to organize. At the end of the service two little girls who were friends of Katherine Moore, Ina and Lena Stillinger, went home for the night with the Moore family. There were eight people that night in the Moore house: J. B. and Sarah Moore, their four children, ranging in age from five to eleven, and the two Stillinger girls.

On the morning of June 10 the house was quiet. At 7:00 a.m. a neighbor noticed that no one was stirring outside, and chores were not being done. The chickens had been left squawking in the chicken coop. She knocked on the door, but the door was locked and there was no answer. She let the chickens out of their coop and called Ross Moore, who was J. B.'s brother. Ross Moore had a key to the house. As the neighbor waited on the porch he forced open the door and went in.

Everyone in the house was dead. Eight people had been murdered with an axe inside a locked house in a small, quiet midwestern town. The Man from the Train had struck again, and vanished once more into the blackness of the night.

# SECTION I

*— 1909 to 1912 —*

# CHAPTER I

# The Bloody Penny

"Buchanan county Va., in which Hurley is located, is very sparsely settled and is very rugged," reported the *Washington Post*. "Communication by telephone and telegraph is decidedly limited and slow, making the scene of the tragedy practically inaccessible, and details of the developments exceedingly hard to secure." The first newspaper accounts of the Meadows family murders, published the day after the crime, state that "bloodhounds were rushed to the scene and in a short time they took up the trail of three supposed murderers in a cornfield which adjoined the home. There the foot prints of three men were found impressed in the soft soil. A posse of citizens, heavily armed, are following the bloodhounds, bent on lynching the murderers if they are captured." The murders occurred in a log cabin on a mountain in Virginia in a place that is about five miles east of Kentucky, about five miles west of West Virginia, and—perhaps of more relevance to our story—within a mile of the railroad.

On the night of September 21, 1909, six persons were murdered, and the cabin that had been their home was set on fire. The man of the house, George Meadows, was found outside the cabin with his skull crushed and two bullet holes in his torso, his head nearly cut off. He was found half-dressed, and with a pencil in his hand. The log cabin had belonged to his mother-in-law, Betty Justus, who was known to the community as Aunt Betty. Her body was inside the charred remains of the cabin, in yet worse condition than George's; her head was found some distance from her body. Lydia Meadows, George's wife, was also inside, also murdered with an axe or a hatchet, as were their three children, Will, Noah, and Lafayette, all less than ten years old.

The scene of the Meadows family murders was variously identified in the newspapers as Hurley, Knox, Knox Creek, and Laurel Creek; let us say that it was Hurley, Virginia, because that at least is a real place that you can find on a map. A road zigzags through the mountains just north of Hurley; the house sat along that road. Newspaper reports filed on the day of the crime say that the posse following the bloodhounds numbered three hundred men. The town's chief employer, the Ritter Lumber Mill, shut down for at least two days so that workers would be free to participate in the chase.

The bloodhounds followed a trail across the mountains for the better part of a day and for ten miles, arriving finally at the mountain cabin of Silas Blankenship. At one point the trail led to a sheer rock wall as high as a man's head, which the hounds and posse had to scramble over. At last they did indeed find three men, Blankenship and his two sons, who were digging potatoes when they heard bloodhounds baying and looked up to see a large mob of angry farmers rushing toward them. The Blankenships fled to their cabin, bolted the doors, and poked shotguns out of "loopholes" in the walls, apparently designed for exactly such a purpose. The Blankenships promised to blow the heads off of anyone who approached the cabin. It was a credible promise, and a six-hour standoff ensued.

Six murders, bloodhounds, an angry mob of hundreds of men with ropes and guns, and three men barricaded inside a cabin with shotguns. It's a hell of a scene; this occurred September 23, 1909, in the mountains near Hurley, Virginia. Many in the posse wanted to rush the cabin and set fire to it. Cooler heads prevailed. The Commonwealth's attorney, a man named Scores, hurried to the scene with a crew of special deputies, well-armed just in case there weren't enough guns already on-site. Eventually the Blankenships were promised safe passage to jail, the mob was dispersed, and the Blankenships surrendered. But the United Press reported the next morning that "the farmers of Buchanan and adjoining counties are gathering at Hurley and it is believed they will attack the jail and lynch the suspects."

The Blankenships were arrested on a charge of murder; it is a measure of how different our justice system was a hundred years ago, that three men could be charged with murder based on nothing but the baying of some bloodhounds. First reports were that blood-soaked clothing had been found at the Blankenship house. The Blankenships were men of good reputation, however, and it is fortunate that they were not hanged or set afire; it turned out they were innocent. They had an alibi for the night in question, and nothing of any substance tied them to the crime.

The governor of Virginia was Claude Swanson. On September 27, Governor Swanson offered a $250 reward for information leading to the arrest and conviction of perpetrators. A process was also established by which citizens could "subscribe," intended to raise another $2,000 to $5,000 in order to pay for detectives to find the murderers. Before the reward was offered, however, the man who would eventually be convicted of the crime was already under arrest in West Virginia.

Howard Little was ironically named. At the time of his execution the newspapers referred to him as a "handsome giant," and a photo of him in custody, guarded by six armed men, shows a powerfully built man a head taller than anyone else in the photo. He was not an inconsiderable man. In his youth he had worked as a United States Marshal in Kentucky or perhaps as an assistant to one, and, after moving to Virginia, had been made foreman of a large lumber company. He was intelligent, assertive, and he worked hard. He was also a lothario—a Don Juan, as the papers said at the time.

Married with four children, Little had made plans to leave his wife. He had been carrying on with a married woman, a Mrs. Mary Stacy; Little and Stacy were making arrangements to skip town together, although it is anyone's guess whether Little actually intended to follow through on this.

Local authorities turned immediately to private detectives for help in the investigation, which was standard practice at the time. The detective agency brought into the case was the Baldwin-Felts Agency in Bluefield, West Virginia—a substantial and professional agency. In this era, good private detective agencies had resources to investigate a crime that vastly exceeded the resources of small-town sheriffs—and, in many cases, exceeded the resources even of the biggest and best metropolitan police agencies. One of those resources was that they maintained good records of known criminals living in the area.

Howard Little had once been convicted of murder in Kentucky—a fact not known to the community in which he lived, but included in the files of the private detectives—so he was immediately of interest to the Baldwin agency. He was, of course, hardly the only known criminal living in the area, but there were other facts against him. On Thursday morning after the murders on Tuesday night, an agent from the company dropped by the Little home for a conversation. The conversation did not go well. Little had spent most of the evening in question away from his home, returning home long after midnight, his jacket wet and carrying a lantern of unknown provenance. He had a cut on his leg. He had no alibi that he could share, and his wife was not supportive. He had recently borrowed a revolver from a friend.

In June 1892, while working as a US Marshal, Little had murdered a man named Jacob Kinney (name also reported as George McKinney) in Pike County, Kentucky, which is just across the border from Hurley. Little and Kinney had been rivals for the affection of a young woman. Little was thirty-eight years old at the time of his death, which would mean that he was twenty years old at the time of the earlier murder. He was convicted of that crime and sentenced to a life term in prison, but had been pardoned by the governor of Kentucky after serving four years.

Little was arrested by six men led by Lee Felts, a brother of the named partner in the Baldwin-Felts Agency; he was arrested in Bull Creek, West Virginia, on September 24. (Lee Felts and a third brother, Albert Felts, were among those killed in the Matewan Massacre in 1920.) Little was held for a week in Welch, West Virginia, thirty-seven miles east of Hurley, his arrest kept quiet for five days to circumvent another lynch mob and also, probably, to allow the reward fund time to build up, so that the Baldwin-Felts Agency would make more money when they stepped forward to claim the reward. Felts told reporters on October 1 that "he believes that Little committed the crime single-handed," although up until—and after—the arrest was made the theory of the investigators was that the crime had been committed by a gang of three robbers. Two friends of Little, named by the newspapers, were investigated for a connection with the crime, but had solid alibis.

Meadows had been buried with two bullets in his body. Detective Felts now ordered that the body be exhumed and the bullets removed. On October 2 investigators dug up the body and removed the bullets, and announced immediately that the bullets fit the revolver that Little had borrowed. There were no ballistics in 1909; what was meant by the statement that the bullets "fit" the revolver was that they were of the right size, the right weight and caliber, that they could have been fired from that pistol, which was a .32 caliber pistol.

Little was moved to a jail in Grundy, Virginia, sixteen miles south of Hurley, and then, fearing another effort to lynch him, to a jail in Lebanon, Virginia, about fifty-five miles to the south of Hurley. Between Grundy and Lebanon is the small town of Honaker, Virginia. Getting word that the prisoner was to be moved, a mob of 75 to 100 armed men gathered in Honaker, planning to intercept the police officers as they came through. The mob cut all the telephone wires between Grundy and Lebanon, to prevent word getting out of their plans, but police officers sniffed out the effort, moving the prisoner thirty miles through the mountains with the aid of horses and mules.

Mrs. Little had told police that she could show them where her husband had hidden the money from the robbery. She was unable to deliver on this promise. The money was never found, and, in fact, there is no real evidence that any money was ever taken.

A lawyer named Bert T. Wilson was retained to defend Little. In prison Little lost weight, a lot of weight in a little time, and spent his hours reading the Bible. Troops were provided for Little's protection before and during the trial. The first witness was Senate Justus, an adult son of the murdered Betty Justus. Justus had worked with Little at the Ritter Lumber Company; Little was his foreman. Justus claimed that Little had asked him "frequently" how much money his mother carried around with her. Another witness—not identified by name in the reports of the trial—said that Little had said to him that she shouldn't keep money around like that, because it would be an easy matter for someone to rob her, murder the family, and set fire to the house.

Mary Stacy, the woman with whom Little had been planning to leave town, testified that Little gave her $20 on the day before the murders in order to buy clothes to get ready for the trip, and had told her that they would be ready to go as soon as he was able to get some money out of his bank.

The most important witness of the trial was a woman named Mary Lee. Mary Lee, for reasons unknown, lived with the Little family; she may have been a governess or housekeeper, or she may have been a relative. The common understanding of the law at that time was that a wife could not testify against her husband, and Mrs. Little did not testify. Miss Lee became the most important witness because she could testify to what the wife could not.

Mary Lee testified that Little had been absent from the home on the night of the murders. A lamp was left burning; she awoke several times during the night, and the lamp was still burning (the implication being that, had Little come home and gone to bed, he would have put out the lamp). She arose about 6:00 the next morning to find Little asleep on a couch. There was a lantern on a table that did not belong to the family, and his jacket was hanging up wet, as if it had been washed. After breakfast he took out a file and began to file on the lantern. She asked him why he was doing that, but he offered no explanation. He went out to work near the house, cutting some brush, and took the lantern with him. After a couple of hours he came back in and asked for some bandages, saying that he had cut his leg. The wound appeared to be dry.

Mary Lee also testified that after the murders Little appeared restless. He would wake up in the night, she said, and he and his wife would have long conversations in their bedroom in the middle of the night.

The lantern became critical. Police found the lantern in a barn outside the Littles' house, either hidden there or simply hung up where a lantern normally hung; in any case the police insisted that it had been hidden. A long string of witnesses, twenty or more, appeared in court to testify that the lantern had belonged to a neighbor of the Meadows family, had been borrowed by George Meadows, and had been in the possession of George Meadows prior to the night of the crime. Witnesses bounced in and out of the witness box quickly, as was common in trials at that time, perhaps fifty witnesses in a day. Reporters didn't get all of their names.

The railroad line that runs through Hurley was the N & W railroad, the Norfolk and Western. On the morning after the murders, Little allegedly bought a newspaper from an N & W news agent named French, and paid for the newspaper with a bloody penny. French saved the penny, and introduced it into evidence at the trial. This apparently had a huge impact, and was said by some newspapers to be the strongest evidence against Little (although the *New York Times* reported, more sensibly, that the critical witness against Little was Mary Lee).

Little insisted that he was innocent, but did not take the stand and did not put on an affirmative defense. His attorney attempted to tear down the prosecution's case by cross-examination. Little offered no explanation for where he was on the night in question. There were two days of testimony, and on the morning of the third day, November 27, Little was convicted of six murders. The jury deliberated for twenty minutes.

He was sentenced immediately, and taken to Richmond under heavy guard directly after sentencing. He was to be executed in Richmond on January 7, 1910. The *New York Times* reported, after the trial, that "the crime for which Little was convicted was a particularly atrocious one. The only motive which can now be conceived by the authorities is that of robbery. They believe Little sought to obtain the money which he thought was in the house, amounting to $1,300, and that murder and arson followed, but since the crime was committed none of the money has been found."

On Christmas Eve, 1909, Samuel Baker, who was George Meadows's neighbor and brother-in-law, was murdered in what is usually described as an unrelated incident. Baker's wife was also wounded in that attack. The murderer of Samuel Baker was strung up by a hundred armed men, and his body, hanging from a steam pipe in the Ritter Lumber Mill, was riddled with bullets. That crime wasn't entirely unrelated; Harry Pennington, the man who was lynched for killing Samuel Baker, was a good friend of Howard Little and had vigorously defended him in arguments about his guilt. He attacked the Bakers because (a) he was drunk, and (b) he blamed them for the prosecution of Howard Little.

The governor expressed deep regret about the lynching, all the more so because it was the first lynching in the state in 1909. Virginia had been the only southern state (up to that point) that had not recorded a lynching in 1909, and the governor had been hoping to get them through the year with a clean record. Little was granted a one-month reprieve by Governor Swanson while his case was appealed. Higher courts affirmed the verdict, and Little was executed in the electric chair in Richmond on February 11, 1910. He went to his death calmly, composed and dignified. He denied any involvement in the Meadows murders until the last moment of his life. He was buried in his family cemetery in McDowell County, West Virginia.

\* \* \*

The puzzle of this crime is that George Meadows was both shot and bludgeoned in his front yard. This doesn't seem to make sense. The other members of the family were murdered in their beds. If Meadows was shot twice *before* the rest of the family was murdered, why didn't they wake up? Somebody hears a noise outside, the father steps out (half-dressed) to investigate the intruder, there are two gunshots, and the rest of the family goes back to bed? Doesn't make sense—yet obviously Meadows must have been attacked before the rest of the family was. I'll try to explain it when we discuss this crime again later in the book.

\* \* \*

I believe Howard Little to have been an innocent man, although I can't explain to you *now* why I believe that. Much later in our book, in chapter XXXV, we will return to the Meadows family murders; by then you will have a great deal of background information that you do not have now. When we return to the story I will explain what I believe happened and why I believe that, and you can decide then whether you agree or disagree. Perhaps, until then, you will be kind enough to suspend judgment? Appreciate it.

# CHAPTER II

# Logan's Turnpike

The Hood family was one of the most respectable of the community, and belonged to that class of our citizens who give offense to no one. That murder was committed seems hardly possible, as they had no enemies and kept no valuables in the home that would tempt the robber.

—*Raleigh Register*, November 4, 1909

In retrospect, it seems strange that the Hurley and Logan's Turnpike murders were not connected at the time. From Hurley, Virginia, to Beckley, West Virginia, is eighty-two miles, a little bit less as the crow flies, but you can't get there as the crow flies unless you are a crow. Even with the wrinkles dictated by the terrain it is less than the distance from Sacramento to San Francisco, less than the distance from Philadelphia to New York. Perhaps this describes the relationship between the two and the nature of the time and place: that if you lived in Hurley or Beckley in 1909 and you went to a bigger town to shop for something special, it is likely (in either case) that the bigger town would be Bluefield, West Virginia. Bluefield at that time had a population of about 11,000, hardly a metropolis, but was bigger than any other city in the area.

West Virginia in the fall is something to see. The mountains still beat back development in concert with generations of poverty, roads underlining its tree-stuffed beauty rather than despoiling it. Beckley, West Virginia, looks like it was built in the late 1980s, which makes it seem new and shiny compared to the prewar structures falling down in surrounding towns.

The murders of the Hood family took place on Halloween night, 1909, a month and ten days after the murders of the Meadows family. The Hoods lived on Logan's Turnpike, which adjoins Harper Road about four miles west of Beckley. Harper Road was a well-used road then and is a major highway now. Train tracks litter the area. Two tracks run parallel to Harper, overrun with trees and weeds, behind a Dollar General, the most recently built structure in town. Less than half a mile from there is what remains of Logan's Turnpike, a curving pathway with just Coal Marsh Missionary Church and falling-down homes. Chickens scratch boastfully in the road. The dilapidated homes actually add to the beauty of the area, the light and the weeds poking through the structures in a kind of evolution. Trains and their ghosts are everywhere, and you can look down on them in the valley below Logan's Turnpike.

A 1909 report from the *Bluefield Telegraph* describes the neighborhood of the Hood family as "an enlightened section of West Virginia." One of the first schools for black children in West Virginia was built in Beckley in 1907, and the area had a sizeable African American population. The Logan's Turnpike neighborhood was occupied by three black families and the Hoods, who were white and lived above a black-owned restaurant. A little way down the road was Glen Daniel, then called Marshes, which was a largely black neighborhood. By all accounts, the Hoods were on good terms with their neighbors. George Washington Hood was a widowed octogenarian and a former Union soldier. Originally from North Carolina, he had lived on Logan's Turnpike on and off since the war. In 1909, he was living modestly with two sons, Roy and Winfield, his daughter Almeda, and Almeda's twelve-year-old daughter, Emma.

Emma was without a known father, as Almeda had never been married. The mother and daughter had recently accepted Jesus at a church revival, and they were baptized on the morning of October 31 at Mount Tabor Baptist Church in Beckley, a few miles away. It was Sunday; the murders occurred on a Sunday night. Roy had attended church with them, to see them baptized. The other brother, Winfield, was out that night visiting some neighboring ladies. The father, George, was reportedly in the restaurant below the home in the early evening, showing off some of the money he had made on the recent sale of horses, but this is merely a "report." It is something somebody said.

Despite being a single mother nearing forty, Almeda had romantic prospects. Her suitor, a coal miner by the name of Mike Ferrell, came by the house the previous evening and stayed until early in the morning. They were supposed to be married in December of that year. Some reports claimed that George Hood had thrown him out that night, that the younger man was drunk, and that they had exchanged words. Ferrell reportedly told Almeda that he would be at the baptism on Sunday if he could find a clean shirt, but he didn't show.

About 11:00 p.m., Winfield Hood and Walter Harper returned to the Hood residence after their dates. They found the house, including the restaurant on the ground floor, fully engulfed in flames. They rushed the doors, trying to break in, but were pushed back by the flames, standing helpless as the roof collapsed and the house burned with no sign of the people inside. Passersby stopped and people drifted in until the crowd numbered in the hundreds. There were no screams. Everyone inside was already dead.

When the fire died down Monday morning, the bodies of the younger members of the family were found in the place where the parlor would have been. Roy had a bullet in his head, but how Almeda and her daughter had died was less obvious; their heads and bodies both had mostly disintegrated. Their remains seemed to have been "stacked" in a pile, as was done in other cases in this series. The Civil War veteran was found in the back room, his head crushed by a blunt instrument. The *Washington Post* reported more extensive axe wounds to Roy and Almeda's bodies, and that "there seems little doubt, though, that Washington Hood's throat had been cut before the fire was started."

There was an odor of oil or gasoline. Some would later offer the explanation that Almeda and Emma had left a lamp burning for Winfield, forgot about it, and the lamp exploded and blocked their exit. Others thought that the culprit had poured oil on the bodies, to speed the fire.

Several people were accused immediately. Mike Ferrell, Almeda's lover, was arrested with three other men in an abandoned railroad lumber yard about eight miles north of Harper, along the railroad and near to where he worked. The four men were separated and sent to different jails in Bluefield and Beckley to avoid mob violence. The men were made to "submit to a rigid examination" and given a "sweating" by the police (you've got to love those 1909 euphemisms for police brutality). They gave alibis; the alibis checked out, and the four men were eventually released.

We are running out of real facts here; that is, we are running out of facts about the murders themselves. There are many facts about the investigation. Whenever there is a tragedy of this nature, people will tell fill-in-the-gap stories to create a narrative. Once these pieces get printed in the newspaper (1909) or circulated by social media (twenty-first century) it becomes difficult to tell the story without them, even though these "gap stories" are generally untrue. We have seen three of them already in this case—the story that George Hood was flashing money on the evening of the murders, the story of the quarrel between George Hood and Mike Ferrell, and the speculation about the lamp exploding. All of these stories are probably false, but we cannot be 100 percent certain that they are false, so we have to include them in our account, just in case.

In the modern world there is a fairly sharp delineation between objective realists and those who believe in paranormal phenomena. Paranormal phenomena are commonly seen in movies, novels, and books, including books framed as nonfiction, and are a major element of cable television. Studies show or claim to show that *most* Americans in the early twenty-first century believe in ghosts, and many believe in psychics, witchcraft, mental telepathy, and other paranormal phenomena—but paranormal beliefs are strictly and almost universally banned from police investigations, courts, and prosecutions, as well as from medicine, engineering, the sciences, and from almost all of the ordinary and mundane practices of well-educated people such as accounting and finance.

In 1909 this was not true. In 1909 discussions of paranormal phenomena intruded casually into serious matters such as police investigations. In a tiny town 120 miles northwest of Beckley lived an invalid, Elizabeth Blake, an impoverished woman who had somehow acquired a national reputation as a psychic. Within a few weeks conventional leads ran out and the investigation began to revolve around meetings between detectives and Mrs. Blake. Mrs. Blake evoked the ghost of the late George Hood. The ghost of George Hood revealed that the murders had been committed by a white man in a mask and three black men. When asked for their names, the spirit of the late Mr. Hood became uncommunicative.

As was true in the Meadows case, the murders of the Hood family were followed quickly by another murder in close proximity; in fact, the "other murder" in Beckley happened three days before the one-off murder in Hurley. A black businessman named A. R. Blakey was murdered and robbed of several gold coins in Beckley on December 21, 1909, murdered by a man named Luther Sherman. Sherman was put on trial and convicted of the murder in a well-publicized trial. In the summer of 1910 Sherman, teasing investigators, would lead them to believe that he had participated not only in the Hood family murders, but also in the murder of the Meadows family. In fact, he was not connected to either the Hood or Meadows murders.

The murder of the Hood family was never solved. It is likely that had Howard Little not been quickly arrested after the murders of the Meadows family, the Hood and Meadows crimes would have been connected by the press and public; likely, but not certain. It is likely that they would have been connected because both little towns were in the orbit of Bluefield, West Virginia, and the similarity of the murders, combined with the extreme rarity of a murder of this type, should have been enough to make people connect the dots. This is not certain, however, because the people of that time and place may not have had any concept of how unusual it is for an entire family to be murdered with an axe by unknown persons in the middle of the night, and consequently, not realizing that such events are extremely rare, may not have seen the connection between the two. There was no similar crime anywhere in the United States in 1909, other than these two, which were separated by only a few miles and only a few weeks. But detectives based in Bluefield were heavily invested in the proposition that Howard Little had murdered the Meadows family, and they would have shot down quickly and emphatically anyone who had suggested a link between the crimes.

# CHAPTER III

# The Scandalous Schultzes

Houston Heights, Texas, founded by Oscar Martin Carter in 1891, was the first planned community in Texas. In 1910 it was separated from Houston by about a mile, but linked by streetcars and railroads. Houston at that time was a city of 78,000. Houston Heights was annexed by Houston in 1918.

On the night of Friday, March 11, 1910, Gus Schultz, a lineman with Houston Electric, hosted a "sort of entertainment" for family and friends with his wife, Alice, at their home at 732 Ashland Street in Houston Heights. The Schultzes lived in an unpainted three-room cottage fifty feet from the Missouri-Kansas-Texas railroad. (The KATY railroad; we will see the KATY several more times in our book.) There was beer, piano, guitar, and good company. The couple partied pretty hard considering they had two young children, a three-year-old girl named Bessie and a six-month-old who may have been a boy and who may have been named Sandy, although accounts are not consistent. The house was in a segregated white area, one block over from the black part of the neighborhood.

Gus Schultz was twenty-three; Alice was twenty-one. At the party she wore a tight-fitting, low-cut pink dress that showed several inches of her legs—provocative in that era, when dresses normally covered the tops of the shoes. For several days following March 11 there was no sign of life around the Schultz house. The house was locked up tight, and all of the curtains had been drawn. An African American woman named Maggie Nelson did the Schultzes' laundry. On Wednesday, March 16, Ms. Nelson found the laundry from the previous week still hanging on the clothesline, the house still locked, and the Schultzes' guns visible underneath their house. Ms. Nelson talked to a neighbor lady, who had also been concerned about the family, and the neighbor lady called the sheriff. The sheriff pulled the guns out from under the house (two rusty rifles and a shotgun) and recognized the smell of death emanating from the residence. Late in the day on March 16, police broke into the house, where they found the bodies of five people—two men, a woman, and the two small children. All five had apparently been murdered with an axe. The bodies had been piled on top of one another, and Mrs. Schultz (Alice) was found nude except for a thin nightshirt. The little girl, Bessie, was also found almost nude. There was blood all over the walls. The crime scene was described as "the most gruesome of all the tragedies that have occurred in and about Houston." The stench in the house was so overpowering that police had to open the windows for several hours before they could begin the investigation. A swarm of flies filled the room where the bodies were found.

The first thought was that Schultz had found his wife with another man, had murdered the two of them, then killed the children and taken his own life. This theory was abandoned when it was discovered that Schultz had been hit in the back of the head with an axe or some other blunt instrument, and also that his body was on the bottom of the body pile, suggesting that he may have been the first to die.

The extra dead man in the house was Walter Eichman, who had been living with the Schultz family and . . . well, we have to get to it sometime . . . was apparently enjoying intimate relations with Alice Schultz. Eichman was not her only lover, nor even her favorite.

Whether their relationship is more accurately described as "open marriage" or "sex work" is not entirely clear, but men who were not her husband often gave Mrs. Schultz expensive gifts.

Alexander Horton Sheffield was one of those men. He signed his name "A. H." and went by the name of Sandy, the same name as the Schultz's baby. Sheffield, although he was a married man with two children, had lived in the Schultz house until Eichman moved in. Sheffield was tall, handsome, and came from a family with money. Shopping recently for jewelry, Alice Schultz had volunteered to the jeweler that Sheffield was the only man she had ever loved, or ever would. Eichman—also married—was the brother-in-law of the man who actually owned the house. While Sheffield lived there they had told neighbors that he was Mrs. Schultz's stepbrother, although this was not true. A previous landlady had evicted the family because of the odd relationship between Alice and Sandy. After moving out, Sheffield had continued to visit Mrs. Schultz frequently.

About twenty-four hours after the bodies were discovered, Sheffield was arrested in connection with the crime. He would live in the shadow of the charges for more than three years, although there was never any real evidence against him. Sheffield had attended the "dance" at the Schultz house on March 11, in the company of a seventeen-year-old girl; Sheffield was twenty-seven. He had returned for a visit on the following Sunday, under somewhat odd circumstances. Passing by the Schultz house, he had seen a cow wandering loose, about to destroy the laundry hanging on the line. He knocked on the door but was unable to rouse the family, because, of course, they were all dead. He had put the cow back in the pasture, and then tried again to get someone to come to the door. That failing, he had made a curious remark to a neighbor to the effect that the family must all have gone boating and had drowned. Sheffield also told police that he had seen the three guns stacked *in* the Schultz house on Friday night, and had seen them under the house on Sunday. None of the weapons had been fired in a long time.

Sheffield, who worked as an engineer for a brewery, emphatically denied any knowledge of the crime, and gave a rational explanation for the curious remark to the neighbor. He said that he knew that the family intended to go boating on Saturday. When the family seemed to have disappeared, his only thought was that they had not returned from the boating expedition. The explanation made sense, and Sheffield was released at the time.

Eichman was found with a mosquito net covering his head, and Bessie with her head shoved down into the bedclothes. The sheriff theorized that either the murderer had spent considerable time in the house after the crime, or he had returned to the house a day later. All of the bodies had been found stacked in one room, but large pools of dried blood were found in a different room. There were no indications of a robbery. The house had not been ransacked, and no weapon was found in the house. *An axe was later found in a nearby well, with bloodstains still visible on the handle, although the axe had been sitting partially submerged in water.*

We will see this syndrome many times in this book: that the sheriff fairly quickly understood what had happened here, but then went into denial about it. Several days into the investigation, the sheriff told a reporter that the only thing he could figure was that the crime was committed by a "fiend who may have developed a homicidal mania and satisfied his lust for blood," and who had disappeared via the train track after the crime. That was, in fact, exactly what had happened: The Man from the Train was a homicidal maniac with an insatiable lust for blood, and he had hopped a freight train and skipped town four days before the crimes were discovered.

Among all of the crimes in this book, this is one of those that we are most certain was committed by The Man from the Train. There are triggers for us, beyond the obvious ones like an axe, midnight, the murder of an entire family in one event, and the extreme proximity to the railroad, things that are like flashing lights saying "this is the guy." This event has four of those markers:

1. The heads of the victims being covered with cloth or other items, both before and after the crime.

2. The house being sealed up tight, with the window shades all drawn, at the conclusion of the crime.

3. The presence of a prepubescent female, essentially nude, among the victims.

4. The bodies being moved around the house postmortem for no obvious reason.

As time passed the sheriff began to feel pressure to solve the crime, and began to rummage about for a prosecutable candidate. The sheriff was Archie Anderson. He was sheriff of Harris County for a long time, colorful, and information about him can still be found on the Web.

Some weeks after the murders a woman named Lydia Howell (name also reported as Powell) had a mental breakdown. She had been at the party the night the Schultzes were murdered and was much affected by the murders. She was convicted of lunacy and sent to an insane asylum.

Later still, a man named Frank Turney was arrested in connection with the crime; he had also been at the party. Pressured by police, Turney "confessed" to his involvement in the murders, and implicated Sheffield as well as Lydia Howell. His story was that the three of them had waited after the dance until the family fell asleep, and that Sheffield had murdered the family with a window weight while he guarded one door and Miss Howell guarded the other. Turney said that he knew nothing about the murders until after the deed was done. In July 1911, more than a year after the crime, Sheffield and Turney were indicted by a grand jury. Sheffield was released on bond in October of that year, and was scheduled to go on trial for the murders on December 4, 1911.

It appears that Turney was a vulnerable man who told police the story they wanted to hear after being pressured and perhaps beaten by the police, and also promised by the police that he would not be prosecuted. Once he was out of police custody he began to say that the story he had told police was not true. After he reneged on the account, the police attempted to prosecute him as well as Sheffield. But without Turney's story, they had no case against Sheffield *or* Turney; all the evidence they had, other than the odd relationship between Alice and Sheffield, was Turney's story, which pretty much everybody knew was a police fabrication.

In December 1911, Sheffield was free on bond, but Turney, who had accused Sheffield under a promise of immunity, remained in jail. Sheffield's trial was postponed from December until the following April, and then postponed until October. The prosecution was stalling for time, still hoping to put together a case somehow. In October 1912, Turney was released from custody, and the prosecutor acknowledged that his confession would not hold up in court. In May 1913, three years after the crime, the charges against Sheffield were quietly dismissed.

Despite his blatant infidelity, Sheffield's wife stuck with him throughout the ordeal. He returned to his employer, had another son, and lived almost sixty years after the crime, passing away in 1968. Lydia Howell regained her sanity, was released from the insane asylum in 1913, and left Houston Heights for unknown places in 1916. The house at 732 Ashland Street no longer stands, and the nearby railroad line is now a bike path.

# CHAPTER IV

# Marshalltown

The Iowa farm of James Hardy, aged sixty-four, rested in a kind of no-man's-land nearly equidistant from a ring of small towns and towns too small to quite be towns: Van Cleve, Melbourne, Baxter, Newton, Laurel, Kellogg, Luray. The farm was about four miles from the railroad—with two exceptions the farthest distance from the railroad of any crime that will be discussed in this book. The railroad angled southwest out of Marshalltown, stopped sometimes in Luray and sometimes in Melbourne, and then headed west.

On Sunday morning, June 5, 1910, James Hardy and his son went to the barn and discovered that one of their horses, a bay horse named Old Kit, had been saddled and bridled, ready for a trip, although no one in the family had done this. They were alarmed by the incident, which strongly suggested that someone had intended to steal the horse, and, at a minimum, demonstrated the presence of an intruder on the farm. They decided to sit up that night and keep a watch on the barn.

Hardy's nineteen-year-old son, Raymond Hardy, was planning to be married on the following Wednesday (June 8) to a lady named Mabel Starnes, who lived three and a half miles away. After supper on the evening of June 5, Raymond went to visit his fiancée at her home. He told her about the bridling of the horse. He was there until sometime after midnight, when he returned home, presumably on horseback.

Hardy reached his home about 1:00 a.m. He struck a match to light a lamp. In the match-lit darkness, before the lamp had ignited, he saw a large pool of blood, and discovered the body of his mother, Lavina Hardy, lying halfway on and halfway off a couch. She was fifty-seven, or not; differing ages are reported for all the members of the family. Moments later he discovered the battered body of his brother Earl, aged twenty-nine. He ran to the phone and cranked the handle vigorously, a distress signal to the neighbors who shared the party telephone line. A neighbor, C. W. Preston, was the first to respond, sometime before 1:30 a.m. By the time Preston arrived at the Hardy farm Raymond had called the county sheriff, A. A. Nicholson, who lived in Marshalltown. Sheriff Nicholson arrived at the farm about 4:00 a.m., but before he did neighbors had found the body of James Hardy in the barn, where he also had been beaten to death. A leaded gas pipe, taken from the barn, was discarded near the body of James Hardy, perhaps indicating that he had been the last to die. According to the *Cedar Rapids Gazette* (June 6, 1910), the neighbors "found the bodies cold, as though they had been dead for some time. All three had been killed with a piece of gas pipe and the brains beaten out." The gas pipe, about thirty inches long, had been sharpened on one end; it was used in the winter for prying frozen manure off the ground. The Waterloo paper says, yet more graphically, that their skulls had been beaten to a pulp; another newspaper ups the ante to "mashed" to a pulp. All of the victims had been struck from behind on the right side of their heads, near the top of the head. On the wallpaper above the couch where Mrs. Hardy died was a handprint in blood, the hand pointing toward the ground, as if the killer had braced himself against the wall while beating Mrs. Hardy to death.

Raymond Hardy was arrested and held "on suspicion that he

knows more than he has told" about the tragedy. The sheriff's first theory was that Hardy's family had objected to his marriage, but this was shown to be untrue; the two families had known one another for years, and had cooperated in planning the wedding.

"Tramps" had been seen in the neighborhood, and some people believed the murders were committed in order to facilitate a robbery. An Associated Press story dated the day the bodies were found (June 6) states frankly that "a motive for the crime is lacking."

The funerals of the Hardy family were in Marshalltown on June 8, the day that was supposed to have been Raymond's wedding day. They were buried in Colfax, Iowa—yet another of the ring of small towns that surrounds the murder site. It is about sixteen miles from the Hardy farm to Marshalltown.

Raymond Hardy was still in custody at the time of the funerals, and a newspaper reported that "he will be placed on trial tomorrow." The "trial" was actually a proceeding of a coroner's jury. Hardy was kept in custody after a search by the sheriff found bloody overalls and a bloody hat "hidden" on the property. Hardy claimed that the blood was chicken blood, but the sheriff alleged that Hardy acknowledged that he had hidden the items, supposedly from the fear that he would be accused of the crime. (A different newspaper says that the sheriff believes Hardy "made an effort to hide the overalls in the house, but was discovered and gave them up.")

The *Atlantic Evening News* (Atlantic, Iowa) wrote that "the father's body in the cow barn indicates that the murder took place early in the evening, probably about chore time." The sheriff also pointed out that the father, murdered in the barn, had not been carrying a lantern, which indicated that the murders had been committed in daylight, which had ended about 8:45 p.m. This, again according to the sheriff, identified the son as the assailant, although an equally plausible explanation is that the murderer stole the lantern to help him make his getaway. I do believe, however, that the murders may have been

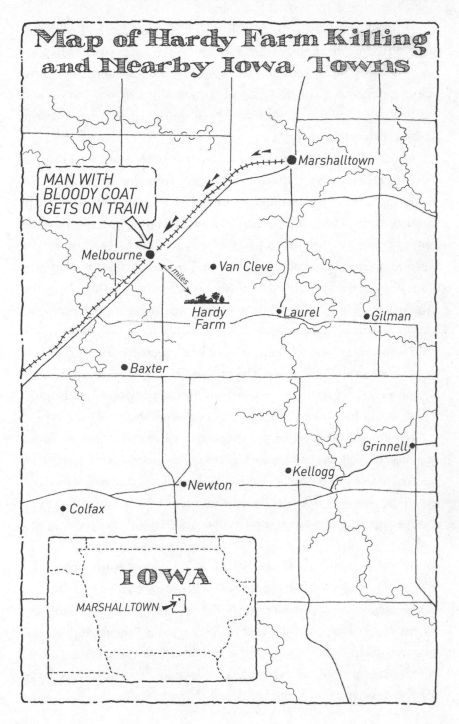

# Map of Hardy Farm Killing and Nearby Iowa Towns

MAN WITH BLOODY COAT GETS ON TRAIN

● Marshalltown

Melbourne ●

● Van Cleve

4 miles

Hardy Farm

● Laurel

● Gilman

● Baxter

Grinnell ●

● Kellogg

● Newton

● Colfax

IOWA

MARSHALLTOWN →

committed about the end of daylight. The murderer had probably been watching the family from a hiding place in an outbuilding all day, trying to puzzle out how he would be able to overpower three adult men. When the only one of those men who was strong and healthy left the farm about a half hour before sunset, he probably sprang into action at dusk.

Milk cans carried in from the barn were scattered near Earl Hardy's body, as if he had been attacked returning from the barn. The most likely scenario is that the murderer entered the house after Earl Hardy headed to the barn, and murdered Lavina Hardy in the otherwise empty house, then waited for Earl Hardy to return. After they were dead he went to the barn, and attacked the senior Hardy, who was a small man with severe arthritis in his left arm. The article in the *Atlantic Evening News*, June 7, is worth quoting at more length:

> Friends of the boy and family declare it is impossible that he could have committed the crime. The bureau drawers of the house were all opened and the contents strewn on the floor. Otherwise nothing about the house was disturbed. The bodies of the young man who was killed and the father had watches on them and money in the pockets. This was undisturbed, so that robbery apparently was not the motive. All the bodies were fully dressed and the father's body in the cow barn indicates that the murder took place early in the evening, probably about chore time.

All of the members of the family had been in poor health, other than Raymond, who was described by all who knew him as likeable and good-natured. The murders were the front-page story in the *Des Moines News* ( June 7), which described the case as "the most profound mystery in the criminal annals of the state of Iowa" and reported that hundreds of people had come to Van Cleve to view the bodies of the slain family. Also from the *Des Moines News*:

The family was respected for the love and consideration shown each other. Earl, the murdered son, was weak and not able to do heavy work, and the younger boy, always strong and rugged, did double duty on the farm to save his brother. The family were renters and had but little means, but they had portioned the hardships, share and share alike. No trouble had been heard of in the family circle at any time. None had an enemy in the community.

The theme of the impoverished family carries through the newspaper coverage of the case despite constant bubbling bits of information to suggest they were not all that poor. Raymond Hardy was arrested with $35 to $40 in his pocket, which was six weeks' wages at that time, and John Hardy apparently had more money than that in his pockets. The house in which they were murdered was decent and substantial, and they at times had hired help. The family owned at least two horses and various other livestock, and we see constant references, in accounts of the crime, to family possessions such as pistols, telephones, and carpets.

There is one mention in a newspaper of someone arrested and held in Sioux City, Iowa, in connection with the crime, and then this is never mentioned again, although it will be mentioned again later in the book. The sheriff continued to insist he had a case against Raymond Hardy, claiming inconsistent statements and that the boy had changed his story under questioning.

Such as?

How he got blood on his hat. He was wearing a grey felt hat when he visited his girlfriend. The next morning the hat had blood on it. Hardy first said that the hat must have gotten blood on it when he hung it up on the south wall of his house, but there was no peg on the south wall, so he said he had hung it on the east wall, near where his mother's body had been found. He said that it must have fallen off and gotten blood on it, but the sheriff said that the peg was a good two feet from the sofa where the blood was. Hardy finally said he didn't know how the blood got there. The county attorney thought that the inconsistent stories about the hat were critical evidence.

The sheriff now asserted that Hardy's motive for the murders was to inherit the family's property—their livestock, machinery, and household goods—and to have a place to live with his new bride.

The sheriff asserted that Hardy changed small details in his story about finding the bodies—but we will note that the sheriff himself has now changed the very essence of *his* story twice, alleging first that the murders were committed because the family opposed the marriage, then that Hardy had quarreled with his father over chores, then that he had committed the murders in an effort to inherit the family's modest possessions. And, oh yeah, what bride *doesn't* want to move into a rental house that has recently been the scene of three grisly murders?

It is immaterial how the blood got onto the hat, since: a) the blood was not on the hat at the time he had visited his girlfriend, and b) the bodies were cold by the time they were discovered. If Raymond Hardy committed the murders, he had to have committed them *before* he visited his girlfriend, not after. That would mean that, if the blood got onto the hat as he was committing the murders, it would have been there when he visited his girlfriend's family. Since the blood had to get onto the hat after the visit, it cannot be evidence about the crime.

A note was found in a drawer in Raymond's room, giving $1,000 from James Hardy to each of his two sons, Earl and Raymond. It was just a gag, said Raymond; the note was a forgery, but it was just a joke. The story about the bridled horse could not be true, said the sheriff, because he had found the bridle and saddle in the barn, covered with dust, as if they had not been moved for some time. Raymond Hardy was arrested with money in his pockets; he could not adequately explain, said the sheriff, where the money had come from. Another spoke in the wheel of evidence surrounding him was a gun. Earl Hardy's pistol had been hanging on a peg near where he was murdered. After the crime it was missing from its holster, but the gun was later found in a locked suitcase in Raymond Hardy's room. It wasn't the same gun, said Raymond. He and his brother had purchased identical pistols. This was his.

The newspapers were now certain that Raymond Hardy had murdered his family. The *Waterloo Courier* reported on June 8 that "developments since Monday . . . have strengthened, rather than weakened, the belief of Sheriff A. A. Nicholson and his officers and County Attorney J. H. Egermayer that Raymond Hardy, the youngest and only living member of the family, committed the crimes."

> Yesterday, the day before what was to have been his wedding day at Newton, Raymond submitted to a three hours' examination and grilling in his cell by County Attorney Egermayer. Under the examination which at times, Egermayer said, was as racking as could well be imagined, Raymond stood calm, and unflinching. Without, speaking figuratively, "batting an eye," and in a calm and even tone of voice he answered every question put to him. Cool and collected, without ever once losing his temper he told and retold details of the tragedy, of the Sunday it happened and of his past life and conduct. Back and forth, crossing and re-crossing and jumping here and there, first touching one detail then another, the prosecutor led him. But the lad faltered but little, although the county attorney said that in details he tripped in his story.

This, again, from the *Waterloo Courier*. On the morning of June 9, the day after the funerals, Hardy was found unconscious on the floor of his cell, bleeding heavily from the nose. It appeared that he may have broken his nose in a suicide attempt, banging his head against the walls. Hardy refused to explain what had happened to him, and the sheriff insisted there had been no suicide attempt. A paragraph quoting neighbors in support of the beleaguered boy—and containing no other information—was headlined ominously "Raymond is an enigma."

Five hundred people crowded into Melbourne to learn what they could from the inquest; teams of horses were tied up along the street in every conceivable place. Mabel Starnes, Raymond's fiancée, was the first witness. She was several years older than the accused, about twenty-four, and in fact she was pregnant, although the newspapers never alluded to this, and always referred to her, throughout the ordeal, in respectful terms. She had worked on the Hardy farm, for Mrs. Hardy, in the past. She said that the last time she had seen Mrs. Hardy, a few days before the murder, she had helped Mrs. Hardy feed the chickens, and Mrs. Hardy had told her that once they were married half of the chickens would be theirs. Mrs. Hardy had never expressed any opposition to the marriage, and did not advise them not to get married. Mabel said that Raymond Hardy seemed in every respect normal throughout the evening. Raymond Hardy was asked whether he sounded the alarm over the telephone before or after finding his brother's body. He said that he couldn't remember; the entire sequence of events was like a dream to him, and he had no firm hold on it. On June 10, 1910, the coroner's jury failed to find sufficient evidence to hold Ray Hardy, and ordered his release.

On June 11, Governor Carroll of Iowa offered a $300 reward for the apprehension and conviction of the murderer(s). A Professor Macy of Highland Park College in Des Moines (now part of Drake University) examined the bloodstained clothes to attempt to determine whether the blood was human blood or chicken blood, but he made no public statement as to his findings. The wallpaper with the handprint in blood was peeled off the wall; this also was to be submitted to experts in an effort to prove that it matched Raymond Hardy's hand. Experts concluded that there was insufficient ridge detail for the prints to be usable.

Within days after the murders, neighbors had moved in and scrubbed the crime scene clean, washing the blood off of and out of anything that could be cleaned. Two days after his release Raymond Hardy returned to the scene of the murders and, assisted by his neighbors, boxed up all of his belongings and cleared out, going to stay with relatives in Des Moines. Sheriff Nicholson was there as this was being done, and newspaper reporters.

Another small town in Marshall County is Luray, Iowa; Luray is southwest of Marshalltown, which makes it to the northeast of Melbourne, and less than five miles straight north of Van Cleve; I'm sure you have that all straight. Anyway, a man named Frank Wickersham, who lived and loved in Luray, came forward belatedly with the information that, on the morning of June 6, he was riding the train north toward Marshalltown, when two men got on the train in Melbourne. No one knew them, and they spoke to no one. One of them had a good deal of blood on his coat, and several of the other passengers remarked on it. However, since none of the passengers knew that the murders had occurred the previous evening, no effort was made to identify the man, who rode the train on north when Wickersham debarked in Luray.

By the end of June donations had increased the reward fund for the apprehension of the murderers to $885. By mid-July Raymond Hardy had moved in with the Starnes family, and was helping them tend to the crops on his old farm. Being only nineteen years of age he needed the consent of a guardian to marry Miss Starnes. A neighbor was named his legal guardian, and they were married in Newton on or about August 12, 1910. On September 12 the possessions of the Hardy family were sold at a public auction. Prices were inflated, as people turned out to bid on relics from the infamous crime. Neighbors pressed for a grand jury to investigate the murders, but officials decided that would be a waste of money, since there was no new evidence to present.

A baby boy, Otis Herbert, was born to Mabel in early October, five months after the murders. The couple moved to Minnesota, where they had two more children and raised a family. Mabel Starnes Hardy died in 1951, and Raymond Hardy passed away on May 24, 1969. The house where the murders occurred still stands, and is occupied today. The Web site "Iowa Cold Cases" has a photo of the house, dated 2012.

# CHAPTER V

# The New Orleans Axeman

The preface to the story of the New Orleans Axeman was a gruesome attack on July 8, 1908, which ended the life of a man named Alfonse Durel, who had lived on Bourbon Street. This appeared, at the time, to be an isolated albeit unusual event, and it is not mentioned in most accounts of the series of crimes by the New Orleans Axeman. As that was the preface, the first chapter, then, was the murder of August Crutti (and the attack on his wife) on August 14, 1910. We're going to skip the details because, frankly, it's not our story.

Five weeks later, whoever had attacked the Cruttis attacked another pair of Italian grocers, Joseph and Vincenta Risetto. Both survived the attack, although Joseph died a couple of years later, perhaps as a consequence of his wounds. The attacks on the Cruttis and Risettos were so obviously similar that the press immediately connected them:

> Exhibiting all the gruesome details of the crime committed at August Crutti's grocery, at Lesseps and Royal Streets, on August 14th, a bloody duplicate of that deed was uncovered yesterday morning when Joseph Risetto, an Italian grocer, was found on the floor of

his bed-room covered with blood from a wound on the face, while his wife lay mortally wounded on the bed.

—*The Daily Herald*, Gulfport, Mississippi,
September 21, 1910

We believe that Mrs. Risetto survived the attack; the newspaper jumped the gun in saying that she was mortally wounded. There were more attacks in New Orleans in 1911 and 1912, and then there was a break of several years in that series, which resumed in earnest in May of 1918, and terrified New Orleans in 1918 and 1919.

The story of the New Orleans Axeman is vastly better known than The Man from the Train; information about it appears in many different books, which some of you have read. Because of this, you may be wondering whether The Man from the Train and the New Orleans Axeman could be one and the same.

No.

Absolutely not.

The Man from the Train and the New Orleans Axeman have five things in common:

1. Both attacked people with an axe.
2. Both attacked in the middle of the night.
3. Both normally used an axe taken from the premises.
4. Both abandoned the axe at the scene of the crime.
5. Neither was primarily a thief.

However, when you look at the small details of the crimes, virtually everything is different. The Man from the Train almost always attacked within an hour of midnight. The New Orleans Axeman attacked later in the morning, 3:00 to 4:00 a.m. The Man from the Train attacked with the blunt side of the axe, almost always; the New Orleans Axeman with the sharp side of the axe. The Man from the Train used a heavy axe, like you would use to chop down a tree; the New Orleans Axeman used a smaller axe, more of a meat cleaver than an axe.

The New Orleans Axeman primarily attacked adults, and walked past children to attack adults on numerous occasions. The Man from the Train attacked everyone in the house, but had a special interest in juvenile females. The New Orleans Axeman attacked in a city, and only one city. The Man from the Train never attacked anyone in a real city, although he did commit attacks that were located on the periphery of smaller cities.

The Man from the Train either sealed the house up tight when he left, or set it afire, or both. The New Orleans Axeman did neither. Almost all of the attack sites of The Man from the Train are within a short walk of the railroad. Some of the New Orleans Axeman's attacks were close to the railroad, but most were not. August Crutti's grocery was within five feet of the railroad, or even less, but the attacker was seen leaving the scene of the crime on foot, walking away from the railroad.

The New Orleans Axeman, although he was not "really" a thief or not primarily a thief, sometimes did steal things, and usually forced victims to open the safe for him or to hand over their valuables, as if he was pretending to be a thief to confuse the police. The Man from the Train never stole anything from the scene of a murder, and is never known to have threatened to do so, which the New Orleans Axeman did repeatedly. They are simply not the same.

Another thing that distinguishes the two is that the New Orleans Axeman was an amateur. There is nothing remotely comical about either series of events, but the New Orleans Axeman was almost comically inept at committing murder, at least compared to The Man from the Train. Keven McQueen (*The Axman Came from Hell and Other Southern True Crime Stories*) says that the New Orleans Axeman attacked twenty-two people, of whom twelve survived and ten died. Every account of those crimes has a slightly different take on which crimes are part of the series and which are not; as is true in our case, it is impossible to know for certain which crimes should be included.

But by any accounting, *most* of the people who were hit in the face, the head, or the throat by the New Orleans Axeman actually survived the event, and that's not including the dozen or more people who were sleeping in an adjoining room and were not attacked. When The Man from the Train broke into your house, you were *dead*. You were *not* going to live to tell the police about it. Let us say that 55 percent of those attacked by the New Orleans Axeman and 70 to 80 percent of those who were in the home at the time of the attack survived. For The Man from the Train, the parallel percentages would be about 3 percent and 6 percent—perhaps lower than that, but not higher.

# CHAPTER VI

# Which Is Not Really a Chapter

On September 20, 1910, the family of John Zoos was murdered with an axe near Byers, Pennsylvania, a town that no longer exists. We will skip over the story entirely for now, but will tell you the story very briefly later in the book.

On November 20, 1910, the family of Oda Hubbell was murdered in their home near Barnard, Missouri. A man named Hezekiah Rasco was arrested for the crime within hours, and was executed by the state of Missouri in March 1912.

For the moment, we are treating this also as an unrelated event. There are several things about the crime that suggest the possibility that it could be a part of our series, but the best evidence is that it is not. You will be better equipped to decide what you think about that after you know more about the patterns of the crimes, so we will hold off for now and tell you about the Zoos and the Hubbells later, in chapter XXXVII.

# CHAPTER VII

# Martin City

Like Byers, Pennsylvania, Martin City, Missouri, was never exactly a town, and is no longer anything. Martin City was about where 135th Street in Kansas City is now, and right next to the Kansas state line. The Bernhardt (or Barnhardt) family lived on a farm within walking distance of Martin City, but on the Kansas side of the line, in Johnson County, Kansas, in an area that was then fifteen miles south of Kansas City, but that has since been swallowed up by urban sprawl. A rail line ran through Johnson County (and still does), coming within a half-mile of the Bernhardt farm, then dodging east a little distance and going through Martin City on the east side.

On December 10, 1910, a rural mail carrier named Gray noticed that the Bernhardt family had not picked up their mail in several days. Finding a couple of road workers repairing a culvert a half-mile up the road, Gray asked if they had heard anything of the Bernhardt family. They said they didn't know anything, but as the three men were talking another neighbor stopped to join the conversation. He said that he hadn't heard anything of the Bernhardts for several days and had been concerned about them, so the four men decided to visit the farm and check on the welfare of the family.

Dogs chained up near the barn had not been fed or watered in days, and were near death. A horse whinnied desperately inside the barn. Entering the barn, they saw the horse straining to feed from a small pile of hay just outside its reach. The pile of hay didn't look right. Approaching the hay, one of the searchers saw a dark piece of cloth. Pushing up the hay, they found what they at first assumed was the body of George Bernhardt.

Rushing to Martin City to use a telephone, they sent a message to the sheriff of Johnson County, Sheriff Stead (or Steed): "A murder has been committed on the Bernhardt farm. Come at once." Sheriff Stead borrowed an automobile from a friend and rushed immediately toward Martin City, where he found four men anxiously waiting at the end of the driveway. Walking the sheriff back to the barn, the men realized that they had been so upset that they had forgotten to tend to the desperate horse. They pushed the hay off of the dead man, and discovered with a shock that it was not Bernhardt, but someone else, someone much younger. The body of Bernhardt lay a few feet away, and near that, another pile of hay, underneath which there was another body.

The three men were George Bernhardt, forty, Tom Morgan, a seventeen-year-old who was visiting the family from his home about ten miles to the north, and a man initially identified as Glenn Cotner, a hired hand. Glenn Cotner turned out to be alive and well on a farm some distance away, but he knew who the hired man was. It was James Graves, a native of Oregon. The victims had been hit in the head with a pickaxe. In the house the searchers found the fourth body, that of seventy-five-year-old Emeline Bernhardt. She was found in a closet on the second floor. Her skull had been crushed by a clock weight, and she had died on the floor of the closet.

The Johnson County prosecutor, C. B. Little, arrived at the farm within hours. Little drove to Martin City to use a telephone, and called Kansas City police officials, asking for their help in investigating the murders.

The Bernhardts were well off; they had a nice farmhouse, and "according to neighbors, Mrs. Bernhardt always kept a large amount of money in the house." They were suspicious, distrustful people who did not associate with their neighbors. When they needed a hired hand on the farm they would contact an employment agency. The normal practice would have been to hire a neighbor, or, even more common, to trade work with the neighbors. The Bernhardts would drive up to Kansas City to an employment agency, hire a complete stranger, and then they would warn the hired man not to associate with the neighbors. The neighbors said that Mrs. Bernhardt did not trust banks, choosing to hide her money in the pan drawer at the bottom of her kitchen range. Later on it would be learned that she had more than $3,000 in banks, which was a good deal of money at that time.

The police thought immediately that they had an idea who had committed the crime. The Bernhardts had had trouble with a hired man, serious enough trouble that it had reached the point of police reports. In addition, there were bloody fingerprints on the outside of the closet where Mrs. Bernhardt had died, large prints that appeared to have been made by a man's hand. But the neighbors also told the newspapers—and presumably the police—that they had seen a strange man hanging around the Bernhardt farm for two or three days.

Edward P. Boyle, chief of detectives in Kansas City, took charge of the investigation. He was a veteran detective and a very savvy guy. Within hours, Boyle had changed the direction of the investigation. *Inside* the closet, which had recently been whitewashed, Boyle found the bloody prints from four fingers and a thumb of a man's left hand. A section of the wall was cut out and taken to Kansas City. Inspector Boyle developed a list of all of the hired men who had worked at the Bernhardt house in recent months, so that their fingerprints could be compared to those found at the scene.

The pickaxe was found in the barn, its handle covered in blood, and a button was found near the victims, a button probably from a man's shirt, while none of the dead men was missing any shirt buttons. The head of the pickaxe had apparently flown off during the last murder in the barn. A clock weight was found in the barn like the one used to murder Mrs. Bernhardt. The search of the house revealed a strong box in which the family's money and their valuable papers had been kept. The box was undisturbed.

Boyle studied the victims. The hired man and the seventeen-year-old visitor, he discovered, had been killed by a single blow to the head—but the Bernhardts had been savagely beaten, as if by someone who hated them. I was shocked to read this, in a 1910 newspaper. In a modern police investigation, if one victim of a multiple homicide bore the main brunt of the attack, the police would immediately focus on this, since it would indicate anger directed at that victim. However, I had always believed that this insight came about in the age of the profiler, mid-1970s on. But here it is, in a 1910 newspaper. Inspector Boyle states quite clearly that he now believes that revenge was the motive for the crime, not robbery, and that the reason for his belief is the level of violence directed at the two victims who lived on the farm, as opposed to those who were more transient.

A newspaper reported "it was learned that on Wednesday, the day on which the murdered persons were last seen alive, a mysterious wagon was seen at the Bernhardt farm. This wagon contained three men. That afternoon neighbors heard screaming coming from the vicinity of the farmhouse. A short time after this the wagon containing the three men was driven rapidly away from the vicinity."

The story of the three men and the wagon and the screaming never comes back up after this first telling. It appears that Inspector Boyle simply ignored this story, treating it as a part of the excited gossip that always occurs after an event of this kind. The central puzzle of the crime, however, is how one murderer was able to overcome three adult men, given that those men were presumably awake, alert, and in possession of their faculties (presumably so, since they were found in the barn, rather than in their beds). Even if the murderer had a gun, he couldn't have done that. He would have had to put down the gun to hit somebody in the head with an axe, and this certainly would have provided the other two men with the opportunity to either fight or flee. If there were three people involved in the murder, that would explain how that could happen.

John Feagle had the next farm over from the Bernhardts. They didn't get along. Feagle had caught the seventeen-year-old Tom Morgan setting traps on his property, and had run him off. Morgan said that George Bernhardt had told him it would be OK. Feagle went over to the Bernhardts and demanded to know why Bernhardt had given Morgan permission to set traps on his (Feagle's) property. Bernhardt said that he hadn't. Emeline Bernhardt came out, joined in the quarrel, and called Feagle a liar. That was the last time the Bernhardts had been seen alive.

Feagle was interviewed at length by Inspector Boyle and Kansas City Chief of Police H. T. Zimmer. Feagle told inconsistent stories, or anyway they said that he did. Feagle said that he had heard cries of distress from the Bernhardt home later that night, and had seen two hunters leaving the property. He recognized the men. On December 12, two days after the bodies were discovered, Feagle was arrested. After his arrest bloody overalls and bloody clothes were found, said the police, hidden in a closet on the second floor of his home.

If I could digress for a minute—alerting you in advance that Feagle will be cleared of the crime—note the use of the terms *hidden* or *concealed* in the above description. (Both terms were frequently used in reporting the discovery of the clothes in the closet.) Feagle and his wife and his father said that wasn't blood, that was paint; he had painted the barn red. As to the clothes being "hidden" in a second-floor closet, do you remember the lantern that was found "hidden" in Howard Little's barn? Where exactly would you expect to find soiled and useless clothing? Hanging in the entryway? Laid out on the kitchen table? Draped over the bannister? Isn't a box in a second-floor closet about where you would expect to find these things?

I am not anti-police; I am pro-police. I am all in favor of the police catching the bad guys and stringing them up by their murderous little thumbs. But I want to point out how easy it is for the police, once they decide that you committed a crime, to start shading the facts to make you look guilty. If dirty clothes are found in the laundry basket, then the accused is in the process of cleaning up the evidence; if they are in a box, they are "hidden" in the box. The accused "gave contradictory stories"; the same was said about Howard Little—as it can always be said; the police can *always* say that you gave contradictory accounts of what happened or of where you were. Learning to filter that stuff out is essential to thinking clearly about the evidence in crime stories. These claims are meaningless shadings of the truth much more often than they are valid characterizations.

Feagle was in custody for five days, which were very colorful and, were it not for the extreme gravity of the situation, almost comic. He implicated a former hired hand, Sam Dailey, in the crime. Dailey was also arrested. A coroner's jury was impaneled in Olathe, Kansas, county seat of Johnson County, on Tuesday, December 13. Feagle testified in front of the panel, as did Dailey, some of the other former hired hands, and the two men Feagle claimed to have seen hunting on Bernhardt's property. Somehow they started talking about chicken stealing. The Bernhardts had been troubled by somebody stealing their chickens, which was probably part of the reason they didn't trust their neighbors. Feagle and the hired men started going back and forth, all of them claiming to have some reason to believe that it was the other guy who had been stealing chickens. It was sort of presumed that whoever had been stealing the chickens might also have been involved in the murders. This went on for two or three days, back and forth, until the jury panel announced that they'd heard as much about the chicken stealing as they needed to hear. When you live that close to the Missouri state line, you should probably *expect* somebody to steal your chickens.

A third man, Walter Button, was arrested 150 miles away, and brought back to testify. The Bernhardts paid their hired men seventy cents a day, whereas a standard wage would have been a dollar, and they were difficult to work for. This led to rapid turnover at the hired man position. The police were trying to play the suspects off one another, figuring that one of them must have done it. If they could get them all talking, the truth would come out. Dailey claimed that he had heard Feagle threaten to kill the Bernhardts. Button told stories about a woman who claimed to be Dailey's wife. Gradually it became apparent that these guys were more blowhards than they were axe murderers.

Walter Button frankly did not like George Bernhardt, who was a hard man and given to confrontations with neighbors and hired hands, but he spoke highly of Emeline, the mother, who he said cared very much for the livestock, and always insisted that the cattle be treated well.

On December 15, Kansas governor Stubbs returned from an out-of-state trip, got off the train, and announced to the reporters who greeted him a $250 reward for the arrest of the men responsible for "one of the most horrible crimes Kansas has ever had." Dailey was released on December 16. At that time it was also announced that the police were looking for "a tramp hired hand" who had been seen in the vicinity, a man with a "bull-dog face," reportedly wearing corduroy clothes.

Feagle was formally charged with the murders on December 15 and then, on December 17, exonerated and set free. Two theories about this: (1) the authorities may finally have tested the paint on those overalls and found that it was, in fact, paint, and (2) the filing of charges may have been a last-ditch effort to sweat a confession out of him. Nothing more was ever said about the overalls; one has to assume that if it was blood, Feagle would not have been released. The fingerprints didn't fit anybody that the police could find.

"I didn't kill them," Feagle told reporters after his release. "Only my gabby, foolish talk got me into this trouble. I'm not very bright. I don't know how to look after myself and keep out of trouble." The man in the corduroy suit was now considered the chief suspect in the murders. A railroad drifter named Harry Ryan—claiming to be named Harry Ryan—was arrested in Iola, Kansas, on December 17, after walking into a poolroom and asking if they had any newspaper stories about the murders. Sheriff Stead went to Iola to question him about the case, and decided that he could not have committed the crime. The man with the corduroy suit and the bulldog face was identified and arrested; he was named Albert Allen. He acknowledged being in the vicinity of the crime on the day before the murders, acknowledged that he had been a friend of the Bernhardts, and was arrested in possession of a watch inscribed with a *B* or an *R*. He was released later in the same day, when he provided a solid alibi for the day of the crime.

After the release of Allen the crime essentially disappeared from the newspapers. On December 29, 1910, the Bernhardt farm and all of the property on it—the livestock, furnishings, farm equipment—was sold at a public auction attended by more than a thousand people. John Feagle was one of the first to arrive, and bought several items.

"With the sale," reported a wire service story, "probably what is the last chapter in the murder mystery was written, for the officers have no clew to the criminal." Eighteen days after the murders were discovered, the property was disposed of, and the press declared the investigation at a standstill and the story finished.

They were not quite correct; even years later, it would occasionally come to light that Inspector Boyle or some other officer had traveled to Illinois or California to see whether a person in custody could be connected to the Bernhardt murders. In late December of 1911 (a year after the murders), a twenty-two-year-old man named Charles K. Bowman was arrested in Indiana in connection with the crimes, and returned to Kansas City to face prosecution.

He was arrested with some fanfare. He was an unstable youth, had talked too much about the murders, and seemed to have revealed knowledge of the murders, which he said he had been given by another person, the "real" murderer. Again, the newspapers all but pronounced him guilty. He was released on February 1, 1912, when it was established that he had been in Louisiana on the day of the crime.

To a modern reader the speed at which the investigation was essentially abandoned is quite astonishing. As twenty-first-century readers of crime stories we are accustomed to narratives of detectives who stick with an investigation through years and even decades of failure and frustration before ultimately unlocking the mystery. The idea of giving up on the investigation of a spectacular crime eighteen days in seems quite bizarre.

We tend to think of the modern world as fast moving, things happen at the speed of electrons. In many ways this is true; in many ways it is untrue. I believe the owner of the Chicago Whales made the decision to build what is now Wrigley Field in January 1914 (perhaps in December 1913) and had it built by opening day. Many things happened a hundred years ago with what now seems like incredible speed.

Into the early 1950s, it was common for murder trials to be concluded within 120 days of the crime. There are numerous instances, into the early 1950s, of people who were executed within 120 days of a crime. The Constitution guarantees the right to a speedy trial. The Warren Court, as an unintended consequence of well-intentioned decisions, reduced the speed of the process of justice from 80 mph to 15. This wasn't necessarily a bad thing, nor was it necessarily a good thing. In this book we will see many examples of gross injustice resulting from the justice system moving too fast.

Lights had been seen in the Bernhardt house on Wednesday night, December 7. Boyle believed that the murders had been committed late Wednesday night or early Thursday morning. My opinion is that they were committed at dusk on Wednesday. I am guessing, right? In December lamps would be burning in the house by five o'clock. A man doing his evening chores in the barn would be carrying a lantern. My belief is that the murderer hid in the barn and found the pickaxe in the barn, where it naturally would be. One of the men, most likely the hired hand, came out to the barn to do his evening chores, milking the cows and feeding the chickens. The Man from the Train jumped out of the shadows and murdered him with the axe, then covered up his body with hay so that it could not readily be seen. After an hour or less George Bernhardt probably wondered what was taking the hired man so long to do his chores, and sent the seventeen-year-old out to check on him. The murderer waited until he had entered the barn, jumped out of the shadows, and murdered the second victim, then covered him up with hay in the same manner.

The two people in the house may have heard and seen nothing at this point, or they may have heard something and thought "What was that?" The true horror of what they were dealing with was beyond anything they could imagine. When the second man did not return from the barn, the third man—probably George Bernhardt—went out to find out what in the Sam Hill was going on out there. He probably supposed that something in the barn had broken, and they were struggling to fix it.

If the murderer had been hiding out in the barn, watching the house, he probably knew how many people were in the house. When the third man was dead he probably knew there was no one left in the house but an old woman. George Bernhardt was hacked up more than the other victims, not because the murderer especially hated him, but because the murderer had time to do that. He knew there was no fourth man coming. The murderer looked around the barn for another weapon, after the head of the axe flew off, and found a pair of old clock weights. Now certainly alarmed and terrified, Emeline Bernhardt looked out the door and saw a dark figure striding toward the house with a bludgeon in his hand. She ran desperately to the second floor and hid in a closet. A woman's gold watch was reported missing from the scene—an indicator, if true, that this was not The Man from the Train, although money and other valuables were left in plain sight. He probably took some towels to clean up with. In the middle of the night he walked back to the train line, hopped aboard a slow-moving freight train, and was hundreds of miles away before the bodies were discovered. This is my conjecture.

Of all of the crimes that will be a part of this series, this one may have had the most professional investigation. Local officials immediately sought help from experienced investigators. Boyle, Stead, and Zimmer did not waste time waiting for bloodhounds or some spurious out-of-town expert. They preserved the crime scene—which was quite often not done at all, and in other cases was poorly done. They developed a list of suspects; they interviewed those suspects in an orderly fashion. They developed leads and worked them out. They realized early in the case that they were not dealing with a robbery, unlike several of the other cases, in which officials asserted in the first hour of the investigation that they were dealing with a robbery and doggedly persisted in that belief, despite the absence of any evidence to sustain that theory.

The police had a plan as to how they were going to solve the case. They examined the crime scene in minute detail. They studied the clock weight, which was one of the murder weapons, so closely that they were able to determine that this weight had been used only to murder Emeline Bernhardt, not the other victims. No one else who investigated any of these crimes studied their crime scene as meticulously. They did accuse innocent persons of the crime, but they dropped those charges when they were unable to develop evidence. They were persistent and determined, relative to the standards of the time. The only thing was, they just didn't have anything to work with, and they ultimately failed to solve the crime.

\*    \*    \*

Postscript: On August 20, 1916, Mr. and Mrs. Henry Muller were murdered on their farm near Stillwell, Kansas. A man named Bert Dudley confessed to murdering the Mullers and was convicted of their murders on September 19, 1916. On September 21, Dudley, who had previous criminal convictions of a serious nature, was dragged from his jail cell by a mob that overpowered the sheriff and battered down three sets of steel doors, and was hanged from a telephone pole south of Olathe, Kansas. It was the first lynching in Kansas in fourteen years, and the next-to-last ever.

Stillwell, Kansas, is only seven miles from the Bernhardt farm. After Dudley murdered the Mullers, stories were published alleging: (1) Dudley had once worked as a farmhand for the Bernhardts, and (2) he had confessed to another inmate that he had murdered the Bernhardts as well as the Mullers. While we think it is unlikely that Dudley murdered the Bernhardts, the possibility cannot be ignored, based mostly on the proximity of the crimes.

# CHAPTER VIII

# The Casaways

The startling thing about the murder of the Casaway family is the almost complete absence of racism in the coverage of the story. Newspaper accounts at the time of his death say that Louis Casaway was born and raised in New Orleans—at that time the only city in America where mixed-race marriages were tolerated and not terribly uncommon—and that he was born about 1860. Census reports suggest that he may actually have been born a free black citizen about 1855 in New Bern, North Carolina, and that in 1860 he was living in New Bern with Matthew and Christiana Marshall, the former a painter. His childhood was pitched into chaos by the Civil War, and he wound up in New Orleans, then moved to San Antonio about 1876 or 1877.

Over the following thirty years he was mentioned at least a dozen different times in the local newspapers. San Antonio in the 1870s was a fairly small town (about 15,000 people), and the *San Antonio Light* was a small-town newspaper. In 1885, an L. Casaway and Charles Casaway were included in an announcement of the Eclipse Minstrels, who were "composed entirely of colored members." In 1887 he joined the "laborer's board," and in 1889 he organized a Juneteenth event commemorating the end of slavery. He was an active member of the Republican Party. He was mentioned often in that role, and in connection to his work as a porter, hall messenger, and janitor at the city hall. A front-page story in 1895 reported that he had been promoted. Later in 1895, his name was listed as part of a group thanking the mayor for taking down wanted posters of local rapists, which were creating a motive for racist violence. Three years later, his name was listed as a delegate in a wonderful report from the July 17, 1898, *San Antonio Light* on a squabble in the local Republican primary. The black caucus within the party walked out over a disagreement of some sort, but then both sides came together to record the following statement to "thunderous applause":

> Resolved: That this convention rejoice in the fact that past differences in our party have been wiped out and we agree to work for harmony and success and for the principles of our party in the future.

In addition to his professional and civic contributions, Louis also kept up a high-profile social life. His thirty-sixth birthday (he probably was actually forty-one) appeared at the top of a list of local events, recording "a stag party of his friends." In 1898, a famous Cuban War vet stayed with his good pal Louis Casaway. In 1902, Casaway was credited with expanding the gymnasium. I believe that the *Light's* editor's theory was that local people would buy the paper if their name was in the paper, so he tried to get as many local people's names in the paper as he could.

Elizabeth Casaway, born Elizabeth Castalow, was from Hallettsville, Texas, a small town a hundred miles due east of San Antonio, and incidentally the only place in the world named "Hallettsville." Born probably in 1874, she was married at about the age of fifteen to a man named Layne, who abandoned her soon after their marriage. The next year she moved to San Antonio, where she worked as a seamstress. There Louis and Elizabeth met, fell in love, and were married, which was not all that easy, considering that Louis was black and Elizabeth was white. He claimed to be thirty at the time of the marriage but was probably thirty-five; she was about sixteen. Unable to get married in Texas, they went to Mexico. According to a later article in the *Chicago Defender*, legal proceedings were begun against them based on the marriage, but a grand jury declined to indict them, and they were, in the words of the *Defender*, "allowed to go unmolested." By all accounts they had a happy marriage, and by 1911 they had three children: Josie, aged six, Louise, aged three, and Alfred Carlyle Casaway, aged five months. After the birth of Josie in 1904 Louis curtailed his political activity, and took a job as custodian at Grant school, a segregated elementary school for black children. In the 1910 census Louis is listed as "W"—white—which may indicate that he sometimes passed as white, but more probably indicates that the census taker interviewed Elizabeth, saw that she was white, and simply assumed that her husband must be white as well.

By 1911 the population of San Antonio was close to 100,000 people. Casaway had grown up with the city; he was one of the old-timers, thus known to all of the people who ran the city. The Casaways lived at 417 North Olive Street in San Antonio, which is four-tenths of a mile from the train track (three to four blocks), and seven-tenths of a mile from the train station, the depot.

Louis Casaway's sister was married to an attorney named R. A. Campbell, also black, and they lived in a house that adjoined the Casaway residence. The Campbells had a renter named Mrs. Drake, and Mrs. Drake had a son who would play with the Casaway children and often spent the night with them. On the evening of March 21, 1911, the Casaways and the Drake boy were playing around the neighborhood, but about sundown she went over to the Casaway house and brought him home, a casual decision that no doubt saved his life. As the children played around the neighborhood that night, we might speculate, a Quiet Little Man was watching them from the shadows, perhaps from a barn or a shed nearby.

On the morning of March 22 Louis Casaway did not report for work. The principal of the school, Mr. Tarver, called the Campbell house to ask if they had any idea why Casaway was not at work. Mrs. Drake answered the phone. She went next door, knocked loudly, and called to the Casaways, but received no answer. She went back and got Mrs. Campbell, Casaway's sister, and Mrs. Campbell circled the house, calling to the Casaways and knocking on the doors and windows trying to find a way in. The house was locked up tight, and no one answered. Alarmed, she went back to her house and got her husband.

R. A. Campbell, unable to enter the house by a doorway, pried off a screen and forced open a window. As he did so a pillow tumbled out. With the pillow out of the way he could see inside the house, and thus he could see the bloody bodies of Louis and Louise Casaway. He ran immediately back to his house, and called the police.

The police from two different jurisdictions (city police and the sheriff's office) rushed to the house in force; the next-day newspaper contains a long list of the names of policemen who responded to the crime scene. The Casaways were all dead. All five had been hit in the head with an axe, which was left in the house, and the walls were spattered with the blood cast off from the swinging of the axe.

The police found that the back door, the door leading off the kitchen, was unlocked; the Campbells had thought that it was locked, but it actually was not. Probably the murderer had jammed the door, wedging something into the door as it closed so that it would be difficult to open.

On the evening of March 21 it had rained hard, starting a little after eleven o'clock at night. The police found no mud or water tracked into the house, but found footprints in the mud leading away from the back door. From this they inferred that the murderer had entered the house around or before eleven o'clock, and had left the house after the rain. The first half of that assumption is not necessarily correct. He may well have entered the house *after* eleven, but not by the door. He usually crawled in a window.

The neighbors had seen and heard nothing unusual. There was, however, an unusual thing that had happened, as there always is in any well-documented murder. Louis Casaway had gone to buy a bucket of beer on the night of the murders, not long before the rain began. Casaway did not drink and did not normally purchase alcohol, and his wife did not drink. From this it was surmised that the Casaways may have been expecting a houseguest, and it was speculated that the beer may have been drugged, which would explain why they did not awaken when they were attacked.

San Antonio in 1911, I mentioned, was a city of 100,000 people. To the best of our knowledge, this is the only time that The Man from the Train committed one of his atrocities in an urban area; he killed a lot of people in towns of five or ten thousand, but never (other than this case) in a city. The railroad line, coming in from the north, just clipped the edge of town. It is our belief that the murderer did not see the city as he came into town, and just did not realize that he was in a city.

Other than that, the murder of the Casaways is a perfect compendium of the signature elements of this series. If there is one crime in this series that we can be absolutely, one thousand percent certain was committed by the same man who committed the murders in Villisca, this is the crime. Consider this paragraph, from the *San Antonio Light and Gazette*, on the day after the murders:

> That the person who committed the crime was deliberate in his fearful work of slaughter is shown by the condition of things found upon the arrival of the officers. The faces of Louis Casaway and his wife were found covered with a cloth. In the window near which

Louis Casaway lay a pillow had been placed. A pillow also was found in the window near the head of the woman and a blanket had been spread across the north window of this room. Josie Casaway was killed while lying on the bed nearest the wall of the north room, as shown by the blood at that spot. The body, however, had been picked up and afterwards thrown near the foot of the bed, the head being bent farther back than was the larger portion of the body. Other conditions found in the room indicated that the murderer was in no hurry to leave. In each killing the blunt end of the axe had been used.

The covering of the faces of the adult victims is a part of the signature of The Man from the Train. He did this in his very first murder, many years earlier, and he did it many times in his career.

The placing of cloth objects such as pillows and dresses in the windows near the victims is a part of his pattern.

The covering of a window or multiple windows with blankets is a signature element of The Man from the Train.

The moving of dead bodies is a part of his normal pattern.

The special attention to the body of the prepubescent female victim, the moving or staging of her body, is an element of his pattern that appears numerous times.

The lingering in the house after the crimes were committed is an element of his pattern.

The killing of the victims with the *blunt* side of the axe, rather than the blade of the axe, is a clear sign that it's him. Again, he did this in his first crime, and he almost always killed people with the blunt side of the axe.

The locking up of the house as he left is another element of his signature. The proximity to the train tracks, the axe, the leaving of the axe in the house, the commission of the crime late at night, probably two to three hours after the victims had gone to sleep . . .

all of this is 100 percent consistent with the pattern of his crimes, and we will see all of these elements again, and again, and again, as we go forward with this story, and then go back to look at the earlier crimes.

The phrase "other conditions found in the room indicated that the murderer was in no hurry to leave" is a euphemism, the real meaning of which, I am virtually certain, is that he masturbated over the body of Josie Casaway, perhaps repeatedly. The "other condition found in the room" was ejaculate.

"The skull of this child" reported the *Light and Gazette*, "was the only one that was not laid open"—further evidence of his special interest in that victim. "It was within two or three feet from where this child [Josie] lay that the axe was found on the floor." After killing the family, probably in a mad rush of events lasting no more than a few minutes, he walked around the house with the axe, making sure that they were dead, and that no one in the house was left alive, hiding under a bed or cowering in a closet. When he was certain that they were all dead, he put down the axe and turned his attention to Josie's body.

From the same newspaper story quoted above:

> That robbery was not the motive, the officers say, is borne out by the fact that nothing in the house was molested. Not a drawer in a bureau or wardrobe was found disturbed. The trousers of Louis Casaway were still hanging on the foot of the bed and several dollars were in the pockets. His watch was still in the vest. The most plausible information gained by the officers is that tending to the belief that revenge prompted the wholesale slaughter.

Of course, revenge was *not* the basis of the crime. Madness was the basis of the crime. They were trying to find a rational basis for a wildly irrational event. The Man from the Train killed people because he hated people, and he enjoyed hitting them in the head with an axe, and he enjoyed dragging their bodies around. It was his favorite thing to do in the whole world. Ghastly and appalling as this is, difficult as this is even to write, the fact is that he *especially* enjoyed hitting small children in the head with an axe. The police simply could not conceive of the possibility that this was what they were dealing with.

Throughout the run of terror created by this man, fifteen years or more, people would try to "normalize" his actions by assigning the crime a rational motive. In most of our cases, the compulsive need to have *an* explanation for the crime expresses itself in the assertion that the victim was in possession of a large amount of cash, even though, in almost all of those cases, there is no actual evidence that there was any money. In this case, because the victims happened to be an interracial couple in a time and place where marriages between black and white people were slightly less common than marriages between horses and butterflies, the police immediately assumed—and asserted—that they were murdered because they were an interracial couple:

> That the murder of the entire Casaway family Tuesday night was the deed of a person crazed by the problem of miscegenation, and in his hallucination wishing to wipe out the entire family, is the belief of several of the detectives who are working on the case. The fact that Casaway was a negro and his wife a white woman, they believed, preyed upon the mind of someone until the wholesale murder presented itself as the only solution.

There is no evidence for this. No one is known to have threatened them because they were a mixed-race couple. No one wrote racist slogans on the walls. The Ku Klux Klan at this time did not exist; it had gone out of business decades before, and was revived three years later in Atlanta.

Several years earlier, perhaps six years earlier, Louis Casaway had been involved in a conflict with another man, a black man, and the man had threatened his life. His feet were about the right size to fit the footprints in the mud, and so he was arrested within a day of the crime. Nothing actually tied him to the crime, however, and he was released within a few days. An elderly relative of Elizabeth, a man named William McWilliams, forced his way into the crime scene and was arrested for suspicion of involvement in the crime. He was held for some time, but it became clear that he was suffering from dementia, and he was not prosecuted.

As to the theory that the beer was drugged, which is presented in some newspaper accounts to explain the failure of the Casaways to rise and defend themselves—ridiculous. To us, looking at the case from our vantage point, it is obvious why the Casaways didn't awaken in time to save their lives. The Man from the Train, by this time, had been killing people in their sleep for more than a decade; he had done it many times. He knew what he was doing.

By far the most likely explanation for the bucket of beer is that it was simply a mistake. The saloon keeper reported that Casaway bought the bucket of beer not long before the rains began, after eleven o'clock. How likely is it that a man who does not drink, and who had to be at work at seven o'clock the next morning, would go and buy a bucket of beer at eleven o'clock at night, *even if* he was expecting a houseguest? It doesn't make sense. It never happened. Either the saloon keeper confused the date of the purchase, or—more probably—he confused Casaway with someone else.

Of course, Casaway may have drunk quite a bit more beer than his sister and brother-in-law *thought* that he did, and he may have purchased the beer and drunk some beer at some other time. I am merely arguing that he did *not* go out and purchase the beer at eleven o'clock on Tuesday night. If we believe the story of the bucket of beer, it distorts the timeline and fractures every other fact with which it comes in contact. People get very excited when an event such as this occurs in their neighborhood, and they say all sorts of things that are not true. This is simply one of those things.

Louis Casaway was a man who was respected and admired by those who knew him, and his murder made a deep impression on his community.

* * *

The 1970s serial murderer Dennis Rader, known as BTK, was sexually fascinated by a young girl, an eleven-year-old girl named Josie Otero. As in this case, he killed the entire family, and then masturbated over the body of the young girl. He had seen Josie Otero playing around the neighborhood, and became obsessed with her. Rader was to say after his capture more than thirty years later that his sexual obsession with Josie Otero launched him into the killings, even though he never again killed anyone younger than twenty-one years of age.

This is relevant to our story in this way: some of you may think that, since the villain in many of these cases was sexually fixated on young girls, those crimes that did not involve the death of a young girl must not be related to the series. But the BTK story shows that this is not always true. A serial murderer may be sexually fixated on young girls, but this obsession need not be the trigger to *all* of his crimes.

The house where the Casaways were murdered is still standing today but is unoccupied and is in such bad repair that it would appear unlikely to last much longer.

CHAPTER IX

# Oregon

In spring 1911, William Hill, thirty-two, a plumber who worked
for the Portland Natural Gas Company, bought a small house about
half a mile up the hill from the streetcar stop. . . . Here, a short
train ride from the city, where William could earn good wages,
he and his family could live the rural life that urban Americans
idolize so much.

—JD Chandler, *Murder & Mayhem in Portland, Oregon*

The first faint realization that what we now call a serial murderer
was at work came about as a result of three crimes in the Pacific
Northwest in the summer of 1911. By that time The Man from the
Train had been murdering families for thirteen years, but up until
then—setting aside two crimes in 1904 which were briefly connected
one to another but not to the series—no one had connected the dots.

On the morning of June 10, 1911, a neighbor noticed the lack
of activity around the house of William Hill. It had been eleven
weeks since the murder of the Casaways. The observant neighbor
asked his wife to go check on the family. She knocked on the door,
got no answer, and tried to look in the windows. The windows had
been covered with clothes, but through a small gap she could see

the bloody body of Dorothy Hill, aged five, laid out on the floor of the front room. She ran screaming from the scene.

Like the murder of the Casaways, although not as much so, the murder of the Hill family was a compendium of the signature elements of The Man from the Train. There were four victims. The house was near the railroad—a half mile from the streetcar line, less than a mile from the railroad itself. The murderer had picked up an axe from a neighbor's yard, where it had been left leaning against the house. The murderer had entered the house after the family was asleep and had murdered the father in his sleep; police believed he had been struck with the *handle* of the axe. His wife had apparently stirred a little bit, but had also been murdered in her bed. Clothes had been hung over the windows. Jewelry and a purse with cash were left in plain sight, although police also believed (probably incorrectly) that some jewelry may have been taken. The house was locked up tight as the murderer left.

The murders are believed to have happened about 12:45 a.m., based on:

1. A clock which was broken at that hour, and

2. The fact that a neighbor's dog launched into a prolonged fit of distressed barking at that time.

The couple's eight-year-old son had been murdered in his bed. The body of little Dorothy was laid out on the floor and was covered with bloody fingerprints. In my view, no reasonable person would doubt that this was the same man who had murdered the Casaways, the man who would go on to Colorado Springs and Villisca. The murders in Villisca occurred exactly one year after the murders of the Hill family, one year to the day.

There was a famous bloodhound up in Seattle, a bloodhound named Brady, who had caught himself a few criminals over the years. After a delay of several days Brady was brought to the scene of the crime, which was actually in Ardenwald, then an unincorporated area seven miles south of Portland. Brady was instructed to trail the murderer. I will trust you to guess how productive that was.

A month later Archie and Nettie Coble were murdered in their beds in Rainier, Washington. Rainier was at that time an unincorporated village of about a hundred people, identified in all sources as a "railroad stop." It is 112 miles due north of Portland, 35 miles south of Tacoma. Archie Coble, aged twenty-five, did not report for work on July 11, and no one was seen stirring around the Coble house.

The scene of the Coble murders seemed very similar to the house in Ardenwald, and police and quasi-policemen almost immediately drew a connection between the two. Coble and his wife had been murdered in their beds by an axe that was left in the room, but not by the blade of the axe; they were beaten either with the blunt side of the axe or with the handle of the axe.

After the accusation of several innocent parties and some interloping from amateur detectives, a man named George Wilson, a neighbor of the Cobles, confessed to murdering them, sort of. Wilson was not of sound mind (no Dennis the Menace jokes, please). His wife told authorities that she feared that he might have committed the crime. Wilson said that he had no memory of having committed the crime, but that he did believe that he had done so. After a few days he retracted this "confession"—most of us remember when we have committed a murder—and began to insist that he had nothing to do with the crime.

Wilson was put on trial in November 1911. There wasn't really any evidence against him as to the specifics of the case, but the prosecution could demonstrate that Wilson had more than the normal number of eccentricities, and . . . well, that puts a nut case in the village at the time of the murders, which is good enough for government work. Wilson was convicted of the murders.

It seems reasonably clear that the Coble murders were a part of the series. Some writers have written them out of the series because:

1. A man "confessed" to that crime and was convicted of it,

2. No children were murdered, and

3. Later accounts of this case state that an adult woman, Nettie Coble, was raped and murdered, which would be a significant departure from The Man from the Train's usual practices, were it true.

But Wilson was a weak link who was convicted of the murders because nobody had any better explanation than that the crazy guy must have done it. Nettie Coble was actually *not* raped before she was murdered, and it's not clear where modern writers have come up with the idea that she was. This is the account of the discovery of the bodies as reported in the most local newspaper, the *Centralia (Washington) Weekly Chronicle*, immediately after the crime was discovered:

> The Cobles had been married less than a year. Coble was a clerk in the Rainier Mercantile Company's store and was first missed when he did not appear for work yesterday morning. As his wife was also not seen about the house, a neighbor, Mrs. W. B. McNett, entered the place but became frightened when she found it empty. She called in an acquaintance who was passing, and re-entering the house they found Coble and his wife laying in bed with the covers drawn over their heads. They lifted the spread and were horrified to find that their heads had been horribly beaten and mutilated. The couple had evidently been dead since Monday night.
>
> A bloody double bitted axe was found under the bed. Coble's watch and valuables were untouched and nothing had been taken from the house. Coroner McClintock of Thurston County arrived in Rainier last night and took charge of the bodies. The authorities believe the outrageous double murder was committed for the purpose of revenge, but say that Coble was not known to have any enemies.

That directly contradicts on two counts the notion that Nettie Coble had been raped: (1) she was found in bed, soaked in blood, with the covers pulled up around her, and (2) local authorities believed that the crime was committed for "revenge." Covering of the heads of the victims with the blanket is a signature behavior for The Man from the Train.

Rainier, Washington, was similar to Hurley, Virginia, Barber Junction, North Carolina, Byers, Pennsylvania, and many other places where The Man from the Train committed his murders. It was also, if accidentally, similar to Scappoose, Oregon, where we will go later in this chapter. The murder house was a short walk from the train. He liked to kill people in semirural settlements too small to have a regular police presence.

The crimes in Rainier were committed thirty days and 119 miles from the murders in Ardenwald, which is a normal time-and-distance gap for The Man from the Train. We know that The Man from the Train had been in the vicinity a month earlier, because of the Hill family murders, and his next five crime scenes show him moving eastward, which presumes that he started in the West.

Authorities and amateur detectives who visited both crime scenes absolutely believed that the crimes were linked. A shoe print at each scene was measured at three and a half inches across (very small), and was believed to be the same shoe. The Cobles were murdered in their beds in the middle of the night. Valuables were left in plain sight, as The Man from the Train often left them.

It does not appear that mirrors or windows were covered with cloth in this case or that a lamp was moved, although it is not clear that these things were *not* done, either. Since Rainier was an isolated community with no local newspaper, reports from the scene are sketchy, and leave many of these details up in the air. It is clear that the Coble house was not locked up after the murders.

I am more inclined to believe that the Coble murders were committed by The Man from the Train than that they were not. However, the evidence of which I am aware is not sufficient to convince a skeptic one way or the other. The press (and the police, up to a point) *believed* that the crimes were linked, and this created a certain level of suspicion that a serial murderer was at work. This is a milestone in our story. There would be fourteen more weeks and fourteen more murders before this suspicion burst into bloom, but a seed was planted. When there were additional crimes, that seed would grow.

A month after Wilson was sent away, another woman was murdered with an axe in Rainier, a Japanese woman identified only as Mrs. Somomura. Rainier was a tiny little village; they should have had about one murder a century. I don't know what happened in that case, whether anyone was ever convicted of it. The real function of the Somomura case—clearly unconnected to The Man from the Train—is to further muddy the waters of an already murky situation.

Going back to the Hill and Coble murders, let me explain the amateur detectives. You have to understand how primitive criminal investigation was at this time. There was no FBI. Almost without exception there were no state investigative services on call as a resource for local authorities, although there were crime labs in some states. The US Marshals Service would not get involved in local crimes. Local police were largely on their own except for the resources volunteered by neighboring authorities, and 99 percent of the local police had little or no experience in dealing with a crime of this nature.

Because local police were on their own, when they were confronted with a high-profile murder case it was common practice to hire private investigators to help out. This was actually the second thing the local officials would do; the first thing they had to do was to raise money to hire a private investigator. There wasn't even an organized, regular system to fund such investigations. Local officials would try to raise funds for an investigation by:

1. Asking the victims' family for financial assistance,
2. Establishing a reward fund to which citizens could contribute,

3. Appealing to the city government for funds, and

4. Asking the state government to help out.

More or less in that order. If the family of a victim had any money, they were expected in the normal case to establish a reward fund. Sometimes the money would be used to hire investigators. In other cases private investigators would flock into the case, working on spec. If the private investigators were able to create a case against someone, they would claim the reward.

This was a dreadful system. It encouraged the framing and prosecution of innocent people. It encouraged kickbacks to elected officials, who could be bought off to make arrests and pursue prosecutions. It wasted valuable time at the start of an investigation, while resources were assembled. It left many crimes essentially uninvestigated, if no one took the initiative to organize an effort to fund a real investigation (and in particular, it left uninvestigated crimes against poor people and against minorities).

In 1911 there existed no organized system of licensing, regulating, and authorizing private investigators, except perhaps in a few larger cities. This left private citizens probing into open murder cases in significant numbers without warrants and without legal authority. Some of them were good, many of them ex-cops, but some of them were just people who had read too many Sherlock Holmes stories and appointed themselves private eyes. They would start poking around in unsolved murder cases, hoping to get the reward money or acting out fantasies of being master detectives. The cream of the crop were the Pinkerton and the Burns detective agencies, but even the Pinkerton and Burns agencies were shot through with shysters, con men, unscrupulous thugs, and rank amateurs. It was truly an awful system.

The Cathey brothers, George and Collins Cathey, were self-appointed private investigators. They seem like reputable people, identified as Dr. George Cathey and Dr. Collins Cathey. Dr. George was a blood specialist, and Dr. Collins had studied the Bertillon system, which was a failed effort to identify criminals by a detailed set of physical measurements. They were amateur detectives who became prominent in this investigation, as private investigators became prominent in many of these cases. The Cathey brothers were the first to insist that these crimes were linked.

Unfortunately, the Cathey brothers also insisted that a man named Swann Peterson had committed the crimes. Peterson was an innocent man who had been accused of involvement in the murders by George Wilson. You wouldn't think that amateur detectives with no background in criminal investigation would make a mistake like that, but somehow it happened.

After most of the murders committed by The Man from the Train, local people were accused of the crime, and there is always a story to be told there. There are always many more facts known about the prosecutions of innocent people than are known about the murders themselves. If we were to relate all of those stories in any detail, this book would go on for thousands of pages.

A man named Nathan Harvey had property that bordered the Hills' house in Ardenwald, and had been involved in a property dispute with them. On the night of the murders Harvey had arrived home late; in fact, apparently he had arrived back at his house near the time of the murder, but he did not go into his house. Not wishing to disturb his family at the late hour—OK, he was probably drunk and didn't want his wife to find out—he had slept in a shed outside his house, emerging from the shed the next morning to discover the neighborhood overrun by police.

Harvey had not lived a spotless life. There had been rumors of his involvement in violent and unsavory acts at other times. It was probably inevitable that Harvey would be charged with murdering the Hill family, and he was, on December 21, 1911.

Harvey's friends immediately went to work on his behalf. Large public meetings were held, rallying against his prosecution, and more than 500 signatures were gathered on a petition calling for his release. On December 27 the charges against Harvey were dropped and a judge ordered his release, although the sheriff, assisted by a private investigator, continued to insist that Harvey had committed the crime.

With the sheriff agitating publicly for his prosecution, the case against Harvey was presented to a grand jury in January 1912. The district attorney's last name was "Tongue," which is a wonderful name for a lawyer. District Attorney Tongue presented the evidence against Harvey to a grand jury, but ridiculed the case as he presented it, and directed the grand jury not to issue an indictment. The sheriff and the private investigator continued to harass Harvey for another month, until a judge issued a cease-and-desist order commanding them to back off.

Over the following years at least four people would confess to murdering the Hill family, including a man named Leroy Robinson, who would confess in 1931 to having murdered the Hill family, and also to having committed the murders in Villisca.

*　　*　　*

In early September 1911, there occurred another two murders in the Portland area that we will have to cover here, although in the end it is clear that they are unrelated to our main story.

A man and woman named Mr. and Mrs. Frank Wehrman lived in an isolated mountain cabin near Scappoose, Oregon; it was not near a railroad track, although the railroad does go through Scappoose. They had recently moved to Scappoose from Marshalltown, Iowa, a small town that also figures in the Hardy family murders (Chapter IV), the Bernhardt murders (Chapter VII), and the aftermath of the Villisca murders. Scappoose is just south of the Oregon-Washington border, twenty miles north of Portland. Scappoose, now a thriving Portland suburb of about seven thousand people, was at that time an isolated, unincorporated village, basically a logging camp with no more than two hundred people. According to the Oregon Supreme Court, "(t)heir little cabin was situated in a lonely place in the mountains, with no means of communication with the outside world, except a wagon road, which during a large portion of the time, was in bad condition."

Frank Wehrman was a chubby, cheerful baker who had a regular job in Portland, spent his weeks in Portland and his Sundays at home with his young and attractive wife, Daisy, and their four-year-old son, Harold. In the week ending on September 3, 1911, a Sunday, he did not go into Portland to work, reporting illness. September 4 was Labor Day. Wehrman returned to Portland that morning. On September 5 a friend and neighbor of Daisy Wehrman, Elizabeth Siercks, knocked on their door and got no answer. Looking in through a window, she could see Daisy lying on a bed with her son next to her, but the cabin was locked with a padlock, and she could not raise Daisy and could not get into the cabin. Returning on September 6, she saw Daisy and Harold lying in the same positions as the day before, and still could not raise them. On September 7 she brought the sheriff to the cabin.

Daisy and her four-year-old son had been murdered with an axe. Actually, they had not been murdered with an axe, but I lied to you for a reason. What appears to have happened is that they were shot three times each with a Colt revolver, and then, after they were dead, they were hacked up some with a hatchet, probably in the hope of linking this crime with the fact that an axe murderer was on the loose. This was entirely successful, as far as the newspapers were concerned; the newspapers immediately reported the case as another in the series of the Portland-area axe murders. The police, however, quickly realized that such was not the case.

Daisy Wehrman's clothes had been pushed up around her midsection. She had apparently been shot resisting a sexual assault. The sheriff, Sheriff Thompson, checked out Wehrman but could not tie him to the crime. Within three days county authorities had hired an experienced private investigator, L. L. Levings, and, in this case, instructed Sheriff Thompson to work at Levings's direction.

Taking the sheriff with him for legal authority, Levings went to the Wehrman cabin, where he noticed a newspaper dated September 4 (Monday) mixed in with a batch of mail. Daisy had not been seen by anyone except her husband since September 2. Levings went to the general store, which served as the local post office, and asked whether Mrs. Wehrman had picked up her mail on Monday. No, said the man in the store; the people up in that area commonly picked up one another's mail. He thought that Daisy's mail had been picked up by a man named Arthur Pender.

Levings found a set of new lace curtains in Wehrman's cabin, unopened. The curtains had been made for Mrs. Wehrman by a woman named Rachel Bates, and had been left in Wehrman's mailbox on September 3. There were no mail deliveries to this rural area. There was a community mailbox on a stump at the entrance to the road, several hundred yards from any house. When somebody went into Scappoose they would pick up everybody's mail, bring it back, and drop their neighbors' mail in the community mailbox. People would also drop other stuff in the mailbox to be distributed later, particularly if the road was wet.

Rachel Bates said she could prove she had left the cloth in the mailbox. "Ask Jack Pender," she said. "He was passing by just at the time I dropped off the cloth. He saw me do it."

John Arthur Pender, known both as Jack and Arthur, was building a cabin near the Wehrmans', and had been living in a tent while he was building the cabin. Levings found Pender in his tent and began to question him. Pender had deep scratches on his face, fingernail scratches probably, covered by two or three days of stubble. Pender claimed that the scratches were a rash. Levings had seen fingernail scratches before. He instructed Sheriff Thompson to place Pender under arrest.

Pender would not confess to the crime. A gun could be connected to Pender by circumstantial inference. Ballistics in 1911 were primitive, but experts were certain that this was the gun that had killed the Wehrmans. The gun had a "gas pit," and there was some rust in the gas pit, which gave bullets fired from this gun a unique and distinctive appearance; we don't understand that, but it's taken from the official report of the Oregon Supreme Court review of the case, which we take to be an authoritative source.

Pender had written a letter to his wife shortly after the murders, urging her to join him immediately because he needed to make a trip out of the area. Additional circumstantial testimony from the neighbors alleged:

1. That Daisy Wehrman appeared to be uncomfortable in Pender's presence, and avoided having contact with him, and

2. That Pender had not done his evening chores at the normal hour on Monday, September 4, but had done them late at night.

Pender's father was the captain of detectives in Ogden, Utah. Jack Pender Sr. went immediately to the Portland area and began trying to disassemble the case against his son. The case now had dueling detectives—two savvy, experienced police detectives, one trying to prove that Pender had committed the crime, the other that he had not. It was a fair fight; there was evidence on both sides. A shock of hair had been found clutched in Wehrman's hand after her death. It could not be matched to Pender's hair. There were bloody fingerprints on a towel in Wehrman's bathroom. They did not appear to be Pender's fingerprints (although how you can get fingerprints off a towel, I don't know).

Pender's first trial resulted in a hung jury. In his second trial, despite the problems with the case and despite his father's efforts, Pender was convicted of the murders based on the circumstantial evidence against him. The case against him was presented by District Attorney Tongue. Hearing his conviction announced, Pender shouted in the courtroom that he was an innocent man who had been framed by Levings and Thompson.

He was sentenced to death.

Pender, during his trials, became known as "The Beast of Portland" or "The Portland Beast Man," either nickname implicitly broadening the accusations against him to include the other crimes. Nothing tied Pender to either of the other crimes, however, so that link gradually evaporated.

Pender's father, having exhausted himself and his fortune trying to clear his son's name, died suddenly in the summer of 1913. Oregon eliminated the death penalty shortly after Pender was sentenced, and Pender's sentence was commuted to life in prison. Doubts about Pender's guilt played an important role in the public debate about the death penalty. In 1915 a man named John G. H. Siercks, an inmate at the Oregon insane asylum, confessed to having committed the murders in Scappoose. Here is an account of Siercks's confession from a 1915 newspaper (edited to remove a few off-topic words):

> John Arthur Pender, convicted of the crime, and, until the recent passage of a bill abolishing capital punishment, under sentence to be hanged, will be freed by executive order in a few days.
>
> Pender was under sentence to be hanged October 25. He always had maintained his innocence. When it was determined to submit a measure for the abolition of capital punishment to the voters, Governor West reprieved him until after the election, saying he wanted Pender to have the benefit of the people's verdict. Pender has been in the penitentiary ever since.
>
> George A. Thacher, a Portland criminologist, brought about yesterday's development. He became convinced of Pender's innocence at the time of the trial. Asylum authorities, as well as Thacher, declare there is no doubt as to the truth of Sierks' confession.
>
> Setting out, after clearing Pender in his own mind, to find

a person capable of committing such a crime as the Wehrman murder, Thacher said he made a canvass of those patients in the asylum who exhibited traits such as were manifested in the case. His investigation gradually led to Sierks, who he said had lived in the neighborhood of Mrs. Wehrman. Unsuccessful himself in obtaining a full confession, he enlisted the help of Rev. W. G. McLaren, the penitentiary chaplain.

Upon making the confession, Sierks puffed on a cigar and said that he felt better than he had for a long time.

Thacher was another of those amateur detectives who, in this era, were routinely allowed to meddle in criminal investigations. Authorities didn't buy Siercks's confession, and Pender remained in prison. Thacher mounted a campaign for Pender's release, and in 1919 published a book entitled *Why Some Men Kill: Or, Murder Mysteries Revealed*, in which he editorialized on behalf of Pender. The book can be read online today. Pender was pardoned by the governor of Oregon in 1920.

On April 22, 1924, telegraphing our story, a fifteen-year-old girl named Martha Gratke was beaten and stabbed to death in Portland. The crime was never solved.

On October 28, 1927, another fifteen-year-old girl named Charlotte Crawford went to police with a story about an older man who had been trying to get her to meet him in a park. Police thought they were dealing with a pervert, not quite realizing the seriousness of the situation. They arranged for two policewomen to shadow the girl as she kept the assignation. This very nearly went terribly wrong. The older man lured the girl deep into the tangled brush, put his hands around her throat, and choked her into unconsciousness. By the time the policewomen reached them he was poised over her with a hammer raised above his head. Another few seconds would have been too late.

The man was taken into custody with the hammer, a large knife, and an imitation handgun. At the police station he was recognized by older policemen as John Arthur Pender.

Pender pled innocent by reason of mental defect (insanity), was convicted of the attempted murder of Charlotte Crawford, and was returned to prison with a life sentence. Police could never tie Pender to the murder of Martha Gratke, and no evidence at all links him to the crimes in Ardenwald and/or Rainier.

Summarizing the Oregon/Washington crimes:

- The murder of the Hill family in Ardenwald on June 10, 1911, was quite certainly committed by The Man from the Train.
- The murder of the Cobles in Rainier, Washington, on or about July 11, 1911, was probably committed by The Man from the Train, even though a man named George Wilson was convicted of that crime.
- The murder of the Wehrmans in Scappoose, Oregon, on September 4, 1911, was an unrelated murder committed by John Arthur Pender, and the crime scene was staged to confuse it with the other two crimes.
- The murder of Mrs. Somomura in Rainier in December 1911 was an unrelated incident, probably a domestic murder.
- The murder of Martha Gratke in Portland in April 1924 is unsolved, but it is a good guess that it may have been committed by John Arthur Pender.
- The attempted murder of Charlotte Crawford in Portland in October 1927 was the work of John Arthur Pender.

# CHAPTER X

# The Double Event

After midnight in the wee hours of September 30, 1888, Jack the Ripper murdered a prostitute in London's East End. Within hours, he had murdered another one. This is known among those who write about Jack the Ripper as the Double Event.

It is common for serial murderers to have a Double Event. Ted Bundy had a Double Event, the Lake Sammamish murders, on July 14, 1974. Many other serial murderers have had double events—killed one victim, and then immediately killed another. The Man from the Train's Double Event occurred on September 17 to September 18, 1911, in Colorado Springs, Colorado.

The little house at 321 West Dale Street in Colorado Springs is just a bit less than a hundred yards from the railroad tracks. It is still occupied today; if you compare photos from then and now it is obviously the same house, with a porch roof now in danger of collapsing. Like few other crimes in this book, the scene is not forgotten. If you stop by the house, the current neighbors will know which one you're looking for and will point it out to you. The unfortunate residents of the house in September 1911 were the wife and children of A. J. Burnham. A. J. had tuberculosis, or consumption, as it was then called. Whatever you call it, in that era it was killing more than 100,000 Americans a year. People who had tuberculosis were advised to move to the mountains, which was 10 percent more effective than telling them to keep their fingers crossed. Colorado Springs was in the mountains, so there was a tuberculosis sanatorium, where people who had TB went to get better or, in most cases, die.

May Alice Burnham had a sister named Nettie Ruth. Nettie and Alice were working together on a sewing project. On Wednesday, September 20, Ms. Ruth walked to her sister's house at 321 West Dale, carrying some clothes that were in need of mending. May Alice did not answer the door. The house was locked up tight, and all of the window blinds were drawn. A grocery bill had been tacked to the front door by a grocer's clerk who had been unable to raise anyone inside the house. Nettie thought that May might be visiting a neighbor who lived down the street, but the neighbor said she hadn't seen May for several days. Concerned, they placed a call to the sanatorium where Albert (A. J.) lived and worked as a cook. Albert said he hadn't been to the house in a week.

The neighbor had a key to the Burnham house. As they placed the key in the lock, Nettie said, "Oh, suppose we find May and her babies dead in the house. It would be terrible, terrible." The lock stuck.

Newspaper reports say that the lock stuck. I doubt that that's actually what happened. The Man from the Train often jammed something into the lock to make the door hard to open. When the door was forced open, whatever it was would fall to the ground, and people would never realize it had been there. I suspect that it was not that the lock was stuck, but that the door was jammed shut. Whatever. As they pushed the door open the stench of death overwhelmed them.

The house was exactly as it had been on Sunday evening, when Nettie had last visited. Sunday night's dishes still sat on the table. Seconds later the two women ran screaming into the street.

There were three victims—May Alice, John, and Nellie Emma. John was a three-year-old boy; Nellie Emma a six-year-old girl. Their skulls had been crushed with the blunt side of an axe. May and John had been killed in their sleep. Nellie either had awakened or her body had been moved after she had been killed; in any case she was not found in the aspect of sleep. Something in the room would later cause the chief detective in the case to describe the perpetrator as a "moral pervert"; what that was was never revealed, but you and I know. The blinds were drawn, and the house, as we mentioned, locked up tight except for a window through which the murderer had exited. There was a bowl of bloody water, where the murderer had probably washed his hands, and there was a small pile of ashes in front of the stove. A crumpled portion of the Sunday newspaper was found on the floor, partially burned, and the lower part of a lace curtain had been burned.

A bottle of ink had been setting in the window ledge through which the killer left the house. The murderer had knocked it over as he left, leaving ink and smudged ink fingerprints all over the windowsill, and printing a perfectly clear ink thumbprint on the handle of the axe.

At first it was assumed that the killer had tried to burn the house down as he left, but a newspaper photographer would say later that he had accidentally set fire to the curtains when he used too much flash powder in taking a photograph. (Many fires, of course, were actually started in this way.) Because of the photographer's statement, authorities would conclude that there had been no effort to burn down the house. It is my opinion that he had attempted to burn down the house, based on these facts:

1. The Man from the Train frequently did set fire to the house after completing his crime, although we have not yet told you about most of the cases in which this had happened,

2. A crumpled Sunday newspaper, partially burned, is just *too*

coincidental. Tinder made from newspaper is what people use to start a fire.

In any case, before the issue of the fire arose the rush of policemen to the scene had drawn a crowd of hundreds. After about an hour one of the onlookers noticed something curious. While every other house in the neighborhood was a hive of anxious activity, the neighboring house—just a few feet from the Burnhams—had about it the silence of the grave.

It was the house—no longer standing—of Henry and Blanche Wayne, ages thirty and twenty-six, and their baby daughter, Lula May, who was two. Henry Wayne, another consumptive, had moved his family to Colorado about a month before the murders. He had met Burnham at the sanatorium, and Burnham had told him that there were houses for rent in his neighborhood. The two families were becoming friendly. Predictable details. Police knocked on the door. No answer. The screen door had been cut open. Police forced their way in. Three more bodies, all murdered with the blunt side of an axe. The bloody axe which had killed both families, borrowed from a neighbor, was found resting against the Wayne house.

Police began a normal course of investigation, starting with Albert Burnham. Burnham was arrested as soon as the crimes were discovered, and the Colorado Springs *Gazette* reported the next morning that "police were working on clews that may make it extremely difficult for him to disprove their theories." Burnham had an alibi, and in any case was too sick to have committed the murders. He would die of tuberculosis a few months later.

The Pinkerton Agency in Denver was hired to investigate the crime, and the Denver chief of police also volunteered his men. They put together what would now be called a task force, and actually, a very good task force—the sheriff, the local police chief and assistant police chief, an assistant district attorney, plus the Pinkerton Agency and the Denver police. In charge of the Pinkerton crew was a man named Prettyman. Prettyman was pretty certain that they would soon solve the case. "No person can commit a crime of this kind without leaving some sort of a clew," Prettyman told the Colorado Springs *Gazette*. "And once we find such a clew, the whole story will unravel like a ball of twine—and with a rapidity that will surprise the men working on the case. It may take a day, it may be several weeks, but sooner or later we will be in a position to announce that we have a footing. From then on it will be easy sailing." (It is unclear whether Prettyman knew that a "clew" was in fact a ball of twine. The modern word *clue* evolved from the word clew, which meant a ball of string or twine.)

A gold bracelet was left untouched on the arm of Blanche Wayne, and a gold watch on the mantel of the Burnham house. *In each house a lamp had been moved, and its chimney had been removed.* A fingerprint expert was called in from Leavenworth, Kansas. He tried to lift fingerprints from the lamps, and photographed the ink fingerprints from the axe and the metal basin in which the murderer had washed his hands.

Although the Burnham house was tiny, it did have a spare bedroom with a door that locked. The neighbor who had the key to the Burnham house ran a boardinghouse a few houses away, and occasionally Alice Burnham had allowed an overflow lodger to sleep in the spare bedroom, and also sometimes in a hammock on her porch. All of these lodgers were now suspects, but as they were just names in the wind, not suspects of any value. Other people became suspects—rejected boyfriends, neighborhood creeps, transients, etc. May Alice had a questionable relationship with an ex-boyfriend who lived in the neighborhood. His personal life wound up in the newspapers. No case could be constructed against any of them, no one was ever brought to trial for the crime, and the investigation stalled out.

The police and Mr. Prettyman explicitly rejected the possibility that the crimes could have been committed by a madman with no connection to the Burnham and Wayne families.

*   *   *

Jack the Ripper's Double Event is often attributed by Ripperologists to his frustration or lack of satisfaction with the first murder. It is believed that he was interrupted in the process of committing the first murder, and driven away from the body before he could eviscerate her or whatever it was that he had in mind to do. He then selected the second victim.

But noting the frequency with which serial murderers who are sexually motivated do have a Double Event, I have always wondered whether it was not the opposite—if, in fact, the murderer was so "high" and so excited after the first murder that another murder was just his way of keeping the good times rolling. We come to these six murders: why, then, did he go from the Waynes to the Burnhams?

It could be either motivation. We're not 100 percent sure that the Waynes were murdered first, by the way; that is police conjecture, and I think it is most likely correct, but we can't be certain. The key is the spilled ink. If he had gone to the Waynes after spilling ink and getting some of it on his hands, there would probably be some evidence of ink in the second house. Therefore, police believe that it happened the other way—but on the other hand, the axe was found resting against the Wayne house, which would suggest that that was the final venue.

The Burnham and Wayne families were friendly, and their children often played together in the yard that joined their houses. The Man from the Train may have been watching the children play, perhaps walked by the house two or three times in the daylight hours, and may have focused on Nellie Burnham as his primary target. He may then have broken into the wrong house and killed the Wayne family by mistake, which is not to say that he didn't also enjoy it. But realizing his mistake, he then broke into the Burnham house and completed his mission. This, I think, is the most likely explanation.

# CHAPTER XI

# Monmouth

Monmouth, Illinois, in 1911 was a town of 10,298 people, a little bit larger then than it is now. It rests in the far western part of the state, eighteen miles from the Mississippi River and a little more than two hundred miles from Chicago. The railroad track cuts into Monmouth from the south, runs through the southern part of Monmouth, and then bends back southward again, putting about 15 percent of the town on the wrong side of the tracks.

The Dawson family lived on the wrong side of the tracks, in an area that was mostly black although the Dawsons were white. William Dawson had been convicted of a serious crime years earlier—stealing horses—and had done hard time. He had moved to Monmouth about 1903 and was working as the caretaker for the First Presbyterian Church. Dawson and his wife (Charity Dawson) had been married in 1875 and had had eleven children, but by 1911 the kids were mostly grown and out of the house, and of the three who were still at home, two chanced to be absent on the fateful night of September 30 to October 1, 1911, which was a Saturday night and Sunday morning.

On Sunday morning Dawson failed to unlock the church and make it ready for services, which was his job. The minister was to say later that he was concerned that Dawson might be ill, and sent the deacons to Dawson's house to check up on him. The first reports were rather different: the deacons were sent to the Dawson domicile to discuss with him his dereliction of duty. In any case, the Dawsons were dead.

There were three dead here: William and Charity and their thirteen-year-old daughter, Georgia. Let us organize our comments as a discussion of whether we should or should not consider this a murder committed by The Man from the Train. There are four reasons why we should not consider it a part of the series. First, we don't have enough information about it to say with confidence that it conforms to the patterns and reflects the fetishistic behavior that identifies our culprit. Second, it is believed now that the murders were committed not with an axe, but with a piece of lead pipe. Third, it is reported in the book *Murdered in Their Beds*, by Troy Taylor (2012), that the back door of the Dawson house was left unlocked, whereas The Man from the Train normally locked up the house as he left. And fourth, a man was eventually convicted of being involved in the Monmouth murders.

Troy Taylor lives in Illinois, and he apparently was able to get access to the Monmouth daily newspapers from the time, which we have not seen. In any case, it is my opinion that the Monmouth murders most likely *were* committed by our principal culprit. For the following reasons:

1. The extreme proximity to the railroad (about a quarter of a mile),

2. The murders occurring in a small town very much like the other places his attacks occurred,

3. The murder of an entire family in a single event, which is rare although it seems common because we're reporting on one after another in this book,

4. The fact that the murders were committed late at night, after the family had gone to sleep,

5. The fact that a young girl was among the victims,

6. The fact that the body of the young girl was found in a "staged" or "struggling" position, whereas the adults were killed in their sleep and their bodies left in that position, as is true in so many other of our cases (in many of our cases, the adults and male children are murdered in their sleep, but the young female is either awake at the time of her death or her body is moved after death),

7. The blinds being drawn and the windows covered after the crime,

8. The complete and absolute absence of any rational motive,

9. The absence of any evidence of a struggle, and

10. The absence of any factor that would make us think that it isn't him.

Getting back, then, to the two factors that might be considered not in keeping with The Man from the Train's habits—the gas pipe and the unlocked door. At the time of the murders, it was reported in all sources that authorities believed the family had been murdered with the blunt side of an axe. Later, a leaded gas pipe was found in an area adjacent to the train track, and it was decided that the lead pipe had been the murder weapon. But (a) it is not clear that this was in fact the murder weapon, and (b) even if it was, that doesn't mean it isn't him. If he was intent on murdering someone and couldn't find an axe, I don't think that would have stopped him from committing murder.

As to the door being unlocked, the reports that emerged at the time state specifically that the Deacons, suspecting that something was wrong, *broke into* the Dawson house. Even if one door was unlocked, again, it's not persuasive that it is not him. All reports agree that the blinds were pulled and that the *front* door was locked, although one report says that the kitchen door was unlocked. He left a door wide open after murdering the Lyerly family (1906), and he would leave a door open after murdering the Showman family two weeks later. It's not a big deal.

As is always the case, a suspect was immediately identified, in this case a man who had once been William Dawson's brother in the horse-stealing fraternity. Dawson had given evidence against this man, it was alleged, and the man had sworn to have his revenge when he got out of jail. The man was investigated and cleared. He was several hundred miles away on Saturday night and on Sunday morning, and could not have traveled to Monmouth and back in the time available.

A man named John Knight was convicted years later, but it is Troy Taylor's conclusion—and ours—that the case against Knight is insubstantial. What happened was this. After the Dawson family murders, no arrests were made and no charges were filed for several years. A local attorney, John Hanley, got interested in the case, and began investigating it as a self-appointed private investigator, which, as I have mentioned, was not uncommon a hundred years ago.

By 1915 John O. Knight, who lived in the neighborhood where the Dawsons were murdered, was in jail for burglary and larceny. John Hanley talked to Knight, who was a black man, trying to see whether he knew anything about the crime. Knight, thinking he could perhaps use this to con his way out of prison, hinted that he *did* know something about the murders. The murders, he suggested, had been committed by a man named Lovey Mitchell, who had been living in Monmouth at that time. He suggested that he might have helped Mitchell commit the crime, but that Mitchell was the chief culprit.

Mitchell and his wife were arrested in St. Louis. By 1915 there was a widespread understanding that there had been a traveling midwestern axe murderer, so the arrest of Mitchell made headlines across the country. Mitchell and his wife were held for several weeks without access to a lawyer or to a reporter, and were pressured hard to confess to the crimes. A grand jury was supposed to hear the case against them—but didn't. There was no case against them. The Mitchells were quietly released.

Knight, on the other hand, had talked his way into a murder conviction. Prosecutors argued that he had confessed to the crime in the process of implicating Lovey Mitchell. They held a trial, convicted Knight, and added quite a few years to his prison sentence. But if there was anything of real substance against Knight, whatever it was has been lost to history.

One more thing here: the flashlight. Months later, months after the murders of the Dawson family, a fence around the house where the murders occurred was being demolished and rebuilt. As the fence was being torn down a pocket flashlight was found, into the handle of which someone had scratched the words COLORADO SPRINGS.

Colorado Springs??!! My God, that's where those other murders occurred!

That's what you're supposed to think—but here's the thing. In early October 1911, when the Dawsons were murdered, no one had seen a pattern in the murders in Oregon and Colorado and Illinois. In mid-October, after the next family was murdered, that changed suddenly. Recognition by the press that these crimes were linked coalesced about two weeks after the Monmouth murders.

The flashlight was discovered months later, after everybody was talking about the murders being linked. But The Man from the Train quite certainly did not carry a flashlight with him to the murders in Colorado Springs, which we know because he moved lamps in both houses there. He *could* have acquired a flashlight later, certainly, and he *could* have scratched COLORADO SPRINGS into the handle of it as a kind of memento of what he had done, I suppose, and he could have accidentally dropped that flashlight near the Dawson house, I suppose, but it seems terrifically unlikely. What seems a great deal more likely is that some mischief-maker or private detective had decided to manufacture evidence that the crimes were linked by scratching COLORADO SPRINGS into the handle of a flashlight "found" (or placed) near the Dawson house.

CHAPTER XII

# Ellsworth

Chicago, Oct. 17—The murder of a man, his wife, and three small children as they slept in Ellsworth, Kan., was almost identical to the slaying of six in Colorado Springs, September 21, and more lately the killing of Wm. E. Dawson, his wife and daughter in Monmouth, Ill., October 1. In each case an ax was the instrument of death. In every case each person in the house was killed apparently while asleep with a single blow of the murderous ax. . . .

In no case can the slightest motive be discovered by the police.

—Associated Press article, October 17, 1911

You have heard, no doubt, of the actor who becomes an overnight sensation after ten years of hard work? So it was with The Man from the Train. After thirteen years of murdering families in relative anonymity and without recognition, in mid-October 1911, there was suddenly a realization that a maniac was traveling the rails. The Associated Press reporter in Chicago made the connection, but he was not alone. Newspapers all over the area, including many not using the AP wires, also immediately connected the stories. The Ellsworth, Kansas, newspaper, hours after the discovery of the bodies, stated as fact that the fiend from Colorado Springs has now come to our city.

93

The Showmans, like the Burnhams, Waynes, and Dawsons, were people of limited means. In 1911 automobiles were relatively new, and much more difficult to operate than they are now. Most adults did not know how to drive. William Showman worked at what would later be called a garage or filling station. He would pump gas and help out the mechanic who owned the garage. He was described at the time as a "chauffeur," but the work he did was closer to what we would call a taxi driver or an Uber driver. When someone got off the train in Ellsworth and wanted a ride to a farm five miles out in the country, Showman would drive them out there in a car owned by the garage. In 1911 you could rent a car and a driver for $1 a day.

Like Dodge City, Deadwood (South Dakota), and Tombstone (Arizona), Ellsworth, Kansas, was one of the signature towns of the Wild West. The railroad lines reached Ellsworth in 1867, and for a few years, until other lines were built farther south and west, the cattle drives from Texas headed to Ellsworth. It was a rough town, with open prostitution, gambling, rows of dance halls, and many gunfights. A hotel built in Ellsworth in 1872 would accommodate 175 guests—one of the largest hotels west of the Mississippi at that time.

That era ended in Ellsworth about the time it began in Dodge City, and the cattle drives were over everywhere by the mid-1880s. On October 15, 1911, the Ellsworth city marshal, a man named Morris Merritt, stayed up late at night, reading the newspaper in his front room. It was a Sunday night. Merritt's house was just steps away from the railroad track. As he read his paper he heard a scratching sound at the back of the house, as if an animal was pawing at his back door. He paused for a minute, wondering what the noise was, but the noise stopped and he went back to his paper. The next morning, the marshal would discover that the screen from a window at the back of the house had been removed, and an effort had been made to pry open the window itself. The screen was left leaning against his house. Someone had tried to break in.

The significance of this became apparent that evening. The Showmans lived two houses up the street, on a small hill overlooking the railroad tracks. Laurie Snook, a friend of the Showmans, lived a couple of blocks away. On the morning of October 16 the Showmans' dog was hanging around her front yard. She shooed him away, told him to go back home. In the afternoon he was back. Mrs. Snook tried to call the Showmans on the telephone, asking what was up with the mutt, but the Showmans didn't answer. In the evening the dog was still there. She called the garage where Showman worked and was told that Will Showman had not shown up for work.

A family of five had been murdered in their beds, their heads crushed with the blunt side of an axe. The axe had been left in the house. The blinds had been pulled tight, although in this case a back door was left open. The murderer had removed a window screen and entered the house through the window.

Mrs. Snook ran screaming from the house. Attracting no attention, she retreated to her own house, where she called Showman's brother on the telephone. John Showman called the police.

The murderer had removed the chimney from a lamp, leaving the chimney under a chair in the kitchen and the lamp still burning in the room where the last of the murders occurred. He had washed his hands, and washed off the axe, in a bucket of water inside the house. He had covered the telephone in the Showmans' house with a dress. He had posed Pauline Showman's body in a disgusting manner postmortem, but had left the other victims in their beds where they were murdered. The axe had been taken from a neighbor's yard.

The sheriff sent for bloodhounds, which were imported from Abilene, Kansas, about sixty miles east of Ellsworth. The dogs led to the intersection of two railroad lines, a short distance west of the Showman house. Taken back to the house and turned off their leashes, the dogs circled the house, sniffed the bushes outside the house, and then returned to the same point as before.

No matter who puts on a Christmas party, they can always find somebody to play Santa Claus. No matter who is murdered, there is always someone who can be cast into the role of First Suspect. If a victim is an ex-con, the natural suspect is someone he knew in prison, or someone that he betrayed during his life of crime. If the murdered woman has ever had a lover, the lover is the First Suspect. If the man has ever been in a fight, the man he had the fight with is the First Suspect. If the dead people lived in a nice house, it will be reported, without evidence, that they kept money hidden in the house. When an interracial couple was murdered in San Antonio, the police were certain they were murdered because of racial animosity. When the husband was absent from the murder house in Colorado Springs, the absent husband was immediately a suspect; he didn't act right, for a grieving husband, you know. In Oregon it was a neighbor with whom the family had a minor dispute. In Washington it was a neighbor who was a bit of a nut. In South Carolina it was tenant farmers. No matter what, there is always some motive that can be inferred from the victims' lives, and some person whom the newspapers can load up with a sinister costume.

The first suspect in the Ellsworth murders was Charles Marzyck. Marzyck was an ex-con who had been married to Pauline Showman's sister. She had divorced Marzyck and remarried while he was in prison (1906 to 1910). It somewhat understates the facts to say that Marzyck was a "suspect" in the Ellsworth murders. For a period of several months, it was widely believed—and was reported in hundreds of newspapers—that Marzyck was probably responsible not only for the Ellsworth murders, but also for the murders in Colorado Springs and in Monmouth. Belief in Marzyck's guilt erupted in Ellsworth immediately after the crime, and spread from coast to coast within the next two days. Ira Lloyd, attorney at law, had defended Marzyck in his 1906 criminal trial. "I believe Marzyck will remain in the neighborhood until he completes his vengeance," Lloyd said. "After his sentence he told me that when he was released he would come back and kill the people who were responsible for his conviction and also their children. 'I will put them all in hell,' he said." Marzyck's ex-wife, now named Minnie Vopat, reported that he had recently been living in Colorado Springs and was wanted by authorities in Colorado Springs on a bad check warrant.

For a month or so, Marzyck sightings outnumbered pigeons. Minnie Vopat, her new husband, and her family lived for months in terror of Marzyck's return—well-founded terror, I might add. Marzyck *had* issued broad death threats against the family in 1906, and Mrs. Vopat's sister and her sister's family had been brutally murdered. While almost all of the information about Marzyck would later prove to be nonsense, it was not at all irrational or paranoid for her to be terrified at the time.

The day after the bodies were discovered it was learned that a stranger had registered at a local hotel on the night of the murders, drunk, signing the register as John Smith. John Smith left the hotel the next morning without checking out, leaving a bundle of clothes in his room. There was blood on the shirt. The investigation immediately conflated John Smith with Charles Marzyck, concluding that it was Marzyck who had signed the register as John Smith. A coroner's jury reached the legal conclusion that John Smith was the person most likely responsible for the crime, a sort of quasi-indictment.

"Back to the salt mines" is not just an expression in central Kansas; there are actual salt mines, which still operate today. Police scrambled for several days on the trail of John Smith, finally arresting him at the salt mines in Kanopolis on October 20. Kanopolis is five miles from Ellsworth, and October 20 was four days after the murders were discovered.

Once in custody, however, Smith no longer seemed like a good candidate for the murders. First—and who would have guessed it?—his name was actually John Smith; Smith or Smitherton, he used both names, but he wasn't using the name as a blind, and he wasn't Charles Marzyck. Second, he had told people where he was going when he left Ellsworth, which is not in the tradition of a fugitive. He had actually gone to Kanopolis, on foot, and had in fact applied for work in the salt mines, as he had said that he was going to. He seemed to have checked into the hotel in Ellsworth about the same time that the city marshal had heard someone trying to break into his house.

Smith was so drunk when he was arrested that the police were unable to question him. After he was given a night to sober up he was interviewed at length. He didn't seem to have any notion what the questioning was about. His story was that he had gotten off the train in Ellsworth on Sunday night (the night of the murders), had found a bundle of clothing wrapped in a blanket, and had picked up the clothing and carried it with him to the hotel room. In the middle of the night he had a nosebleed, and had used the shirt from the bundle of clothes to wipe his nose. He had abandoned the clothes in the hotel room. He apparently thought that he was being questioned about stealing the clothes, and seemed shocked to learn the real reason he had been arrested. His wife confirmed that, when he drank a lot, he would have nosebleeds.

The Man from the Train quite certainly did not check into local hotels when he was going to commit murder. If he had, he would have been put out of the murdering business very quickly, since looking for strangers in town was one of the first things the police always did while waiting for the bloodhounds to arrive.

There is, however, something tremendously interesting in the John Smitherton side story, overlooked by everybody who has written about the case. The clothing. If he hopped off the train and found the bundle of clothing, we may assume that the clothes had been left or "dropped" down by the railroad tracks, perhaps by someone else who had hopped off the train earlier in the evening. Who do we know who might have left a bundle of clean men's clothing down by the railroad tracks?

We don't know an awful lot about how The Man from the Train escaped detection, but we do know:

1. That a person who hits people in the head with an axe is going to be hit by flying blood,

2. That no one was ever caught fleeing the scene of one of the crimes with blood on his clothing, and

3. That if The Man from the Train had been caught in the vicinity of one of the crimes with blood on his clothes, it is extremely likely that he would have been executed.

It is a reasonable guess, then, that when he was ready to "hit" a house, he would hide a change of clothing down by the railroad track, so that he could get out of the bloody clothes, perhaps within minutes after leaving the scene of the crime. John Smitherton was not The Man from the Train—but he may have picked up The Man from the Train's escape clothes.

Once Smitherton was cleared, the focus returned to Charles Marzyck. Marzyck was finally located on April 30, 1912 (six months after the murders), living in Canada. Living in relative isolation, he was unaware that his name had been published from coast to coast in the forty-six states.

Once Marzyck was located the case against him collapsed. Although Marzyck was from Ellsworth and was well known there, no one had seen him around Ellsworth near the time of the murders. He denied that he had ever been to either Colorado Springs or Monmouth, and there was in fact no evidence that he had. The story about his being wanted in Colorado Springs for writing bad checks was false, as was an oft-repeated story that Marzyck's brother lived in Colorado Springs. He had been in Canada at the time of the murders.

The book *Murdered in Their Beds*, by Troy Taylor, states that "he was brought back to Ellsworth and put on trial for the murders. . . . despite planted evidence in the form of a cigar cutter that he supposedly left in the Showman house, Marzyck was cleared of the crimes and a not guilty verdict was returned by the jury." In fact, there was no trial; Marzyck was brought to Ellsworth but released after a preliminary hearing. Newspapers in this era sometimes referred to preliminary hearings as trials, which I would assume accounts for the confusion.

*　　*　　*

In discussions of the murders in the Colorado Springs newspapers after the Showmans were killed, letter writers began referring to the culprit as "Billy, the Ax man," or, more commonly, as "Billy, the Ax Smasher." In 1911 a vaudeville comedian, known as Billy Van, the Assassin of Sorrow, had a brief burst of popularity. He was not a huge star, but he was popular in Colorado Springs. He had appeared there in early September 1911, about two weeks before the murders, getting nice write-ups in the local papers. The nickname given to the murderer was almost certainly derived from Billy Van, as well as, of course, being a reference to Billy the Kid.

The nickname "Billy, the Ax Man" has been picked up in the twenty-first century and is sometimes used to refer to our criminal. But while we have tried to minimize the gore, we are dealing here with perhaps the most despicable criminal in American history, a truly ghastly felon who enjoyed hitting small children in the head with an axe, and who may have killed around a hundred people. Giving him a cutesy nickname that sounds like it came from a kid's cartoon seems to us not fitting, and there will be no further reference to that nickname in this book.

In 2006, a woman named Beth Klingensmith wrote an academic paper about these murders for a college course. The paper was published on the Web and has since been used as a resource by almost everyone who has written about these events, including us. It is a very good paper, but Ms. Klingensmith draws a line between the midwestern murders and the murders in the Northwest, ruling those out of the series, based on her own misunderstandings about the murders in the Northwest and her lack of knowledge about them. In any case the public was aware, from mid-October 1911 onward, that someone was traveling around the Midwest murdering families. They got it, but they didn't get it. From a modern perspective it seems very strange. On one level, the public and the newspapermen and the police now understood that these crimes were linked. They understood that some nut was running around murdering people—but they didn't understand it at all. They were entirely unable to make that short walk . . . what seems to us now to be a short walk . . . from realizing that these crimes were linked to realizing that these were *random* crimes, rather than crimes that arose from conventional motives. They couldn't process it. Does not compute. Random, but not random.

The city cop in Ellsworth, Kansas, had direct, personal knowledge of the random nature of the crime. He had heard the culprit *with his own ears* trying to break into *his* house. One might think that this would have provided persuasive evidence, at least to that cop, that the Showman family was a target of opportunity—and yet the investigation went on as before. The investigation leaped instantly to the assumption that the Showmans were the murderer's intended targets, despite the fact that the city marshal had direct knowledge that should have led him in a different direction.

This continued to be true. When the next family was murdered—even though many people immediately recognized that it was part of the series—the investigation instantly began to revolve around the lives of the victims. The only way that authorities could conceive of to link the crimes was to find some person who knew the Showmans and had some grievance against them, and who also knew the Dawson family, and had some reason to hate them, and who also knew the Wayne family or the Burnham family, and had some reason to kill them.

Borrowing again from Ms. Klingensmith's paper, a quote taken from the Colorado Springs *Gazette* of October 18, 1911:

> Is another family, somewhere, slated for massacre . . . on Sunday, October 29? If there is anything in sequence or in the theory now accepted by the authorities of five states, one family, perhaps two, living in a small, two-room cottage on the outskirts of some town in the United States, will be murdered with an ax sometime be-tween midnight, October 28 and midnight October 29 to satisfy the seemingly insatiable thirst for blood of the most cruel and heartless beast ever known in the history of crimes.

The Man from the Train didn't care anything about the two-week interval, and he didn't care anything about the size of the house, and he didn't care much about it being a Sunday night. He just enjoyed killing people; the rest of it was incidental. These assumptions—as much as the assumption that there must be some connection between the murderer and the murdered—are a denial of the true nature of what was happening. They are a way of trying to put limits around the edges of the crimes, limits that were not there.

Random, but not *really* random. They're not really random; they happen only on Sunday nights. They happen only at two-week in-tervals. They happen only in the Midwest. There is an explanation here, they told themselves; there is a logic to the crimes. It is just a little different from the normal logic. The press and the author-ities "understood" that the Monmouth, Illinois, case was a part of a pattern—and yet, all the same, another man was put on trial and convicted of participation in the Monmouth murders.

When there were additional murders, the investigations into those murders went on exactly as before. Suspects were rounded up, exactly as before, from ex-lovers and family members and business rivals and neighborhood crazy people. All they did was, they occasionally stretched the pool of suspects so that it included multiple murder sites.

To a large extent, this is still true *today* in discussing these murders. There are still people today who are trying to blame the Villisca murders on someone from Villisca—even though it could not possibly be more obvious that this is merely one crime in a series that stretches in both directions.

You will read in some accounts of this series that panic and paranoia were spreading throughout the Midwest. The exact opposite is true. The people who were afflicted by this one-man plague didn't *over*react. They *under*reacted. They underreacted by a wide margin. They didn't begin to do what reason would have told them needed to be done.

When they realized that there was a madman on the rails, they had a choice between panic and denial—and they chose denial. Pretending that the Showmans had been murdered not by a random crazy person but by an ex-brother-in-law was a part of that denial. Pretending that the murderer worked on a clockwork schedule, every other Sunday night, was a part of that denial. Pretending that the Oregon crimes were unrelated was a piece of that denial. They simply were not able to face what they were actually dealing with.

CHAPTER XIII

# Paola

A fact worth remembering in this case is that the details were carefully arranged, even to spreading the sheet over the heads of the victims apparently to keep the blood from splashing on the murderer. This denotes a calm preparation which would not be likely in one inexperienced in this line of work. The similarity in the crimes gives rise to the question, were they all done by the same party? Another fact is that nearly all of them were committed during the warm months. Was it a crazy tramp?

*—The Miami County Republican*,
Paola, Kansas, June 14, 1912

The neighborhood in Paola now swarms with children; probably it did even in 1912. It is a neighborhood of small "first houses." The neighborhood rises up above the railroad lines at a steep grade, as if presenting itself to the viewer; the street is wide and open, the houses are tiny and packed together and they stagger up the hill. The old train depot is gone, but if you stand where the depot was you can see all of the houses where the people in this story lived; they're maybe 150 yards from the railroad line. And if you stand in the yard of 710 West Wea and a train goes by, it feels like the train is 10 feet away.

Rollin and Anna Hudson were married in Massillon, Ohio, in April 1910. Hudson was nineteen years old at the time of their wedding, Anna twenty. After their marriage they moved to Centerville, Ohio, where they boarded with Mr. and Mrs. George W. Coe. (We might say they coe-habited with them; it's a very dark story, and we're desperate for relief. Anna's maiden name was "Axxe"—really— but we're going to let that pass without comment.) Mr. Hudson, a young man without education or professional skills, worked as a cone grinder in a factory, a job that involved breathing metal dust. He quit that for health reasons, did some manual labor for a railroad. Rollin and Anna had problems. They split up for a while, and Coe would say that Rollin had told him he had three times found Anna with another man.

Later, spinning perhaps off of a few ill-chosen words, the legend of Anna's unfaithfulness would grow to epic proportions, obscuring the more relevant facts of the case, but that is later. In March 1912, Mr. and Mrs. Coe moved to Paola, Kansas, a town (then) of 3,300 people. Two railroad lines met in Paola, the Frisco line and the M. K. & T., which stood for Missouri, Kansas, and Texas. The Hudsons joined them in April. They bought a few pieces of cheap used furniture and rented a small house across the street from the Coes, at 710 West Wea Street. The house still stands, is in good condition, and is occupied today.

About June 4, 1912, a large, pig-faced man appeared in Paola, staying at a rooming house, and asking questions about Rollin and Anna. He said that he was an old friend from Ohio. Around 8:30 p.m. on June 5, a Wednesday evening, the pig-faced man appeared at the Hudsons' door, wearing a blue suit. He was greeted warmly by both Hudsons and invited in. Whether or not the man was seen leaving the house is in dispute; in some reports he was seen leaving the house about 11:00 p.m.; in other reports he was not.

One of Hudson's coworkers on the M. K. T. was named Longmeyer.

The Longmeyer family lived three houses up the street. A little after midnight on June 5 (the wee hours of June 6) Mrs. Longmeyer was awakened by the crash of breaking glass. Stumbling into the hallway, she saw the dark shadow of a man fleeing from her kitchen. She ran into the kitchen; the kitchen door banged open, she heard footsteps crossing the wooden porch, and he was gone.

Mrs. Longmeyer had an eight-year-old daughter named Sadie. Panic-stricken, she rushed into Sadie's room, and discovered that Sadie's bed was empty. Sadie was huddled in a corner, terrified but unharmed. There was a man, she said. She had seen him crouched over her mother's bed. Mr. Longmeyer had slept through the intrusion, and was groggy when awakened.

Returning to the kitchen, Mrs. Longmeyer found that the broken glass was the chimney from an oil lamp, shattered on the floor; its wick was turned low so that it emitted but a faint glow. Also on the floor of the kitchen she found a woman's kimono-style dressing gown that did not belong to her. The man had broken into the house by prying off a window screen, which was left leaning against the house next to the window. When dawn came Mrs. Longmeyer walked to the courthouse, reported the break-in, and handed the kimono over to a deputy sheriff.

Also that morning, Rollin Hudson did not report to work. I wince to use this phrase again, having used it so many times, but no one was moving around at the Hudson house. Knowing of the break-in at the Longmeyers' and concerned about the Hudsons, a group of three neighbor women gathered at the Hudsons' front door. Pushing the door open a little they could see into a back bedroom, where they could make out the forms of two people lying in the bed. As they looked nervously around—one of the three women had reportedly already fainted on the front lawn—they saw a buggy coming down the street, which they recognized as belonging to Herman Hintz, a deputy city marshal. He had another man with him. Hintz and the other man went into the house, where they discovered, in the words of the *Miami Republican*, "a ghastly sight. Turning back a coverlid and sheet that covered their heads, they found Mr. and Mrs. Hudson dead. Mr. Hudson was lying on his right side with the left side of his head and face crushed. He was evidently murdered while he slept, without having made a struggle. Mrs. Hudson was apparently awakened when her husband was killed and raised her head, when she was struck of the back of the head and of her face with some partially sharp instrument an inch or an inch and a half wide."

Sitting on a box next to the bed was a lamp without its chimney. A window was open in the other bedroom, and the screen had been removed.

The previous night's dishes were undone, serving dishes for three people, and photo albums were opened, as if the doomed couple had spent their last hours reminiscing with an old friend. A box of letters sat on the table next to the photo album. Of course the pig-faced man in the blue suit was the first suspect in the case. From comments made later by the county sheriff, Sheriff Chandler, I would infer that he had identified the stranger and eliminated him as a suspect; however, this is never quite explicitly stated. Police were to decide that the kimono found in the Longmeyer house had belonged to Anna Hudson.

The subsequent newspaper stories focused heavily on the rumors about Anna Hudson's love life, but from a logical standpoint there wouldn't seem to be any doubt that this crime was committed by The Man from the Train, and not by either the pig-faced visitor or Anna's alleged "affinity," which was the term used by newspapers to refer to a lover. There are three levels of evidence that lead us in that direction. First, the circumstances of the crime are consistent with The Man from the Train. By "circumstances of the crime" I mean the following:

1. A two-minute walk from the intersection of two railroad lines,

2. Multiple murders without apparent motive,

3. No robbery (Anna Hudson's jewelry was left in her bedroom),

4. Access to the house through a window,

5. Crime committed in the middle of the night,

6. Murders committed with an axe or some similar instrument,

7. Clear and obvious evidence that the criminal was experienced at committing crimes of this nature,

8. Crime committed in the time and place where The Man from the Train was most active.

This crime was committed four days before the murders in Villisca. Paola is in the northeast corner of Kansas. Villisca is in the southwest corner of Iowa. Northeast Kansas almost touches southwest Iowa. You could probably walk from Paola to Villisca in four days; it is 177 miles. Villisca is slightly to the *west* of Paola—odd, since Iowa is almost entirely east of Kansas.

Second, there are the telltale clues, the criminal signature of The Man from the Train—the lamp without its chimney, the removed window screens at both houses, the bodies being covered with cloth (preventing the blood from flying), the fetishistic moving or carrying of clothes, sometimes for no apparent purpose.

Third, the assumption that the Hudsons were murdered either by an ex-lover or by the pig-faced man in the blue suit seems to be trumped by the break-in at the second residence. If Anna Hudson's lover had killed the couple, why would he wander up the block and break into the Longmeyer house, apparently bent on continuing the mayhem? And if the evening's visitor had committed the crime, why was the Hudsons' window screen pried off, after the visitor was seen entering through the front door?

The sheriff—Sheriff F. Marion Chandler of Miami County—very specifically and repeatedly stated that it was his belief that the crime was committed by a stranger who had no connection with the Hudsons.

The quote with which we began this chapter is one of the most incisive comments made by a journalist in any of the places where The Man from the Train committed his atrocities. The writer's observation that "the details were carefully arranged, even to spreading the sheet over the heads of the victims apparently to keep the blood from splashing on the murderer" is the exact same observation that six decades later would become the foundation stone of criminal profiling: the realization that this criminal was unusually well organized, that he had thought through the crime and was taking steps he had planned in advance. The newspaper editor infers from this—consistent with modern criminal profiling, and also correctly—that the murderer was experienced, that he had done this before. (This, again, seems inconsistent with the crime having been committed by someone emotionally involved with the Hudsons. The angry lover would not likely have experience as an axe murderer.) In part of the paragraph not quoted the writer listed the "linked" crimes, including the Bernhardt murders, which modern writers often overlook. The writer then realizes that the "linked" crimes almost all occurred in warm weather—a fact that I myself did not realize until I had been working on this book for more than a year—and then speculates, correctly, that the murders were committed by what he calls a crazy tramp. In the hundreds of thousands of paragraphs of old journalism that we reviewed in writing this book, that one stands out.

* * *

The assumption that the public should give a wide berth to the process of justice is a recent phenomenon in human history, and is a by-product of the complex and sophisticated police networks that we now take for granted, but that began to develop less than two hundred years ago. In almost all of the history of the civilized world, and in America up until the middle of the nineteenth century, it was an *obligation* of private citizens to arrest and detain those suspected of crimes until they could be given over to officials. With the development of robust police services, beginning about 1840 but not reaching maturity until about 1940, came a gradual acceptance that police investigations should be left to police professionals.

In Kansas in the nineteenth century there were 200 documented lynchings, all of them of persons believed to have committed crimes; the actual number of lynched persons is 200, not 199 or 201 or rounded off to 200. (The number of separate events is somewhat less.) In the twentieth century there were six such cases, three of those from 1900 to 1902. By 1912, when these murders occurred, lynching had essentially ended in Kansas, but was part of the state's recent history. A lynching is, of course, the ultimate example of an inappropriate involvement of the public in the process of justice. We might expect, then, that where there are so many extremely inappropriate interactions between the public and the process of justice, there would also be many other inappropriate, if less dramatic, interactions between the public and the process of justice.

And, in fact, there were. Not only did much of the population of Paola go by the murder house to see what they could see, but hundreds of people from Kansas City jumped on the train to come join in the excitement. The understanding that it was inappropriate to involve oneself in a criminal investigation was a new phenomenon, an idea promulgated by some police since about 1880 but not yet adopted by the public, in the Midwest or beyond; two murders that occurred in New Brunswick, New Jersey, in 1922 so captivated the public that throngs of New Yorkers rushed out to invade the scene of the crime.

We tend to write about these murders that the police failed to protect the scene of the crime. They did, but the more important truth is that the public failed to observe boundaries. It is not that the boundaries keeping the public away from horrible crime scenes were violated; it is more that they did not exist. Those restraints had yet to be constructed. We see this in dozens of ways. In almost every case we see curious spectators flocking to the scene of the crime, often by the thousands. When a house burned down after one of our murders, a story to be told later, hundreds and hundreds of people stopped by the house in the following weeks and picked through the burned-out wreckage, looking for souvenirs.

In 1912 it was normal for newspaper reporters to be present when suspects in serious crimes were interrogated; if not present during the interrogation, reporters were often allowed to interview suspects in custody after the police interrogation was finished. Suspects in some cases were paraded to news conferences. Newspapers in many cases came into possession of items of evidence such as letters, wills, and other documents. Again, this is an inappropriate interaction between the public and the process of justice.

In *The Great Detective*, Zach Dundas quotes Paul Collins as saying that "Hans Gross published the first standard forensics text in 1893, and by the next decade police knew how to preserve crime scenes, maintain chains of evidence, proceed in an orderly and scientific way—all the staples of procedural detective stories now. They staffed cases in teams, with specialist bureaus taking on different aspects of investigations. It wasn't just Inspector Lestrade coming out to 'take the case in hand' anymore."

Well . . . in London, maybe. In New York, maybe maybe. *Some* police may have known how to do these things. In the places where The Man from the Train committed his crimes, no way in hell. What Collins describes, with teams and specialist bureaus, is an urban police force. The towns where these crimes were committed had a one- or two-man police force—if they had any police force at all.

In most of the cases covered later in this book, the scene of the crime will be invaded by large numbers of private citizens— sometimes thousands of them—before the first policeman is on the scene. And when the police do arrive, there quite certainly are no teams or squads or specialist bureaus. Eventually, these states would form state investigative bureaus, which were basically squads of former county sheriffs, who could be called in to assist the small-town police—but that would happen thirty to forty years after the crimes in this series. Of all of the dozens of crimes in this book, there are only four that were investigated in anything like the manner described by Mr. Collins, those four being the Schultz murders in early 1910, the Bernhardt family murders in 1910, the Casaways in 1911, and the Double Event in Colorado Springs in 1911.

In many of these cases, but in the Paola case more than any other, it is difficult to be sure what actually happened. You would think that people would have the common sense not to tell whoppers that place them in the middle of a terrible crime story, but people like to tell stories. Without the boundaries that we have now, people told stories that put themselves in the center of the action. I believe that two people in our cases (George Wilson in Rainier, Washington, and John O. Knight in Monmouth, Illinois) accidentally talked themselves into murder convictions. This still happens occasionally in the twenty-first century, but it was more common in a more primitive system.

There are facts in this case the size of a pea, and a layer of gossip surrounding them that is the size of a grapefruit. I wish that I could simply ignore the grapefruit, but there could be something useful in there, and I would feel I was cheating you if I just let it all slip away. One of the problems is that Paola at this time was served by two local newspapers and by several other regional newspapers. The two local papers were intensely competitive, and they printed different and sometimes irreconcilable accounts of the investigation.

The gossip can be sorted into two magazines: those stories that allege Mrs. Hudson's involvement with another man, and those stories told by neighbors about the night of the crime(s). In our judgment, the stories about Mrs. Hudson may or may not be true, but they are irrelevant to the murders. Most of the stories told by the neighbors are probably not true.

The narrative about Anna's involvement with another man began with comments allegedly made by George Coe shortly after the crime. Coe certainly was in a position to know intimate details of the Hudson marriage, but it is not clear what exactly Hudson said to Coe, or what exactly Coe said to a reporter. Coe is reported as saying that Hudson told him he had three times found Anna "with" another man, but what exactly did that mean? Did it mean that he had three times found them naked in the bedroom, or did it mean that he had three times found them walking together on a public street, or sitting and talking in a manner that he (Rollin) felt was inappropriate, but she (Anna) didn't think was wrong?

People who have written about the case, in 1912 and in the twenty-first century, have generally rushed to the conclusion that it was the former. I think the latter is a better guess. We don't know the character of George Coe. The fact that he would spill slanderous gossip about the couple to a newspaper reporter hours after their murder certainly speaks poorly of his judgment, but we don't know whether he was a reliable man, or whether he was a fool and an inveterate gossip. Rollin Hudson's father was a successful attorney; according to a newspaper of the time he "is a prominent attorney at North Industry [Ohio] and has been prominent in politics there. He knew the late President McKinley and Judge Day well and was counsel in cases there with them and against both of them. He is a man of education and refinement." Mr. Hudson—also in a position to know—came to Paola after the murders, denounced the rumors against his daughter-in-law, and told reporters that she had been a good wife and a virtuous young woman (according to *one* of the local newspapers. According to the other one, he was surprised to learn that Anna and Rollin were back together).

The printed speculation about the event sometimes links the pig-faced man to Anna's supposed paramour, but this is unlikely. Rollin Hudson worked on the day before his murder. The pig-faced man waited until Hudson was at home to knock on their door. For a man to visit a married woman alone in her house in the middle of the afternoon starts rumors—then and now. This man was observing propriety.

Anna and Rollin Hudson had had a loud argument in public just days before they were murdered—an argument related in some stories to a letter she had received. This is my take on all of this, and you can make of it what you want. Rollin and Anna were married when they were very young, and, as is generally true of those who marry too young, they were working through things inside of their marriage that are better worked through before marriage. They were still growing up. Rollin was insecure, jealous, and suspicious of Anna; Anna resented it, and probably told Rollin that she would talk to whomever she wanted to talk to and it was none of his business.

These stories mushroomed from a thin factual record. Quite similar stories are told about young wives connected to many of the crimes recounted in this book. It is the back side of Victorian prudishness, that women who are expected to be above all suspicion are condemned to live perpetually in the shadow of the suspicion cast by the most ordinary events.

In relating the story of the break-in at the Longmeyer house, I left out a relevant detail. Mrs. Longmeyer insisted that she, her husband, and her daughter had been drugged with chloroform before discovering the break-in at her house. Not only did Mrs. Longmeyer insist that she had been the victim of an attempted drugging, but another neighbor, Mrs. Cora Pryor, also claimed that she and her two children had been chloroformed by the assassin before he broke into the Hudson and Longmeyer houses. "I had a hard time wakening up Thursday morning," Mrs. Pryor said. "My head ached terribly and the two children complained of the same thing, we were sick all day yesterday. Just as if we had been chloroformed."

Mrs. Pryor lived two doors down from the Hudsons, next door to the Longmeyers. Myrtle Coe, who lived across the street, reported hearing a scream coming from the Hudson house just about midnight, and the woman who lived between the Hudsons and the Pryors reported that she had seen the shadow of a man pass by her back window shortly after midnight. The whole damned neighborhood appears to have been vaguely aware that the chloroform monster was on the prowl.

Mrs. Pryor was probably loopy and nobody paid much attention to her, but the police bore down hard on Mrs. Longmeyer, who, since she had reported the break-in before the murders were known and had come into possession of an item taken from the Hudson house (the kimono), could at least be suspected of having had some involvement in the crime. She was interviewed repeatedly by police, who tried to make her back off her statement about the chloroform, which she adamantly refused to do. A detective named JL Ghent, detailed to the case from the Kansas City police, told reporters at one time that he believed the murders were the work of a jealous woman, bent on revenge at Anna Hudson.

One newspaper is deeply into the chloroform stories and Anna's love life, while the other observes quietly that "it is thought both were chloroformed before the fatal blows were struck." Really? Let's think that one through.

The reports about The Man from the Train using chloroform began after the Ellsworth murders; someone who was in the house in Ellsworth thought that he smelled chloroform, and then chloroform would become a standard element of the narrative of subsequent crimes. But we know that The Man from the Train was carrying an axe. The question is, was he carrying an axe *and chloroform*? If so, *what did he need the chloroform for*? If you have an axe and you're intending to kill people with it, and you're comfortable doing that, what exactly is the purpose of the chloroform?

The use of chloroform as a weapon was a hot-button topic in this era. From 1899 to 1901 a criminal gang in Pennsylvania known as the Chloroform Gang used chloroform to subdue their victims for the purpose of robbery. The leaders of the Chloroform Gang were brothers Ed and Jack Biddle. One of their victims died, and they were arrested for murder, convicted, and sentenced to death. They became famous eight decades later because the warden's wife, Kate Soffel, helped them to escape from prison and ran away with them; she had fallen in love with Ed Biddle. *Mrs. Soffel*; maybe you saw the movie. William Marsh Rice, for whom Rice University is named, was murdered with chloroform in 1900, a very famous crime. As a result of these events and a few others, the use of chloroform as a murder weapon was prominent in the imaginations of naïve people.

Of course it is stupid to suggest that The Man from the Train was carrying chloroform, but nonetheless this is instructive. What I believe to be the first paragraph ever published about the murders in Villisca, published on the day the crimes were discovered, says that no one smelled chloroform in the house—not that *someone* had smelled chloroform in the house, but that *no one* had. What this tells us is that the reporters had immediately connected the murders in Villisca to the earlier crimes, and this assumption is what made the Villisca crimes instantly famous: the immediate realization that this was not merely an isolated crime, but rather, the latest in an ongoing series.

On June 10, five days after the crime, a rambling, four-page letter was found on the stairway of a restaurant in Paola; it was dated May 27, addressed to Anna Hudson, and pinned to it was a note asking that the letter be turned over to the proper authorities. The contents of the letter were never released, but those who read it described it as a passionate love letter, obviously from someone other than her husband.

That's bogus. It's a mischief-maker's prank, like the flashlight planted at the house in Monmouth, Illinois. Prudish people will get themselves all worked up about illicit sex. When the rumors about Anna Hudson's infidelity became a part of the story, people ran wild with it.

\* \* \*

The Man from the Train murdered fourteen people in fourteen weeks in late 1911, then was inactive for seven months, then was hyperactive again in the summer and fall of 1912. The last murder in 1911 and the first murder in 1912, separated by seven months, were both committed in Kansas.

This suggests the possibility that The Man from the Train was incarcerated somewhere in Kansas from October 1911 until June 1912. Serial murderers who are incarcerated in the middle of their run spend their time in prison fantasizing about killing people and often have a burst of murderous activity beginning hours after they get out of prison. Ted Bundy did this, and Arthur Shawcross, and Kenneth McDuff, and others. The Man from the Train killed ten people in a week in early June 1912. This suggests to me that he may have gotten out of prison just before then.

He would not likely have been incarcerated at the Kansas State Prison in Lansing, because people sent to Lansing were usually held for more serious crimes, and usually more than a few months. But he could have been held in any of a hundred county jails, or in any of dozens of city jails. We made an effort to find the records of people released from prisons in Kansas in the first days of June 1912, but we came up empty. We don't know what name he was using at that time; we don't know what he was arrested for; we don't know exactly when he was arrested, or where. There just isn't enough information to work with.

This is a chronology of the forty-nine murders that are discussed in this first section of the book, omitting the murders that we believe not to have been connected to the series:

| SECTION I | | | | |
|---|---|---|---|---|
| *Where* | *Who* | *No.* | *Date* | *Year* |
| Hurley, Virginia | Meadows family | 6 | September 21 | 1909 |
| Beckley, West Virginia | Hood family | 4 | October 31 | 1909 |
| Houston Heights, Texas | Schultz family | 5 | March 11 | 1910 |
| Marshalltown, Iowa | Hardy family | 3 | June 5 | 1910 |
| Johnson County, Kansas | Bernhardt family | 4 | December 7 | 1910 |
| San Antonio, Texas | Casaway family | 5 | March 21 | 1911 |
| Ardenwald, Oregon | Hill family | 4 | June 9 | 1911 |
| Rainier, Washington | Coble couple | 2 | July 11 | 1911 |
| Colorado Springs, Colorado | Wayne family | 3 | September 17 | 1911 |
| Colorado Springs, Colorado | Burnham family | 3 | September 17 | 1911 |
| Monmouth, Illinois | Dawson family | 3 | September 30 | 1911 |
| Ellsworth, Kansas | Showman family | 5 | October 15 | 1911 |
| Paola, Kansas | Hudson family | 2 | June 5 | 1912 |

# SECTION II

*Summer* 1912

CHAPTER XIV

# Villisca 2

June 9, 1912, was a Sunday, and the lights were out. Villisca, Iowa, was a town of 2,000 to 2,200 people; it was technically a city, and in 1912 such a place was normally referred to as a city. Villisca had installed streetlights in 1888, but the streetlights had been turned out due to a dispute between the city and the power company over the cost of electricity. Overcast skies had returned Villisca to a medieval darkness.

There was a Children's Day service at the Presbyterian church, starting at 8:00 p.m.; the family of Josiah and Sarah Moore attended and participated in the service, which Sarah had organized. Two little girls who were friends of Katherine Moore, Ina and Lena Stillinger, spent the afternoon playing at the Moore house. They lived outside of town and were supposed to spend the night with their grandmother, who lived in Villisca, but before the service Joe Moore called their house and asked if the girls could stay the night with Katherine. The Stillingers' parents were not in the house, but an older sister gave permission for the change of plans.

The service ended about 9:30 p.m. At about the same time the city marshal, Hank Horton, was standing in the city park, talking to one of the night watchmen, when a man they did not recognize passed by a little distance away. Horton spoke to the man, but the stranger did not reply. The night watchman was holding a flashlight, and Horton said, "Why don't you throw your light on that man, and make him face around?" But the man was disappearing rapidly into the darkness, and the moment passed.

Joe Moore, also known as J. B. and more formally as Josiah, was the owner of the local John Deere store. He was a moderately prosperous small-town businessman raising a large family in a small, plain house. Joe was a cheerful, well-liked, simple man who, in the words of the Iowa attorney general, was "at peace with everybody."

About 7:00 a.m. Monday morning a neighbor noticed that no one was stirring outside the Moore house. The Moores had two horses, two cows, and some chickens, all of which needed attention, but the chickens had been left squawking in their coop. The Stillinger girls had not called home after daybreak, as they had been instructed to do. The neighbor knocked on the door, but the door was locked and there was no answer. She let the chickens out of their coop and called Joe Moore's brother, Ross Moore. Ross then called the John Deere store, where he was told that Joe had not come to work that morning. The clerk who answered the phone, the second-in-charge, walked to the Moore house, banged on the door, but then walked back to the store, the house still locked up tight. Ross Moore had a key to his brother's house, and by a little after 8:00 a.m. Ross was concerned enough that he went to the house.

There was no one around, the neighbor and the store clerk both having given up and gone home. Ross Moore checked on the livestock and then circled the house, banging on windows, trying to see in the windows and yelling out to see if anyone would answer. The neighbor returned. Ross unlocked the front door and/or forced it open. The house inside was very neat and entirely clean, but tainted with a foul odor and a terrible stillness. Across the parlor there was a small bedroom, called the parlor bedroom, where Katherine Moore normally slept, although on this night she was upstairs with her brothers. Ross Moore opened the door to the parlor bedroom, saw blood everywhere and the dead bodies of two young girls, obviously bludgeoned to death. He staggered back across the parlor, and moments later, sitting on the steps of the front porch, would utter the exact words that appear in countless crime books: *Something terrible has happened*.

The Villisca police force consisted of the city marshal, Horton, and a staff of at least two night watchmen. In support of these was a county sheriff, eighteen miles away in Red Oak, which was the county seat of Montgomery County. None of these men had any training to be a police officer, and none of them had any experience in dealing with any situation remotely like this.

Hank Horton rushed to the scene. The house, he said, was as dark as night. Lighting matches and holding them in front of him and armed only with a nightstick, Horton crept carefully from room to room, not knowing whether a madman might still be lurking somewhere in the house. In the match-lit darkness he found the bodies of the rest of the family, eight dead in all: Joe Moore (aged forty-three), Sarah Moore (forty), Herman (eleven), Katherine (nine), Boyd (seven) and Paul (five), and Lena Stillinger (eleven) and Ina Stillinger (nine). I apologize for the need to write this sentence, but the heads of all of the victims had been beaten to a pulp; it appeared that all had been hit in the head repeatedly with the blunt side of an axe, and that Joe Moore, in particular, had been hit many times. Sarah Moore had been hit at least once with the sharp side of the axe. A rusty axe, taken from the family's coal shed, was left in the parlor bedroom with the Stillinger girls. A kerosene lamp without its chimney was found on the floor of the upstairs bedroom where the parents slept; on the ceiling above there were marks made by the backswing of the axe, apparently by someone who was very short, as the ceiling was low, and a man of average height would have difficulty swinging an axe in the room. A second kerosene lamp, also without its chimney, was on the floor of the parlor bedroom. Multiple mirrors in the house had been covered with cloth or clothing, and all of the windows in the house not already covered with window shades had also been completely covered with cloth. Every outside door had been locked or wedged shut. A washbasin with bloody water sat on the kitchen table, and a slab of bacon, taken from the ice box, was on the floor of the parlor bedroom, where it had apparently been used as a masturbatory aid.

When Horton exited the house there were neighbors gathering near the door, including one of the night watchmen. Horton pulled the door shut and spoke to Ross Moore, saying, "My God, Ross, there's somebody murdered in every bed." He instructed the watchman not to allow anyone into the house, then ran for the center of town, looking for a doctor, Dr. Cooper. Pausing briefly at city hall to ask a clerk to call Red Oak and ask for help, he found Dr. Cooper in his office, finishing his morning coffee. Cooper and Horton returned to the house before 9:00 a.m., but a crowd was already gathering. Neighbors had called friends and relatives of the Moores, and their minister was there. After escorting Dr. Cooper around the house Horton returned to city hall, where he called a private detective he knew who had experience in investigating murders (Thomas O'Leary, of the Kirk Agency), called the county attorney, the coroner, and a couple of other local doctors. He located city officials, informed them of what had happened, and got authorization from them to call out the National Guard, and order them to surround the house, and to send for bloodhounds.

A local drugstore owner who had expensive photography equipment took the equipment to the house to document the scene, but after taking some pictures he may have been ordered out of the house by the coroner. (Sources conflict on this point.)

Horton's instructions to keep unauthorized people out of the house were not zealously enforced. Horton estimated in a subsequent hearing that at least twenty people had been through the house before the National Guard arrived about noon; others have estimated that the number could have been fifty to a hundred. Horton canvassed the local hotels, asking about any strangers in town, and met with the other people who had been through the house to document what they had seen. Volunteer posses were organized to search through all the outbuildings in town, looking in particular for bloody clothes that may have been discarded.

The bloodhounds were ordered from Beatrice, Nebraska, 134 miles to the west; the Nofzinger bloodhounds were regionally famous. It took hours for them to arrive. On Monday or Tuesday Horton questioned every neighbor who lived within sight of the Moore house and made notes of what they had to say, which in every case was that they hadn't seen anything unusual.

The bloodhounds didn't arrive until about 9:00 on Monday evening, a little more than twelve hours after the murders were discovered. They picked up the scent of someone at the scene of the crime, trailed it down the block, stopped briefly at the house of a neighbor, Frank Jones, and then, with hundreds of people trailing behind them, led the mob out into the country, where they lost the scent at the Nodaway River, which is more accurately described as a creek. It being nightfall the operation was shut down until the morning, when the bloodhounds repeated the process and traced the same route.

A coroner's jury went through the house and viewed the bodies late on that day. The coroner called undertakers from several nearby towns, and the bodies were removed to a makeshift morgue at the fire station late that night.

Roy Marshall, the most authoritative source on the events of the day, says that the crowds that arrived on the day of the tragedy were mostly local people and were of manageable size, but the crowds swelled enormously on the following days. Reporters came from many newspapers, of course, as well as thousands and thousands of people from out of town, drawn to the spectacle, and, again according to Marshall, dozens and dozens of private detectives. Photos taken later in the week show the streets of Villisca swarming with people, no doubt many times more people than actually lived in the town.

At the same time, we should point this out: that there were people living twenty miles from Villisca who heard nothing of the murders for at least some weeks, and knew nothing about them. Certainly the events in Villisca were a huge statewide sensation, but it was a different world: no television, no Internet, no radio. Many people either never read the newspaper or skipped disinterestedly over stories about out-of-town murders. Some people were illiterate. Farmers spent long days in the fields, particularly in midsummer, and went irregularly into town. Not everybody got the news.

The coroner's jury began hearing testimony (which was properly recorded) beginning on Tuesday, one day after the discovery of the bodies. The funerals were on Wednesday, June 12, attended by an estimated seven thousand people. The coroner and the other doctors who had been to the scene all believed that the victims had died shortly after midnight on Sunday night. All of the victims had been murdered in their sleep except perhaps Lena Stillinger, aged eleven; according to the testimony of Dr. F. S. Williams, Lena "lay as though she had kicked one foot out of her bed sideways, with one hand up under the pillow on her right side, half sideways, not clear over but just a little. Apparently she had been struck in the head and squirmed down in the bed, perhaps one-third of the way." Lena's nightgown was pushed up and she was wearing no undergarments. It appeared that the killer had used her underpants to wipe the blood off of his hands and off of the axe handle, as there was lint clinging to the handle of the axe. There was a bloodstain on the inside of her right knee, probably a handprint, and a defensive wound on her arm. Although the coroner did not say this as part of the official record, he would tell a private investigator (C. W. Tobie) that Lena Stillinger had been sexually molested after she was dead. All of the bodies had been completely covered with blankets, except that Lena's arm protruded out from beneath the blanket.

The Moore house had a barn. Found in the barn was a depression in a pile of hay that looked as if someone had made a bed there, and if you lay down exactly where that depression was, there was a knothole in front of your eye that enabled you to watch the Moores' house. It is presumed that the murderer lay quietly in that spot and watched the house go dark. Some people have theorized that the murderer entered the Moore house during the church program and hid in a closet until the family returned and went to bed. The authors, how-ever, believe that this is enormously unlikely.

The Villisca murders remain famous in the Midwest. Almost everyone from Iowa knows the general story. The Moore house is on the National Registry of Historic Places. It is used today as a haunted house for Halloween and for similar macabre events, a sort of low-level blood tourism like the famous Jack the Ripper walking tour in London. The county historical society has said that 80 percent of their requests for information concern the murders. The axe with which the murders were committed could be seen in the city hall from 1987 to 2004, although it is not currently on display. Books have been written about Villisca, and still are.

The doctor(s) who examined the bodies believed that each had been hit *repeatedly* in the head with an axe. We question whether this is true, and frankly believe that it probably is not. Our opin-ion is that these doctors had never seen anyone who had been hit hard in the head with a heavy axe before, and they had no idea how completely the human head could be destroyed by one blow from a heavy axe.

But as to the actual facts of the case, what I have told you is really all that is known. There is another story about Villisca, a rich and complicated story that goes on for years, goes on for decades, and we will tell you that story in chapters XV through XVII, because it is an interesting story that we believe you will enjoy reading, and also because that story has never been told in print the way that it deserves to be told. But as to the actual facts of the Moore case, we're pretty much done here.

# CHAPTER XV

# Villisca 3

After a day or two the tourist ghouls went home, leaving Villisca in meltdown shock. Children long accustomed to running all over the innocent little town with minimal supervision were suddenly on a three-foot leash, never again out of their parents' sight; those children would say decades later that Villisca was never the same. For the rest of the summer families would bunk together so that one father or the other could sit up through the night with a loaded shotgun. The words *gossip* and *speculation* no longer describe the conversations that followed; this was *Terror*. Gossip is a rapier, slicing quickly and leaving its victims to bleed from small cuts; this was more on the scale of a bomb, creating a crater where the heart of the town had once been.

But let us call it gossip; *Who do you think it was? What did you see? What do you know? What have you heard? Who do you suspect?* There is a contrast here between Villisca and Paola, the two atrocities unquestionably committed by the same man in essentially the same manner, only days apart. Paola buried the event and moved on immediately; two months after the murders you can't find much interest in them in the local papers. The body count was much higher in Villisca and the town not as large, but more to the point, the victims in Villisca were well-loved members of the community, people everybody knew, whereas the Hudsons were barely acquainted with Paola. Some people decided the Hudsons had been murdered by someone who knew them before they came to town; others, that it had been someone from the train. In either event it was over. It was never *over* in Villisca; it hung around the town like a wounded monster, an unwelcome guest at every gathering. The reporters and most or all of the police had instantly connected the Villisca murders to those in other towns, but the people of Villisca never accepted that. It was the connection to the other murders which made an immediate sensation of the Villisca crime; it was the realization that these crimes were part of a *series* that sent the press running to Villisca. When the murders happened the police immediately sent for bloodhounds, but when the bloodhounds told them that the killer had left town, they just ignored that and went on. The private detective who was called by Marshal Horton hours after the discovery of the bodies, Detective O'Leary, clearly and absolutely believed the murders had been committed by what we would now call a serial murderer (page 46, Roy Marshall; Villisca sources explained in chapter XVII). That wasn't enough to make the townspeople feel safe. The Montgomery county sheriff, Oren Jackson, believed that the crime was committed by outsiders, not by people from Villisca (page 79, Roy Marshall). It didn't get through.

What happened in Paola was on the fringe of town, and what happened in Villisca was at the heart of the town, but more than that, the people of Paola did not know the Hudsons, mostly had never met them and never heard of them, whereas Joe Moore—a business owner in the center of town—was known to everyone, liked by almost everyone, and loved by many—as was his wife, as were his children, as were the Stillinger girls. The people of Paola thus naturally perceived what had happened as coming to them from the outside, whereas the people of Villisca perceived what had happened as coming from within. They never accepted that they had been hit by a moving force; they saw themselves as betrayed by someone within, someone who was still there.

Frank Jones was perhaps the most successful man in Villisca at the time of the murders. Beginning modestly, he had built a substantial fortune based around a hardware and farm implements business, and then later, a bank. At the time of the murders he owned a car dealership as well—not a big deal in 1912, when not so many cars were sold. In 1912 he represented Montgomery County (in which Villisca sits) in the Iowa state legislature, and he was among the leaders of the state legislature. At the time of the murders he was running for the state senate; he would win the seat. I'm not saying that without the murders he would have been governor in ten years, but I wouldn't have bet against it, either.

Jones was a leader in his church and in the community. He had never taken a drink of liquor, even a sip of beer, and people who had known him for decades would say that they had never heard him use a curse word. When terror was the bread of Villisca and gossip was the wine, however, Jones became one of the targets of the gossip; one among many, but one of them. Joe Moore had been Frank Jones's assistant in his hardware and farm implements store, his right-hand man. Moore had left to start his own business, becoming Jones's competitor. Moore was more likeable than Jones, friendlier and more approachable, and he had taken a good many of Jones's customers with him when he left. There may have been some ill feeling between them, or not, and the bloodhounds did stop briefly at Jones's house as they were trailing the scent, but there is no real evidence that Jones ever disliked Moore or was ever angry at him for leaving and starting his own business; Jones, after all, had done the same thing to *his* employer years earlier. In any case some years had passed since Moore had left Frank Jones's employment, and normalcy had settled over their long relationship. Small-town business rivals are often friends.

Have you ever seen the 1962 movie *The Music Man*? It's a delight, if you haven't seen it, a movie in the tradition of *It's a Wonderful Life* and *Field of Dreams*, rather than *Psycho*.

Villisca happened in the exact time and place depicted in *The Music Man*. *The Music Man* is set in a small city in Iowa, and the first scenes of the movie are in the last days of June 1912. The movie is useful for helping to understand the time and the place—for illustrating the way, for example, that the trains connected the small town to the world at large. The opening scenes of the movie are Harold Hill on the train and jumping off the train, and there is constant talk, throughout the movie, about getting back on the train and getting out of town. In *The Music Man* the tranquil lives of the half-sleeping burghers are disrupted by a roguish con man intent on making a few bucks and getting out before he gets caught; in Villisca the tranquil lives of the half-sleeping burghers were devastated by as evil a man as has ever walked the face of the earth.

But there was a con man who came to Villisca, too, not in June of 1912 but in April 1914, almost two years after the murders. His name was J. N. Wilkerson, James Newton Wilkerson. He was a private detective, in the employ of the Kansas City office of the Burns Detective Agency. We could not quite say that he was as reprehensible as The Man from the Train himself; that is an extraordinary standard. Wilkerson was intelligent, charming in one-to-one conversation, and charismatic from the stage. Wilkerson saw in the Villisca tragedy a chance to make some money.

The Burns Agency had been hired by the state of Iowa to investigate the murders in the first days after the crime. The Burns investigator assigned to the case was C. W. Tobie. Tobie preferred to work undercover, so the fact that he was a private detective was kept secret. He worked the case through the end of August 1912, filing daily reports with the agency, but in early September Tobie was promoted to head of Burns's Chicago office, and the Villisca investigation was taken over by W. S. Gordon. He made no secret of the fact that he was a Burns detective employed by the state, and sometimes talked to the newspapers to explain what was being done. This was preferable, from the standpoint of the state, because Tobie's secrecy had left the people of Villisca convinced that the state was doing nothing to help.

By the winter of 1912 to 1913 the Burns Agency had run out of leads and had stopped actively investigating the case. In late 1913, a year after the murders, the relatives of the victims met with the mayor of Villisca, a local dentist, who was in charge of the Villisca reward fund. The mayor set up a meeting with the county attorney and Iowa Attorney General George Cosson. The attorney general's office still had the arrangement with the Burns Agency. It would cost $8 to $10 per day to put an investigator on the case, but Sarah Moore's father had agreed to put up $250, the attorney general's office could kick in a little bit of money, and the Villisca reward fund could be repurposed to pay for a detective. Montgomery County officials attended the meeting but did *not* agree to underwrite the investigation, which later became significant. Among the four parties, they decided to contact the Burns Detective Agency and get the investigation going again.

The Burns Agency now assigned J. N. Wilkerson to the case. Where others saw tragedy and horror, Wilkerson saw opportunity. Wilkerson heard the rumors about Jones's involvement in the murders, as he heard similar rumors about many others, but he was much more interested in Jones because Jones had money. No doubt the rumors about Jones were included in the file that Wilkerson was given when he was assigned the case. Just like an advertiser or a salesman or a lawyer, Wilkerson studied the file that had been assigned to him, looking for an angle that he could play. Frank Jones was an angle. Wilkerson was in fact a lawyer, having been admitted to the bar in Texas in 1890, but let's not dwell on that; the reputation of lawyers doesn't need the hit.

Jack Boyle wrote crime stories for the *Kansas City Post* and other publications. In 1914 Boyle went to Villisca to do a story about the murders. He called the Burns Agency and asked to talk to whoever was in charge of the investigation. They denied that they had any connection to the investigation—standard practice, probably—but Boyle returned to Villisca and was able to make a connection with J. N. Wilkerson.

Wilkerson and Boyle became partners in the con, Newman and Redford in *The Sting*, Wilkerson in the lead and Boyle as his accomplice. In the summer of 1915 Boyle confronted Frank Jones, claimed that he was in possession of evidence that proved Jones was involved in the murders, and offered him a chance to tell his side of the story before the reports were published. He invited Jones up to his hotel room. Wilkerson was hiding in the hotel room, and had set up a Dictaphone (a recording device) to make a record of whatever was said. Jones was blindsided by the accusation—up to that point there had been nothing but some essentially innocuous rumors—but he refused to go to Boyle's hotel room; he offered to talk to Boyle about the case, but not in the hotel room, they would have to go to his store. Boyle said No, it had to be the hotel room; Jones said No, it had to be in the store, and the interview never happened.

Weeks later, another newspaper reporter approached Jones with an offer; this reporter was named Bell, but he was using the name Daley. Bell/Daley said that he had come into possession of the reports from the Burns Agency concerning the murders. The reports were very damaging to Jones, said the middleman, but for $25,000 Jones could purchase the reports, and if he did, he could be assured that all investigations of him would never see the light of day. $25,000 in 1915 was roughly equivalent to $600,000 in 2017.

There is no doubt that this meeting took place; Bell said that it did, Jones said that it did, and Wilkerson acknowledged that he had cooperated in setting it up. But, Wilkerson insisted, it was not blackmail; it was merely an investigative ploy. If Jones expressed an interest in purchasing the packet, that would show that he had something to hide. This kind of "blackmail by newspaper" was quite common in that era. There were newspapers—dozens of them—which were essentially extortion rackets; their reason for publishing was to extort money for the stories they agreed not to publish. There is a very good book about the practice called *Minnesota Rag: Corruption, Yellow Journalism, and the Case That Saved Freedom of the Press* by Fred Friendly. Often, within that practice, a private investigator or a city cop would team up with a newspaper "reporter"; the private eye would dig up dirt, and the newspaper guy would offer not to publish it in exchange for money. Dividing the action between them, they were trying to create a situation in which neither of them could be shown to have committed a crime.

Wilkerson also did things like this in other cases; I'll explain later. Jones knew that he hadn't done anything, so he told Wilkerson, Boyle, and Bell what they could do with their threats. He wasn't going to pay them a dime.

But Wilkerson was not making an idle threat. Wilkerson began a campaign to prosecute Jones for the murders, a devious, energetic, and resourceful campaign that he would sustain for several years. Perhaps he thought that Jones would succumb to the pressure and pay off the blackmail; perhaps he simply switched strategies and decided to play another angle. Wilkerson worked with the rumors, mined the gossip as if it were gold. He worked with the weak, the excitable, and the irresponsible. He ingratiated himself to the families of the victims, becoming their spokesman and their advocate. He loved the widows, and the widows loved him. He would sit and talk with the people who had no one else to talk to; he would talk to them for hours, waiting for them to say something he wanted to hear. *You saw what?! Oh, my God; that's incredible. That's amazing. What else did you see? What else did you hear? Oh, you have to share this with the public. What you have told me is so tremendously important. You have to do the right thing here. You have valuable information about this terrible crime. I know this is hard for you, but I need you to talk about this at my next public meeting.*

Wilkerson gave vulnerable people praise and reinforcement for telling ridiculous stories that would have drawn a scornful look from any legitimate investigator. When he had two facts, two claims, he would go for three; when he had three witnesses, he would go for four. The fountainhead of Wilkerson's case was a nutty woman from Marshalltown, Iowa, two hundred miles away, Vina Tompkins. Mrs. Tompkins claimed that she had been raised and had lived all of her life among a gang of criminals who committed terrible crimes from coast to coast, that her ex-husband, her current husband, and all three of her brothers were members of this gang. She claimed that she had spent time in Villisca (in fact she had not), that she knew the Moore family, that she had been in the Moores' house, and that she knew the full story of the murders.

Wilkerson, a highly intelligent man, had to know that Vina (Vine-Uh) had no actual information about the case. But Vina Tompkins could be manipulated to say almost anything that he wanted her to say. He thus began to bolster her reputation for credibility, in the same way that he worked to destroy the reputations of those who opposed him. Vina Tompkins would ultimately deny that she had ever said most of the things that Wilkerson claimed she had said, but that was years later, and by that time Wilkerson had developed many other "witnesses."

In early July 1914, a family was murdered with an axe in Blue Island, Illinois. As nearly as we can tell that case was unrelated to The Man from the Train, although we can't be certain of that. William Mansfield had been married to a woman murdered in the Blue Island massacre, and had abandoned her and her family. Mansfield got his wife and another woman pregnant at about the same time, and abandoned his wife to live with the other woman. He was a suspect in the murder of his wife's family.

J. N. Wilkerson traveled to Blue Island, looked into the case, and adopted Mansfield as part of his case against Frank Jones. Wilkerson claimed that he could prove that Mansfield was in Villisca on the night of June 9, 1912, and that he was in Paola on the night the Hudsons were murdered, and also that he could tie him to another murder. None of this had any foundation in fact; Wilkerson was just making it up as he went along.

Frank Jones's son, Albert Jones, was married to a young woman named Dona. Dona was quite a looker, and she had a reputation; she had been around the block a few times. A rumor spread that Dona had been involved in a secret relationship with J. B. Moore, and that this had provoked Frank Jones to set up the murders.

No evidence for any of that, really; Dona Jones had almost certainly been a little bit free with her embraces, and perhaps had married Albert Jones, who was basically a walking pumpkin, to share in the family's money. To me, this is just like the stories about Anna Hudson's lover, and Alice Schultz's lovers, and May Alice Burnham's lover. Sex is always suspected of inspiring every dark and secret act—for good reasons; sex *is* at the origin of many murder plots; every cop will tell you that. Sex was at the root of this case—but not the kind of inappropriate-but-normal sexual impulse that leads a man to sleep with his neighbor's wife; rather, it was sexuality of a horribly twisted kind.

I am of necessity leaving out steps and stages; Wilkerson's case against Frank Jones et al. evolved from one set of accusations to another. Con men talk in circles. To present these accusations as a cohesive, logical case would be inaccurate, since they never were, and to present them in the stages that Wilkerson presented them would require years, since Wilkerson shifted his narrative constantly over a period of years. But in short form: Frank Jones was allegedly upset at J. B. Moore not only because of business competition, but also because Moore was canoodling his son's wife. Jones hired Mansfield to murder the family; Albert Jones helped them do it, and a vast network of city and state officials were involved in a conspiracy to cover it up and obstruct prosecution.

Through the second half of 1915 and the first half of 1916 Wilkerson worked to indict Frank Jones, but the county attorney, Ratcliff, wouldn't hear it; he knew that Jones had nothing to do with the crime. In the summer of 1916 Frank Jones was running for reelection to the state senate, in a hard-fought Republican primary contest against the same Ratcliff. In early June, days before the Republican primary, someone mailed a flyer to hundreds of potential voters, showing large pictures of William Mansfield and Frank Jones, and bluntly accusing Mansfield of the murders and Frank Jones of setting up the murders. There is no doubt that Boyle and Wilkerson were behind the flyers, although there is no direct proof of this. Ratcliff, the "beneficiary" of the smear, was horrified by it. The flyers were mailed from Kansas City, where Boyle and Wilkerson both operated, and used a photo of Mansfield that was a part of the Burns file on the case. On learning of the flyers Ratcliff went immediately to Villisca, went to Jones's home, and met with him.

Following that meeting, Frank Jones denounced the libel and stated that he would file suit against anyone who publicly accused him of being involved in the murders. He had said the same thing before, but that was private, and off the record. This was public, and in the newspapers.

Jones lost the primary election, although Villisca still voted for him. (The Villisca area had a population of three to four thousand people, including farmers near the town; the senate district that Jones represented had a population larger than thirty thousand.) The purpose of the flyers was not merely to impact the election but also to set the stage for other actions. The fact of the flyers broke down the resistance of other publications to publishing the allegations. The year 1916 is four years after the murders; not a lot has happened within the legal system in those four years. The next two years would see an avalanche of lawsuits, arrests, and prosecutions. A week after the Republican primary, Jack Boyle published a story in the *Kansas City Post* directly alleging that William Mansfield was connected to sixteen murders, and that warrants had been issued in Red Oak, the county seat, for his arrest in connection with the Villisca murders. The second half of that was true; warrants had been issued for Mansfield's arrest in connection with the Villisca murders.

The story told by the *Kansas City Post* article was essentially the Vina Tompkins story. The story was preposterous on its face, and embroidered with elements literally lifted from fiction. Boyle had published a series of fictional detective stories under the pen name Boston Blackie. Now Boyle claimed that Mansfield had long been called Blackie—totally untrue—and he dubbed Mansfield "Insane Blackie Mansfield." Boyle's story was picked up by dozens of other newspapers, and thousands of people now came to believe that the Villisca murders had been solved.

With Ratcliff running for the Iowa senate, the county attorney's job had been filled by a young, inexperienced lawyer who was heading into an election of his own. A resolution to the Villisca mystery might secure his reelection. Wilkerson persuaded the rookie prosecutor to charge Mansfield with the Villisca murders, promising him evidence to be produced later. Mansfield was arrested by Wilkerson and other Burns operatives in Kansas City two days after Boyle's story was published. They spent the night trying to sweat a confession out of him; according to a lawsuit later decided in Mansfield's favor, Wilkerson and other Burns detectives on the day of the arrest punched Mansfield repeatedly, loosened several of his teeth, threatened his life, held an axe over his head, and while driving over a bridge, threatened to pitch him into the river. Mansfield was a tough guy who had spent time in Leavenworth; he wasn't giving anything up, and, in fact, he had no knowledge of the murders.

The Mansfield case went to a grand jury in Red Oak in mid-July 1916. The county attorney presented the case with J. N. Wilkerson sitting at his side, staging the witnesses; they were asking for indictments of William Mansfield and another man not named by the newspapers. They got nothing. Numerous witnesses refused to say what Wilkerson had promised they would say; others told stories so improbable it was hard not to laugh. The jury returned no indictments, and Mansfield was released on July 21. Mansfield's legal involvement with the Villisca case from the time he was accused until the time he was legally cleared was just a few weeks.

Villisca citizens had read in the newspapers a month earlier that the case was solved. Now the accused murderer was free, and the man supposed to have been pulling the strings remained in the clear. The young county attorney lost his reelection bid. Undaunted, Wilkerson told everybody who would listen that Frank Jones had fixed the grand jury. He just needed another grand jury, he said; he needed another shot at it.

Frank Jones now hired his own detectives and began to fight back. On August 3, 1916, Wilkerson held a public meeting of his supporters on a farm near Villisca. Numerous speakers accused Jones of arranging the murders. Jones had said that he would sue any man who said this in public, and he followed through, filing a slander suit against J. N. Wilkerson and numerous other people, including Joe Moore's brother, Ross, who had discovered the first bodies. Later the suit was refiled to dismiss Ross Moore and all of the other defendants, leaving Wilkerson as the lone defendant.

Filing that slander suit, Jones would say, was the worst mistake he would ever make. The reputation of the Burns Agency was under attack, and the Burns Agency would send in the marines. The agency rushed an expensive and experienced lawyer to Villisca, backed by a squadron of private detectives. Out-lawyering Jones's team ten to one, they converted the slander suit into a prosecution of Frank and Albert Jones. Witness after witness now came forward with stories to tell about Frank Jones—all of them later discredited, but Jones and his attorneys were caught off guard by the charges, and were unprepared to rebut them. Every seat in the courtroom was filled. People stood in the back of the courtroom and flowed into the hallway. Every hotel room in town was sold; every newspaper in the region was represented. Wilkerson had organized a group of his followers to sit in the center of the courthouse, to murmur appreciatively at points made in his favor and to laugh aloud at statements made by Jones's attorneys. The first vote of the jury was six to six. Gradually they swung toward Wilkerson. The slander suit not only failed, it left large sections of the public convinced that Frank Jones had in fact arranged the murders.

This set the stage for another grand jury to look into the case, this time looking not at William Mansfield but directly at Frank Jones. We'll get back to that in a moment. In 1915, J. N. Wilkerson had begun a series of public meetings. The public meetings initially were small, informal, and infrequent. Over a period of three years they grew larger, more enthusiastic, and more frequent.

> The small, private meetings he began conducting well before the Mansfield arrest, events that often included guards to keep out the unwanted, were now public events. He was a charismatic speaker and people wanted to hear what he had to say, and in 1917 they came in droves. The popularity of his meetings was enormous, attracting more and more people.
>
> —Roy Marshall, *Villisca*

People were still excited about the case years after the murders. Wilkerson could fill a house with people anxious to talk about the murders, and fill another one two weeks later. These meetings are brilliantly described by Troy Taylor in *Murdered in Their Beds*:

> The program went on for more than two hours. Eventually Wilkerson returned to the stage and spoke about the investigation he was conducting and how dangerous it was, what a great service it did for the people, how good he was at it and of course, how he needed money to keep it going. He claimed that many people were afraid to tell what they knew about the murders and would only come to him in secret. Because they would not talk publicly, he said he was unable to use what they told him, due to the fact that he was an impeccable and honest investigator. Anyone who claimed that he brought questionable evidence into the case, he told the crowd, was lying.

One meeting, in January 1917, drew 1,200 people—more than half the population of the town, although of course many of those who attended were not from the town itself. That meeting was organized in an effort to force Montgomery County to pay an unpaid bill for Burns's services in investigating the case, about $2,800. The investigation had been funded by $250 from Sarah Moore's father, a Villisca reward fund, and the Iowa attorney general's office. The money from Sarah Moore's father and the reward fund had long since run out, and after Wilkerson and Boyle charged the attorney general's office with covering up the investigation to save Frank Jones, the attorney general's office wasn't paying their bills. The county had never agreed to pay for Burns's investigation, although (after another large, loud public meeting lasting for several hours) they agreed to pay part of the bill. But during this battle over who would write the checks, a wealthy farmer started a "subscription list" of citizens who agreed to collectively underwrite the investigation. In a sense this was the worst-case scenario; it meant that Wilkerson had an unlimited line of credit to keep the investigation going—as long as he could keep people angry, as long as he could keep the public riled up and demanding justice.

Over the course of three years and more of these tent-revival-type meetings, Wilkerson built his case against Frank Jones. People who had told police investigators in the days after the murders that they had seen nothing and knew nothing now were willing to swear that they had seen things and knew things. A widow named Margaret Landers lived across the street from the murder scene. On the day after the murders, she had told Marshal Horton that she had seen nothing. Four years after the murders, under the guidance of Wilkerson, Mrs. Landers began to claim that she had seen things, important and meaningful things, on the night of the murders. Her son stepped forward to support her story. On the day after the murders he had said that he had seen someone walking near the house on Sunday evening, but didn't know who it was, but now he knew who it was. It was Albert Jones, he said. He had known Albert Jones all of his life; they had grown up together.

Wilkerson had prepared a "dope sheet" outlining his case against Frank and Albert Jones. But after Wilkerson beat Jones in the slander suit at the end of 1916, Iowa officials decided that another grand jury was in order. That grand jury—the second grand jury to look into the case—was called in the last week of February 1917 and began hearing evidence on March 5.

The waters had now been flowing in favor of J. N. Wilkerson for almost three years. Animosity against Jones was at such a fever pitch, by early 1917, that there was a serious fear that he might be lynched (although lynching was unheard of in Iowa by this time) or that he could be shot by some justice-seeking farmer.

# CHAPTER XVI

# Villisca 4

Wilkerson will not be accused of being ashamed of himself. So much of his stuff is so utterly silly that it would not be given credence except by those who are living under the spell of extreme excitement. The situation in Villisca and Red Oak is as terrible as it is absurd.

—Storm Lake *Pilot-Tribune,*
July 1917, Storm Lake, Iowa

In late February 1917, J. N. Wikerson instigated an effort to burglarize Frank Jones's store. This act would contribute somewhat to Wilkerson's eventual undoing, but not right away.

Until 1917 Wilkerson had never lived in Villisca; he worked the case a few days at a time with other cases, in and out on the train. While in Villisca he stayed with a woman with whom he had developed a relationship; at least one woman, or at least one woman at a time. In the summer of 1915 a young schoolteacher named Nellie Byers was raped and murdered in central Kansas. It was relatively obvious who had committed the crime. The crime occurred in an isolated area but near a farmhouse, and a man who was staying in that house was a convicted felon with a history of violence against women. Although other people also lived at the house, the suspect acknowledged that he was there alone on the day of the murder. Nellie Byers had expressed a fear of him, and would try to avoid him. The suspect, Archibald Sweet, acknowledged being within two hundred yards of the spot where the crime had occurred, but claimed that he had seen and heard nothing. Men's footprints at the scene of the crime were of the same size as Sweet's shoes.

The county attorney, however, knew that he needed more to secure a conviction. He contacted the Burns Agency, asking for a private detective, and the Burns Agency sent him J. N. Wilkerson.

Wilkerson, within hours of arriving on the scene, enquired as to whether there was a reward in the case. No, the prosecutor said; the suspect is already in custody. Why would there be a reward?

Well, said Wilkerson, what if it wasn't him? If that suspect was released, could there be a reward then? After meeting with Archibald Sweet and "interrogating" him for about three hours, Wilkerson announced that Sweet was innocent, that another man had committed the crime, and that they needed to write to the governor and see if they could arrange for a reward fund for the proper solution of this case.

Over the next few weeks, it became clear that Wilkerson—being paid by the county—was actually working hand in glove with Archibald Sweet to try to manufacture a case against another man, and that this was being done in order to pursue a reward. On several occasions, Wilkerson generously offered to split the reward with the county attorney, if a reward could be arranged.

Within a few weeks, the county attorney fired the Burns Agency, but Wilkerson hung around and gave interviews to the local newspapers, insisting that Sweet was innocent and that he was being framed by the county attorney. The prosecutor was able to convict Sweet of the murder, despite Wilkerson's interference, but refused to pay the Burns Agency for Wilkerson's services.

In 1917, about the time that Wilkerson's program in Villisca was finally collapsing, Archibald Sweet signed an affidavit confirming that Wilkerson had proposed that the two of them work together to frame an innocent man, and outlining at every step what Sweet should say and how he should act to help bring this about. When Frank Jones and those on his side finally had Wilkerson on the run, this affidavit (and others related to the Nellie Byers case) became one of their weapons.

\*    \*    \*

Frank Jones had lived among the people of Montgomery County all of his life and had won election to the Iowa senate by carrying a huge percentage of the Villisca-area vote. He was quite astonished, at first, to find himself outmaneuvered by an outsider, his reputation torn to shreds by a lowlife con man.

But after he lost the primary election in June 1916, Jones began to fight back, and in early 1917 the tide seemed to be turning. The town's businessmen rallied around him. Jones hired his own private detective; that private eye, posing as a newspaperman, deeply infiltrated Wilkerson's operation. By February 1917, Jones had a safe stuffed with affidavits about the Nellie Byers case and with other information damaging to J. N. Wilkerson. Wilkerson—who had almost certainly stolen files from the county attorney's office in an earlier incident—now located a burglar who could break into Jones's store and into the safe. It was a cloak-and-dagger operation; Wilkerson hired people through intermediaries, arranged to be out of the area and with an alibi at the time of the crime, and surreptitiously handed off the keys to the getaway car without actually going to the car, doing everything he could do to keep his hands clean.

Frank Jones's spy within Wilkerson's operation, however, had become one of Wilkerson's trusted assistants, and was in on the plot. When the burglars showed up at Frank Jones's store in the predawn hours of a bitterly cold February night, Frank Jones and Hank Horton were waiting for them inside the store with loaded shotguns. Horton's shotgun misfired and the burglars escaped, but again, Jones had spies in Wilkerson's nest; the escape was temporary. Wilkerson's men ratted him out. Wilkerson acknowledged arranging the burglary but claimed that it had been merely an effort to recover evidence that would incriminate Jones in the murders.

The Burns Agency was now plagued by legal troubles around the nation. By early 1917 James Burns himself was under indictment for several different forms of illegal surveillance, and a judge in Florida had declared that the Burns Agency was "a menace to the public." The Burns Agency lost $2,500 and got another black eye when William Mansfield successfully sued Wilkerson for assaulting him at the time of Mansfield's arrest in June 1916. Wilkerson's involvement in the break-in at Jones's store was now suspected, although Wilkerson would not be charged with that crime until several months later. Jack Boyle, Wilkerson's publishing partner, was arrested in Kansas City in January 1917 for possession of drugs, an offense with which he had a long acquaintance; that arrest took Boyle permanently out of the story.

Wilkerson hadn't liked the previous grand jury, July 1916, which had failed to indict Mansfield or Frank Jones, but when Montgomery County and the state of Iowa took Wilkerson's case back to the grand jury in late February 1917, there were two things that were significantly different—two things beyond this accumulation of hickeys. First, the second grand jury had access to Wilkerson's dope sheet, outlining his case against Jones, explaining what each witness would say that would support the case. And second—in large part because of this case—the Iowa state legislature had authorized the Iowa attorney general's office to hire a permanent staff of professional investigators.

Within days the members of the grand jury had begun to notice that witness after witness was saying things different from what Wilkerson's dope sheet had promised they would say. In some cases they backed off what they had said before, in some cases witnesses flatly denied that they had ever said what Wilkerson claimed they would say, while in other cases they took what Wilkerson said they would say and ran on down the field with it, making new allegations that went well beyond the old. A man who was reported by Wilkerson to have seen Albert Jones and two other men standing outside the Moore house about midnight on the night of the murders now traveled back to Iowa from Montana to say that he had seen nothing of the kind and had never said that he had. Other recantations or denials were just as stark. The one constant was that the testimony never matched what was supposed to be said.

Wilkerson's witnesses could be sorted into two groups. One group—70 percent of the witnesses, and more—seemed reliable enough but testified about matters peripheral to the case, not really damaging to Jones. The other group, the truly damaging witnesses, consisted of obviously and fantastically unreliable witnesses—notorious liars telling remarkable stories about how they happened to witness Jones and his partners plotting and carrying out the murders. In every case except one (Warren Noel) these people had withheld crucial information about a terrible and infamous crime for years after the fact, in almost every case denying at the time that they had seen or heard anything. None of these witnesses had ever reported having any information about the crime until interviewed by J. N. Wilkerson.

And when the professional investigators from the Iowa attorney general's office checked out details from their stories, nothing checked out; nobody seemed to have been where they claimed to have been at the crucial times.

As the slander suit filed by Frank Jones against Wilkerson had switched poles and become a trial of Frank Jones for the murders of the Moore family, the grand jury proceeding looking into Frank Jones now flipped and became an investigation of J. N. Wilkerson. Noting remarkable discrepancies between the dope sheet and the testimony of one witness, Wilkerson was called to the witness stand to explain the discrepancies. Wilkerson refused to answer questions and was ordered to spend twenty-four hours in the county jail for contempt of court. His legion of supporters stormed around town demanding his release, but Wilkerson did his twenty-four hours in jail.

The grand jury report excoriated Wilkerson and debunked his allegations. The report stung Wilkerson, but he still had hundreds of passionate supporters in the small town. Wilkerson submitted a bill to the county for his investigation, $595.29; there was another contentious public meeting about whether the bill should be paid, but it was paid. The Burns Agency fired Wilkerson, apparently in April 1917. That didn't finish him, either. He stayed in town and continued to hold public meetings.

A bill was passed by the Iowa legislature, the Thompson Bill, aimed directly at putting an end to Wilkerson's operation. Wilkerson and a troupe of his supporters traveled to Des Moines and met with the governor, William L. Harding, pleading with him not to sign the bill. Wilkerson told the governor that the bill was aimed at him, in particular, and would restrict his freedom of speech. All of that was true, but on April 26, 1917, Harding signed the bill into law.

\*　\*　\*

This was the same era in which Rasputin was murdered, and J. N. Wilkerson was harder to stop than Rasputin. Under attack, Wilkerson attacked. In court on charges of arranging the burglary, Wilkerson filled the courtroom with his supporters, who cheered for him and snickered at the points made against him, just as they had during the slander litigation. He accused the attorney general's office of stealing his investigative file, which he had worked on for years. He referred to Iowa Attorney General Horace Havner as a shyster, and began to mock him and deride him in his public meetings—just as he had done to Senator Jones, to Marshal Horton, to the previous attorney general, and to anyone else who opposed his operation.

It is a poor idea, for a con man, to make a mortal enemy of the state attorney general. If you are in the con man business, I would not recommend that you should do this. But Wilkerson had become a very serious problem. Theoretically banned from holding his public meetings in Iowa, Wilkerson moved his operation across the state line into Nebraska, at one point booking a special train to take people from western Iowa over to Nebraska to see the show; Wilkerson's operation sold tickets for the excursion. He drew large crowds, but after a couple of meetings Wilkerson realized that the Nebraskans were just there to watch and wouldn't give him money to support the investigation, so he moved back into Iowa; the Thompson Bill, aimed at stopping the public meetings, was unconstitutional and unenforceable, and Wilkerson just ignored it.

By now Wilkerson had convinced a large share of the area's population—almost certainly over half of them—that the elected officials were conspiring to hinder the prosecution of Frank Jones. Rather than discontinuing his public meetings, Wilkerson increased their frequency. He held court in every little town and small city in the area. His supporters organized themselves as the "Citizen's Investigative Committee," also known as the Montgomery County Protective Association. They had dues, they had officers, they had committees, they had projects. They had an oath. *I hereby promise under oath that I will not disclose the secrets of this organization, and that I will assist every effort this organization may make to uphold the law and further the cause of justice. I further pledge myself to defend this organization and its members against injustice of any kind.* Wilkerson no longer had to reserve the hall and post flyers about his upcoming meetings; that was done for him by his support group. His organization collected dues, passed the money to him, and kept records of how much money was raised at each event. Wilkerson had a list of "100 questions" that he wanted to ask Frank Jones; the list was a regular feature of his meetings. His organization got copies of the questions bound into a pamphlet and sold copies at his rallies, giving the profit to Wilkerson. He no longer needed the Burns Agency or the county; he no longer dreamed of extorting a payoff from Frank Jones. He was living off the land.

And the Iowa attorney general was about to do him a tremendous favor.

Iowa Attorney General Horace Havner had taken personal control of the 1917 grand jury (the second grand jury). Havner became fascinated by the crime. He knew that Wilkerson's case against Jones was a house of cards. But if Jones and Mansfield didn't commit the crime, he wondered, who did?

Enter Reverend Kelly.

The term *pathetic loser* will hardly do him justice. Born in England, Reverend L. G. J. Kelly, Lyn Kelly, was a tiny little man who was weak in every facet of his nature. He was physically very weak, he was mentally weak, and he was morally weak. These categories miss his central liability, which was a weakness of will, of focus, of energy, of determination. Almost all of us are weak in some of these ways and stronger in others. Reverend Kelly was that rare and unfortunate man who was weak in every area. He was not stupid, exactly; but his mind was so disorganized that he acted stupidly. Married to a stern, dour woman who towered over him, he would occasionally be caught peeping into his neighbor's windows and fleeing across the lawn, chased by an angry husband. When he got excited Kelly's speech became so disorganized that it was impossible to tell what he was talking about. In his letters, portions of which were published and thus survive, he would lose his train of thought in midsentence.

Reverend Kelly had attended the Children's Day service in Villisca, organized by Sarah Moore and attended by the Stillinger girls hours before the murders. He was not a real minister; he was a man in his forties who decided, after he had failed at numerous other professions, that he would try his hand at preaching. Although the word *intern* wasn't used across the map then as it is now, he was essentially an intern, taking classes at a seminary in Omaha and traveling around the circuit of Presbyterian churches in the area, trying to learn the preaching business. He had absconded repeatedly to avoid paying his debts. After the murders but before he was prosecuted he had been thrown out of divinity school and denounced by the Presbyterian churches association of South Dakota.

On the night of the murders Kelly was a block away, sleeping at the house of the minister who had invited him to the Children's Day service. He became fascinated by the Moore family murders as soon as he heard about them, obsessed by them at a disturbed level. He wrote to the Moores' minister, explaining his background as a detective and begging the minister to arrange for him to tour the murder house. Pretending to be a private detective, trained in England before he came to the United States, he wrote many letters to the governor of Iowa and to others concerned with the crime, explaining his theories about the case. He tried to work with the two most legitimate private investigators in the case, C. W. Tobie of the Burns Agency and Thomas O'Leary of the Kirk Agency, who was brought in on the day of the murders. Tobie wrote Kelly a blunt letter, telling him to butt out, while O'Leary, privately suspecting that Kelly might be involved in the crime, indulged him and would listen to what he had to say. One time, in the lobby of the Villisca hotel, Reverend Kelly acted out his theory of how the murders had occurred with such intensity that the night watchman was called to tell him to go back to his room.

In December 1913, Reverend Kelly, by now trying his hand as a writer, advertised for a secretary. He had no money to pay a secretary; he was just acting out a fantasy, just as he was acting out a fantasy in trying to be a preacher or a detective. When a sixteen-year-old girl answered his ad for a secretary, through the mail, he wrote back to her, explaining to her that in this position she would sometimes be expected to pose for him in the nude; in typical fashion he rambled on for several paragraphs about the ins and outs of posing in the nude in places where they would be completely alone and no one would know where they were and it was critical for her to keep this secret, and how did she feel about that?

She felt that she should contact the police. Actually, she felt she should talk to her minister, and her minister felt that he should contact the police, but the outcome was the same; the police contacted postal authorities, and the postal authorities began to investigate Reverend Kelly for using the United States mail to solicit a minor female. In early 1914 Reverend Kelly was arrested, after which he was involuntarily confined for several months in a mental institution in Washington, D.C. While he was there Reverend Kelly impressed those who were in charge of the place as being perhaps not one of the crazier people in the house, but certainly one of the most annoying. He ranted, attempted suicide, asked others to kill him, groped other prisoners, and talked endlessly about the Villisca murders. One of his jailers reported that Kelly said that he had committed the murders. The jailer reported this up the ladder, and the Washington authorities contacted people in Villisca.

For what it is worth, I'm not convinced that Kelly ever told anyone, before he was arrested, that he had committed the Villisca murders, although numerous sources say that he had. Kelly, when he was excited, babbled incoherently. He talked a great deal about being suspected of committing the crime; that was part of his every-day, every-hour conversation. Somebody thought he said that he had committed the murders himself; God only knows what he had actually said.

Sheriff Jackson and the county attorney had interviewed Kelly before and concluded that he had nothing to do with the murders, but they now traveled to Washington to interview him again. Kelly pulled himself together, vigorously denied that he had committed the crime, denied that he had ever said that he had, and gave a largely coherent interview consistent with his earlier statements. The sheriff and the prosecutor once more concluded that Kelly had nothing to do with the crime. Those holding Kelly decided that he was not a menace to society and released him, and he was never prosecuted for sending the salacious letters to the sixteen-year-old.

There were, however, two consequences to the episode. First, the press got wind of the fact that the investigators had made the trip to Washington. And second, Kelly, fired up again, began again writing letters to Iowa authorities explaining his theories of the crime. He was now being targeted as a suspect in the crime, Kelly said, because of his work as a detective; he was getting too close to the truth, and the real culprits were getting nervous.

Iowa Attorney General Horace Havner was intrigued. In May 1917, Havner reconvened the Montgomery County grand jury—the same grand jury which, in the previous month, had failed to indict anyone. In four days, they returned an indictment, charging Reverend Kelly with the murder of Lena Stillinger. Of course, it could be presumed that whoever killed Lena Stillinger had also killed the other people in the house, but Kelly was charged with only the murder of Lena. This was done as a hedge against double jeopardy. If Kelly was acquitted of the murder of Lena Stillinger, he could still be prosecuted for any of the other murders.

The indictment was supposed to be sealed, but everybody had spies. J. N. Wilkerson had a spy on the grand jury, so he knew that Kelly had been indicted. Havner didn't know exactly where Kelly was and didn't want him arrested right away, because he needed time to assemble his case against Kelly.

Wilkerson, however, tracked down Kelly and informed him that he (Kelly) had been indicted for the murders. Wilkerson befriended

Kelly and persuaded him to return to Iowa, present himself to the county attorney, and demand that the prosecution begin immediately.

It is impossible to explain how crazy this story is, but here's a detail that may help. When Wilkerson located Kelly in St. Louis, he whisked him away to a small town in Illinois, to make it harder for the prosecutors to arrest him. After a couple of days he went back to St. Louis, boxed up Kelly's possessions, and mailed them to a storage center in Kansas City. When he did that, though, he signed the receipt "F. F. Jones"—Frank Fernando Jones.

Why?

Wilkerson wanted to claim that Frank Jones was the puppet master behind the prosecution of Reverend Kelly. He was trying to set up a claim that Jones, operating in conjunction with the prosecutors, had seized Reverend Kelly's belongings in St. Louis, and had taken control of them, when in reality he himself had done this. That done, Wilkerson then escorted Kelly to Chicago, where Kelly stayed in a good hotel for a couple of days (at Wilkerson's expense) and met with attorneys before heading back to Iowa. Arriving in Red Oak on May 14, 1917, Kelly presented himself to the county attorney. This was a complete shock to the county attorney, since Kelly's indictment had been sealed, and Kelly wasn't even supposed to know that he was under investigation.

After Kelly was arrested, awaiting trial, he was housed at a prison in Logan, Iowa, ninety-two miles northwest of Villisca. According to Dr. Edgar V. Epperly (web post):

> The "Little Minister" had been interrogated repeatedly throughout the summer, but as the trial drew near, the state officials decided on one final all-out effort to get him to confess. Late in the afternoon of August 30, Kelly was brought into an interrogation room in the Logan, Iowa Jail and confronted by Attorney General Horace Havner, State Agents O. O. Rock and

James Risden, and the Harrison County Sheriff, M.D. Meyers. Thus began a grilling that was to last throughout the night. All big men, they played the bad cop role with the diminutive Reverend Kelly, breaking occasionally to return him to his cell. In jail with him he now found two "thieves" who assured him from their long criminal experiences it would go easier on him if he confessed. One of these "criminals" was actually a deputy sheriff from Pottawattamie County, G.W. Atkins, and the other a newspaper editor from Missouri Valley.

Around 5:00 a.m. Kelly broke and dictated a confession. He claimed to have had difficulty sleeping the murder night, so he went for a walk. While walking down the middle of the street he saw a light in a house and two children (Lena and Ina Stillinger) getting ready for bed. He heard the Lord's voice commanding him to "Suffer the children to come unto me," and, in another portion, "to slay and slay utterly." In a trancelike state, he walked to the back of the house, picked up the axe from inside the Moore family's coal shed, went in the kitchen door, and proceeded to kill everyone. He stayed in the house until first light, then let himself out the front door and left town.

The confession was retracted as soon as Kelly got a lawyer and a good night's sleep. It was inconsistent with the crime scene in numerous ways, and Kelly vigorously denied it for the rest of his life, but . . . there it was, a confession.

One of the mysteries of the murders is that the staircase in the Moore house creaked so loudly that investigators could never understand how the murderer reached the upstairs without waking the parents. I understand that and will explain it later, but one of Kelly's stories had him running up the stairway twice before he killed the parents—upstairs to kill the boys, downstairs to kill the girls, back upstairs to kill the parents.

The evidence against Kelly was:

1. The confession,

2. The fact that he was certainly in Villisca on the night of the murders,

3. Some claims that he talked about the murders before they were publicly known,

4. Allegations that he had sent a bloody shirt to an out-of-town laundry, and

5. The clear and convincing evidence that he was a weirdo who throughout his life had dealt poorly with his sexual urges.

Also, Kelly was left-handed, and there were some investigators who believed that the murderer might have been left-handed (as, in fact, he was).

The day of the murders was Kelly's first visit to Villisca. He was living at that time in Macedonia, forty miles northwest of Villisca; Macedonia was about one-tenth the size of Villisca. Kelly had preached at revival meetings in two settlements much smaller even than Macedonia on the Saturday before the murders, then had come to Villisca on the afternoon of the crime, where he attended the Sunday-evening service and spent the night at the home of the Moores' minister. He caught a train back to Macedonia at 5:19 a.m. on the morning of the murders. An old couple on the train and one man in Macedonia claimed that Kelly talked to them about the murders before the bodies were discovered.

These allegations, however, arose years after the murders. Kelly had come to Villisca without a change of clothes. When he boarded the 5:19 a.m. train those clothes were clean, or at least without obvious blood. The wife of the minister with whom he spent the night in Villisca testified that his bed had been slept in, and that there was no evidence that he had gone anywhere or done anything. To get back to Macedonia had required two train rides. Kelly had taken the same train passage two weeks later; after five years it was difficult to be certain that the conversation had not occurred on the latter journey.

Kelly went to the murder house, told those watching the house that he was a private detective, and was allowed to go through the house as dozens of other private detectives had been. The real evidence was that Kelly was a goofball, a pervert, and a petty criminal. He had no job skills; he was too weak to do manual labor and too unstable for anyone to hire him to be a store clerk, so he was unable to earn money in any conventional manner. He skipped out on his debts, because it is unclear what else he could have done. This speaks, again, to his quite unusual incompetence, but the Villisca prosecutors didn't need a hopeless incompetent; they needed a murderer; actually, a supercompetent murderer. Kelly was brought back to Red Oak, charged with murder, bullied into an obviously bogus confession, and put on trial.

Reverend Kelly's first trial (telegraphing the story) began on September 4, 1917. There were four lawyers on each side of the case, which a regional newspaper promised would be "the hardest fought legal battle ever staged in the middle west." On the day the trial began, Iowa Attorney General Horace Havner was arrested at the courthouse. One of Wilkerson's nutty witnesses was a prostitute named Alice Willard; I am sorry, a lady named Alice Willard, who, according to her own testimony, was hiding in a plum thicket with a traveling salesman when she witnessed a conversation between Frank Jones and one of his coconspirators. Havner had examined Willard very roughly during the grand jury proceedings of the previous March, and she alleged that Havner had met with her later, at a hotel, and had threatened to charge her with perjury if she repeated her stories under oath. A grand jury decided that this was witness tampering—"oppressing the witness"—and indicted him for it. Havner posted his own bond and returned to the courtroom for the prosecution of Kelly.

The first Kelly trial lasted three weeks and went to the jury on September 26. Wilkerson's supporters disrupted the trial constantly, crowding around Kelly to offer encouragement, patting him on the back and shaking his hand. The judge lectured the bailiff to put a stop to it, but the emotional crowd was uncontrollable. Two more bailiffs were added to the courtroom, and still the disruptions continued.

Within hours after the testimony ended the jury deadlocked, eleven to one; one juror stuck on not guilty by reason of insanity, while the other eleven were all committed to an outright acquittal. The judge, as he would do today, ordered them to go back and complete their assignment. After two more days and twenty-one ballots, all of them eleven to one, the judge accepted the impasse, and a hung jury was declared.

Despite the obvious impracticality of it, Havner had committed the state to a retrial. First, though, Havner had to fight his own legal battle, against the charge of oppressing the witness Alice Willard. The trial was an odd one. With a change of venue back to Logan, Iowa, Havner was back in the courthouse where he had extracted the confession from Reverend Kelly, with Reverend Kelly now housed in the same building awaiting a second trial—while Havner, the Iowa attorney general, was being prosecuted by the same Montgomery County attorney who was his cocounsel in the prosecutions of Reverend Kelly. After a few hours of testimony the judge ruled that even if everything Alice Willard said was true there was no crime, and threw out the case.

The trials were flying fast and furious now. About the same time, a grand jury in a neighboring county refused to indict Wilkerson for arranging the burglary attempt at Frank Jones's office. Wilkerson acknowledged that he had arranged the break-in but claimed that it was a lawful effort to obtain evidence about the murders. This was transparently false; one cannot presume that there is evidence about a murder in your neighbor's safe and steal the safe, and in any case

Wilkerson had taken elaborate precautions to cover his tracks. It was nonsense, but it created a smoke screen. Actions had been taken in several different counties to plan the burglary. Because half of the population of Montgomery County regarded Wilkerson as a knight in shining armor, prosecutors attempted to indict him in an adjacent county where elements of the crime had occurred, but the residents of that county were well aware of the madness that had consumed Montgomery County, and understandably regarded the prosecution as an effort by Montgomery County to dump their trash over the backyard fence. They refused to indict Wilkerson.

On November 12, 1917, Kelly's retrial began. The crowds were gone this time. At his first trial spectators had lined up at 5:00 a.m. to get into the courthouse. At the second trial, in the same courthouse, there were empty seats. On November 24, Kelly was acquitted on the first ballot.

I don't mean to demean those who prosecuted Reverend Kelly by suggesting it was all a put-up job to take the pressure off of Frank Jones; those who were involved in the prosecution appear to have sincerely believed that Kelly was guilty. But the Wilkerson investigation was becoming a serious problem for Iowa officials; it was eating into the politics of the state. Villisca itself was hopelessly, and angrily, divided between pro-Wilkerson and anti-Wilkerson factions. Customers who were pro-Wilkerson would not shop at stores that were pro-Jones; children from families that were pro-Jones were not allowed to play with children from families that were pro-Wilkerson. The schism tended to divide along lines of religion. Since Jones was a Methodist, most of the Methodists supported him. Since the Moores had been Presbyterians and their minister was in Wilkerson's camp, most of the Presbyterians supported Wilkerson. Havner and the others who arranged the prosecution of Reverend Kelly almost certainly hoped that putting another suspect in front of the town would divide and weaken Wilkerson's support.

Far from it. The prosecution of Reverend Kelly was a wide-open door for Wilkerson, and he rushed through it. In a political campaign, in a debate, in a trial, the worst thing you can do is to hand the truth to your opponent. It is vastly easier to defend a true proposition than it is to defend a lie. The prosecution of Reverend Kelly, which bordered on being silly, allowed Wilkerson to say things that were true. He would describe Kelly as a "poor nut," which was true, and would say that Havner was trying to railroad him, which was essentially true.

Now living full-time in the Villisca area, Wilkerson set up the Reverend Kelly Defense Fund, and raised money on behalf of Kelly's defense. As long as Kelly was in legal jeopardy, Wilkerson was paid by the defense fund. When Kelly was acquitted that pipeline dried up. Wilkerson looked for some way to sustain his campaign. He decided to run for office. He was going to be the new county attorney.

Actually that understates it; not only was Wilkerson running for county attorney, but one of his chief supporters was running for Sheriff, and another for county supervisor. They all ran as Republicans. Wilkerson by now was the most famous man in the county. He had conducted dozens and dozens of high-profile public meetings. His picture had been on the front page of the newspapers countless times. He had fantastic name recognition, and while it was true that many people hated him, at least as many and probably more regarded him as a hero. He wanted to be the county attorney, a modest goal for such a man. If he could attain the office, Wilkerson could finally prosecute Frank Jones for arranging the murders of the Moore family, but first he had to get licensed to practice law in Iowa. That's when the part about being mortal enemies with the Iowa attorney general raised its head.

In April 1918, J. N. Wilkerson petitioned for a license to practice law in Iowa. Horace Havner acted immediately to deny the petition. That battle was still being fought out when the Republican primary came around in June. Wilkerson was originally listed on the ballot, despite not being legally eligible to take the office he sought, but then was taken off the ballot after it was decided that this was a problem. No problem; Wilkerson was a fantastic campaigner. He started a write-in campaign, and won the primary easily, while one of his supporters won the election to be the Republican candidate for sheriff, another, the candidate for county supervisor.

Frank Jones was now fighting for his life. If J. N. Wilkerson was elected the county attorney, Jones was in serious, serious trouble. There was, however, another step in the process; there was a county nominating convention, which had the authority to resolve disputes. This was a dispute: Was Wilkerson eligible to appear on the ballot, or wasn't he? This dispute would be resolved by the Montgomery County Republican Party, and if there was one place left where Frank Jones still had friends, it was the Montgomery County Republican Party.

\*     \*     \*

This finally came to an end in late June 1918.

There were crime scene photos taken of the Villisca murders, although only one photo is known to survive. Warren Noel was the owner of the crime scene photos, having purchased them with a photography business. J. N. Wilkerson, learning of the photos, visited Noel, who became one of Wilkerson's most active supporters. He was an excitable young man with an attractive young wife.

In late summer of 1917, Warren Noel purchased a flashy automobile that he fairly obviously could not afford. In September 1917, Noel was being investigated by the county sheriff on charges of writing bad checks. In the course of that investigation, investigators learned that Noel was also suspected, by the other officers in Wilkerson's operation, of not turning over to the group all of the funds that he had collected. He was stealing the money before Wilkerson could steal it.

In October 1917, Noel staged an incident in which he claimed to have discovered a plot to derail a train and thus murder Wilkerson, who would be on the train. He thought there should be a reward, from the railroad, for his having prevented the train derailment. Officials from the railroad didn't even consider paying the reward, but didn't have enough information to prosecute. About the same time, officials from Wilkerson's band confronted Noel about holding back money. Unable to come up with the money, Noel sold his flashy car, reported it stolen, and filed a false insurance claim. The insurance company, like the railroad, didn't give a thought to paying the claim but didn't have enough information to prosecute.

On October 31, 1917, Noel took a train east from Villisca, getting off the train several times for various reasons. He mailed a letter back to his wife, claiming that he had been seized and was being held hostage by a mysterious group of ruffians. The next morning Noel was found on the platform of the freight depot in Albia, Iowa, 120 miles east of Villisca, with a bullet in his head. His revolver was on the ground beside him.

Noel was well insured, overinsured, and his suicide left his young widow a wealthy woman. In late June 1918, as the battle raged over whether Wilkerson would be allowed to practice law, thus allowed to become the county attorney, Mae Noel and J. N. Wilkerson traveled together (with her baby) to Ottumwa, Iowa, southeast of Des Moines. Arriving about eleven o'clock at night, they walked to a hotel, where they registered under assumed names in two adjoining rooms.

If it now occurs to you Warren Noel may actually have been murdered, welcome to the club; this has occurred to others as well. The coroner ruled it a suicide. But entirely by chance, Wilkerson and Mae Noel were spotted on the street by state agents. The state agents were low-level police officers, generally assigned to bust up poker games, hassle bootleggers and prostitutes, and enforce other laws of a type that, in the modern world, we would classify as "why don't you people mind your own business?" One of those laws prohibited adultery. Wilkerson was a married man. In 1918 it was a violation of the law, in Iowa and probably every other state in the nation, for him to get too friendly with a woman not his wife.

The agents who spotted Wilkerson knew immediately who he was, and the state agents worked indirectly for Horace Havner; that is, they worked for somebody who worked for somebody who worked for Horace Havner. When they spotted Wilkerson with a woman not his wife, they got interested fast, and in a few minutes there were three state agents hiding in the next room, ears pressed to the door, and standing on furniture so that they could watch the hallway from behind the transom of a darkened room.

Wilkerson and Mae Noel were found to be sharing a hotel room and arrested on a charge of adultery. The next morning that charge was dropped, but they were rearrested on a charge of *conspiracy* to commit adultery; apparently the agents, in their eagerness, had jumped the gun and arrested the couple before they had actually got around to adulterizing each other. It was a violation of the manual; the agents were supposed to wait until they heard the bedsprings creaking—again, I am not making up these details—but they got anxious and moved in too early.

Wilkerson's arrest made headlines across Iowa. Perhaps it was not a serious law and not a serious violation, but to do this with the widow of a man who had been completely devoted to you and who had recently killed himself was seriously unseemly.

At long last, Wilkerson's support melted quickly away. The Montgomery County Republican Convention decided that Wilkerson would not be their candidate. Wilkerson dropped his petition for a license to practice law in Iowa and filed instead for a license to practice law in Nebraska. Nebraska turned him down.

In late 1918 there was one more trial, Wilkerson's trial for conspiracy to commit adultery. Horace Havner personally prosecuted the case; Wilkerson, as always, was active and aggressive in his own defense. The trial was nasty but brief and ended in a hung jury identical to Reverend Kelly's, eleven to one for acquittal. Havner could have retried the case but chose not to, and the case against Mae Noel was never brought to trial.

The great J. N. Wilkerson left Villisca in disgrace. He came back at least one more time, about Christmas 1918. He ran into Frank Jones on the street; they were both headed to the same bakery. They snarled at one another, spat insults, and made motions as if they were ready to fight. Frank Jones pulled back his foot and kicked Wilkerson, so they said, like you would kick a dog, and then they were pulled apart.

# CHAPTER XVII

# Villisca 5

In this era, private detectives were the nation's premier investigators. The private eyes were better funded than the police networks, better organized, more experienced, better paid, and more flexible. Between 1930 and 1950, the private eyes were pushed out of this business by the development of state investigative agencies.

There were four large national detective agencies in that era—the Pinkerton Agency, which was the largest, the Thiel Agency, the Kirk Agency, and the Burns Agency, which was the second-largest. It may seem surprising that the Burns Agency would work with a man like Wilkerson, but actually it isn't. Nineteenth-century detectives were essentially spies. The term *detective* entered the English language in the middle of the nineteenth century and was in common usage after 1860, but early detectives basically infiltrated criminal communities, befriended criminals, and ratted them out. Of course, police occasionally do that now, but in the nineteenth century that was a detective's job description. James McParland of Pinkerton's, the most celebrated detective of the nineteenth century—still alive and still active in 1912, and peripherally involved in this case—infiltrated criminal conspiracies as a young man and ran spy networks as an older man. This is not to deny him credit for what he was; he was also clever, well-organized, and an outstanding interrogator. He would get everybody's story on record, and then he would systematically check out the details of each narrative, just as a modern police investigation would.

By 1912 the detective business was becoming more sophisticated; it was no longer merely spying on criminals and betraying them, although that remained an important part of the trade. When Wilkerson was on assignment for the Burns Agency he drew a salary, drew a per diem allowance, and (of course) had all of his expenses paid. But otherwise, when he was not on assignment, the usual arrangement was that the detective had to drum up his own business; otherwise he didn't get paid. The Burns Agency and the other agencies ran ads in local newspapers, and their employees trolled for high-dollar thefts and other serious crimes, as well as, of course, taking walk-in business: missing relatives, people who absconded without paying debts, and cheating husbands.

For a detective to make money by investigating a tragedy was normal—as it is for any detective, or for a prosecutor—and Wilkerson probably rationalized it as such. This is what I have to do to fund this investigation, I have to hold these meetings. It's normal for a detective. He probably did not see how corrupt he had become because, of course, he did not want to.

It would be nice to report that J. N. Wilkerson was punished for his actions and died under a bridge, but he wasn't and he didn't. He landed on his feet; he would spend much of the rest of his life traveling around the Midwest, lecturing about the assassination of Abraham Lincoln. He developed complex and convoluted conspiracy theories about the assassination, and his theories survive to this day. An old man who died in 1903, in his last years, claimed to be the "real" John Wilkes Booth. After he died his body was mummified and exhibited at carnivals and in sideshows as the body of John Wilkes Booth. Wilkerson purchased the mummy sometime in the 1930s and toured the Midwest with it, giving lectures about the assassination and supposed cover-up. A long and entertaining history of J. N. Wilkerson and his mummy "John" was published in the *Saturday Evening Post* on February 10, 1938.

Years later, the county attorney who assisted Havner in the prosecution of Reverend Kelly was walking down a street in Kansas City, when he heard someone call his name. He turned around; it was Wilkerson. Wilkerson said his apartment was just across the street, and he invited the attorney up for a drink. "You've got yourself a real nice place here," said the attorney.

Wilkerson smiled broadly and said, "Well, you can thank the citizens of Montgomery County for that. They paid for about sixty thousand dollars of it." Wilkerson died in Oklahoma either in 1937 or in 1944; we are unsure which is accurate.

Wilkerson's stepson married Blanche Stillinger, the older sister of the Stillinger girls, who gave permission for them to stay overnight with the Moore family. They had a long and happy marriage, and raised a family.

Frank Jones lived another twenty-five years, into his mid-eighties; he died in 1941, in Villisca.

Horace Havner served as attorney general of Iowa from 1917 to 1921, being reelected in the midst of his war with Wilkerson. Havner in 1917 was traveling around the state, speaking everywhere, trying to lay a foundation for a run for the governor's office in 1918. Suffering setbacks associated with this case, he skipped the run in 1918, ran for governor in 1920, and lost in the primary. Havner slipped into obscurity after leaving the attorney general's office, and we have been unable to locate the time and place of his death.

The much maligned (and unfairly maligned) Hank Horton died in Villisca in 1923, aged sixty-two.

William Mansfield became a labor organizer. Later in life he would claim that he was targeted for prosecution in this case because of his labor union activities, although actually he didn't become active in his union until years after his involvement in this case. He died in Milwaukee in the 1950s.

Reverend Kelly talked constantly, during his trials, about writing a book, explaining his view of the case, but of course he never did. He was in and out of Montgomery County for a couple of years, trying to borrow money to file a lawsuit against the county, but that never happened, either. Eventually he went back to England, where he disappeared. He may or may not have returned to the United States. It's rumored that he died in a mental hospital on Long Island in the 1950s.

The axe with which the murders were committed was taken on the night of the murders to the home of Montgomery County Sheriff Oren Jackson. It was kept at the Montgomery County Courthouse, and was introduced into evidence in the Kelly trials in 1917. Sometime between 1923 and 1930 the axe was given by the then sheriff Arthur Baker to James Risden, who was an investigator for Horace Havner in 1917, one of the crew that bullied Kelly into confessing, and who later became head of the Iowa Bureau of Criminal Investigation. A 1945 article in the *Des Moines Register* mentioned the axe being in the possession of Mr. Risden. Two young men interested in the murders in 1961, Edgar Epperly and Donald Brown, located the axe in the possession of Mr. Risden's widow, and she expressed a willingness to give it away. Donald Brown gave her a box of chocolate-covered cherries, not exactly in exchange for the axe, but as a gift in recognition of a gift. Later, Mr. Brown gave the axe to Dr. Epperly, again in exchange for a box of chocolate-covered cherries. Epperly loaned the axe to a Villisca city official, and it was displayed in the Villisca city hall from 1987 to 2004, at which time Dr. Epperly reclaimed the axe and placed it in a secure location. Plans are for the axe to be donated to the Villisca Historical Society.

If you want to know more about Villisca there is a documentary movie, *Villisca: Living with a Mystery*, which I am tempted to say is of the highest possible quality. Of course, nothing is of the highest possible quality, but certainly this is far above the normal standards of crime documentary. *Living with a Mystery* includes interviews filmed over a good many years by Kelly and Tammy Rundle, edited and released in 2004. The Rundles talked to everybody they could find who was extremely interested in the case, talked to old people (in the 1980s and 1990s) who were in Villisca at the time of the murders, assembled all of the facts of the case, and boiled it down into an immensely interesting 116 minutes. The Rundles worked with Dr. Edgar V. Epperly, a retired educator who has been interested in Villisca, and working to understand what happened, since the 1950s; Dr. Epperly is in a sense the author of the documentary. Much of the documentary is oral history, and oral history involves inevitable distortions, so some things that are said in the movie are not exactly right. But if you're not really, really interested in the Villisca murders now, you will be by the time you finish watching.

Roy Marshall was the state fire marshal of Iowa from 1989 to 2000; that's right, Marshal Marshall. He had a fifty-year career investigating fires in Iowa. As a result, when he turned his attention to writing a book about Villisca (*Villisca: The True Account of the Unsolved Mass Murder That Stunned the Nation*) he had both investigative skills and relevant connections. Marshall is quite intelligent, very professional, and entirely serious in his approach. The book was published by Aventine Press, a vanity publisher, in 2003; Marshall knows more about the murders in Villisca than I am ever going to know, and I have great respect for his work.

A couple of quibbles. While Marshall recognizes and clearly states that there is good evidence connecting the Villisca crimes to others in the series, he devotes almost all of his book to the "follow on" stories about Villisca, the prosecutions of innocent men in Villisca. This seems to me a curious choice. He pays little attention to the question of who might actually have committed the murders, instead writing for hundreds of pages about the prosecutions of two innocent men, and the horrible battles created within Villisca by these corrupt prosecutions.

Second quibble, which is related to the first. While Marshall is extremely well informed about Villisca, and I take his book about Villisca to be a credible and authoritative source, when he touches on murders in other towns he often doesn't know what he is talking about, and much of what he says is just completely wrong. It is more than that; he seems curiously ill informed on those topics. His account of the Pfanschmidt murders (chapter XVIII) is irretrievably garbled, and he doesn't seem to have ever heard of Clementine Barnabet (chapter XXXVIII), although her story was well known at the time and shaped the thinking of many others about the murders. Marshall almost ridicules the Montgomery County sheriff, Oren Jackson, because Jackson kept coming back to the belief that a religious cult was behind the murders:

> Jackson favored the cult theory: a group of fanatics, perhaps religious, traveling the country and killing at the bidding of their leader, or if not that, a traveling maniac, riding the rails, killing and then moving on, waiting for the urge and the opportunity to kill again.
>
> —Roy Marshall, *Villisca*, page 79

Jackson's thinking was obviously influenced by the Clementine Barnabet episode, which we will tell you about later in the book. While I like both the Rundles' documentary and Marshall's book very much, the two sources do differ on hundreds of facts about the case. Since Marshall worked mostly from documents, while the Rundles are working largely from oral history, I have taken Marshall's book to be the more accurate source in almost every case.

There is another book about the case, *Morning Ran Red*, by Stephen

Bowman, but that's a fictionalization, so I haven't read it and don't know anything about it.

The autopsy report from the Villisca murders can be found online or purchased. The Crime Library (crimelibrary.com) has a nineteen-part series on the Villisca murders, by Katherine Ramsland, which is really awful.

In addition to the books and materials about Villisca itself, there are also books about what I call The Subsection. There was a long string of murders committed by The Man from the Train, and of that long string a Subsection is relatively well known. The Subsection begins in 1911 and ends in 1912. Before this book, no one has known that the series of murders actually goes on much longer than that, but many people in that era were aware of the Subsection, and a good amount has been written about the Subsection.

We should mention, again, the college term paper of Beth Klingensmith, which was instrumental in restarting interest in this series of crimes, and which has been used since 2006 as a resource for information about them. Also, we should mention again the book *Murdered in Their Beds*, by Troy Taylor, published by Whitechapel Press in Decatur, Illinois, in 2012. This is subtitled "The History and Hauntings of the Villisca Ax Murders," but it is about the series of crimes beginning where Klingensmith thought that they began.

Dr. Edgar Epperly has also written extensively on the Web about the murders; when you find his name associated with postings connected to Villisca, you should regard those as authoritative.

*   *   *

The central question, of course, is whether Jones or Kelly could actually have committed the murders. It is my view that it is entirely impossible that either Jones or Kelly had anything to do with the crime.

To believe that Jones committed the murders, first of all, you have to separate the Villisca murders from all of the other murders in the series. I believe that it is apparent that the Villisca murders were a part of a series. If they were, then the Jones and Kelly theories are out the window at the start.

Getting past that, there is no actual evidence linking Jones to the murders, or, at best, the evidence is of such poor quality that it can hardly be called evidence.

Third, whoever committed these murders was crazy, vicious, mean, and consumed with hatred. Jones was a clean, thriving, honest businessman in his late fifties, a leader not only of the community but of the state. It's hard to reconcile the two. Dr. Edgar Epperly put it well, in an interview with CLEWS, a Web site:

> The one conclusion I do confidently draw is that F. F. Jones, Villisca banker and state senator, was not guilty. He lacked motive, did not have a sufficiently disturbed personality to contemplate the act, and his supposed hired killer William Mansfield can prove with sworn testimony and documentary evidence he was in Montgomery, IL, working on the railroad on the night of the murder.

The Villisca murders are not rational; they are psychotic—highly organized, but psychotic. It is H.O.P.B.—Highly Organized Psychotic Behavior.

Regarding Reverend Kelly, I absolutely do not believe that he was capable of committing a crime of this nature—not that he was not *morally* capable of great depravity, perhaps, but that he was simply not capable of it in the same sense that he was not capable of playing quarterback for the Green Bay Packers. And to the same degree; these murders were far, far, far beyond anything he was capable of pulling off.

Whoever committed these murders was a horrible person, but he was also cunning, strong, organized, and relentless. Serial murderer expert Robert Ressler, interviewed for *Villisca: Living with a Mystery*, stated that the murderer would have had to be physically strong and agile. Lyn G. J. Kelly was timid, weak, and mentally disorganized at an extremely high level. Lyn Kelly, when people said bad things about him during his trial, would bury his face under his arms and sob uncontrollably. His wife, towering over him in the next chair, would cradle him like a child and pat him on the head.

You think it is *easy* to break into somebody's house in the middle of the night, kill eight people, and get away with it? You think that is something that just anybody could do? Even if it was something that 95 percent of men *could* do, Reverend Kelly would be in the other five percent—but in fact it is something that 99 percent of us could *not* do. Pardon the scatology or skip the rest of the sentence, but I'd shit in my pants if I found myself breaking into somebody's house with an axe. Almost all of us would.

And as to Reverend Kelly being a pervert . . . well, let me make this argument. It is actually quite common for men to like to look at young women naked. There are whole industries built on this fact—lots of them. It's pretty much universal. All men are creeps; didn't your mama ever tell you that?

What is unusual about Kelly is that *he was so bad at it.* He was so bad at it that he got himself arrested and locked up for several months in a mental hospital for merely *trying* to do what tens of millions of men in every generation quite successfully do without any negative consequences. Kelly approached a common problem from a position of completely absurd incompetence, picked a young woman almost at random, and made a proposal to her that would make a hooker queasy. And left her with evidence that she could turn over to the police. Do you *really* think this man was capable of murdering eight people in a locked house and walking away from it clean?

Reverend Kelly absconded on his debts because he was incapable of earning money, and he engaged in poorly conceived sexual misadventures because he was incapable of getting sexual satisfaction in the normal ways. (His wife once told an investigator that the two had never had "normal sexual relations".) The prosecutors in this case, who had little experience with sexual abnormality, thought about sexual deviance in a primitive way. They lumped together Reverend Kelly's sexual peccadilloes—highly inappropriate but essentially normal—with abnormal behaviors of the most extreme nature. They thought that one pervert was the same as another.

As to the possibility that Kelly could have committed other murders in the series, Dr. Epperly said (in the interview with Laura James, no relation to the authors), that "I have thrown away a lifetime trying to place Kelly in one or another of the murder sites at the crucial time." Horace Havner dictated a memo in April 1917 in which he said of Reverend Kelly that he "was in some ways a brilliant man. He was erratic but at times would preach really brilliant sermons." This sentence has justified later writers in exaggerating Reverend Kelly's preaching skills, and in presenting him as an intelligent man. But Havner had never met Kelly at the time he wrote this memo, was working from third-hand and fourth-hand knowledge about him, and makes a number of statements about Kelly in this memo that are clearly false. Reverend Kelly never made it beyond an apprentice stage, as a minister, and the only preaching he ever did was to small audiences in rural areas.

Hank Brewster, who wrote a book about the case, believes that Kelly committed the murders. Epperly has said that Roy Marshall believes that Kelly committed the murders, although Marshall's book does not say so. Most of the political and cultural elite of Villisca one hundred years ago, because they were allied with Frank Jones, bought into the theory that Kelly was the real culprit, and a recent episode of *The Dead Files* promotes the belief that Kelly committed the murders.

I am astonished that *anyone* would believe that Reverend Kelly could have committed these murders, so I am going to hit this one more time. People believe that Kelly could have committed these murders because the truth is so horrible that, when confronted by it, they avert their eyes. But let's not avert our eyes here; let's look right at it. We know three things about the man who committed these murders. We know:

1. He was sexually attracted to prepubescent females.
2. He preferred them to be dead and covered with blood.
3. He loved doing violence to others.

Let's compare that now to Reverend Kelly. There is no evidence that Reverend Kelly was attracted to prepubescent females. His sexual misconduct, to the best of our knowledge, was directed at a sixteen-year-old girl that he had never met, and at wives of his neighbors. Strike one.

There is no evidence that Reverend Kelly had an attraction to dead people or people who were covered with blood. Strike two.

There is no evidence I am aware of that Reverend Kelly was ever violent.

One of the arguments made against Reverend Kelly at his murder trial is that he hated children, that he was grumpy around children, that he was annoyed by them and didn't want them around him. *This is the exact opposite of the behavior of a man who is sexually attracted to children.* Child molesters are *over*friendly with children. Child molesters are able to get on a child's wavelength, in order to befriend, and then take advantage of, the child. They don't hate them, and they're not annoyed by them.

After the sixteen-year-old turned Reverend Kelly's letters over to the postal police, they responded, pretending to be her, and Reverend Kelly responded with yet more graphic letters, apparently outlining some extremely unattractive sexual opportunities for the young woman. These letters were introduced against him at his murder trial, but they were not read aloud in court because they were so obscene. The specific contents of those letters is now unknown.

Dr. Epperly has said that he doesn't believe that Kelly committed the crime, but he half-believes it, and he would like to know what those letters would reveal about Kelly's perversity. But (1) that content was heard and known by the jurors, who were completely unpersuaded, and (2) this argument suggests that we have 80 percent of what we need to hang Kelly, but we are missing that last 20 percent. The reality is that we have 2 or 3 percent of a case against Kelly; we are missing 97 or 98 percent.

Reverend Kelly had socially unacceptable behaviors wrapped around psychologically normal sexual desires. Even if Kelly was sexually attracted to children (no evidence), and even if he was focused on postmortem sexuality (which is extremely unusual, and for which we have no evidence), and even if he was prone to violence (no evidence), and even if these three were all true, *he still was not capable of having committed these murders.* The murders required boldness, focus, and self-possession, which were beyond his capacity.

\*     \*     \*

Almost every modern source of information about the Villisca murders will say that the small-town police failed to secure the crime scene, and one source says that "it was among the most mishandled crime scenes in American history." In fact, the handling of the Villisca crime scene was well *above* the normal standards of the time.

The mistake is based on three misunderstandings. First, huge crowds of people did go through the house on Tuesday and Wednesday of the critical week, after the bodies had been removed late on Monday. Oral history, in my view, has conflated the events of June 11 and June 12 (Tuesday and Wednesday) with those of June 10, when the crime scene should have been documented (and was, to a limited extent). Second, critics tend to assume that modern standards about the preservation of a crime scene can be applied to 1912, when of course they cannot. While the concept of preserving the crime scene to preserve the evidence was not entirely unknown in 1912, this understanding was primitive at best. Even the concept of a crime scene *yielding* evidence was at a primitive level in 1912. Combining that with the public's lack of acceptance of the need to stay away from the scene, it was normal for citizens to overrun a crime scene. This happened in almost every case discussed in this book.

Third, modern writers seem to assume that Marshal Horton had available to him a police network that *could* have immediately rushed to the scene and taken control. In fact, there was no such network. Marshal Horton:

- Displayed immense courage by going through a dark house filled with dead bodies, holding a match in front of him for light, with no reason to believe anything other than that the murderer was still in the house.
- Called the county sheriff, who was the only off-site police official available to him.
- Immediately called a private detective experienced in investigating homicides.
- Instructed the night watchmen—his only assistants—not to let anyone into the house without good reason.
- Sent immediately for bloodhounds.
- Sent immediately for a fingerprint expert.
- Almost immediately called out the National Guard to establish a perimeter around the house.

He met with the people who had been through the house and made notes about what they had seen, and he organized a volunteer search of all the outbuildings in the city. Within the first thirty-six hours, he canvassed the neighborhood to see what evidence the neighbors might have. He made notes about those conversations, which later proved to be vital in obstructing the malicious prosecution of Frank Jones. What more could he have done? What other options did he have?

None. He did everything he could have done, except that probably he should have insisted that the photographer be allowed to finish his work, and he should have taken possession of the crime scene photos. It has been written that Horton and the county sheriff, Sheriff Jackson, spent the day waiting for bloodhounds to arrive. When I started writing about the case I believed that to be true, but when you bury yourself deeply in the details of the day, you can see that they were actually very busy, that they worked hard, and that everything they did was reasonable and appropriate.

Two years later, when J. N. Wilkerson came to town, Horton immediately spotted him as a con man, and refused to cooperate with him. Wilkerson treated Horton as he treated Jones, as he later would treat Horace Havner; he ridiculed him in public meetings, trying to destroy his reputation so that Horton would not be an obstacle to Wilkerson's operation. He would claim that Horton was a part of the criminal conspiracy that was obstructing the investigation of the crime.

I'm not saying that the control of the crime scene was perfect, merely that it was above the standards of the era. Some people were permitted to enter the crime scene who should not have been there. Items in the house were handled that should not have been handled.

But modern writers act like they are shocked, *shocked* that perhaps fifty people went through the crime scene before noon on the day the bodies were discovered. If similar murders were committed tomorrow in New York or Chicago, I would bet that more than fifty people would go through the crime scene before noon—and I would bet that items of potential evidentiary value would be mishandled.

The people who would go through the crime scene in a modern investigation would be police, crime scene technicians, an official photographer, medical personnel, police supervisors, and prosecutors. The people who went through the crime scene in Villisca were mostly in parallel positions—doctors, police, local officials, a photographer. There *were* some people who went through the murder house who were in other categories—a minister, relatives, family friends. This may be interpreted as a difference in crime scene protocol; it is hardly an outrage.

Large numbers of people did go through the murder house after the bodies had been removed, and this is different from a modern crime scene; in the twenty-first century we don't do that. There *were* people who went through the Moore house who had no business being there, but there is no reason to believe that any evidence was lost as a consequence of these extras going through the crime scene, or that any subsequent act of the tragedy would have been different if the crime scene protection had been perfect.

Fingerprints? Give me a break. Fingerprints in 1912, although everybody talked about them and everybody was aware of them, were not far beyond the level of a theory. Villisca authorities *did* send for a fingerprint expert on the day of the crimes; he showed up drunk and had nothing to offer, but they did send for him. There were no murders very much like this solved by fingerprints in 1912, or for many years after 1912. Even sixty years later, it was immensely difficult—and extremely rare—to solve a stranger-on-stranger homicide based on fingerprints. Fingerprint powder and fingerprint tape had not yet been invented in 1912. The cases in that era in which fingerprints proved vital were cases in which the perpetrator (1) was an obvious suspect, and (2) left fingerprints in blood. The Man from the Train was aware of fingerprints and had begun several years earlier to wash fingerprints from the handle of the axes that he used (although he had spilled a bottle of ink in Colorado Springs, and may have left his fingerprints there in ink). He had wiped the axe with Lena's underwear; there was lint clinging to the axe, and blood on the underwear, as if it had been used to wipe away blood, and also the axe had been wiped on the sheets of one of the beds. Other than fingerprints and possibly a shoe size, what evidence exactly would have been at the crime scene? You think maybe he dropped his wallet?

What needed to be done to solve this crime was vastly beyond the level of "securing the crime scene." What needed to be done was more on the scale of locking down the railroad system in a range of 150 miles to limit the criminal's ability to flee, organizing a multi-state, multimillion-dollar investigation to piece together information from many different crime scenes, and systematically identifying and checking out tens of thousands of men who lived on the rails to see what they might have heard, might have seen, where they might have been. Unless those things were done, securing the crime scene wasn't going to do anything.

# CHAPTER XVIII

# Dynamite Pfanschmidt

C. C. related a conversation from the following evening, Monday, September 23. "Ray, I understand you are going into the auto business too." He said, "Yes, there is lots of money in that." I said, "Yes, with you it is always money, money, money."

—From Beth Lane, *Lies Told Under Oath*

On Friday night, September 27, 1912, the family of Charles and Mathilda Pfanschmidt was murdered in a farmhouse near Payson, Illinois. Four persons died in the crime—Charles, Mathilda, their fifteen-year-old daughter, Blanche, and a nineteen-year-old schoolteacher named Emma Kaempen, who was boarding with the family while she taught school nearby. The murders were probably committed with an axe, and the house was set on fire after the family was murdered.

Just across the Mississippi River from Hannibal, Missouri, is an area that is famously, and rather weirdly, isolated. The second time you drive through there, you *will* remember to fill up your gas tank before you leave Hannibal. You pass towns and cities every few miles, farmhouses everywhere around you, and then you hit this big infarction where there is just *nothing*. You don't see houses, you don't see little side roads with an occasional car on them. It's like western Kansas, or southern New Mexico, or the Dakotas. If it's nine p.m. and you notice that your gas gauge is hitting empty, you're in big trouble because you're not going to see an open gas station for a hundred miles.

The Pfanschmidt farm was in that area, and was probably six to eight miles from the nearest railroad. Quincy, Illinois, was well served by railroad traffic. The Pfanschmidts lived eight to nine miles southeast of Quincy, and the railroad line did head south and east out of Quincy. It missed the Pfanschmidt farm by a good distance. If The Man from the Train committed this murder, I think we have to conclude that he departed from his usual pattern in this respect.

Ray Pfanschmidt, the twenty-year-old son of Charles and Tildie, was three times put on trial for committing some or all of the murders and was eventually exonerated. Ray was the very definition of a young man on the make. Twenty years old, he had established a small business moving dirt around. He had taught himself to use dynamite by studying the sales instruction materials, and he used a lot of dynamite. He used dynamite to blow tree stumps out of the ground, loosen the ground for digging wells, and loosen the ground so he could move it around more easily. He had several contracts with other businesses to grade land for roads and for coal mining and for other purposes, and he had numerous workers, older men that he hired to run teams of horses that leveled land and hauled dirt. He had been referred to in the local newspapers, before the murders, as Dynamite Pfanschmidt.

He was also getting into the auto sales racket. There were dozens or perhaps hundreds of little car companies around the nation, building automobiles of different types. Bright young men were trying to get a foothold in the automobile business in every way you can imagine—opening garages, selling gasoline, fixing autos, selling tires, selling auto parts, selling the cars themselves, etc. Ray Pfanschmidt was trying to shoehorn together enough money to become the local car magnate in Quincy, Illinois. He had already signed some contracts (with Rambler) to take possession of cars for the purpose of reselling them, and had borrowed money here and there—including from his father—to be in position to fulfill the contracts. Had not the tragedy intervened, Pfanschmidt Motors would very probably be selling cars in Quincy, Illinois, today.

At the time that the Schmidt hit the Pfan he was living in a tent at a job site in Quincy. On the evening of September 27 he had visited his sweetheart, to whom he was engaged, at her house, several miles from the scene of the crime. He left there about 10:45 p.m. and was seen on the roads going in the direction of his tent, which was the opposite direction from the crime scene. The prosecution argued that, after going some distance in that direction, he had pulled off the road and doubled back to the house where his family was murdered.

This was problematic, in that he was seen in Quincy before 1:00 a.m. (Saturday, September 28), and perhaps as early as midnight. There wasn't much time there, but several people testified that they saw what they thought were Pfanschmidt's horses and his buggy on the road that he would have taken to do this at about the time that he would have had to do it.

On Saturday morning, Ray Pfanschmidt took his watch to a jeweler's in Quincy to have it repaired. The prosecution would argue that the watch clasp and casing were broken during the murders. On the other hand, the man set off dynamite for a living; it's not difficult to imagine how he could have broken the watch; 99.9 percent of people who break their watches are not committing murder when they do so.

Throughout Saturday, September 28, no activity was seen around the Pfanschmidt farm. Their mail, delivered early on Saturday, was never picked up from the mailbox. Their chores were never done, their horses not fed and not watered, the cows not milked. Several phone calls to the Pfanschmidt farm went unanswered.

As the day went on, more and more people who passed by the farm began to smell something burning, something like burning flesh. The farmers supposed that the Pfanschmidts were probably burning some hogs, since there had been an outbreak of cholera, and people were burning livestock to stop the spread of the disease.

Nothing was seen of the family that entire day, however, and in the early-morning hours of Sunday, September 29—after midnight on September 28—the house burst into flames. Even though it was the middle of the night a crowd gathered outside the house, watching it burn and making some futile efforts to put out the fire by carrying water from the animals' watering tank. Ray Pfanschmidt and many of his cousins, aunts, and uncles were awakened by middle-of-the-night phone calls and were on the scene before sunup, as were a crowd of neighbors and passersby. The police chief from Quincy arrived not long after the sun rose. By early Sunday morning, according to some estimates, a thousand people were at the farm.

Going back to the first hour of the fire, when neighbors saw orange flames bursting from the roof and raced to the house, terror stricken, hoping against hope that the Pfanschmidt family was not inside. It had rained about ten o'clock on Saturday night, not much, just enough to settle the dust. Giving it every possible benefit, let us suppose that glistening in the moonlight and in the glare of the fire, there is a flat, damp driveway, and through that driveway there is the muddy track of a single carriage entering the property, circling around and then leaving—a track apparently left after the ten o'clock shower and before the fire. Under the circumstances, one can see how spectral and sinister that track would appear to be.

We don't know that this was exactly what happened, but we do know that there was a track, and that the neighbors who were thrust into the role of first responders focused on that track at once, and took action almost immediately to preserve the track for its value as evidence.

The Track became the basis of suspicion against Ray Pfanschmidt. By 6:00 a.m., when there were perhaps a hundred people on the scene, the gossip among them was that that was the track of Ray Pfanschmidt's buggy and the track of Ray Pfanschmidt's horses, that one could tell that it was by the width of the track and the tread of the wheels and the hoof prints of the horses and the peculiar sharp turn that the vehicle had made, which a conventional carriage could not have made. Once they were able to get inside the burned-out house and determine that the family had been murdered before the fire, the police and the gossiping neighbors immediately began to suspect—based mostly on The Track—that Ray had committed the crime.

On Friday, September 27, the Pfanschmidt family had been in Payson, returning to their farm not much before midnight. The family must have been murdered soon after that, and the house must have been set on fire as the murderer left the house.

On Monday morning, thirty hours after the house was found engulfed in flames, bloodhounds were brought in. The bloodhounds were given the scent from the suspected track, and they tracked the scent to Ray Pfanschmidt's horses, nine miles away in Quincy. Sort of. What actually happened was, they tracked the scent a certain distance to a public road, where the bloodhounds were put into a vehicle and driven to the next intersection, then they were taken out and tracked the scent across the intersection, then they were put back in the vehicle until the next intersection, etc. When the dogs lost the scent along oiled streets in Quincy, they were put in the car and released a mile away along the same street. It was estimated that of the nine miles the bloodhounds had tracked the scent to Ray Pfanschmidt's horses, about six miles were spent in the vehicle.

Ray Pfanschmidt's clothes were central to the mystery. Pfanschmidt—a nice-looking young man—was a clothes horse, and he owned several "suits" of khaki clothes, which he normally wore with a red bow-string necktie. A week after the murders an outdoor toilet near Ray's job site was being destroyed, and as it was tipped over a set of Ray's khaki clothes was discovered in the vault of the privy, wrapped in newspaper and spattered with blood.

To a demanding modern reader, the blood-spattered clothing is the essence of the case. The rest of the evidence against Ray Pfanschmidt can be easily dismissed; it is the clothes that matter. The trials of Ray Pfanschmidt revolved around endless, repetitious, conflicting, and confusing testimony about what clothes he was wearing at what time.

Pfanschmidt's defense attorneys argued that they could account for all of his khaki clothes on the Monday after the murders; in other words, all of his clothes were clean and accounted for at that time. No one is convinced by this argument. His defenders believed that one of the many private investigators hired to help out in the case had stolen a set of Ray's clothes from his tent, splattered some blood on them, and hid them where he knew they would be found. This argument cannot be easily dismissed. On its surface, it does seem powerfully convenient that Ray supposedly hid his clothes in an outbuilding that was scheduled for demolition just days later. The clothes were found wrapped in an out-of-town newspaper and tied with string, but Ray Pfanschmidt did not subscribe to that newspaper and did not have copies of that newspaper in his tent, nor did his family subscribe to the paper. Some of the red marks on the clothes were tested and found not to be blood but red dye (although others were in fact blood). The sheriff believed that the red dye had come from Ray's red bow-string necktie, but another witness alleged that he had overheard a private investigator talking about putting red ink on the clothes.

A private detective sent by a neutral third party testified that he had searched the toilet thoroughly days after the murder, including the privy vault, and the bloody clothes were not there. That P.I. was the former chief of police in Quincy, and the future sheriff of the county. The real problem, though, is the amount of blood; there were spots of blood on the khaki clothes. The defense argued—and I believe—that if Ray Pfanschmidt had been wearing those clothes at the time he murdered four people with an axe, there should not have been "spots" of blood on them, but large splotches of blood, at a minimum.

While most of the Pfanschmidt clan supported Ray, his grandfather, C. C. Pfanschmidt, believed that Ray had committed the crime. Ray and his grandfather had clashed before, and C. C. had come to believe that Ray was way too interested in making money. The grandfather had more money than the rest of the family, and he hired private detectives to assist in the investigation.

The Track was the basis and foundation of the prosecution of Ray Pfanschmidt. But it is clear, from a careful study of the evidence, that Ray Pfanschmidt was not at the farm on the Saturday evening before the fire broke out—not clear that Ray was innocent, not clear that The Track was not made by his vehicle at some other time, but absolutely clear that the prosecution's theory of the case, founded on and derived from The Track, was bubkes.

The prosecution's theory was that Ray Pfanschmidt, having murdered his family on *Friday* evening, returned to the farm on *Saturday* night to set the house on fire. This never happened, and we know that it never happened for the following reasons:

1. Ray Pfanschmidt was alerted to the tragedy about 4:00 a.m. on Sunday, September 29, 1912, had his horses brought to him, and raced to the scene. The prosecution put on a string of BS witnesses to say that Ray's horses were excessively fatigued after he raced the nine miles to the farmhouse, more tired than they should have been had they made only that one nine-mile trip. But two young men who handled the horses in the morning, getting them ready to go to the fire while Ray talked hurriedly with his relatives, both testified

that the horses were fresh and full of energy at that time. There is no reason whatsoever not to believe them.

2. Ray's time is well accounted for in Quincy until about eleven o'clock on Saturday night. The prosecution's theory is that after eleven o'clock, Ray raced to the farm, set fire to the house, and then raced back to Quincy.

But dozens of witnesses had smelled fire and smelled the odor of burning flesh hours earlier—as early as ten o'clock that morning. By six o'clock that evening the smell had become thick and pungent, although no one could place where it was coming from. It is obvious that the house was set on fire on *Friday* night, but that the flame had burned out, then the fire had smoldered within the walls of the house for about twenty-four hours before it reignited. The Track of the single vehicle after the rain, spooky as it was, had nothing to do with the fire, because the fire was already burning long before the rain.

3. What the prosecution alleges—that Ray drove his team to the house and back to Quincy in two and a half hours on Saturday night/ Sunday morning—borders on being impossible. The prosecution put on witnesses to demonstrate that it was *possible* to drive a team of horses that distance in that amount of time, and I don't doubt that it was possible—but it would have been highly unusual. It is not clear that it was even possible with Ray's team and Ray's buggy.

4. About eleven o'clock on Saturday evening, Ray Pfanschmidt attempted repeatedly to persuade his cousin, who sometimes stayed with him at the tent, to come out to the tent with him. There are multiple witnesses who testified that this happened. But the prosecution's theory of the crime is that, by 11:15, Ray was racing toward the farm to set the fire. This doesn't make any sense.

There is little or no evidence supporting the prosecution's theory of a Saturday-night return to the farm. They started with that, so they stuck with it.

Were the Pfanschmidts murdered with an axe? Well, the first people on the scene believed that the family had been hacked to death with an axe, and an axe was introduced into evidence against Ray Pfanschmidt. However:

1. The fire did a pretty effective job of destroying the crime scene, and

2. The investigation of the crime was completely inept.

We don't know what the murder weapon was. We know that at least two of the victims were murdered in their beds, because their bodies were found in their beds, burned almost beyond recognition. Parts of the body of Charles Pfanschmidt were never found.

Ray Pfanschmidt's first trial was a local sensation, with so many people crowding into the courthouse that it compromised the structural integrity of the building. The trial lasted three weeks. Ray Pfanschmidt was found guilty in the first trial, and sentenced to death. The Illinois Supreme Court threw out the conviction, citing numerous errors in the trial, and stopping inches short of stating that there had been insufficient evidence to submit the case to a jury. The county retried Ray, charging him only with the murder of his sister, Blanche, and, when he was acquitted of that charge, tried him again, charging him only with the murder of Emma Kaempen. He was acquitted again.

The Illinois Supreme Court ruling established a legal precedent which is still observed and still cited today, the precedent being that the actions of bloodhounds are not evidence against the accused. Bloodhounds may be used to uncover evidence; bloodhounds may lead the police toward evidence or toward a suspect. The tracking of the bloodhounds is not evidence in and of itself, since no one knows what is in the bloodhound's mind that causes him to go one direction or another.

Ray Pfanschmidt did have some criminal tendencies. While taking a short course at the University of Illinois he had been accused of stealing $35 from a roommate, and later, after he was acquitted, he was arrested a couple of times for things like dealing in stolen auto parts and stealing tires. The real problem with the prosecution's case is not that it is contradicted by other testimony. The problem with the prosecution's case is that, even if there was no conflicting evidence of any kind, even if you assume that everything the prosecution says is true and add in the fact that Ray Pfanschmidt was later shown to be a petty criminal, it still falls short of a convincing argument.

The prosecution argued that Ray Pfanschmidt, at the scene of the crime, seemed detached, that he did not act appropriately at the time for an innocent person. This is an argument that prosecutors always make, but it is contradicted by the best evidence on the subject. The Pfanschmidts were stoic German people who were trained from birth not to display emotions in public. Pfanschmidt testified that at the time of the fire he had gone into an outbuilding, out of view of the other people, and was in there crying when his aunt came in and told him to brace up. The aunt and another relative testified that this did in fact happen. His fiancée and his other relatives all testified that he was distraught about the murders, but that he had fought hard to maintain his composure in public. Numerous family members caught him crying (and trying to hide it) over the course of the next week.

Days after the crime, a man and his young daughter were poking around in the remains of the house where the tragedy had occurred. The daughter pulled out of the wreckage a burned clockface, with wires wrapped around the hands. This was immediately turned over to authorities.

Because Ray Pfanschmidt was experienced in the use of dynamite, the prosecution presumed he was capable of using a clock as a detonation device. But Pfanschmidt testified that he had never used any form of delayed-detonation device, had never been trained to do so, and wouldn't know how to do so. There is no evidence to the contrary.

If a delayed-detonation device was used, that certainly would discourage us from believing it was The Man from the Train. But in the prosecution of Ray Pfanschmidt, a delayed-detonation device simply makes a further hash out of an already incoherent prosecution timeline. The prosecution argued that Ray Pfanschmidt had murdered his family on Friday night, and had returned to the house to set the fire on Saturday night. I understand how the clockface/ bomb was of use to the prosecution, but of what exact use was it to Ray Pfanschmidt, assuming that he committed the crime? The family was dead; why do you need a delayed device to set fire to the house?

A dollar bill with blood on it was found in a local bank. The bill was discovered in the bank more than a month after the crime, and more than a week after Ray had been arrested. The county sheriff seized the bill, a story was constructed about how Ray Pfanschmidt *could* have given that bill to a particular person, and that person could have deposited it in the bank. There was no evidence that this had happened; it was merely possible. This was introduced as "evidence" against Pfanschmidt in his first trial.

The first trial started six months after the crime, in March of 1913. Days before the trial, a private investigator reported finding an axe head in the wreckage of the house, its handle burned off. Literally thousands of people had poked through the wreckage; one private investigator testified that he had been through the burned house, looking for evidence, virtually every day since the fire. Days before the trial started, they found the axe head.

But of what use is the axe head anyway? Somebody murdered the family; we know that. How does the axe head tie Ray Pfanschmidt to the crime?

It doesn't.

A gasoline can, supposedly from Ray's work site, was found in the wreckage of the house. That testimony cannot be entirely discounted. Of course, one old gas can looks a lot like another one, and it apparently was Ray Pfanschmidt himself who found the gas can in the wreckage of the house and pointed it out to the police, but it's possible that this means something.

Ray Pfanschmidt was put on trial in his hometown, in an emotionally charged atmosphere, and a silver-tongued lawyer was hired with money provided by Emma Kaempen's father to present the case to a jury. That jury found him guilty. The Illinois Supreme Court told them:

1. To move the trial out of town.
2. That the bloodhounds were not evidence.
3. That the dollar bill with the blood on it was not evidence.
4. That the hiring of defense lawyers was not evidence, either.

And there were numerous other flaws in the trial. This led to two more trials, in which the juries said, "I'm sorry. Did I miss something here?"

Some people have written that Pfanschmidt's clever lawyers got him off. The truth is exactly the opposite: the slick lawyers in this case were the prosecutors. The prosecutors used smoke and mirrors and legal tricks—some of which were actually illegal tricks—to create the illusion that there was a substantial case against Ray Pfanschmidt where the mere outline of a case existed in fact. We can't say with confidence that Ray Pfanschmidt did not commit the crime; it is just that three prosecutions produced almost no reason to believe that he did.

If Ray Pfanschmidt did not commit the crime, then we have the motiveless, inexplicable murder of a random farm family, in the time and place in which The Man from the Train was doing a lot of that kind of thing. I won't argue that it is him, because we don't have any idea what happened here, even though there were several highly publicized trials. It could be that the murder weapon was not an axe, it could be that the family was systematically dismembered, it could be that a delayed-detonation device was used, it could be that Ray Pfanschmidt committed the crime. It was several miles from the railroad track. We couldn't convince a skeptic that it was related to the other crimes in the series.

*   *   *

A good bit of Beth Lane's book *Lies Told Under Oath*, about the Pfanschmidt case, deals with the love story between Ray and the woman to whom he was engaged at the time of the murders. Her handling of that story is extremely skillful and tremendously powerful. I regret that I can't share any of the love story with you here, but:

- It unfolds very slowly,
- It is outside the compass of our narrative, and
- I could never match the skill with which Ms. Lane has told that story, and I certainly don't want to retell it and make a hash of it.

For us, the central question of this crime is whether or not it could have been committed by The Man from the Train. The following facts argue for its inclusion in the series:

1. A family was murdered, probably with an axe, without warning and for no apparent reason.

2. The crime occurred in the time and place where The Man from the Train was most active—about a hundred days after the murders in Villisca, and a little less than three hundred miles from Villisca. The farm where the murders occurred is about forty miles from the closest point of Iowa, and is just over a hundred miles from Monmouth, Illinois, where The Man from the Train had murdered a family almost exactly one year earlier.

3. After the crime was committed the house was set on fire, which argues strongly against this being a copycat murder or an effort to

throw authorities off the track by linking it to the series of unsolved crimes. While some people did realize at this time that a murderous stranger was riding the rails, he had not set fire to the house in any of the recent murders with which he was connected, and absolutely no one, at that time, realized that he had also committed a large number of similar crimes earlier in his career in which he did complete the crime by setting fire to the house.

4. The Pfanschmidt murders were probably committed at the time of night at which The Man from the Train usually attacked his victims, and were committed on a weekend, as most of his crimes were.

5. Although this may be a personal reaction rather than evidence, I did not become convinced that the Pfanschmidt murders were a part of the series until I had almost finished writing this book. I had given a speech in Davenport, Iowa, and on the way back to my home in Kansas I decided that I would drive through Payson again (I had visited the area earlier) to look at something I had missed on the previous visit. But trying to drive to the scene of the Pfanschmidt murders, I *accidentally* drove directly through Monmouth, Illinois, where another family had been murdered earlier. That drove forcefully home to me how closely connected those two crimes are geographically, and I became convinced that they were probably linked. It's a hundred miles, yes, but it's a hundred miles in an area with very, very few towns and cities.

Arguing against the inclusion of the Pfanschmidt murders in "our" list of crimes are the following:

1. The farmhouse was not near the railroad—certainly not *extremely* near the railroad, as all of the recent crimes had been.

2. The murders may not have been committed with an axe or similar instrument.

3. A clock may have been used as a "bomb" to trigger the fire.

4. Because the house was destroyed, there is limited evidence of the idiosyncratic behaviors that identify The Man from the Train,

such as breaking in through a window, locking the house up tight, or covering windows and/or mirrors with cloth.

Having studied the crime as best I am able to do, it is my personal opinion that the crime was a part of the series. However, I do not believe that I could convince a skeptic of this, so I won't make a definite claim that it is related.

# SECTION III

— 1900 *to* 1906 —

# CHAPTER XIX

# Stepping Backward

We are all aware of the ways that inventions and developments that are like inventions can quickly reshape our lives; that is, we are aware of the way that this happens in the years that we remember. We tend to forget that the same waves of innovation rolled over society—and reshaped it just as rapidly—before we came along.

It is difficult to describe how far-reaching the changes were that occurred in the first decade of the twentieth century. There is probably no other decade in American history, or even human history, that witnessed changes as profound as those which reshaped American culture between 1900 and 1910. In 1900 very few houses had electricity, but in this decade new houses were built with electricity, while millions of existing houses were retrofitted with light switches and lightbulbs and plug-ins (in urban areas. Electrification of rural areas didn't gain traction until the 1930s). The endless development of household electronic devices began. In 1900 nobody had cars. In 1902 it is believed that fewer than 6,000 American vehicles were on the road. By 1910 there were 130,000 automobiles, 35,000 trucks, and 150,000 motorcycles—a fiftyfold increase in vehicular traffic in eight years, and of course the numbers continued to skyrocket. The roads had to be built and rebuilt to accommodate the new world; the laws had to be rewritten. In the small city in which I live, a law was passed in 1906 requiring an automobile to pull over to the side of the road when encountering a horse, so that the automobile did not frighten the horse. Less than three years later the law jumped to the other side of the bridge, and residents were banned from bringing new horses into town. If you had a horse you could keep him as long as he lived, but if you didn't have a horse you couldn't get one without special permission. Nineteenth-century roads were almost all unpaved; now they needed to be paved. Tens of thousands of American cities added either bus service or trolley car service in this decade, or both. The New York City subway system opened on October 27, 1904. Car dealerships were being built in every city in America, and tire stores, and auto parts stores, and gas stations. (In the early days of automobiles, gasoline was sold through drugstores and was sold in containers, rather than through pumps.) Livery services, which were called taxis, were being rapidly driven out of business, replaced by what we call taxis.

In 1900 there was essentially no movie industry. By 1910 the movie business employed many thousands of people, nickelodeons were available in every town, and movie theaters were being built alongside the gas stations and the car dealerships. While sound recordings have more of a history before 1900 than do movies, the popular music industry by 1910 was being rapidly and radically reshaped by record players, which were becoming more affordable.

In 1900 zero percent of American houses had telephone service—not zero houses, but zero percent, rounded off to the nearest one percent. By 1910, in the era in which we have been writing about, many people had telephones. Villisca had two competing phone systems; you couldn't call from one system to the other. J. B. Moore's John Deere store, like many businesses in Villisca, had telephones from both systems so that anybody would be able to reach them from either system. Few houses had indoor plumbing in 1900; certainly few houses had indoor plumbing in the small, semirural areas where The Man from the Train liked to attack. By 1910 many more houses had indoor facilities (although most still did not).

It is reported in some places that violent crime rates exploded in this decade, although this is not well documented. Of course, the history of the airplane begins in this decade, but that didn't have real impact until World War I, which is after our story. But the sweeping changes in American society from 1900 to 1912 invaded every corner of our story. Fingerprints. While the knowledge that fingerprints were unique dates back to the ancient world, and a murder was solved by fingerprints in Argentina in 1892, fingerprinting as a modern forensic enterprise began in 1900 or 1901, and awareness of fingerprints exploded in the middle of the decade. In 1900 few people were aware that the skin ridge patterns on their fingers were unique to them and could theoretically be traced to them. By 1910 everybody knew that.

In 1900 the basic blood groups (A, B, AB, and O) were unknown; by 1910 there had been two breakthroughs in that field, and by 1912 police were beginning to study the blood at crime scenes.

The flashlight was invented in 1899 and commercially marketed beginning in 1904. In 1900 night watchmen carried lanterns. In 1910 they carried flashlights. One of the ways we can surmise that The Man from the Train was probably over thirty-five in 1910 is that he lighted his way around dark houses by carrying kerosene lamps, rather than by using a flashlight, as he would probably have done had he been ten years younger.

Let me break now from the disembodied narrative voice that we normally use to write books and speak to you one on one, writer to reader. I need to explain my problem to you, and I don't know how I would do that, other than in the first person.

I began researching this series of crimes with the murders that center around Villisca, the murders in 1911 and 1912. In doing that, I realized there must be other murders that were part of the series but that had not been associated with the series at the time. Many writers have written about the series as if it began in Colorado Springs, but that can't possibly be right. The murderer in Colorado Springs, who killed six people in two houses in one night, is way too comfortable in what he is doing to be a first-time explorer. This was *not* his first rodeo.

So if this wasn't the first time he had done this, let's look for the others. I started walking backward in time from September 17, 1911 (Colorado Springs), looking for other events that could be related. We have tools to conduct that search now that were beyond the imagination of people trying to connect the dots in 1911. In 1911, what happened a hundred miles away from you might as well have happened on the dark side of the moon; that's not exactly true, but I have a point and I'll get back to it in a moment. Anyway, I started walking backward from 1911, and I found several similar cases in 1910, and at least one in 1909.

But then I hit a wall; for more than a year before the murder of the Meadows family in 1909, I could find no record of a similar case. So this is where the series starts, OK?

Except that it isn't. It isn't for two reasons. First of all, the Meadows family murders, as much as the Colorado Springs murders, do not look like the work of an inexperienced, out-of-control amateur getting his sea legs in the homicide industry. It looks like he knew what he was doing. And second, in the interest of thoroughness, I hired my daughter, Rachel, to search for similar murders occurring before 1909. And she found one.

And another one.

And another one.

And another, and another.

At first, of course, I thought she was just seeing monsters in the shadows, that these wouldn't turn out to be related cases—but no;

when I finally made the time to look into her stack of cases, it seemed much more likely than not that at least some of them were related.

So the series begins somewhere before 1909, but where? We have a string of crimes before 1909, some of which probably are connected to The Man from the Train and some of which probably aren't.

But here's the thing: the year 1900 is very different from 1912. The world changed enormously between 1900 and 1912. One of the things that changed tremendously from 1900 to 1912 was small-city newspapers.

Although the Associated Press has a prehistory dating back to 1846, until 1893 it was basically a cooperative arrangement among a few big-city newspapers. Between 1893 and 1921, under the leadership of Melville Stone, the AP grew enormously, embracing thousands of small-town newspapers, providing news services to them but also, and perhaps more importantly, taking news from them and circulating it around the nation. Wireless news transmission began in 1899, and greatly increased the speed and ease with which news could be shared. The United Press Association, later UPI, United Press International, was founded in 1907 and grew rapidly as a competitor to the Associated Press. By 1912, most small-town newspapers were either AP papers or UPI papers.

The invention of the Bildtelegraph (1900) greatly eased the transmission of photographs. In 1900 small-town newspapers printed few photographs, and almost never printed photos taken a long distance away. Many newspapers illustrated their stories with drawings— some detailed, others crude. By 1910 some small-town newspapers routinely printed photographs taken far away. In 1900 no American college offered a degree in journalism. By 1910 there were journalism programs. In 1900, small-town newspapers were stand-alone operations. They stole stories from big-city newspapers and from nearby towns, because copyright restraints were weak or nonexistent, but for the most part their stories were self-generated, and for the most part they ended where they began. Information had little ability to move around the country.

By 1912 small-town newspapers were plugged into a nationwide network. The story of a spectacular murder in a small town would be picked up and discussed coast to coast. It was this development that facilitated the recognition that a horrible axe murderer was traveling around the country; not that this could not possibly have happened earlier, but it did not. It was not until the newspapers were plugged into the national network that people connected the dots.

Newspapers in that time period grew rapidly in their depth and sophistication. By 1912 newspapers were bigger, physically bigger. They had more pages. They had room to cover more stories and to cover them in more depth. They had more room to allow and encourage comment from their readers. Newspaper reporters became more professional.

Public literacy was advancing rapidly. In 1900 50 percent of white children and about 29 percent of black children aged five to nineteen were enrolled in school—meaning that most children in those age ranges were *not* in school. By 1910 the percentages were slightly over 60 percent for white children, and about 43 percent for black children. By 1920 we were at about 65 percent for white children, and probably over 50 percent for black children.

Education and newspapers, of course, go hand in hand. If you can't read, you don't need a newspaper. In 1900 a significant percentage of the population was illiterate. By 1912 this was less true.

So stepping backward in time from 1909, in small-city newspapers, is almost like stepping off a cliff. In the stories that I have told you about, from 1909 to 1912, we have good detail; we can find hundreds of newspaper stories about many of these crimes, and the newspapers provide leads to documents and other sources. But in 1902, we have nothing like that in many cases (although some cases, in some towns, are well documented even back to the beginning of our timeline).

The murders at the Moores' home in Villisca and the murders of the Ackerman family in Milton, Florida, in 1906 highlight the contrast. The murders of the Moore family are quite famous; magazine articles are written about them, television shows are made about them, and the case is often described as the greatest unsolved crime in American history. But in fact, the eight members of the Moore family killed by The Man from the Train in 1912 are probably not even the most people he had killed in one event. Nine members of the Ackerman family were killed in Florida in 1906, probably by the same man.

But whereas the Moore family murders are famous, the murders of the Ackerman family are so obscure that we were unable to come up with more than a basic outline of what happened. The murders of the Ackerman family are so unknown that I was unable to find anyone *in the historical society of the county in which the murders occurred* who had ever heard of them. Without a few old newspapers, they would be totally and absolutely forgotten.

In part, this is the difference between 1906 and 1912, but in the larger part it is the difference between the Midwest and the rural South. Not wishing to speak ill of the South or to denigrate southerners in any way, but the fact is that literacy in the South, in that era, lagged far, far behind the rest of the nation. In 1912, according to a Web site maintained by the school of education of Chesapeake University, southern states accounted for 34 percent of the American population, but only 3 percent of state funding for education.

In 1911 and 1912, The Man from the Train was killing people in the Midwest. But in the years 1900 to 1908, he was killing families mostly in the South—in Florida, Georgia, and South Carolina. Literacy in those areas was at a low level, and if you don't read, you don't need newspapers. Many or most of the areas in which he committed his atrocities, in the years just before 1908, had no newspaper coverage in the immediate vicinity.

Not only that, but . . . I know you are going to find this difficult to believe. Many of these crimes were never really investigated. I don't mean that there was zero investigation, but for many of these crimes, there is no evidence that there was ever any real effort to find the murderer.

You have to understand how primitive the system was. There were no investigative agencies at the state level in most states. Investigating a murder was the responsibility of local and county authorities—who normally would have no murders or maybe one murder a year in a county, and who had no budget to investigate a mysterious homicide. A study of Montgomery County, Iowa, where the Moores were murdered, found that in the twenty years before the Villisca murders were committed, the county had averaged about one homicide a year. When those murders had an obvious solution, then someone was convicted, but when they had no obvious solution, they were never solved. Half of the murders in the county had no obvious solution, so they were never solved. Montgomery County was probably no different in this respect from any other rural county.

Rural counties had no budget to pursue an investigation, so the first thing they had to do, even to make an *effort* to solve the crime, was to come up with the money. If the relatives of the victims had money, they might offer a reward fund, or the city or the county might kick in some money, or, in many cases, the governor would put up a reward. But if, like the Ackermans, the murdered family was poor or new to the area, there was less pressure to mount an effort. They'd talk to the neighbors, talk to the family, hassle a few local criminals, and then they would shrug their shoulders and put it aside.

So can you see why it was not practical for us to begin the book with the earlier murders? By starting the sequence in 1909, we were able to talk to you about cases that we actually know quite a lot about. By doing that, we were able to establish a base of knowledge about The Man from the Train, sufficient for you to make your own educated guess about whether these earlier cases, that we will tell you about now, are a part of the series or are not a part of the series. We told you about those later cases in chronological sequence, and now we are going to go back in time, back to 1900, and tell you about more cases, again in chronological sequence, but starting from a different point, several years earlier.

# CHAPTER XX

# Trenton Corners

When Bob Hensen visited the Van Lieu family on November 6, 1900, he brought them a chicken. I am certain they didn't ask where he got the chicken. The Van Lieu family were honest, upstanding, hardworking people. Hensen, on the other hand, was infamous, notorious. Which is worse, infamous or notorious? Whichever one was worse, that was what Hensen was. The newspapers would say that he had a bad reputation. He had a bad reputation in the same sense that Michael Jordan had a jump shot. He was fine when he wasn't drinking; he had a temper even then, but he was likeable, and he would take jobs and he would work hard—when he wasn't drinking.

On November 6 a dispute erupted between Hensen and Mary Elizabeth Van Lieu. Hensen left clothes at the Van Lieu house, and he would often stay there, even when George Van Lieu was away. Mary told him that she was tired of taking care of his clothes, and he needed to get them out of her house. In the subsequent argument Hensen may have threatened to kill her, although it is impossible to determine whether this crucial detail is fact or merely gossip.

Van Lieu was a working weekend musician, a violin player, and on November 17, 1900, which was a Saturday night, he had a gig in Trenton (although the term *gig* is not known to have been used until the 1920s). In the early afternoon he met up with a friend and neighbor, Stephen Williamson, and the two of them walked to Trenton Junction, where they would catch the train into Trenton. It was about a three-mile walk into Trenton Junction. At the edge of Trenton Junction they ran into Bob Hensen, who had spent the morning drinking.

The place where the Van Lieu family was murdered no longer exists. The story of the Van Lieu family murders is rich with references to bars and roadhouses, to small settlements that hoped to grow into towns, and to roads which had names, before the roads had merely numbers, and to hills, when even the hills had names, and the creeks had names, but none of these things exists anymore, not the bars, nor the small towns, nor the roads, not even the hills or the creeks.

In 1900 the population of Trenton, New Jersey, was 73,000 people—actually not very different from the population of Trenton now, but whereas modern Trenton sits in the lap of a giant metropolis, in 1900 it was surrounded by farms and fields. In 1900 the population of the rest of Mercer County was 22,000; now it is more than 300,000. Seven miles northwest of Trenton was the settlement of Trenton Corners. Trenton at that time was almost 100 percent white, whereas Trenton Corners was a mixed-race enclave, and every person mentioned by name in this story was black except Ellen Quinn. Leaving Trenton Corners there was a lonely road called the Birmingham-Harbourton road. The Van Lieu family lived along that road.

Hensen said that after meeting Van Lieu and Williamson he visited a couple of taverns in Trenton Junction and in the evening, at dusk and after, took a nap under a bridge. He was awakened when a team of horses and a heavy cart rolled over the bridge, and about the same time some dogs started barking loudly. He wandered aimlessly, heard a violin playing but didn't know where it was coming from. Hensen didn't have any idea what time this was (he may not have been able to tell time), but the eleven-year-old boy who was practicing his violin at that hour was one of the Williamson family. The boy testified that he started playing the violin about 10:30, and that the dogs broke out in a ferocious barking spell shortly after that. A little bit before 11:00 the Van Lieu house was discovered to be on fire. By the time the neighbors got to the scene the house was entirely engulfed in flames. The neighbors salvaged a clock and a table, but otherwise the house and contents had burned to the ground within an hour.

At the time, it was assumed that Mary Van Lieu and her two-year-old son, Willie, were in Trenton with their father/husband, but when George Van Lieu got off the train about 1:00 a.m. another man, also named Williamson, met him on the road and informed him of the fire. Van Lieu asked where his wife and baby were. Investigating further, the neighbors now found a large pool of blood at the back of the house and a bloody axe, taken from the coal shed, discarded in the backyard. After that, they found the remains of the wife and child in the burned-out basement, charred beyond recognition. There was a pump at a well in the yard. The wooden handle of the pump was covered with bloody handprints. The murderer had washed his hands before he fled the scene.

Police arrived. When Van Lieu told the sheriff that he had met Robert Hensen near Trenton Junction and that he assumed Hensen was headed toward his house to pick up his clothes, that for all practical purposes was the end of the investigation. It would be an understatement to say that Hensen was suspected of the crime. He was immediately assumed guilty. One of the first newspaper accounts contained the following rather memorable summary:

Robert Hensen, a Trenton colored man with an unsavory reputation, is the one suspected of having done the shocking deed. He is now confined in a cell in the county jail and the civil authorities are at work collecting evidence which, it is expected, will fasten on him, beyond a doubt, the monstrous crime, and send him to the gallows to expiate the lives that were sacrificed to a murderer's lust.

—*Trenton Times*, November 19, 1900

We don't have the evidence yet, but we know who did it. Two days later:

The fact that the evidence so far brought to light is entirely of a circumstantial nature is in favor of the prisoner. . . . Hensen's life of crime is so well known all over Mercer county that it will be difficult to secure an unbiased jury to try the case. A close and careful watch is kept over the accused by the authorities because they know that he is dangerous and must be watched.

—*Trenton Times*, November 21, 1900

Hensen had been prosecuted for larceny or petty larceny in October 1888, May 1892, and October 1898, and for assault or atrocious assault in January 1885, October 1898, and January 1900. "Atrocious assault" sounds as if it could mean "rape" and it could mean that, but usually didn't; it was a term used in New Jersey law that meant "aggravated assault," which means assault leading to injury. Atrocious assault meant that the skin was broken. He had also been arrested in regard to the murder of a white woman, Ellen Quinn, in 1888. Not blowing that off, but he was a black man suspected in the death of a white woman; if they had had any evidence against him at all, they'd have hung him for that.

Hensen had no permanent address. He slept under bridges and left clothes with friendly families. He was arrested the next day, ten miles away, at the home of another friend—also named Williamson, the fourth Williamson we have encountered. The papers note that the arrest occurred in the same house next to which another man had frozen to death the previous winter.

Van Lieu told the police that when he met Hensen at Trenton Junction, he *assumed* that Hensen was headed to his house (the Van Lieu house) to pick up the clothes that he had left there. Police surmised that this must have led to a renewal of the earlier dispute, and that Hensen must have erupted in anger and murdered the family. Hensen insisted that he never went to the Van Lieu house on that day; he was never there. There is no independent evidence that he was there; no one saw him at the house on the day in question or saw him leaving the house. His presence there, and the resulting dispute, is conjecture, and the prosecution timeline has a six-hour gap. If Hensen had gone directly from meeting Van Lieu to Van Lieu's house he would have been at the Van Lieu house about 4:00 p.m.; the house was found in flames more than six hours later.

Hensen also left clothes at the house of Ann Smith, who lived in Trenton Junction. At some time that evening Hensen went to Ann Smith's house. He knocked on the door and was admitted by a man named John Skillman. Hensen thought this had happened about nine o'clock; Skillman thought it was about midnight. Since Hensen had testified to hearing the barking dogs and the violin playing—things that are known to have happened around 10:30—he must have arrived at Ann Smith's more likely around 11:00. Asked if he was friends with Skillman, Hensen replied, "He is not with me." Hensen told Ann Smith that he was hungry, washed his hands, and was served a meal.

The Mercer County sheriff took pride in treating his prisoners with dignity. The grand jurors saw Hensen sitting in a clean, newly whitewashed jail cell with some furniture, apparently well fed, and remarked that "Well, I must say that the prisoners are made very comfortable." Hensen jumped out of his chair, swore violently for several seconds, and attempted to assault the man who had made the remark. It was a futile gesture, as he was separated from the juryman by iron bars, but Hensen, exhausting his supply of profanities, suggested loudly that if the jury member thought this looked comfortable he should come stay with them for a few days. Retreating across the cell, the "burly negro" turned and hurled a book at the bars. The outburst probably didn't help his cause.

The other facts against him were shoe tracks and bloody clothes. There were three hundred yards of foot tracks across a field, leaving the scene of the crime. These were not bloody tracks; the implication was that because whoever left those tracks was cutting through the field, rather than using the road, he must have been fleeing the scene of the crime. We were spared the bloodhounds this time; we were spared them, actually, because the sheriff had already decided it was Hensen, so . . . why bother with the hounds? The sheriff said that the footprints exactly fit Hensen's shoes. His lawyer said that there was nothing unique about the shoes, they were common shoes of a common size, with no broken sole or anything of that nature to identify them.

There was blood on Hensen's clothes; not a whole lot of blood, but some blood. Hensen said that it might be muskrat blood; he had trapped and skinned a muskrat earlier in the month. He also trapped and skinned rabbits and squirrels; it might be rabbit blood or squirrel blood, and also he had smashed his hand earlier in the week helping somebody move a piano, and his hand had bled. And he had constant nosebleeds. I know, that's too many explanations; when somebody gives you four reasons for having blood on his clothes, it looks hinky. Two Princeton scientists testified that the blood was from a mammal, but muskrats and squirrels are mammals; rodents are mammals. At that time it was difficult to distinguish human blood from the blood of other mammals, although ten years later that was no longer true. The pump handle was sawed off and introduced into evidence; it was covered with bloody prints, which would have been highly significant six years later, when people understood fingerprints, but in 1900 fingerprints hadn't yet arrived.

Hensen had a five-day trial with very good defense lawyers. He chewed tobacco constantly, even on the witness stand, and chewed nervously on the ends of his little mustache. He was convicted in early March and filed an appeal, asking for a new trial. The appeal being rejected, he was executed on December 27, 1901, a little more than a year after the trial.

The case against Hensen is poor, and it rather sets my teeth on edge when people decide who committed a crime in the first twenty minutes of the investigation. At the same time, there is nowhere near enough evidence for us to conclude that The Man from the Train had anything to do with these murders. The indications that it could be The Man from the Train are:

1. The crime did occur within walking distance of the intersection of two train lines.

2. The small, isolated village near the murders is exactly the type of place favored by our criminal.

3. There was no robbery, and no apparent motive, other than the supposition that a dispute from eleven days earlier might have reignited.

4. The Man from the Train's previous (known) murders were in the Northeast, in 1898, and his next suspected or possible murder is in the Northeast, in 1901.

5. Of the few known elements of the crime, some do appear to resemble his patterns that would be established by future crimes such as taking an axe from the scene of the crime: leaving the axe at the scene of the crime, and washing his hands at the scene of the murders.

He may have been in the Northeast at this time; he may have committed the murders. We don't know. The absence of a young female at the scene is against the theory, and there is no convincing evidence that he was criminally active between 1898 and 1903.

Hensen's alleged motive is pretty slight. The Van Lieus were his friends, and he visited them regularly. His story is that he was asleep at the time, a half-mile away. Given his drinking and his normal habits it is not unreasonable to suggest that he might have lain down to sleep it off, and the rest of his story, about the dogs barking and the violin playing, is consistent with the accounts of others. The day-of-the-crime quarrel is pure speculation. But there's a lot here we don't know.

What remains of Trenton Junction is now called West Trenton. What is now the Trenton-Mercer County Airport opened in 1929 as the Skillman Airport; the lonely road along which the Van Lieus lived was regraded to serve as the first landing strip. During World War II General Motors built bombers near the airport, which became such a hive of activity during the war that everything recognizable in the area was obliterated. The Trenton-Mercer County Airport has two landing strips, which intersect almost at right angles. As nearly as I can reconstruct, the house where the Van Lieus were murdered stood exactly at the point where the two landing strips intersect.

Notes about the case:

1. Discovered on an old map but never mentioned in the newspaper coverage of the crime: the scene of the murders was within easy walking distance of the New Jersey state insane asylum.

2. Many of you probably know that there is a file that catalogs data on all known executions in the United States; it is called the Espy File. The Espy File lists Hensen's name as "Henson"; however, all or almost all newspaper articles that we found spell the name as "Hensen."

3. Asked under oath how old he was, Hensen said that he might be "forty-three or forty-five."

4. The witness who talked to Hensen shortly after Van Lieu and Williamson did was named "Stubbs." During Hensen's trial there occurred this exchange between Stubbs and the defense attorney:

*Attorney*: How long have you known [Hensen]?

*Stubbs*: About three years.

*Attorney*: What time did you say it was?

*Stubbs*: Between four and four-thirty.

*Attorney*: How do you know it was that time?

*Stubbs*: I just left Jones.

*Attorney*: What time was it then?

*Stubbs*: Four o'clock.

*Attorney*: How do you know?

*Stubbs*: I looked at the clock.

*Attorney*: Can you tell the time?

*Stubbs*: Yes.

*Attorney*: What time is it now, by the court clock?

The witness walked down from the stand and after looking at the clock said "Nine o'clock." At the time it was 10:45. This raised a big laugh in which Hensen joined. "Look again," said (the lawyer). "It is half-past ten," said Stubbs, and again there was a big laugh at the witness' expense. This seemed to please Hensen immensely and he laughed immoderately.

It doesn't matter what time the encounter on the road happened; it's just color. The pertinent facts are:

1. That Stubbs couldn't tell time, and

2. That the attorney and the spectators all felt that it was appropriate to laugh at him because he could not tell time but had pretended that he could.

Van Lieu and the Williamsons were certainly literate, could tell time, and could read music, but it appears that most of the other people in the story, including Hensen, may not have been able to tell time. But Hensen may have been literate, since we know that he kept books in his jail cell.

# CHAPTER XXI

# Standing by Henry

Never before has this section of Maine had a case which is so mysterious in every way as the horrible affair which took place at the Allen home. . . . The country around here has been infested by tramps for several weeks. [Mary Allen] always kept quiet when there was a rap at the door, and in her stead Mr. Allen would answer the knock. The little girl was handsome and attractive.

—*Boston Globe*, May 15, 1901

Piscataquis County, Maine, is the sort of place where Bigfoot could settle down and raise a family of little Bigfoots without anyone coming to film their morning romps for cable TV. The county is the size of Connecticut, but has a population of 17,000 people—then and now; 115 years ago the population was the same as it is now. This works out to about four persons per square mile, which is less than half the population density of North Dakota, but even that image is somewhat misleading, since most of those people were concentrated in the southern part of the county. 99 percent of the population of the county is trees.

J. Wesley Allen, his wife, Mary, and fourteen-year-old daughter, Carrie, had lived for decades on a hundred-acre farm south of Shirley,

Maine (which is also called Shirley Mills). The Allen house was just a few steps off of a sparsely settled road, so people walking the road would sometimes knock on the door to ask for water or something to eat. Mr. Allen was not friendly to strangers. He was a big, strong man—two hundred pounds, which would have made him much larger than the top athletes of the day—and he was physically fit at the age of fifty-three. According to the *Boston Globe*, "He was very much opposed to visits from strangers, and the neighbors say that on more than one occasion tramps who called at his house made up their minds quickly that they better do business with some other person." Mary was not in good health. The nearest neighbors were three-quarters of a mile away, and there were so few people who used the road that the murder of the family and the subsequent burning of their house and barn went unnoticed for eleven hours.

The road on which the family lived was called the stage road; it is now called the Greenville Road, Maine highways 6 and 15. Although of course nothing is left of the Allen house, the Appalachian Trail passes within an eighth of a mile of where the house was, just to the south of what are called the Spectacle Ponds. May 12, 1901, was a Sunday night. At about 9:45 p.m. a "neighbor" saw a reddish glow in the sky over by the Allen house. He thought nothing of it at the time. The next morning a man driving his children to the village school saw the burned-out house. Upon investigation he found the remains of Mr. Allen in the barn, two large pools of blood nearby. He went for help.

The charred bodies of Mrs. Allen and her daughter were found in the ruins of the house, in separate rooms, in neither case in their bedrooms, from which it is inferred that the family was attacked in the evening, while they were still up and around. The house had burned to the ground and a large barn had burned out, but a stack of firewood between the two had not burned. On this basis it was believed that the assailant(s) may have set two separate fires. Note the stack of firewood; contemporary accounts of the case mention the firewood only because it failed to burn, but where there is a stack of firewood, there is an axe.

After the murders were discovered it required more than twenty-four hours for the sheriff and county coroner to reach the scene of the crime. Mr. Allen, while a prosperous farmer, never kept money in his house and was not known to have enemies. The head of an axe was found in the yard, missing its handle but covered and caked with blood. What looked like the cap of a liquor bottle was picked up outside the house and was taken to be evidence, since the Allens did not drink.

The first suspects were stagecoach robbers. A stagecoach ran periodically up the long, empty road beside the Allen house, and there were highwaymen who operated along the road, refugees, no doubt, from the sixteenth century. A stagecoach had been robbed at Willimantic, seventeen miles to the east, two days before the murders, and a man named William Johnson reported that he had been robbed by four drunk guys near the stage road on Monday morning.

This story, however, turned out to be smoke; the "robbery" by the four drunk guys was nothing more than some mildly aggressive panhandling. Johnson had been walking along the train track two miles west of the Allen house when he encountered a hobo camp, a group of four tramps lying on abandoned mattresses, smoking and drinking. One of the tramps asked Johnson for tobacco to fill his pipe; Johnson refused and went on his way.

Four tramps were arrested and hauled in for questioning—it is unclear whether they were *exactly* the same tramps—but even before they were arrested the sheriff had more or less announced to the press that he didn't believe they had anything to do with the crime. Johnson had exaggerated his report and had tailored his description of the four men to match the suspects from the stagecoach robbery. The sheriff thus concluded that the four men had nothing to do with the stagecoach robbery, were not criminals, and were not legitimate suspects in the murders, all fair enough. From our standpoint, 116 years later, the fact that a hobo encampment stood along a railroad line two miles from the scene of the crime, in an area in which the houses were literally a mile apart one to another, is immensely interesting, but let's move on for now, and we'll circle back to this.

On the day the crime was discovered, before the sheriff and the coroner arrived, the neighbors and newspapermen had decided that the purpose of the crime was to sexually assault the two women of the house; the newspapers left out the word *sexually*, but it is clear what they meant. The sheriff signed on to this theory. On the back of the Allen property, some distance from the house, stood a cabin called the Huff cabin. Neighbors rushed there, hoping to find Mary and Carrie Allen safe. The cabin had been broken into, a bolt removed. They informed Mr. Huff, and he replaced the bolt, but the cabin was broken into again that night. A revolver was stolen from the cabin, and some odd matches were abandoned there, matches of a type investigators had not seen before. When two crimes are committed on the same property on the same day, you figure they're related.

When the sheriff and the sheriff's men arrived on Tuesday morning, they went to the neighbors to start asking questions. To their astonishment, one of the neighbors, Mrs. Telos Smith (Ida Smith), emerged from her house in high dudgeon and barked at the officers that "we are going to stand by Henry." The officers didn't know what Mrs. Smith was talking about, but she explained that people were saying that Henry had something to do with this, but she and her husband knew better and they were standing by Henry.

Henry Lambert was an illiterate twenty-six-year-old French Canadian who worked as a logger and occasionally as a hunting guide. Despite the isolation of the farm, hundreds of people had swarmed the property after the discovery, and they had gossiped among themselves as to who did this. Henry Lambert was the first target. Lambert had built the Huff cabin in the fall of 1900, months before the murders, after living for four years in a camp or cabin across the road from the Allen house, but on the Allens' property. About a year before the murders, Allen had told Lambert that he wanted to farm that piece of property, but that Lambert, if he wished, could build a camp on the back end of the property. Lambert built the cabin, but after living in it for a month or so he sold it or gave it to a man named Elmer Huff, and spent the winter of 1900 to 1901 lodging with the family of Telos Smith.

If you're thinking it is unusual to build (and sell) a cabin on someone else's property, you're not into the mind-set of the era. In this book we have encountered (and will encounter) *numerous* people who were living in temporary shelters, tents, or crude cabins—Ray Pfanschmidt, and John Arthur Pender in Oregon, and others. Many farm people in that era were generous with their neighbors; it was normal for them to share things like horses, labor, and farm implements. It was normal for people to assume personal responsibility to help care for those who were less able to care for themselves. We saw that in the last chapter, in which numerous people helped to feed and care for Bob Hensen, knowing full well that he was a derelict with anger management issues—just as you might drop two dollars into the cup of a homeless man, knowing full well that his mental condition was unsound. As to the ownership of the land, there was (and is) so much unused land in that area, thousands of square miles of unused land, that to concede usage of a small portion of land was really nothing. Lambert would do fieldwork to balance the scales.

On the Saturday before the murders, which occurred Sunday night, Lambert had gone twice to Greenville, which is about ten miles north of the murder scene. There was a woman in Greenville. Lambert spent Saturday night and most of the day Sunday in Greenville, returning to the Smiths, they said, about 8:30 Sunday night. Lambert had bought a bottle of whiskey in Greenville, and the whiskey was all gone by the time he was interviewed the next Tuesday.

Footprints at the scene of the crime appeared to have been made by new or nearly new "rubbers"—rubber boots. Lambert had recently purchased new boots, but the boots were missing and could not be directly compared to the prints.

Lambert was arrested and charged with the crime on Thursday, May 16.

> The officers claim to have found prints from new rubber overshoes near the Allen house and also near Lambert's log cabin, and, in addition, a trail from one building to the other, marked by spots of blood. Just what actual evidence there is against Lambert is not known. Lambert is not disturbed by his arrest, and said last night that he had been very friendly with the Allens, visiting them evenings with considerable frequency.
>
> —*North Adams Evening Transcript*, May 17, 1901

There were rumors that Carrie Allen, the fourteen-year-old girl, was uncomfortable around Lambert; Lambert denied this. The boots now became central to the case, and the alcohol; the theory was that Lambert had shown up at the Allen house under the influence of alcohol, and gotten into a dispute with Mr. Allen.

With regard to the blood spots, let me point this out. What we now know, but what people did not know until about 1950, is that "transfer blood"—that is, blood carried from the scene of the crime on clothes or on a weapon or on the body—will not drip off for more than the first few feet. Transfer blood coagulates quickly. You get a blood trail only from an open wound. Henry Lambert did not have open wounds. If, in fact, a blood trail linked the Allen house and the cabin, that would be strong evidence that Lambert was *not* the murderer.

Lambert was convicted of the crime, and if I have said too often in this book that someone was convicted based on weak evidence, I will nonetheless say it again here, because this is not a case in which anyone would argue with me. Lambert was convicted and appealed. The state supreme court upheld the conviction, and Lambert would spend more than twenty years in the state prison, which, you will be surprised to learn, was not actually Shawshank; it was Thomaston.

Lambert was a model prisoner but continued to insist that he was an innocent man. Over the years a few people began to listen. He became a cause célèbre: justice for Henry Lambert. A number of lawyers worked to try to set him free but, until 1923, without success. In May 1923, a very good lawyer named Charles S. Hichborn persuaded the governor to appoint a panel of leading citizens to listen to Hichborn's arguments on behalf of Lambert, while the attorney general's office appeared on behalf of the state. The panel concluded that Lambert was innocent in fact, that he had been wrongly convicted, and the governor issued him a full and complete pardon based on a claim on actual innocence. Hichborn's plea on behalf of Lambert was published as a pamphlet, entitled "Henry Lambert, a plea for humanity and an argument for justice before the Governor and Council." The introduction to the pamphlet was written by one of Maine's most prominent journalists.

This is quite rare. In the history of Maine there are only four cases in which convicted murderers, incarcerated for years, have been declared to be innocent in fact.

Let's go back now to the trial. In July 1902, when Lambert's appeal was being heard at the state supreme court, the *Boston Globe* printed this summary of the case against him:

> The case of the state summed up is as follows: That Lambert was guilty because of these facts and circumstances, that certain matches were found in a camp formerly owned by him on the Allen place

which were purchased by him, as it is claimed; or certain tracks which were made by some person who wore rubbers, and it is claimed these tracks were made by Lambert; of the story which Maj. Hartnett, the detective, claims was told him by Lambert, which shows that Lambert was the guilty party; that Lambert cannot give an account of himself from 4 o'clock until late in the evening of the 12th of May. The motive which the government claims was infatuation for the daughter Carrie Allen.

It was a long, hard-fought trial; every point made by the prosecution was vigorously opposed by the defense—perhaps too vigorously. The possibility exists that the jury convicted Lambert in part because they disliked his lawyer. The trial, starting November 16, 1901, lasted into December and was reported at that time to be one of the longest murder trials in the history of Maine. The jury convicted him in two hours once the lawyers finally shut up.

The boots in question were missing; Lambert had purchased boots recently, but the boots were missing. The man who sold him the boots testified that they were a size six and a half, which would make them too large to have made the prints in question. The men who found the prints and measured them—men who had known Lambert for years—testified on his behalf, insisting that the dimensions of the prints they measured were inconsistent with the boots brought into court by the defense, identical to those Lambert had purchased. The president of the company that manufactured the boots testified for the defense. The defense also presented evidence that Carrie Allen had recently been given new rubbers, and that the prints were more compatible with her boot size than with Lambert's.

Henry Lambert was wearing a white shirt at the time most in question; he had put on the white shirt with a high collar in order to go to Greenville to see the "girl," but he was wearing a kind of dress shoes, and his feet had gotten blistered, so he had ripped a strip off of the bottom of the shirt, from the part that tucks into the pants, to wrap up his blistered toes. Lambert testified that he had purchased the shirt a little more than a year earlier, and that *the shirt had never been washed*—not relevant, of course, but instructive as to how Lambert lived, thus as to how he was perceived by the community. The prosecution claimed, fairly incredibly, that a piece of charred cloth found in the ruins of the home was the strip of cloth torn from the bottom of Lambert's shirt.

The description of Henry Lambert overlaps with that of Bob Hensen on many points. Both were unmarried men, essentially homeless; both stayed with people who were good enough to give them a bed to sleep in. Both men drank; Lambert was illiterate, while Hensen may have had some very limited literacy. Both hunted and ate small game. Both did odd jobs to pick up a few dollars. When a terrible crime occurred, the police in both cases looked at those people who were *known to be in the vicinity*, and focused on Hensen and Lambert not because there was any real evidence against them, but because—like Reverend Kelly—they were the weakest links among those people known to be near the scene of the crime. In both cases, police arbitrarily discounted the possibility that the crime was committed by someone with no links to the community, and focused instead on the most marginal persons who were members of the community. But whereas Hensen did have a history of violence, and thus was a more reasonable target, Lambert had no history of violent or aggressive behavior.

The real question for us, of course, is whether these murders could have been committed by the main subject of the book. I believe that in fact these murders most probably *were* committed by The Man from the Train—not that there is overwhelming evidence for that proposition, but that it seems to me the most reasonable explanation.

A serial murderer often has an isolated event that occurs several years before he begins regularly killing people. That first event is rushed, amateurish, unplanned, or badly planned. The Allen massacre was not that first, isolated event—and neither is it the first of the planned, deliberate, and systematic murders that he would commit over the next eleven or twelve years. This is a transition event, a murder that resulted from a sudden burst of uncontrolled anger.

The basic fact of the case is that a family was murdered, with an axe, without any robbery and with no reason to believe that anyone held a grudge against the family.

In addition, there are four factors here that strongly suggest The Man from the Train: (1) proximity to the railroad tracks, (2) the fact that it was a logging area; (3) the presence of a large number of railroad tramps; and (4) the presence of Carrie Allen among the victims.

The murders occurred two miles from the railroad track, through relatively dense woods, and the sheriff spoke about that as if nobody could possibly cut through two miles of woods to commit a motiveless murder. But the hobo camp sat just two miles away, and there were trails through those woods, and people cut through them all the time.

Many, many of The Man from the Train's murders were committed in logging areas, presumably because he worked as what we would now call a lumberjack. Logging was then and is now the dominant industry of this area.

Third, the early newspaper coverage of this crime states repeatedly that the area had recently been plagued with tramps.

Fourth, Carrie Allen was just two or three years older than Lena Stillinger (I think), and the newspaper coverage states specifically on many occasions that she was an attractive young girl. Her age is reported in various places as twelve, thirteen, fourteen, fifteen, and sixteen, and I don't honestly know which is correct, but fourteen seems to be the age given most often.

I will note also that it was a Sunday night, which was the most common night for The Man from the Train to attack, and that it occurred in warm weather.

Against the argument that this is our fiend is the fact that not enough is known about the crime to reach that conclusion, and also the fact that this family was apparently murdered about nightfall, whereas The Man from the Train preferred to wait until the middle of the night, when the families were asleep. But if this crime resulted not from a plan and pattern, but from sudden anger, then we would not expect it to conform to the patterns that developed in later years. In 1911 there were two murders (in Marshalltown, Iowa, and in Johnson County, Kansas) in which the murderer hid out in the barn until the man of the house came out to do his evening chores, attacked the man of the house in the barn, and then attacked the rest of the family. This, it appears to me, is what most likely happened here: the murderer was hiding out in the barn when J. Wesley Allen went out to do his evening chores and attacked him from behind with an axe before he had a chance to defend himself.

The Web site Victims of the State, an anti–death penalty information source, makes this the last paragraph of their summary of the Lambert/Allen case:

> In 1923, after serving more than 20 years in prison, Lambert was granted a pardon based on innocence. It was felt that Lambert was convicted on insufficient evidence and that other evidence showed Allen had had a dispute with a tramp who may have committed the alleged murders.

I think that this is roughly right. Some speculation here, OK? Speculating. The Man from the Train acted—committed murders—out of a combination of hatred and a horribly perverted lust; I don't want to call it "lust" because that makes it sound normal, so I will refer to it as "perversion." In the end, these two fused so that he simply enjoyed killing people; he enjoyed committing murder in the same way people enjoy roller coasters or mountain climbing—in the end.

But in the beginning, it was hatred and perversion. My best guess is that, having done some logging work somewhere in the area in the previous weeks, he was spending the weekend tramping around the area, drinking and fantasizing about killing people, when he happened somehow to see Carrie Allen, perhaps just walking across her backyard. He walked down the road a ways, circled back, picked up an axe in the barn, and hid out in the barn until Wesley Allen began his evening chores.

But it may not have been Carrie; it may also be that he knocked on the door and asked for a drink of water, and Wesley Allen came out at him in a bad temper, and told him to get on down the road and be quick about it. The Man from the Train, although very strong, was a small man who felt that he had been mistreated by the world, that he was smarter than other people, and that he was better than other people, but that he had been denied his rightful place in the world.

There is a scene in the TV series *Dexter* in which the friendly suburban serial murderer has a confrontation with a neighbor who is committing some petty vandalism, and the neighbor threatens him, and Dexter says to himself, in his internal-monologue voice, "Believe me, you are definitely messing with the wrong man here." Wesley Allen, a large, powerful man, angrily drove tramps away from his door, but he was messing with the wrong man here. Most likely The Man from the Train, given his small stature and his hatred of humanity in general, particularly hated large men who tried to push him around. So he walked down the road a ways, but as he walked he worked himself into a blind rage about the way that he had been treated.

In the process of this attack, however, The Man from the Train may have suffered a significant injury, causing him to shed blood at the scene. I believe that the two patches of blood in the yard are difficult to explain unless the murderer also suffered injuries. Because he was injured the murderer perhaps spent that night and possibly the next night hiding out in the Huff cabin, retreating into the woods in the daytime. It may be that the injuries suffered by the assailant in this case helped persuade the murderer, in future attacks, to wait until the families were asleep before he began his assault.

CHAPTER XXII

# An Uncertain Set of Names

The population of Florida now is twenty million, but in 1903 it was about 500,000 people, most of whom lived near the northern border of the state, as did the Kelly family—Kelly, or Caffey; we can't be certain of the name. The village of Cottondale, eight to nine miles west of Marianna, was at that time unincorporated, just a few dozen people living around a rural railroad stop, where two lines met; it would be incorporated as a town two years later. The primary industries of the area were cotton farming, logging, and mining.

Henry Kelly, a black man, was most likely a sharecropper. Of the nineteen newspaper accounts of this incident that we could locate, eleven say that the murdered family was named "Kelly," four say "Caffey," two say "Smith," and two do not give any name. We will use the name "Kelly"; however, the best account of the murders uses the name "Caffey," so that could be the actual name.

In any case, the family lived in an isolated cabin near Cottondale; Henry, his wife, and three small children. The Kellys were last seen about October 31, 1903. On November 9 Kelly's mother-in-law, who lived in Marianna, made her way to Cottondale to check up on the family, having not heard from them. The front door was secured from the outside with a padlock and a chain, and she could see blood

230

on the outside of the house. She got a neighbor, and, with difficulty, they were able to break in.

The Kelly family had been dead for several days, and their bodies were already somewhat decomposed. Mr. and Mrs. Kelly were found in bed, their heads crushed by "some blunt instrument." Their baby was in bed with them, his throat slit, and the young children had been decapitated, their bodies on the floor and their heads on a mattress. An unwashed axe had been left in the room.

Two men, perhaps only boys, also black, were "arrested on suspicion." Their names were Albert (or Allen) Roulhaes and Joe Gordon (also called George Jordan and George Jerdan. The name "Roulhaes" is probably misreported, as well, since no other person in the United States is known to have that surname). Since there are no reports of a trial, we have to assume that these young men were released.

This is all that is known about the case. The area where the crime occurred was thinly populated with low levels of literacy and essentially no newspaper coverage. There is no indication that anyone from any newspaper ever visited the scene of the crime, and it is unlikely that there was ever any meaningful police investigation of the crime.

We believe that the mother-in-law, who found the bodies, was named "Smith." The confusion over the other names almost certainly results from the poor quality of long-distance telephone service at this time; the phones were so scratchy and faint that in many cases it was all you could do to make out what was being said by a person on the other end of the line.

Obviously this is a low-information event; we don't know enough about it to draw any solid conclusions. There is a substantial possibility that the crime was committed by The Man from the Train, based on the following facts:

1. It was close to the railroad tracks, and to the intersection of two railroad lines.

2. It was a logging/lumber area.

3. The Man from the Train liked this area, and would murder several other families very close to here over the next few years.

4. The Man from the Train almost certainly went south when the weather turned cold up north.

5. The crime was presumably committed in the middle of the night, since the victims were found in bed.

6. The victims were hit in the head with the blunt side of the axe.

7. The axe was left in the room.

8. Nothing of value was stolen (since the victims had nothing of value to steal).

9. The incident has no characteristics consistent with it being a hate crime.

10. There is no apparent motive.

11. The house was locked up tight as the murderer left, as The Man from the Train would often do.

# CHAPTER XXIII

# Just When You Thought This Story Couldn't Possibly Get Any Uglier

The *Statesboro News* defended these attacks and advertised "PHOTOS OF THE STATESBORO HORRORS FOR SALE." Pictures of the Hodges family, the burned home, Cato and Reed dying in flames, and other lurid prints were available at 25¢ each. Understandably, Blacks began a considerable exodus from Bulloch County, and many white farmers with cotton and corn crops in the field began efforts to stem the violence and quiet the fears of the Black population. In time, a degree of orderliness returned to rural Bulloch County, but the community was never the same. Three-quarters of a century later in the prosperous, progressive college community, most of the great-grandchildren of that earlier generation still cite the lynching of Will Cato and Paul Reed as the best remembered event in the history of Bulloch County.

—Charlton Moseley and Frederick Brogdon,
"A Lynching at Statesboro"

I t rained hard in Georgia on the afternoon of July 28, 1904, and Kitty Hodges and Sallie Akins were caught in the thunderstorm as they walked home from school, a half-mile from the rural schoolhouse to the Akins home on what is now called Isaac Akins road. Kitty and Sallie were nine-year-old girls. They changed out of their wet clothes at the Akins home, Kitty putting on some of Sallie's things. It would have been another mile or more for Kitty to walk on home and it was still raining, so her father, Henry Hodges, hitched up his horse to his buggy and went to fetch his oldest child and only daughter. The wet clothes were wrapped into a bundle and stored under the seat of the buggy. Kitty would be murdered that night, wearing the clothes she had borrowed from Sallie Pearl Akins, and the wet bundle of clothes would be found the next day still tucked under the seat of the buggy, their owner no longer on this earth.

From Cottondale, Florida, to Statesboro, Georgia, is 275 miles, most of that east. Cottondale is near the northern border of Florida, and Statesboro is in the southern part of Georgia, but Statesboro is well to the east of where the previous murders had occurred. A few miles west of Statesboro was a railroad stop known as the Colfax stop, and a small, unincorporated settlement had grown up around the stop.

On July 28, 1904, a family of five was murdered with an axe on an isolated farm near Colfax. The house, which was three-quarters of a mile from the railroad track but a mile from the nearest neighbors, was set on fire. The family was (a) white, and (b) yes, this is certainly relevant. Two black men were arrested the next day, were put on trial, were lawfully convicted of the crime, and were themselves murdered by a lynch mob in an appalling manner a little less than three weeks after the crime. (The house is said to be a mile from the nearest "neighbors," although there were sharecroppers who lived within a mile of the house. In that era it would never have occurred to a white farmer to think of a black sharecropper as a "neighbor.")

There are three subjects here: the first set of murders, the lynching, and the chain of evidence that links the persons who were lynched to the murders. About the first set of murders facts are scarce, but what is reported is clear and consistent with the exception of two issues. Henry Hodges was murdered outside his house about nightfall, presumably as he was doing his evening chores. Hodges's hat was found some distance from the house, along the road near the house, and the marks of a scuffle could be seen in the dirt near where the hat was found. Clotted pools of blood were found near that place, although Hodges's body was found inside the house, indicating . . . well, we'll discuss later what that indicates.

Hodges's wife, Claudia, and his daughter, Kitty, had also been hit in the head with the axe. From evidence found at the scene, it was concluded that both had been sexually assaulted, although newspapers of that era were too circumspect to spell out what the evidence was. Two other small children, a baby and a toddler, had perished in the flames. A purse with several dollars in it was found resting near Claudia's body.

A kerosene lamp *without its chimney* had been placed on a gatepost near the scene of the crime, and was still burning about eleven o'clock that morning, when the crime was discovered.

From what I have told you so far, you might think that this crime was committed by The Man from the Train, and in fact that is what I think; I think it was him, based on:

1. The isolation of the farmhouse, which is consistent with the other related crimes in this time frame.

2. The proximity of the crime to the previous event, to the next event, to other crimes in the series, and to the railroad.

3. The sexual assault on the nine-year-old girl.

4. The bludgeoning of the family, apparently with an axe.

5. The absence of any apparent "normal" motive.

6. Mrs. Hodges's jewelry (including her wedding ring) was left at the scene of the crime, and a purse with money in it was left at the scene of the crime.

7. The house was set on fire, as was The Man from the Train's

usual practice when the scene of the crime was isolated enough that he would have time to make a clean getaway before the fire was discovered.

8. Bodies being moved postmortem for no purpose.

9. The lamp burning without its chimney, which, as much as any one thing, is the signature of The Man from the Train.

We have much more information available about the second set of murders, the lynching of Reed and Cato, than about the first—truly horrible information, by the way. Reed and Cato were bound, soaked with ten gallons of kerosene, and set on fire, alive, begging to be shot, and in the presence of hundreds of people including children. There were photographs taken of the scene, and the photos were printed and sold as postcards.

The murder of the Hodges family became the occasion for a sort of pogrom directed at the black population of Bulloch County. Paul Reed was accused of the crime and taken into custody the next day. His wife, Harriet, gave a confession implicating Reed and his friend Will Cato. Several days later Reed also confessed to his involvement in the murders; he would confess repeatedly to involvement in the crime, which he said was a robbery gone wrong, but not to actually committing the murders. With every confession, he gave a different story about who else was involved with him and who actually committed the murders. In his first story he implicated John Hall and Hank Tolbert, his coworkers from a turpentine distillery in Statesboro, and said that Will Cato was not involved. A few days later he changed his story to say that the murders were actually committed by Will Rainey and Will Cato. Later, he said the murders were committed by a "club" formed for the purpose of raising money for two black preachers named Gaines and Tolbert. Another statement implicated a man named Dan Young; later statements included Handy Bell and an unidentified black man called "The Kid." Just before his death he would add to the list the names of Bill Golden, Mose Parish, and Alex Hall.

The local police arrested these people as they were named, although Sheriff Kendrick expressed doubt about their involvement even as he arrested them. The Moseley/Brogdon article quoted earlier (and later, at greater length) says that fifteen black people were lodged in the local jail, but a newspaper headline in the *Atlanta Constitution* (August 1, 1904) reported that "scores" of black people had been taken into custody; the number fifteen, which appears numerous times in newspaper accounts from the era, may actually be the number who were still in custody weeks later. The sheriff arrested everybody that he thought might be involved and then gradually released those who could not be connected to the crime.

Paul Reed, in some of his many stories, talked about a "Before Day Club." The Before Day Club was said to be an assemblage of rogue black men who plotted crimes against white people, robbing and killing white people. Reports of "Before Day Clubs" now popped up all over the region; there were supposed to be Before Day Clubs in several other Georgia counties, in Salem, Alabama, and as far away as Homerville, Virginia. Three buildings were burned to the ground in Palo, Georgia, a hundred miles from Statesboro, because whites believed they were meeting places for the local Before Day Club. A white farmer (N. W. Epps) was murdered near Tallahassee; the black man who shot him would claim to be a member of the local Before Day Club.

Reed claimed that by leaving the Before Day Club in the middle of the Hodges family murders he had saved the lives of three other white families who had been targeted for murder that same night, and that he himself was now a target of the club because he had broken ranks. In Bulloch County a man was shot and killed because he was misidentified as Handy Bell, one of the named members of the BDC.

Reprisal groups formed in response to the Before Day Clubs. The Before Day Clubs almost certainly never existed anywhere except in Paul Reed's imagination, but the reprisal clubs were very real. In

Register, Georgia (about ten miles south of the scene of the murders), two black men were ambushed and shot. In Portal, Georgia (seven miles west of the murders), a black man was shot, and his wife whipped. According to Moseley and Brogdon's "A Lynching at Statesboro," "numerous other beatings and attacks on Blacks occurred. The *Statesboro News* defended these attacks." Violence against people of color reached a level such that substantial numbers of black families fled the area. As farmers and turpentine mill owners began to find themselves short of black workers, they began an effort to calm the situation. The *Statesboro News* admitted that the Before Day Clubs had never existed.

Reed and Cato were convicted of the murders of the Hodges family after brief trials and jury deliberations that could have been measured in seconds. After the trials Hodges's brother, a minister from Texas, did what he could to prevent the lynching, exhorting the lynch mob at several points to stand back and allow the system of justice to run its course. Claudia Hodges's mother, on the other hand, urged the mob to burn them alive. There is a great deal of information available about the sequence of events leading up to the capture of the victims by the mob, the efforts to protect them from the mob, the decisions made by the mob, etc., but it is a ghastly and pathetic story and in large part parallels another event that I will tell you about later in the book, so I'm going to give that story the back of my hand at this time. This is not a book about lynching or racial violence; the murder of the Hodges family is much more relevant to our subject.

When I told you the story of the crime at the start of the chapter, I told it to you as if these murders were a part of our series, ignoring the evidence that led to the convictions of Reed and Cato. But if you read other modern accounts of the crime, they tend to leave no doubt that the murdered men were the murderers of the Hodges family.

The best account of the crime is a fourteen-page article by Charlton

Moseley and Frederick Brogdon, published in the *Georgia Historical Quarterly* in the summer of 1981. The article is scholarly in nature, documented with footnotes, and extremely well written. All other modern accounts of the crime are based on the information provided by Moseley and Brogdon. Although they don't directly say so, Moseley and Brogdon accept that Reed and Cato murdered the Hodges family and present the story of the murders as if this were clearly true. With the permission of the authors, I am going to reprint here selections from their article, with the goal of helping you to understand that point of view:

> Had the catastrophe been an act of God and nature?
>
> As the small cluster of men pondered the awful scene they began to suspect that more, much more, was involved. Woodcock and Woodrum, the first men at the scene, had noticed even in their excitement a shadeless kerosene lamp burning on the gatepost of the Hodges home, a flickering witness to whatever horrors had occurred there. As some of the men began to draw water from the well to cool the embers around the bodies, others examined the yard and began to discover disquieting evidence of a violent crime. Down the road they discovered the hat of Henry Hodges and near it, towards the cane patch, pronounced scuffling marks in the dirt. Most frightening of all they found several puddles of clotted blood. Then, in the still bright light of the dying fire someone discovered the bare footprints of a man and bloody hand smears on the fence.
>
> Next day, Friday morning, 29 July, a large crowd of people gathered in the road at the Hodges farm. Two bleak chimneys stood like sentinels in the yard, cold black ashes at their feet. On the gatepost the lamp still sat, its fuel exhausted and its flame extinguished. . . . At daylight on Friday following the murders, neighbors had investigated the scene of the crime. Scouring the

area, they had turned up vital clues. Tracks of four strange men were found around the farm, one of them barefoot and three of them wearing shoes. The neighbors brought dogs to the scene and put them on the trail. The tracks led to Fishtrap Bridge on Lott's Creek where a large group of picnicking Negroes destroyed the spoor. In the woods near the burned home searchers discovered a pair of shoes near a log. The shoes were mismatched, one a brogan and the other an elastic dress shoe. Tar coated the heel of one of the shoes and in the tar were several strands of hair, believed to have been from the head of Claudia Hodges. A farmer identified the shoes as mates to two pairs of shoes which he had bought for a Negro tenant living on his farm, one Paul Reed. In the road near the spot where the shoes were found another neighbor discovered a knife. The knife was also identified as belonging to Paul Reed. Hence the self-constituted posse had its first suspect.

Interrupting for the sake of clarity, the shoes and the knife were not found on the Hodges property; even the hat and the "marks of a scuffle" may not have been found *on* the Hodges property. The hat and the marks of a scuffle were found outside the gatepost where the lamp was, and on down the road a little bit. The shoes and the knife were found after the search was extended beyond that. The observation that the hair was "believed to have been from the head of Claudia Hodges" seems instructive about the mind-set of the investigators, since there is no possible way that anyone could have known where that hair came from, or could even have made any educated *guess*, other than to *assume* that it came from one of the five victims. Also instructive as to the mind-set of the investigators is the term "the tracks of four strange men." Really? How do we know that these are "strange" men? How do we know that they are not merely the footprints of neighbors or sharecroppers, passing by in the most ordinary way?

I'm also not sure why Moseley and Brogdon believe that these shoes were "bought for" Paul Reed. The newspapers that I have seen say these shoes were *given to* Paul Reed, which I interpret to mean that they were given to him after they had been worn by their original owners. Anyway:

On Saturday morning a number of the men went to Paul Reed's home and searched it. In the house they discovered a shoe that matched one of those found near the Hodges's home and under the house another that matched the other shoe found at the murder site. The posse also found a bolt of calico and a calico dress that matched the shoe strings found in the shoes. Besides this the men discovered what they believed was blood in the hip pocket of a pair of Reed's trousers. Reed denied involvement in the crime though he readily admitted that the shoes were his. He claimed that the blood stains in the pocket of his pants had come from a partridge which he had killed and placed there. . . . The story that Harriet Reed told damned her husband and their neighbor Will Cato. Will Cato and her husband, said Harriet, believed Henry Hodges to have $300 in coin buried in a kettle behind the chicken coop at the Hodges home. On Saturday night before the murders Reed and Cato had gone to the Hodges home to dig for the money but were discovered and to cover their intentions told Hodges that they had been on their way to a crossroads store to buy banjo strings when Cato had been grazed on the leg by a snake. They asked Hodges, said Harriet, for turpentine to put on the wound. Then, the following Thursday night, Cato and Reed had gone back to the Hodges home determined to get the money or kill the family. Once again Cato and Reed were discovered, said Harriet, and this time a struggle resulted which led to the murder of Hodges and then his wife when she came to her husband's aid. Frightened by their deed, Reed and Cato dragged the bodies of Henry and Claudia into the house. Terrified, they left the scene but upon reflection decided to return and burn the house to destroy the evidence of their crime. Accordingly, approximately an hour later, they returned and while searching the premises for money discovered the oldest child, nine-year-old Kitty Corinne, hidden behind a trunk. Harriet now told a story which became the most often repeated legend of the entire episode. Little Kitty, said Mrs. Reed, offered Will Cato and Paul a nickel to spare her life but they callously bashed in her skull with a lamp base. The two smaller children, Harmon and Talmadge, were left alive to die in the flames. Pouring kerosene from the lamps Cato and Reed put the house to the torch.

Paul Reed may not have been an exemplary citizen, and this may be why he was suspected of the crime. For what it is worth, I do believe that Paul Reed and various friends may have talked among themselves, at some point or on several occasions, about the possibility of robbing the Hodges family—not murdering them and burning down their house, but just about stealing some money rumored to be buried on their property. I believe that this may have happened because Will Cato, during his trial, admitted that he had witnessed these conversations, although he denied everything else that he had been charged with, and he insisted that he told Reed and his friends not to do it. And second, if there had been such conversations, that would explain why Harriet Reed turned on her husband so quickly after she was arrested: when she was told that the Hodgeses had been robbed and murdered, she actually thought that he might have done it (although in fact the Hodges family had not been robbed).

Let's talk about the knife (which is described in some modern reports as a "bloody" knife, although I have not seen any contemporary newspaper which says there was blood on the knife, and Moseley and Brogdon do not say that there was blood on the knife). In its first report on the case, July 30, the *Washington Post* stated that "the skulls of Hodges, his wife, and one child had been broken, apparently with an axe." Almost all first reports of the crime state that the three oldest victims had their skulls crushed by an axe and the two youngest perished in the fire, and the *Washington Post* in their last article about the crime, after the murders of Reed and Cato, still reports specifically and at some length that the Hodgeses were murdered with an axe.

Well, what is the relevance of a knife to an axe murder? Who was the knife used to kill? Moseley and Brogdon avoid this problem by never mentioning an axe in their account. They never say that it wasn't an axe murder; they just ignore the reports which state specifically that it was—and for good reason. Either you follow the theory of the axe in this case, or you follow the theory of the knife; it isn't both. If we follow the theory of the knife, then the murders were committed by Paul Reed and others chosen from the long list of those that Reed accused. If we follow the theory of the axe, then the crime was more probably committed by The Man from the Train. If we follow the theory of the knife, it was a robbery; if we follow the theory of the axe, it was not a robbery. The question is, Which theory, taken as a whole, is more credible?

*   *   *

Backing off for a second, do you know the difference between a kerosene lamp and a kerosene lantern? Some of you who are younger will not catch the distinction, so I had better explain. The lamps used at this time were almost always made of glass, and ordinarily were never taken out of the house. A *lantern* was sturdier, made of metal with glass panes, and was built for outdoor use. A lamp was designed to sit on a flat surface, whereas a lantern was usually designed to be held or suspended from above; it often had a "point" on the bottom so that it could not stand upright on a flat surface.

When I first saw reports of this case talking about a lamp on the gate post, I assumed that they meant a lantern hanging from the gatepost, which would be not uncommon—but no; they meant a lamp, and we know they meant a lamp because they talk about a lamp without its shade (what was called a "chimney" in the North, a "shade" in the South). That's a part of a lamp; it's not a part of a lantern. Now let's look at this paragraph from the *Atlanta Constitution,* August 1, 1904:

> Evidence has developed that tends to show a still more heinous crime was committed upon the persons of Mrs. Hodges and her 9-year-old daughter, Kittie, before they were killed. That robbery was not the prime motive of the crime is shown by the finding of a purse containing several dollars near where the body of Mrs. Hodges was discovered. The theory that now has most adherents is that Mr. Hodges was first attacked and killed at the stable. Then little Kittie was assaulted. Her screams attracted her mother, who ran out with a lighted lamp, which she set down upon a gate post. When Mrs. Hodges ran to the aid of her daughter, the theory is, she was knocked down and outraged and then killed. Then all of the bodies, living and dead, were dragged into the house and the torch was applied. This theory fits in with the confession of the wife of one of the accused men.

Well, no, actually, it doesn't; we just quoted the summary of that confession, and in Mrs. Reed's account, robbery was the entire motive for the crime, no one was raped, Kitty was killed long *after* her parents, and she was killed inside the house, not in the yard. It doesn't actually fit at all.

This failed reconstruction of the crime scene is driven by the questions "Why is that lamp out here on the gatepost?" and "Why doesn't it have its shade?" A man would never carry a kerosene *lamp* out to the stable to do his chores; he would carry a lantern—but a woman might grab a lamp, perhaps, to rush hurriedly into the yard in an emergency (apologizing for the sexist role assignments, but farm people a hundred years ago had strongly defined gender roles). Those speculating about the crime thus designed a scenario around the assumption that Mrs. Hodges must have rushed hurriedly into the yard, carrying the lamp. In other places, they would speculate that the heat from the burning house must have shattered the shade from the lamp.

But there are two huge problems with that scenario. First, it assumes that Mrs. Hodges carried the lamp to the yard in a desperate situation, responding to the screams of her daughter or perhaps searching for her missing husband, but that she somehow had the opportunity, what we might call the leisure, to set the lamp carefully on the gatepost before she herself was attacked. It is difficult to visualize how that happens. Run scenarios in your head, and you will see that within a few moments she is either attacked without warning or she finds a bloody body. In neither of those events is she likely to have the opportunity to carefully place the lamp on the gatepost. Why would she set the lamp on the gatepost before she was either (1) attacked, or (2) found something? And if she found something, why would she then go put the lamp on the gatepost? It doesn't make sense.

This scenario also speculates that three victims were killed outside the house, and their bodies were dragged inside the house before it was set on fire. But it had rained heavily on the afternoon and evening of the Hodges family murders; neighbors initially assumed that the house must have been struck by lightning, starting the fire. If three victims had been killed outside the house and their dead bodies dragged back into the house, there should have been obvious drag marks in the muddy ground, intermingled with deep footprints. If the victims had been either hit in the head with an axe or stabbed to death with a knife, there would have been blood trails along with the drag marks, making them yet more obvious.

This scenario assumes that the first on-scene investigators, the neighbors, found the "marks of a scuffle" some distance from the house and four sets of footprints in the lane outside the house, but that they failed to notice three sets of bloody drag marks with deep footprints in the soft ground leading into the house.

Dragging around dead bodies is hard work; I've never actually dragged a dead body, but I am told that it is damned hard work—and why? It's an isolated farm and they're dead and it is nighttime and you're not going to stay around here anyway, why on earth would you drag the bodies back into the house?

What those attempting to reconstruct the crime scene did not know, could not possibly have known, was that there was a serial murderer traveling the eastern seaboard, murdering families with an axe in circumstances much like this, and that that serial murderer very often sexually assaulted prepubescent females as a part of his crime. And that a peculiar signature of that serial murderer was that he often left a lamp, without its chimney, burning at the scene of the crime.

Moseley and Brogdon, while recounting the story of the robbery at some length, treat the allegation of rape as if this were thrown against the wall to enflame the public's emotional reaction:

On Monday the Savannah Morning News and the Augusta Chronicle printed stories that were not calculated to cool inflamed spirits. Basing their evidence on the discovery of a melted gold ring and several coins near Claudia Hodges's body, the News and the Chronicle discounted robbery as the motive for the killings and openly stated that the "flames concealed a darker crime" and that a "nameless offense" had been committed before the torch was applied. The Savannah and Augusta papers strongly intimated that both Claudia and Kitty Hodges had been sexually assaulted either before or after they were murdered.

Well, no, they didn't "strongly intimate" that this might have happened; they stated directly that this had happened, although, in keeping with the journalistic practices of the day, they did not use the words *rape* or *sexual assault*. What is reported as several *dollars* in all contemporary newspapers has become several *coins* in this article, diminishing its significance. Moseley and Brogdon are writing more about the lynching than they are about the murders; to them, the critical import of this information is the role that it plays in further enflaming the passions of a public that was already in a murderous mood. But the critical information here is not merely that there was a rape; it is also that *there was no robbery.* The Man from the Train, in dozens of cases, left jewelry and money in plain sight untouched at the scene of the crime. Persons committing a robbery do not normally do this. Moseley and Brogdon acknowledge that "much of the confession of Harriet Reed was contradictory and if the killers obtained any money, as she claimed, it was never discovered in the investigation nor could she account for it." This was not a robbery.

The community could have known that the little girl was sexually assaulted, it would seem, *only* if her body was staged in some manner suggestive of sexual assault—for example, if her underwear was missing and she was found with her limbs in an unnatural position. Which, of course, is exactly how The Man from the Train left young girls, in a number of other cases.

In this book we have seen that there is always someone who can play the role of first suspect. *There is always someone who can be immediately identified as having probably committed the crime.* In many of these cases, most of these cases, that first suspect is able to clear his name when given the opportunity to do so. Paul Reed, at the beginning of the investigation, was pitched into the role of first suspect because of some thrown-away shoes and a poor reputation in the community. The question I would ask is, Was Paul Reed ever given any real opportunity to clear his name?

The belief in Reed's and Cato's guilt, I think, is sustained by the belief that innocent people would not confess to a crime that they did not commit; therefore, while these stories are clearly not true, they must include some basic truth. Take that away, and the case against Reed and Cato collapses like a tent without a tent pole.

But, in fact, innocent people confess to crimes that they did not commit all the time. I believe that, in the aggregate, there are more confessions to murder by innocent people than by guilty, although most of these false confessions are accounted for by crazy people. If you take almost any fifteen- to eighteen-year-old boy and put him in a room with a bunch of police officers and tell him repeatedly that "don't you lie to us, boy, we know that you committed this crime, and we've already got all the proof we need about that," that young man *will* confess to the murder, even if he is completely innocent. Vulnerable people will confess to murder, in that situation, because they are afraid of the authority figures, and they have been prohibited by the authority figures from saying that they did not commit the crime.

As people get older, more mature, more confident, they gradually gain the ability to resist being bullied into false confessions. But from the moment they were accused, Paul Reed, Harriet Reed, and Will Cato would have known that they were in serious, serious danger of losing their lives. I am aware of the risks of speculating based on negative stereotypes—in this case negative stereotypes of segregation-era southerners—but is it unreasonable to speculate that Paul Reed was put into a roomful of men, one of whom said, "Don't you lie to us, boy. We know that you are involved in this, and you had better tell us the whole truth right now or you are not going to see the sun come up tomorrow morning."

We cannot *assume* that this happened, but it is reasonable to think that Paul Reed, Harriet Reed, and Will Cato were all interrogated in this manner. Harriet Reed was the weakest link; she broke first, telling a story that fit the facts of the Hodges family murders as best she understood them. Reed and Cato said the things they did after that in an effort to minimize the damage. Probably Reed accused one person after another because he was trying to *guess* who might actually have committed the murders, in the hope that that person would then be arrested, would confess to the crime, and would admit that Reed was not involved. It was a lost cause. Once Harriet Reed had implicated her husband and Cato, they were Dead Men Walking. At that point it was merely a question of whether they would be executed by the state or murdered by a mob.

# CHAPTER XXIV

# Hughes

Two railroad lines crossed in Trenton, South Carolina; actually, because of the consolidation of rival lines in 1894, two branches of the same railway system, the Southern Railway. In 1904 something less than 200 people lived there, in what was normally called a railroad stop. When the Hughes family was murdered in Trenton on December 8, 1904, the first reports immediately connected the crime to the murders of the Hodges family:

### Another Crime Laid to Blacks

**Family Murdered in South Carolina Under Peculiar Circumstances**

TRENTON, S. C.—Dec 8. An entire white family, living near here, has been murdered. Meager details received resemble the killing of the Hodges family at Statesboro, Georgia last August. The Hodges family was murdered by an organized band of negroes formed for purposes of wholesale murder.

—*Decatur (Illinois) Daily Review*,
December 8, 1904

Early in the morning of December 8, the residence of Benjamin Hughes, in Trenton, was discovered by neighbors to be on fire. (Almost 100 percent of newspaper reports say that the crime occurred on December 9, 1904, but it was, in fact, December 8.) By the time the neighbors gathered it was too late to get into the house and save anything. Once the fire had died down, however, searchers found the charred, mostly unrecognizable remains of Mr. Hughes, aged forty-two, his wife, Eva, same age, and their daughters, Emma, aged nineteen, and Hattie, aged fourteen. The bodies of all three women were found in their beds and were undisturbed, suggesting that they had been murdered in their sleep. Their heads had been crushed, probably (according to contemporary news reports) with an axe. *Eva Hughes's face had been covered with a pillow.*

The confounding fact of the Hughes family murders is that Mr. Hughes was shot, and also that he was clothed, rather than wearing pajamas or some such. Setting aside that one circumstance, it would be perfectly clear that these murders were a part of our series. Trenton, South Carolina, is almost exactly a hundred miles due north of States-boro, Georgia. The Hughes family was murdered 133 days after the Hodges family, a normal space-and-distance relationship for the series. The Man from the Train was moving, as he almost always did, in a consistent geographical pattern, drifting north from Florida to Georgia, from Georgia to South Carolina, from South Carolina to Virginia, where a family would be murdered (and a house set on fire) two weeks later.

The Hughes family was murdered without warning and without any rational explanation. The house was set on fire. A young girl was among the victims. Money and jewelry were left in plain sight. The murders were apparently committed sometime after midnight.

If we believe that this crime was committed by The Man from the Train—which I do—this crime becomes a "first" in two ways. Early in his run, The Man from the Train murdered farm families living near small towns but never actually committed a murder *in* a small town. Later, of course, that became his dominant pattern; later on almost all of his murders were committed in towns too small to have a regular police force, like Trenton, but this would be the first.

Also, this would be the first time that two crimes committed by The Man from the Train were connected by the newspapers. Of course, neither of these is any barrier to believing that the crimes were part of the series, since, if he was committing murders early on in rural areas and later on in small towns, *some* murder has to be the first one in a small town.

But Mr. Hughes was shot. In the case with which we began this book, the murders in Hurley, Virginia, in 1909, a man was shot, apparently outside the house, while his family was murdered in their beds, with an axe. It is difficult to understand how this happened. If the man was shot first, why didn't the family wake up? And if the family was murdered first, well, where was the father, and why was he found outside the house? This is the same problem exactly: neither scenario seems to make sense.

The scenario that does make sense was summarized nicely by the *Eau Claire Weekly* (Wisconsin) December 9:

> Investigation revealed the fact that unknown parties, believed by the tracks to be three men, entered the house through the rear door, murdered Mrs. Hughes in her room with an axe, then went to the room occupied by her daughters Emma, aged nineteen, and Hattie, aged fourteen, and murdered them in like manner without the girls awakening. Hughes evidently heard the noise and went from his room into the hallway, where he was shot down, a revolver being found by his side.
>
> A special train was sent to Columbia for bloodhounds to track the murderers. Citizens are guarding the ground about the rear door of the house, where the tracks were found, to prevent disturbing the only means of arriving at a clue.

You may be surprised to learn that the bloodhounds didn't find a damned thing. I don't believe there were three murderers; I believe there was one, but otherwise I think the Eau Claire report has it right—he entered through the rear of the house (as he always did), murdered the women in the rear bedrooms, and then was confronted by the man of the house, who slept in a different room, but who happened to be awake. And armed. The Man from the Train sometimes carried a gun, and would use it if he had to. We have seen indications of that on other occasions, but this seems more definitive. Also, in many of these cases it is unclear whether the young girls were assaulted while alive or postmortem, but if we accept this scenario we have evidence about that issue. Hattie's body was not staged or molested because, just after she was killed, the murderer was confronted by an armed man and had to shoot his way out.

Many newspapers would speculate, because Hughes was killed with a gun and a gun was found near his body, that Hughes had killed his family and then set fire to the house before committing suicide. That crime, of course, is much more common than for a family to be murdered by an intruder for no known reason. The human mind searches for the familiar; we always tend to believe that what has happened is what usually happens. In the words of a wire service story about this case: "The theory of suicide rests largely on the absence of motive for murder and the fact that bloodhounds were unable to discover any trail leading from the house."

But that's not right, and we know that it's not right for several reasons. First, the coroner's inquest ruled that the Hughes family was killed by intruders, not that I would be hesitant to argue with them if I didn't agree. (Parenthetically, the county solicitor who presided over the inquest was John W. Thurmond, the father of South Carolina's most successful twentieth-century politician, Senator Strom Thurmond.) Second, it would be extremely unusual for a man to murder his family *with an axe* and then kill himself with a gun; in fact, I have never heard of that happening. A man will kill his family with an axe (on rare occasions) if he doesn't have a gun, but if he has a gun . . . well, why would he do that? Third, the fire was set some distance from where Mr. Hughes's body was found, which, again, would be unusual in a murder/suicide scenario. And fourth, there is no indication that Hughes was a troubled man or an unstable man, no indication that he had a drinking problem or his wife was running around on him or anything like that. He was not in financial trouble; he was well-off, well-to-do. There is no indication that the family was unhappy. A ship will sink in a storm; it doesn't sink in calm waters. Murder/suicides do not normally happen without context.

# CHAPTER XXV

# The Christmas Day Murders

James Linkous was six foot four and weighed 170 pounds, a string bean who had settled in a mountain town of 3,500 people and was making a living painting houses. He had small, beady eyes and an exceptionally long mustache. He walked slowly with his arms swinging at his side in a way that reporters associated with people from the mountains. He was fifty-five years old in 1904, married to a woman the same age who had the same name as his state, Virginia Linkous.

Several years earlier a man named Frank Vaughn had abandoned his wife and three small children at a time when their mother was terminally ill. Destitute and near death, she had given her children away. One of the three, Willie, had been adopted by Virginia Linkous. In 1904 he was nine years old, and Willie and Virginia were entirely devoted to one another. The Linkous family lived in Radford, Virginia, in a building that had been built as a store with an apartment on the second floor. The store had failed, and the lower half had also been converted to living space; the Linkouses lived in the upstairs apartment, which was nicer, and a woman named Mrs. Texas Butterworth lived in the lower half with her mother and son; that's right, the women of the house were named Texas and Virginia.

I'll let you snicker about that as long as no one says anything about pancakes. There were no locks inside the house or on the outside door; the landlord would say at trial that "the tenants" had requested locks but that they had not been installed.

There are no reports of Linkous being abusive or difficult to live with or of strife within the family; in fact, the reports are entirely the opposite—he was kind, sober, and he treated his wife and adopted child very well. Mrs. Butterworth said that she had heard no arguments between the couple with whom she had shared a house for several months. Christmas Day in 1904 happened to fall on a Sunday. On Saturday night Virginia Linkous was cheerful and in good spirits, and invited the Butterworths to share Christmas dinner with her family.

A little before 4:00 a.m. on Christmas Day, Mrs. Texas Butterworth awoke to find the house filled with smoke. The next thirty minutes were divided between confusion and terror. She rushed upstairs, pounded on the door of the Linkous apartment, and tried to rouse the family, but the doorknob was red hot. Returning down the stairs she got her aged mother out of the house, but the old woman went back in to find her grandchild, got disoriented, and couldn't get out. Eventually the grandson found her and led her to safety. Everyone downstairs got out of the house.

The same was not true of the upstairs, however, and in that half hour Mr. Linkous's behavior would cost him his life. His story was that he was awakened by screaming, perhaps someone screaming "Fire," and, choking through the smoke, exited the house, believing that his wife and child were following behind him. Apparently the couple slept in separate rooms, which many couples did at that time. Reaching the ground, he rushed to the stable, which was near the house, to take care of his livestock, to get them to safety; this was his story.

But the story from others was different, or told in a different way;

to others he seemed indifferent to the fate of his wife and adopted son and worried only about the livestock and about some "fodder"—firewood—that was stacked up next to the house. He seemed very concerned to get the fodder away from the house, lest it should feed the fire, but unconcerned about his family.

Mrs. Butterworth is always referred to in the papers as Mrs. Texas Butterworth, except occasionally she is called Texas Shelor, Shelor being her maiden name. She also had apparently been abandoned by her husband, and it appears that she drank a bit. Mrs. Texas Butterworth—the most damaging witness against Linkous—testified that when she got out of the house she called to Linkous to go save his family, but he ignored her and continued to move his fodder away from the house. A town policeman testified that when he appeared on the scene the fire was "no larger than a railroad torch" and that he tried to get Linkous to focus on saving his family, but that Linkous ran past him and ran a block away to sound the fire bell. Numerous other neighbors reported to the scene quickly. Several of them insisted that when they arrived on the scene, the fire was such that they still could have gone into the house and would have done so, had they known that the Linkouses were still in there, but they assumed that the Linkous family—like the Butterworths—had already taken shelter with the neighbors. One neighbor said that he asked Linkous why he did not go back into the house, the fire still being fairly small, but that Linkous said it was too late.

When the fire was brought under control, it was learned that the victims had been bludgeoned to death with "some dull object" before the fire was set. Immediately on learning this, a lynch mob began to form, and in the evening of Christmas Day Linkous was brought to a jail in Roanoke, fifty miles away, to protect him from being lynched. At first some suspected that Linkous might have been involved with Texas, but that suspicion went nowhere, leaving Linkous with no apparent motive.

Linkous was charged with the murder of his wife and adopted son and was put on trial about three weeks after the murders. The evidence against him consisted entirely of support for these two facts:

1. That if he didn't kill them, it would be a complete mystery who did, and

2. That his behavior in the half hour or hour after the fire was discovered seemed to numerous people to be inappropriate.

That's it; there was no testimony against him of any other kind. The judge instructed the jury that they did not need to know what Linkous's motive was if they were convinced that he had in fact committed the crime. Linkous was convicted of first-degree murder after two days of testimony and fifteen minutes of deliberation, and was sentenced to death.

After Linkous was convicted the community split as to his innocence or guilt. During the trial he had sat motionless, holding his head in his hands. Away from the trial he made an exceptionally good witness for himself. As he neared death he spent time with two local ministers, who reported to the community that either he was entirely innocent or he was "the best hypocrite they had ever met." On the night before he was to be executed he asked that Mrs. Texas Butterworth be brought to his cell so that he could ask her some questions. "Have I ever done wrong to you?" he asked. "Have I not always treated you with kindness?" She agreed that he had always been kind to her, and that he had done her no wrong. On Christmas Eve he had given her a bottle of whiskey. "And now I am to pay for my kindness with my life," he said. Old friends arrived late in the night to say their good-byes. He was served a "sumptuous" breakfast, which went untouched. He was informed that morning that his body was to be sent to Richmond for study by medical students. "My God," he said. "I did think the Governor would allow me to be buried by the side of my wife."

He was executed in Radford at 7:39 a.m. on March 17, 1905,

258

St. Patrick's Day. On the day of his execution he conducted himself with courage and dignity, his head held high. On the scaffold he shook hands with his jailers and executioners, and thanked them for the kindness with which they had treated him. About fifty people were there to witness the execution. Before his death he made the following statement:

> I am a man condemned to die. I am going to meet my God an innocent man. May God bless you people who have sent an innocent man to the gallows. You can believe me or let it alone. Oh that a poor innocent man should be murdered. I pray God to hold me up. How much better off am I than those of you who are standing about hearing my voice. I hope that no other poor man will meet my fate. I am now passing through life to death, and will soon meet my God. All of you meet me in heaven. There you can learn all about it. There I will see one I know.

He had also left a statement to be opened after his death:

> I honestly did not kill either my wife or child. I speak this in the fear of God. I know nothing of how the fire occurred or the cause of it.

To this he had signed his name.

For what little it may be worth, I believe that James Linkous was probably an innocent man—not because he said that he was, but because the evidence against him is so poor. What convicted him was excitable gossip. In a moment of horror and shock, Linkous was expected to act in a certain way, and did not act in that way. His perception of the scene was different from those who came to help. His thinking at first was that his family was safe; later, that it was too late to save them. He was confused and disoriented. He had inhaled smoke. He focused on points at random—the firewood, the livestock, the fire bell—and did what seemed to him appropriate, in his confusion and distress.

The least that one may say is that in the modern world no one would be charged, much less convicted, on such evidence; of course, in the modern world, if he was guilty, we might be able to find much better evidence. Some witnesses didn't seem to understand that fires can grow larger and smaller and then larger again. This obviously seems to have happened here, since the Butterworth/Shelor family reports being trapped in a smoke-filled, burning house, the door-knobs too hot to touch, some time before the policeman arrived on the scene, but the policeman reports a fire no bigger than a torch. Either the witnesses are confused, or the fire took an uneven course.

But our underlying question is not whether Linkous was guilty but whether the crime was connected to our series of crimes. These facts tie the case to our criminal:

1. The crime was committed very near to a railroad stop—and, in fact, near the intersection of two railroad lines. A two-minute walk or less.

2. The crime was committed in the type of small town often favored by our criminal, beginning in 1904.

3. The crime was committed in the middle of the night.

4. Multiple people were murdered.

5. There is no apparent reason for the attacks.

6. The scene of the crime lines up geographically (and perfectly) with the three previous attacks. (If you look at the three previous crimes and ask, "Where is this criminal likely to strike next?" Radford, Virginia, is about as good an answer as you can get. Radford is three hundred miles almost straight north of Trenton, South Carolina. He had murdered families in Florida, Georgia, and South Carolina before Virginia; he had just skipped over North Carolina.)

7. The door to the rooms where the victims died were apparently jammed shut.

8. There is no evidence of theft or the intent to commit theft.

9. The house was set on fire, as was our perpetrator's usual practice in this era.

Also, I will note that the crime did occur on a Sunday and on Christmas Day, while most of the connected crimes also occurred on weekends, and many of them on Sundays, although this may be too weak a connection to be considered a link to the other cases. The temperature in Radford, Virginia, on December 24 and December 25, 1904, was in the mid-fifties. If the temperature had been in the twenties or even the thirties, that would be an indication that it is not The Man from the Train, because he rarely went out killing in cold weather.

The following facts, however, are different in this case from the others:

1. In no other case did he attack persons living in part of a domicile also occupied by another family.

2. When The Man from the Train broke into a house, he killed everybody in the house.

3. The Man from the Train normally killed the adult male or adult males in the house first, before he attacked the women and children. In this case the adult male was not attacked.

4. There is no specific mention of an axe here, just "some dull instrument." (There was, however, a woodpile next to the house.)

5. There is no evidence *in the information we have seen* of the ritualistic behavior that identifies our criminal—carrying lighted lamps around the scene of the crime, covering bodies and windows with cloth, etc. There may be evidence of such behaviors in material that we have not uncovered.

6. There is no juvenile female among the victims.

The evidence is not sufficient to firmly link this crime to the others, but I will note this as well. In Paola, Kansas, a few days before the murders in Villisca, The Man from the Train murdered a couple in a house that sits above the railroad track, almost as if on a perch. If you look at it on a map, it looks like the house in Paola is some distance from the track, but if you stand at the door of that house and a train goes by, you feel like you can reach out and touch it.

The murder scene in Radford sat above the railroad track in exactly the same way, and from the same distance. Although of course the building is no longer there—it burned down in 1904—it sat above the railroad line on a sharply ascending hill, so that the house would have *seemed* much closer to the railroad track than it actually was. And the actual distance was only two hundred to three hundred yards.

\* \* \*

The September 7, 2009, edition of *The New Yorker* contains an excellent article by David Grann about a fire in Corsicana, Texas, on December 23, 1991. In that case a father, Todd Willingham, was executed by the state of Texas for setting a fire that killed his three children. Willingham, like Linkous, went to his death proclaiming his innocence; Willingham turned down an offer of life in prison for a plea of guilty. The cases are eerily similar, and you can gain a lot of understanding of this case by reading Grann's article about that one. Willingham was criticized for moving a car away from the house, in the exact way that Linkous was second-guessed for moving the firewood, but gave the same explanation: he didn't want the gas in the car to explode and feed the fire. Willingham, like Linkous, asked to be buried next to the victims of the fire but was denied that privilege. Even the day of the year is almost the same. Willingham is now believed by many people to have been innocent—but I would point out that the case against Linkous was far weaker even than the case against Willingham.

\* \* \*

From 1900 to 1915 houses in America were usually heated in one of three ways: by coal, by kerosene, or by wood. No houses at all were heated by electricity in this era, and no houses were heated by natural gas or propane.

Large, well-built houses and public buildings such as churches and schools were usually heated by burning coal. The coal would be burned in a furnace in the basement, and the furnace would create either steam or hot water that would circulate around the house. Smaller houses with relatively prosperous residents often burned kerosene, which was often called "coal oil" (kerosene is derived from coal). Many smaller houses also burned coal in small stoves, although that's dangerous; if a coal stove isn't properly vented the fumes can kill you.

Burning wood was the downscale, entry-level heating system, also used by older houses that had not been converted. No data is available as to what the percentage distribution was of houses that burned coal, kerosene, and wood in 1910, but in 1940 55 percent of houses were heated with coal, 23 percent with wood, and most of the rest with kerosene. In 1910 the percentage heated with wood would have been higher than 23 percent. But when The Man from the Train was wandering around a small town, scouting for the "right" house, the first thing he looked for was a woodpile with an axe.

When you read accounts of these crimes, there is often *incidental* mention of a woodpile, which no one recognizes the significance of at the time. In one case, there is a woodpile which is mentioned only because it didn't burn; the house burned, and the barn burned, but the woodpile, which was between the house and the barn, did not burn. In this case, the woodpile is mentioned only because Linkous was moving the wood away from the house at a critical point in the story. It is very spooky to be reading these old newspaper reports and find an offhand reference to a woodpile, and then you think, "Uh-oh. The guy who wrote this story doesn't have any idea what the significance of that woodpile really is."

Later on, after he stopped setting fire to the houses, the axe would be found next to the last victim, and then people understood what that meant. But in this era, when he was burning the houses down, they didn't get it; the handle of the axe would burn, and the head of the axe was just a small piece of junk in a large pile of burned-out junk. No one would notice that the axe was missing from the woodpile. I'm not sure that any crime in this series was *not* committed in a house that burned wood for heat, although there may well have been.

The news reports of the Linkous crime don't say where the woodpile was; it was against the house, but we don't know on which side. But since the house sat up on a hill above the railroad line, if the woodpile was on the west side of the house or the north side, a man standing at the train depot a block below would have seen the woodpile as soon as he got off the train. The moon was almost full—the full moon was December 22—and the sky was clear.

# CHAPTER XXVI

# West Memphis

Memphis, Feb. 9—Boylan and his wife were both well known in Memphis. He was regarded as one of the best negroes in Crittenden County.

—*Bryan (Texas) Morning Eagle*, February 10, 1905

The Mississippi River is deep and wide. Here in the Midwest we will build bridges every couple of miles across a less imposing river, but you don't do that to the Mississippi; it is a monster. Only a few railroad bridges cross the Mississippi, so the railroad lines all converge at those bridges and fan out from them on the other side. There are not one or two railroad lines there, but a large number, joining forces as they near the river.

Memphis, of course, is in Tennessee but on the edge of the state; when you cross the river you are in Arkansas. West Memphis is in Arkansas. On May 5, 1993, three eight-year-old boys were murdered in West Memphis. Three teenagers were convicted of those murders and spent twenty years in prison before they were freed; they are known as the West Memphis Three.

In 1900 there were more than five hundred sawmills within a hundred miles of Memphis. The Boylan family lived west of Marion,

Arkansas, inside this thinly populated latticework of railroads and lumber mills. On Tuesday, February 7, 1905, the Boylan family was murdered with an axe in the middle of the night—father Albert, mother Ann, and a son named Rush. The son was found outside the house, the mother at the front door, and the father inside the house. The axe was left inside the house.

This is a low-information event; this will be a short chapter because we don't know very much about the crime. A week before the murders the Boylans had sold their house and land—apparently the house in which they were murdered—for $1,500 cash. They had put $1,000 in the bank; the other $500 was unaccounted for, and some presumed the money was stolen at the time of the crime.

The Boylans had two adult sons who lived on the property, some distance from the house; they may have lived in a tent or some similar temporary structure. The adult sons claimed to know nothing about the crime. The sons were arrested; however, there is no report of their being prosecuted, and other reports said that a posse of more than forty men, almost all of them black, was searching the area for clues.

There are several reasons to suspect that this crime was connected to the series—the proximity to the railroads, the fact that it was a lumbering region, the unexplained murder of a family with an axe in the middle of the night, and the axe being left in the house. There are a similar number of reasons to think it was not connected: a speculative theft of $500, reports saying the heads of the victims were "severed" as opposed to crushed, as would be the case if it were The Man from the Train. We just do not know.

There was no young female victim here; there was no fire. We do not know whether the house was locked up as the murderer fled. There are connections missing that would be necessary to reach a conclusion. But I will also note this: that once these cases stopped, they stopped. In late 1912 The Man from the Train fled the country, or died, or was put in prison, or something. Once that happened, you just don't find cases like this—random farm families killed with an axe in the middle of the night, near a railroad. Before 1898, you don't find cases like this. And that is certainly a reason to believe that the cases we do have are somehow connected.

# CHAPTER XXVII

# Jacksonville

When the house of the Wise family was seen on fire in the pre-dawn hours of September 22, 1905, the neighbors assumed that Lula was burning rubbish. We will start there, because this is one of the few instructive facts we have about the crime. If the neighbors mistook a house fire for someone burning rubbish, then we may say with confidence that the house was isolated, that the neighbors were not ten feet away or a hundred feet away, but at some distance measured in portions of a mile.

Lula Wise and her four children had all been murdered in their beds, their skulls crushed by an unknown intruder before the house was set on fire. An axe was found among the charred remains. She had three daughters, Maggie, Ida, and Sister, and a son who is known to us only as "Son." The children ranged in age from three to thirteen.

Two or three years before the murders, Mrs. Wise had had her husband, Sam Wise, arrested for beating her. Sam had either (a) served a short prison sentence, or (b) escaped from prison, but in either case he had left the area with no forwarding address. It was easy for reporters to speculate that he had returned to the area to murder his family, and a few of them did, but of course there is no evidence for that.

This is all we know about the case; even the location of the house is missing from the record. The newspapers say that it was "near" Jacksonville, Florida, and that is all that they say; whether it was west of Jacksonville or north of it, whether it was a mile from Jacksonville or five . . . we don't know. It is one of two cases in the book in which we are unable to determine fairly precisely where the house was located; the other will be along shortly. Jacksonville in 1905 was a city of about 25,000 people, but some of those were seasonal residents who came south to escape the cold. The newspapers tell us the race of the victims; they were black.

This is one of two family murders in the series that occurred during the night of September 21 to the morning of September 22; the Meadows family was also murdered on September 21, 1909. The Double Event in Colorado was on September 17, and other crimes occurred on September 27 and September 30, making late September the busiest time period for the murders, as this region is also the busiest place. The Zoos family, which was possibly a part of the series, was murdered on September 20. Sawmills in this era often shut down or cut back in early September. Home building was a seasonal activity, focused in the summer months, so the busiest time of the year for the sawmills was March through May. It is possible that our offender often committed an atrocity at the time that he was laid off from a job, as he was preparing to move on and find work somewhere else. There are several other dates that repeat themselves in the series of murders. The next crime in the series will be on the first anniversary of the last one.

We are all heirs to the racism of the past, and unable to decline the legacy. The harsh reality is that contemporary authorities did not treat the murder of a black family as seriously as they would a white family, nor half as seriously, nor a third as seriously. The newspapers didn't care much about the crime or the victims; they ran a note, then let it go. In fairness to the police, the investigation of a crime of this nature was immensely difficult, and a serious, intense, well-funded investigation of the crime would likely have failed—just as it did in all of these other cases.

A serious investigation would not have found the culprit, probably, but it would have documented the facts, which would have been a step toward identifying the culprit. We would like to take the murders of the Wise family as seriously as we have taken, let us say, the murders of the Moore family in Villisca, but since the case was not documented at the time, we can only tell you what we know and move on.

# CHAPTER XXVIII

# Cottonwood, Alabama

L ike so many of the places bloodied by The Man from the Train, Cottonwood, Alabama, in 1906 could barely be described as a town. It was a whistle-stop of two hundred to three hundred people which had been incorporated just three years earlier. On the night of February 7 to February 8, 1906, the Christmas family was murdered on a farm just outside Cottonwood. Cottonwood is in Houston County, and the county seat of Houston County is Dothan, Alabama, birthplace of Willie Mays. The sheriff of Houston County, Sheriff Crawford, was informed of the murders late in the day on February 8 and left for Cottonwood on the first train out on the morning of February 9.

He found the town in an uproar. Jeremy Christmas was sixty-one years old, and a Confederate veteran. Three people were dead—Jeremy, his wife, Martha, aged fifty, and their youngest son, Slocum, aged eleven. The three had been sleeping in a single room, and had all been murdered in that room. Their heads had been bashed in with an axe, which was left in the room; reports are that their throats had been slit after they were dead, which, if accurate, would be atypical behavior for The Man from the Train. Several dollars were left in plain sight in the room where the murders occurred, and a safe, in the hallway outside, was also untouched.

The Christmas family was well liked—and white, besides—so an intense investigation began immediately. Jeremy and Martha had had ten children, six of whom had passed on before the attack, three of whom were left after the attack. Bloodhounds were brought up from Marianna, Florida, but it had rained hard before the hounds reached the scene, and they were unable to find a trail. A reward fund of $2,500 was raised by donations. A private detective named W. C. Franklin rushed down from Chicago to Cottonwood.

This particular private detective was a real lulu.

Dothan, Ala., March 18.—Following the arrest yesterday of Will Christmas, a son, and Walter Holland, a son-in-law, in connection with the triple murder of the Christmas family, new and sensational developments were brought to light today through the medium of a detective, his assistant, a ventriloquist, a superstitious negro, and the negro's mule.

The detective, who has been at work on the case, declared the whole mystery is solved.

Hokay; well, I don't know why anyone would have any trouble with *that* story, but let me tell you the whole story, and you can be the judge. As I have said before, private detectives in the nineteenth century were essentially spies; the basic job description of a nineteenth-century private detective was to infiltrate criminal communities and sell out his confidants. Since there was a reward fund for the solution of the Christmas family murders, Detective Franklin decided to see what he could do. To infiltrate the criminal population of Cottonwood, he hid out in the woods near the small town, pretending to be an escaped murderer from Georgia. Since the escaped criminal couldn't go into town to get his meals, he hired a black man to bring him his meals, out in the woods, and the black man had a mule. After a week or so the wily detective began to sense that the black man knew something about the case, but wouldn't tell him what it was. So the detective snuck back north, where he knew this guy who could throw his voice. He brought the ventriloquist back with him to his hideout in the woods; not making any of this up. The ventriloquist hid behind a tree or a rock or a bush or something, and threw his voice to the mule, convincing the humble pizza delivery guy that his mule was talking to him; the black man is described in the newspapers as "superstitious," although I don't know that believing that your mule is questioning you about an unsolved murder is *exactly* a superstition. Also, he wasn't really delivering pizzas; I just said that to help a modern reader relate to the role.

Anyway, the black gentleman explained to his mule that the Christmas family had been murdered by Will Christmas, an adult son, acting in concert with a son-in-law. The detective and the ventriloquist overheard this explanation, so they went to the sheriff and explained to him what had happened. Since the information came from an unimpeachable source—that mule had never lied to anybody—the sheriff then arrested Will Christmas and Walter Holland, and also Mr. Holland's wife, who was Will Christmas's sister, and charged them with the murders.

We assume that these three were released; we assume this because we can find no record of their being prosecuted. In 1906 police would arrest you for murder based on no evidence at all; it wasn't like it is now. In this case, several people had been arrested in connection with the murders in the first two days after the crime, but they had all been released. Perhaps the mule refused to testify against them.

The story of the mule and the ventriloquist was reported coast to coast at the time, with no skepticism detectable between the lines. This pathetic effort to claim the reward fund was, as far as we know, the closest that Houston County ever came to solving the murders. And we could tell you that they are a part of the series, but there is a problem with that, too, as you will discover in the next chapter.

\*   \*   \*

If this series of crimes was a one-man epidemic, then the epicenter of the epidemic was Marianna, Florida. At that time Marianna was a town of about a thousand people. In 1903 the Kelly or Caffey family was murdered eight miles west of Marianna. Cottonwood, Alabama, is twenty-four miles north of Marianna, and what may be The Man from the Train's worst atrocity would be committed three months later near Milton, Florida, which is a hundred miles due west of Marianna, just north of Pensacola. Jacksonville is two hundred miles east of Marianna.

\*   \*   \*

Several crimes in this series were committed within five miles of a state line; in this case it is about three miles from the Florida state line to Cottonwood, and about fifteen miles to the Georgia state line. This may not mean anything, but Ted Bundy, as a college student, wrote a paper about jurisdictional issues in investigating related crimes. Bundy realized that if two crimes were investigated by different police agencies, the police most often would never connect the dots. The Man from the Train may have had a similar thought, in a less sophisticated fashion; that is, he may have realized that once he crossed a state line, different authorities would be involved, and they would probably not make any connection between the crimes. He probably was riding north from Marianna on the Chattahoochee and Gulf Railroad, and he may well have thought, "OK, the first little town I come to after I get into Alabama, that's where I'm going to get off." The first little town he came to would have been Cottonwood.

Of the last five murders that I have told you about, at least three and possibly four were committed in what could be described as the first little town you would come to after you crossed the state line.

A mule interrogates a witness in the Cottonwood murders.
(*Logansport [Indiana] Pharos-Tribune*, April 7, 1906)

# CHAPTER XXIX

# Murder in the Cold

The attempt at rape by Snelgrove in the absence of Mr. Stetka caused much talk, and the Stetkas felt the position keenly, and said they were going back to Austria where they formerly belonged.

—*St. John Daily Sun*

S ydney, Nova Scotia, is about six hundred miles due east of Shirley, Maine, where we had an earlier incident. If you are a real 'merican and not from Maine, you will probably think that that's impossible; if you go hundreds of miles east of Maine you would be in the middle of the ocean. But actually you would not; you would be in Nova Scotia, on Cape Breton Island, which is not exactly an island; it is a finger of land detached from the mainland by a river or two and long, long stretches of empty roads. Surrounding Sydney and running underneath much of the island is a large underground seam of high-sulphur coal, the Sydney Coal Field. Eleven miles northwest of Sydney is a coal mining area, and in the mining area is (or was) a small town called Dominion. Dominion was incorporated in 1906, the year of our tragedy, and was dissolved in 1995. Prior to its incorporation it was also called Old Bridgeport.

The Stetka family lived not in Old Bridgeport but south of it;

they were one of a few families living scattered among the coal mines. There were a cluster of five or six houses right next to the Sydney and Louisburg Railroad. Anton Stetka had a wife and two children; unfortunately the newspapers did not choose to share their names with us. There was a boy, aged four, and another child, aged two, who we are guessing was a girl because the newspapers mentioned that the other one was a boy.

The Stetkas had been in Dominion for several years and were respectable, hardworking people living in a tiny five-room one-story house. The house was sixteen feet by twenty feet. As a frame of reference, a living room area rug commonly is seven by ten feet. The Stetkas were purchasing the house from the mining company. It may be presumed that almost everything the Stetkas bought was purchased at the mining company store, which was the only store in the area. In March 1925, this area would become a flash point in a notorious union dispute; local clergy would describe "children clothed in flour sacks and dying of starvation from the infamous 'four cent meal.'"

One of the other miners who lived in this desperate settlement was named Snelgrove. In January 1906, weeks before the murders, Snelgrove attempted to rape Mrs. Stetka while her husband was away. Snelgrove was arrested and jailed in Sydney, but the incident ruined the relationships among the neighbors, some of whom felt that Mrs. Stetka was trespassing conventions of community trust in prosecuting Snelgrove. Snelgrove's mother lived just sixty feet from the Stetkas. It was horribly awkward, and after the rape attempt, the Stetkas had begun planning to return to Europe.

In fact, on the day before the murders Mrs. Stetka had met with the president of the mining company, Henry Mitchell, to ask about getting their money back out of the house. Mitchell said he would pay back their investment in the house, but he couldn't do it right now because he had something else to take care of. Come back tomorrow.

Lamps were seen burning in the house as late as 10:30 p.m. on February 15, perhaps because they were packing for their impending departure, and perhaps Mr. Stetka may have worked until late in the evening; the miners often worked twelve-hour shifts. He picked up his pay late in the day.

A little after 1:00 a.m. on February 16, Engine 661 was pulling a string of empty coal cars into Dominion when the engineer, Alexander McKinnon, saw that a house was on fire. McKinnon "sounded the alarm," presumably giving several blasts of the train whistle, and brought the train to a halt. McKinnon and his fireman rushed to the house. The Stetkas' house was fully engulfed in flames, which could not be extinguished until the walls collapsed, around three in the morning. According to the *St. John Daily Sun*, February 17, 1906, "Between the places where the two beds had been placed was the remains of a sewing machine and close by it lay an axe. The back part of the man's skull was separated from the head and the woman's skull was fractured and also those of the children. . . . Near by lives a partially demented man. The matter thus far is merely one of conjecture. An inquest has begun."

Another report, not entirely consistent with the first, notes that a miner named McAulay saw the fire at 1:30 a.m., "returning from his shift at Reserve as he approached the house." McAulay observed that the porch to the house was on fire and ran to a neighbor's house to ask for help. The neighbor reported that she had heard a dog barking. About this time the train crew arrived, and the group of them ran to the house and pounded on the door, which was locked or jammed shut. A dog was barking ferociously inside. McKinnon covered his face with his jacket and smashed the door. As it broke open the dog rushed out, nearly knocking McKinnon flat. Due to the heat and flames, he was unable to enter the house.

The coroner's inquest lasted for eight days, and thirty witnesses were called. Several of the witnesses were recalled for further testimony. According to the *Manitoba Free Press*, February 24, "the enquiry was very careful and exhaustive and exploded the accident and suicide theories completely, but has not located the murderers." The coroner concluded that there was no evidence to connect the deaths of the Stetkas to the upcoming prosecution of Snelgrove.

There were three front-row explanations for the murders. First, it was suspected, as is always true in these cases, that Mr. Stetka had murdered his family and himself. But since Stetka's head had literally been knocked off of his shoulders, this could not be true.

The second explanation was that the crime was somehow connected to the upcoming trial. But the Stetkas had made plans to leave the area and return to Europe *before* the trial; Mrs. Stetka had decided not to testify. Setting that aside, Snelgrove was in jail, and it is unclear who else might have acted on his behalf. There are no good candidates.

The third obvious explanation, to which speculation turned when the first two failed, was that the crime had been a robbery. In this connection it was mentioned that Mrs. Stetka had gone to the mine president, Mr. Mitchell, to get back the money that they had put into the house—and then noticed that she had failed to get the money. Mr. Stetka had picked up his last fortnight's pay just the previous day, and it was noted that no coins were found in the ashes of the house, nor was Mr. Stetka's watch. On this basis, some concluded that the crime must have been a robbery.

"Robbery" is a theory that fills the void for motive when a crime seems otherwise without explanation. Halifax, Nova Scotia, was the nearest city large enough to have a police force. The chief of police in Halifax, Nicholas Power, came to Dominion after the coroner's inquest. "I am here at the request of the attorney general," Power reported; who the attorney general was and what he was attorney general of was assumed background knowledge, not mentioned in the *St. John Daily Sun* of February 28. We will assume that he was attorney general of Nova Scotia. Anyway, Mr. Power's report concluded (1) that Mr. Power was a great detective who had solved other cases that seemed beyond solution, (2) that he had done a thorough investigation of the crime, and (3) that there was no murder here; it was just an accidental fire.

This appears to have been a one-man investigation; a detective as great as Nicholas Power, chief of police in Halifax, Nova Scotia, does not require the assistance of subordinates. The investigation by Mr. Power tied a bow around the case, reassuring the citizens of Nova Scotia that they could go on about their business and quit worrying about an axe murderer being on the loose. But since this very thorough one-man investigation was done after the coroner's inquest was reported to the crown, and since the results of this investigation were in the newspapers three days after the coroner's inquest was completed, we might perhaps wonder how thorough the investigation really was.

The murders of the Stetkas have eight characteristics suggesting that they may have been committed by The Man from the Train:

1. An entire family was murdered in a single event, without warning, and obviously not by a member of the family.

2. The murders were committed, it appears, within twenty-five yards of a railroad line.

3. The murders were committed with an axe.

4. The axe was left in the room.

5. The front door was left locked or jammed shut.

6. The house was set on fire as the murderer left.

7. The family was murdered between midnight and 1:00 a.m., the time period most favored by this criminal.

8. The crime was committed in a semirural settlement too small to have a police force, as many of the other crimes were.

Simple as these eight circumstances may seem, there should be zero "random matches" to this bundle of facts in a normal year, in all of North America. We might also note

- That it does appear from the words used that the murders were committed with the blunt side of the axe,
- That this was a mining area, as were the locations of a few other crimes; it is likely that the criminal worked primarily as a lumberjack and as a miner, and
- That Mr. Power reported that the children's faces were covered with their blanket—a signature behavior of The Man from the Train.

But at the same time, there are four conditions here that would make us wary of declaring this crime to be a part of the series:

1. Nova Scotia in February is wretchedly cold. The Man from the Train hated cold weather. Other than his breakthrough crime in 1898, we know of no other crime in the series that was committed in cold weather.

2. There is the possibility of another motive, either robbery or the other crime story in which Mrs. Stetka was a victim. Of course, side stories like that crop up in almost every case and alternative explanations are proffered in every case, but this side story is more credible than is, say, the pig-faced man in Paola or the alleged business rivalry with Frank Jones in Villisca.

3. The presence of the dog at the murder scene could be taken to indicate the possibility that the dog was familiar with the murderer. The dog was reported to have been barking loudly, but it is unclear when. It appears that the dog started barking after the murders had been committed and the house set on fire.

4. The first three contra-indicators are weak and wouldn't cause us to question whether the crime should be considered a part of the series. The only real problem is this: this crime occurred just eight days after the murders of the Christmas family in Cottonwood, Alabama, and just over two thousand miles away.

If we ask the question "Would it have been possible for our culprit to have traveled that distance in that amount of time, in 1906,
by hopping trains?" the answer is yes, it was clearly possible. It is
possible that he might have made that trip in as few as four days,
conceivably three, certainly in six. It is also entirely possible that
The Man from the Train committed the murders in Nova Scotia but
not the ones in Cottonwood.

But one of the things that normally identifies crimes that are a
part of our sequence is that they have simple and obvious time-and-
distance connections. If one crime is committed in Florida, the next
tends to be in Georgia or Alabama; if one is committed in Colorado,
the next is committed in Kansas, and most often after an interval of
a month to six months.

We find occasional spatial gaps, such as the 1911 jump from
Texas to Oregon, of course, and there are other cases in which one
crime follows quickly after another. Obviously we should not expect a
criminal's patterns to be rigid. My point is, though, that if we argue
in other cases that the sequence of crimes is knit together by time
and place creating a logical line of march, we obviously have to note
that this is very much *not* true with regard to these two crimes, or to
these three crimes, if we include the next one, which will take place
back in northern Florida.

It is possible that The Man from the Train may have worked in
the mines in this area in warm weather at some earlier point; he may
even have known the Stetka family and may have nurtured a dislike
of them for some reason, and he may have returned to this area as he
was fleeing northward after committing the crime in Alabama the
previous week, deciding to commit a quick atrocity in the far north,
and then go back south.

Also we have to clear this up: the word *lumberjack* was not used
a hundred years ago the way it is now. People who chopped down
trees for lumber at that time were generically called woodcutters,

and the word *lumberjack* was used only to indicate certain tightly knit communities of woodcutters who were ethnically distinct; in other words, it applied more to the community than to the job. Most woodcutters in that era were *not* called lumberjacks, but that is the term we use now, so that is the term I have generally used and will continue to use.

\*　\*　\*

At the far, far end of the wealth-and-privilege spectrum, President Teddy Roosevelt's daughter Alice was married to Nicholas Longworth III on the morning of Saturday, February 17, 1906, which was the day after the crime. It was the closest America has ever had to a royal wedding, a beautiful young woman marrying a charismatic bald man destined to become Speaker of the House. The marriage was not great; she would have affairs whenever she chose, and she would survive him by almost half a century, living almost to the end of the Carter administration and presiding over Washington's social registry as no one else ever has. She was a close friend of the Nixons.

Late in the day on February 17, Big Bill Haywood was arrested in Idaho in connection with the murder of former governor Steunenberg. I know The Man from the Train did not kill Steunenberg; I am just trying to help those of you whose knowledge of history is mostly from crime books keep track of where we are in time.

# CHAPTER XXX

# The Worst One Ever

What may have been The Man from the Train's worst murder ever, in terms of the body count, occurred near Allentown, Florida, in May 1906.

About no other case in our book is the absence of solid information so frustrating. It is exactly as if the Villisca murders had happened, but no one had bothered to write about them. Allentown, to begin with, is not and never was a town, a village, or anything of the sort; it is, rather, a name used for an area where someone once had ambitions of building a city, but failed. The area has a general outline but does not have a downtown or streets or city services. There are roads, and the roads have names, but in 1906 the houses had no addresses. The Ackermans lived not *in* Allentown, but *near* Allentown—but we don't really know where; obviously their house was rural, but then Allentown itself is rural. It is a rural area which has a name as if it were a town.

Allentown is in Santa Rosa County. Less than five miles southeast of Allentown is now Whiting Field, which is the busiest naval air station in the world. The railroad apparently never went through Allentown, although it went up to where Whiting Field now is.

Whiting was built during World War II. According to the US Navy's official Web site (http://www.mybaseguide.com/Navy/1-539):

> Once known as the most industrialized county in Florida, Santa Rosa's history is abundant with the lore of the logging, sawmill and shipbuilding industries around which life evolved. The area around Milton gained distinction as the site of the first cotton textile mill in the South. The Shortline Railroad was the primary hauler of the nation's first paper-mill supply of logs, run by the Bagdad Land and Lumber Co., in operation from 1828 until 1939.

The name of the railroad is another wrinkle. A "shortline" railroad is a generic term applied to thousands of little railroads that once existed and some of which still exist, but in this case it is also the actual name of the railroad. This makes the railroad difficult to research; it is a little like researching a person whose name is "name" or a town which is named "town." Anyway, when they built Whiting Field in the late 1930s they built it to where the railroad ran, for obvious reasons, and later, when they needed to expand their runways, they tore up part of the old railroad to make room.

More relevant to our story is not what Allentown is now but what it was in 1906—a quiet rural area of indefinite dimensions, nestled inside the vast pine forest that still covers large areas of the south. Ackerman was a preacher, much more successful at making babies than at gathering a flock. The family, like the Stetkas, lived in extreme poverty, with nothing worth stealing. They were murdered on the night of May 13 to May 14, 1906—a Sunday night. I will quote the account of the crime from a wire service story, since the account is straightforward, and I don't see how I can improve upon it:

## Nine Are Murdered

**Whole Family Wiped Out in Santa Rosa County, Florida**

**Then Fiends Apply Torch**

**Skull of Each Victim is Crushed, and Body of the Wife with her Infant Child is Found Outside the House— Head of Family was an Itinerant Preacher**

PENSACOLA, FLA, MAY 15—One of the most horrible crimes in the history of the State, if not the history of the South, was committed in Santa Rosa County, ten miles north of Milton, Sunday night, when a man by the name of Ackerman, an itinerant preacher, and his wife and several children, the oldest 14 years of age, were murdered and their bodies cremated in the home, which was fired by the assassins. The crime was discovered yesterday by parties with whom Ackerman had an appointment, who found the home a mass of ruins and the charred bodies of Ackerman and his family among the ruins.

Details indicate that the father, mother, and each of the seven children was murdered before the building was fired, as the skull of each was crushed and the body of Ackerman was found near the location of the door leading from the location in which he slept. By his side was a revolver.

The body of Mrs. Ackerman, who gave birth to a child on Friday last, was found with that of her infant child outside of the sill at the front of the house. The oldest child was found near the door leading out to the front porch. All of the bodies were badly burned, practically only the trunks remaining. The bodies of the three boys were found practically where the bed upon which they slept had stood previous to the conflagration.

When a party from Milton reached the scene about 11 o'clock the sills were still burning, which seemed to indicate that the fire had been started several hours after midnight. The country nearby is sparsely settled, the nearest neighbor residing about one and a quarter miles away. This neighbor says he knew nothing of the fire until early this morning, when he saw that the building had been destroyed and notified other neighbors before trying to ascertain the damage.

The feeling in Santa Rosa County is high over the act and every effort is being made to apprehend the guilty parties.

Ackerman moved to the settlement which is known as Allentown from Opp., Ala., about three years ago and has always been considered a good and peaceful citizen. While he had no regular charge it was his custom to preach throughout that section of Santa Rosa county. He was not known to have had any enemies, and the motive for the atrocious crime is a mystery.

> —Quoted from *Herald*, Tuesday Evening May 15,
> 1906, Syracuse, N.Y.; extremely similar stories
> appeared in many other papers.

Other articles specifically state that the murder weapon was an axe, although this article does not. The article refers to "fiends" and "assassins" because that is what you would ordinarily think in these circumstances, that multiple criminals would be required to do this work. The *Hutchinson (Kansas) News* of May 23, 1906, used the sub-headline "How the Family was Killed Will Probably Never be Known." It won't, but with your indulgence, let me speculate. The Man from the Train entered the house from the rear, we assume, and we assume this because:

1. He almost always did.

2. The mother and oldest child ran toward the *front* of the house, presumably trying to escape from him.

No doubt he broke into the house quietly, noiselessly; he was quite good at that. It was Florida in May, long before air-conditioning; a window was surely open. He expected to find what he usually found inside a house—about four people, two adults and two children. It was probably about 1:00 a.m.

The Ackermans had probably left a kerosene lamp burning in a back bedroom, and likely the first thing he did was to take the shade off the lamp and put it quietly on the floor, then start to examine the layout of the house. Mrs. Ackerman, however, was awake nursing her baby, inside one of the other rooms. I am speculating that she was awake, if you have ever had a two-day-old baby, you will know why, and also her body was found outside the front door, which indicates that she was attempting to flee. The Man from the Train probably killed three or perhaps even four of the children very quickly, probably within sixty seconds of beginning the attack, although, I am guessing, he probably took a couple of minutes to find the lamp and to place it on the floor where it would shed light on what he was doing. Let us assume there are three dead. Mrs. Ackerman now heard something; she heard unfamiliar sounds coming from down the hallway, and poked her head out of whatever room she was in. She screamed, awakening the oldest child and her husband.

Four people are now awake—the parents, the two-day-old baby, and the oldest child. The situation is on the brink of chaos. The father grabs his gun but doesn't have time to load it before he is hit with the axe. He is hit in the side of the head with the blade of the axe; we know this from other accounts. It is not The Man from the Train's "controlled" swing, which is an overhead power strike with the blunt side of the axe, but he is running down the hallway, simultaneously pursuing two people and fending off an attack from a third (the father). He does this with a backhand blow. The mother and the oldest child run for the front door, pursued by an axe-swinging maniac in full flower. He catches the fourteen-year-old at the door, and fells him with one blow. The mother, carrying her baby, looks back for a second in horror, and then she, too, is hit by the axe.

We are assuming a very competent murderer, but he is a lumberjack; he swings an axe a thousand times a day. The axe, to him, is an extension of his body. He is outnumbered nine to one, yes, but the nine include seven children, as young as two days old. He is the only person in the conflict who is fully awake, the only one who actually knows what is going on. He is the only one wearing shoes. He is the only one who has been through events like this before. He is a professional, contending with half-asleep amateurs.

There are now six people in the house who have been hit by the axe, and the two-day-old baby is obviously not a problem. Only two children and the bloodied father now remain. Some of the victims may not have been killed by the first blow, but once they are out, they're no longer problems. The entire assault was probably over, I would guess, five minutes after it began. At least one of those still alive is a prepubescent female, and he does what he does with her. The skulls of all nine victims had been crushed before the house was set on fire.

By the time he is done it is 3:00 a.m. He sets the house on fire, watches it burn for a while, and walks back toward the railroad track— which, in this case, we do not know where it is; we don't know whether the railroad is a hundred yards away, a mile away, or two miles. But as he always does, he will hop a train and be out of the area before the crime is discovered. (Some news stories describe this crime as being near Allentown; others, as near Milton. The Shortline Railroad ran north of Milton but not all the way to Allentown. It is possible, though not certain, that this crime occurred close to the railroad.)

Again, this is my speculation about what happened, and it is surely not accurate on every point. From various other newspapers we learn: (1) Ackerman's first name may have been "Edward" (although other names are also given), and (2) that of the seven children, three were girls and four were boys. The oldest girl was thirteen; the oldest boy was fourteen. Two of the girls slept in the same bed and had been murdered in their bed. One source says that Mrs. Ackerman's maiden name was Mary Simmons and that she was Ackerman's fourth wife; that source, however, is spectacularly unreliable.

Within a week of the tragedy Allentown residents had raised $1,000 toward the solution of the case, while others—probably the governor's office—had kicked in another $2,000. According to the *Hutchinson News*, "The suspicion is that shiftless negroes traveling from one turpentine camp to the other committed the crime, inspired simply by a fiendish desire to take human life." Pretty sure he was a white guy.

On May 6, 1907—about a year after the murders—a private detective named R. C. Beagle filed a warrant for the arrest of two men on a charge of having murdered the Ackermans. The two men were named Joe Stanley and M. C. Smith, both white men; both had lived in the Allentown area at the time of the crime but had since moved away. Stanley was arrested in "Samson," which we are guessing may be Sampson, Florida—north of Gainesville—while Smith was arrested in Gonzalez, Florida, fifteen miles west of Milton. In that there are no reports of the men having been prosecuted, we assume that they were released within the next few days.

CHAPTER XXXI

# The Lyerly Family

This is a horrible story to tell, but it is true so far as words can
reproduce the scene, and its record should not be lost from the
annals of crime.

—John Charles McNeill,
Salisbury, North Carolina,
July 14, 1906

Barber Junction, North Carolina, was a railroad intersection with
a name. There was a line going east and west, and a line going
north and south, and where they met in a rural area of Rowan County,
eleven miles west of Salisbury, there was a small depot, where passengers riding in one direction could change trains and wait out the
time difference. The depot still exists; it was moved to Salisbury, a
little north of Salisbury, in the 1980s. If a westbound train stopped
at Barber Junction and a tramp hopped off the back end of a long
train, he would have seen the house of Isaac and Augusta Lyerly just
across the road, perhaps a hundred yards from the spot where his
feet hit the ground.

Let us say that on the evening of July 13, 1906, a man hopped off
the train at Barber Junction. It was Friday the thirteenth. The Lyerlys

lived in a somewhat run-down hundred-year-old plantation house that had been in their family through generations of slaveholders and generations of sharecroppers. A family of seven lived there in 1906—Isaac and Augusta, a young boy and a young girl, and three older girls who worked hard on the farm during the day and slept on the second floor at night.

Sometime before midnight Addie Lyerly awoke to the smell of smoke. Addie was the middle of the three older girls. She had asthma, and the least amount of smoke would disturb her breathing. She ran down the stairs into a nightmare. Her father was dead; he had been hit in the head with the blunt side of an axe. Her mother lay dead, halfway out of the bed; she had been hit, apparently, both with the blunt side of the axe and the sharp edge, although Addie did not see all of this at first, since Augusta, her mother, had been covered by a pillow.

I will spare you the ghastly descriptions of her brother, John; let us just note that he was dead. John slept in the bed with his father, a common practice of the time, and that bed was on fire. A bureau drawer had been saturated with kerosene, dumped over John's body, and set ablaze. The youngest daughter, Alice, was not dead but dying, moaning in pain; Alice apparently slept in the bed with her mother. The other bed in the room was not on fire, and the room was not on fire. Not certain who was alive or dead, Addie pulled her father and brother off of the blazing bed, and ran screaming up the stairs.

The three girls poured pitchers of water on the fire. The house did not have indoor plumbing, but they got the fire under control with the water that was inside the house, and threw the smoldering bedding into the yard. They carried Alice, the six-year-old girl who was clinging to life, into the yard, and tried to tend to her wounds, but the bedding was setting fire to the yard, so they had to draw water from the well to put out the fire.

The front door had been left open, and a window was also open. Money and other valuables were left in the house, a good bit of money, actually. Some of the money was in plain view, in the bedroom where the murders had occurred. *A lamp that had been on the bureau in the murder room—and which had been seen there by two of the daughters after Isaac Lyerly was sound asleep—had been moved to the mantel.* A bloody axe, last seen resting in the woodpile nearby, had been discarded near the open door.

The girls pulled themselves together and went for help. Carrying Alice, they walked in a group to the house of Filmore Cook, a neighbor who lived about three-quarters of a mile away. Alice would die at the Cook house the next afternoon. Other neighbors lived closer (including a son of Isaac Lyerly, a half-brother of the sisters, who did not get along with his father's second wife, the murdered Augusta), but the Cooks were people that the daughters knew well and trusted. Their pathway through the night took them right past the house of a sharecropper, Jack Dillingham, close enough to reach out and touch the house. As they passed the Dillingham cabin they fell silent, fearing that it could have been Dillingham who had attacked their family. When they reached the Cook house near midnight, the Cooks loaded up horses and rushed back to the Lyerly home.

By the early hours of the morning a crowd of neighbors had encircled the house. There was a grove of huge sycamores and elms in the front yard; a reporter on the scene early in the morning reported the grove filled with buggies and saddle horses, the crowd murmuring softly. A telegram was sent to the county sheriff, who drove to the scene at breakneck speed, arriving about four-thirty a.m. A telegram to the governor's office put in motion an effort to get bloodhounds, which arrived about 8:00 a.m. At least two sets of bloodhounds were brought to the house, but the hounds proved useless, perhaps due to the crowd that had encircled the property or, more probably, because the scent could only have led as far as the railroad line, which was across the road.

Before the sheriff was even on the scene, suspicion had settled on the sharecroppers. The sharecroppers, of course, were all black. The Lyerly girls mentioned that they had tiptoed quietly past the Dillingham house, and it was discussed as well that there had been some words passed in the previous week between Isaac Lyerly and another sharecropper, Nease Gillespie. Jack Dillingham was arrested about 5:00 in the morning of July 14, about six hours after the murders. Nease Gillespie's cabin was raided, and some of his possessions seized, about 6:00 a.m. Reporters from at least three newspapers were on scene not long after sunup.

Nease Gillespie was not quite likeable enough to be called a "character." Whereas most of the other sharecroppers in the area had lived near Salisbury for generations, Nease had moved there (or moved back there) after he had matched up with Fannie Gillespie. He took her name, probably because her name was known in the area. Fannie had an eleven-year-old grandson named Henry Mayhew. Henry Mayhew had a white father, was blue-eyed, and looked almost white, but he lived with Fannie and Nease. (The book about this case, A Game Called Salisbury, insists, apparently based on a census record, that Mayhew was Fannie's son, rather than her grandson, but this cannot be correct.)

Nease was abusive to Fannie and Henry, and although Nease had lived with Fannie for many years and had married her about 1902, he had fathered a son, John Gillespie, with Fannie's daughter. Nease was a hardworking man, a nervous, intense, excitable man, and probably an intelligent man, but he lived an extremely hard life and drank a lot of hard liquor and had a temper, and he was hell on those who lived with him. Fannie would say in court that she and Nease hardly ever spoke, and that she would stay away from him as much as she could.

The telegram sent from the depot at Barber Junction to the governor's office early that morning began with the words: "An unknown man entered the house . . ."—a supposition, but a reasonable supposition. But later that afternoon, a coroner's jury would conclude that "the Lyerlys were murdered with axes in the hands of Nease Gillespie, his son, John, Jack Dillingham and wife and George Ervin and Henry Lee."

They forgot to indict Booker T. Washington. Later that afternoon, Henry Mayhew, an eleven-year-old boy, was "subjected to a severe examination" (*Salisbury Post*). He said he had heard Nease confess to committing the murders. It was worse than that; in Henry's stories, not only had Nease confessed to the murders, but he had also implicated Jack Dillingham and the other four accused. As is pointed out by Susan Barringer Wells in *A Game Called Salisbury*, this story can't reasonably be true; there couldn't plausibly have been four to six people in that bedroom swinging axes, or they would have killed one another. Mayhew's story is irrational, changed numerous times in the following weeks, and was completely contradicted by every adult involved, but . . . this is the South, and it is 1906. When a terrible crime occurred, people immediately assumed that black people had done it, and some members of the press literally said and absolutely believed that Mayhew was telling the truth because he had white blood in his veins. He may have been black that morning, but when he accused his relatives of the murders, his white blood came through.

So began the struggle to avoid a lynch mob. Some of the newspapers began immediately, in the first twenty-four hours after the crime, to refer to the accused sharecroppers as murderers—not alleged murderers, not accused murderers, but murderers. The accused were moved immediately in secret to a prison in Charlotte, beyond the reach of the outraged people of Rowan County. A mob formed in front of the Rowan County jail anyway, and refused to believe that the prisoners were not there. A delegation of the would-be lynchers searched the prison, and then a second delegation, and then a third. At length the mob came to accept that they had been denied blood, and broke up.

A grand jury was scheduled for early August. Assuring state officials that local passions had cooled and that the accused could be protected, Rowan County moved the prisoners back to Salisbury on August 6. It was an insufferably hot day, still and stifling inside the courthouse, and extraordinarily tense. At 3:40 that afternoon, the grand jury returned a true bill, indicting all six of the accused. The trial was scheduled for the following day.

The accused had an attorney; according to *A Game Called Salisbury*, they had an extremely good attorney. Within an hour, the attorney filed for a continuance, claiming that (a) it would be impossible to get a fair hearing in the emotional cauldron of the time and place, and (b) he had been denied any opportunity to interview possible defense witnesses, who were being held by the state. Within moments, the motion for continuance was denied, and the trial was set to begin the next morning.

The attorney demanded a special venire of two hundred. The judge expressed the opinion that this was unnecessary, but, being the fair-minded jurist that he was, granted the special venire and ordered the sheriff to have two hundred potential jurors in the courthouse at ten o'clock the next morning. The court adjourned about 5:30 that afternoon.

Ms. Wells, in her book, debates whether the responsible parties were genuinely trying to prevent a lynching, or whether they were complicit in the tragedy that occurred that night. Myself, I don't question their sincerity, merely their competence. By "responsible parties" I mean the sheriff, the jailers, the judge, the mayor, and other local officials.

In the 1880s lynching was quite common, and was widely equated with justice in the minds of many Americans. By 1906 it had acquired a bad odor and was much less common. It is my experience that people have an immense capacity for self-delusion. I think that the responsible parties, for the most part, had merely deluded themselves about their ability to manage the situation. They wanted to believe that the people of Salisbury were progressive, forward-looking citizens in step with the rest of the nation, rather than that they were backward, ignorant louts who would do the wrong thing. I don't doubt that most of the people of Salisbury *were* forward-looking citizens in step with the nation; it's the other 25 percent you need to worry about.

Anyone could have foreseen the second tragedy approaching. The newspapers wrote editorials, urging the public to stay calm and allow the system of justice to work. The sheriff issued statements to the same effect and sent telegrams reassuring the governor's office that he would and could protect the lives of the accused. The judge spent much of the day, August 6, repeatedly lecturing the courtroom about the need to remain calm and respect the law. They all saw it coming, and they all insisted that they had things under control.

Jake Newell was the very good attorney assigned to the accused. "I reached Salisbury and saw the crowd at the courthouse and heard it talk," Newell told a newspaper two weeks later. "I knew that trouble was brewing." The sheriff warned him to stay in his hotel room, that it might not be safe on the streets. About eight o'clock that night, Newell went to the Rowan County jail to confer with his clients. "Already a crowd had gathered," he said. "But there was practically no demonstration . . . The guards at this time were thoroughly rattled and totally inadequate and incompetent." Newell informed the judge of the conditions, but the judge refused to wire the governor's office for help. He conferred with local officials. They decided that the sheriff, the mayor, and the prosecuting attorney would address the crowd. Anticipating a lynching, nearby towns had sent reporters to the scene who were filing regular dispatches. People were gathering at newspaper offices in nearby cities, following the situation from the wires. The *Charlotte Observer*, reporting in a dispatch sent out at nine o'clock that night: "At this time things look blue for the negroes. Swarms of people are congregating in the streets, and all they lack is a real plucky leader. At this very minute 500 men have congregated in front of the jail, where a dozen or more deputies sit with their guns across their knees. A few keen yells would set the crowd on fire and it would storm the jail. If the deputies do their duty they may have to kill some of their fellow men."

Salisbury had installed a railroad car system in 1905. With every railroad car that passed the jail, a few more men would join the mob. Others tied up their horses and walked in, people filtering down from the mountains and arriving on trains from nearby towns. A lone man jumped the fence surrounding the jail yard and was arrested. A man stood up, a man about forty with a strong voice. "C'mon boys," he said. "Are we going to let our white women die and not fix the niggers that killed 'em?"

There was an exchange of gunfire, shots fired from the crowd, but the guards stood their ground. A local militia, known as the Rowan Rifles, were ordered to report for duty. The judge, the mayor, the sheriff, the solicitor (county attorney), and others repeatedly addressed the mob, imploring them to disperse.

While the main action was at the front of the jail, three rioters with a sledgehammer broke down the back door. They were taken into custody. The judge had ordered that floodlights around the jail be kept on through the night. The mob now began to break out the lights one at a time.

The man who had emerged as the leader now rose again. "Let our men out and we will leave!" he shouted. The sheriff and the crowd negotiated a deal: the sheriff would release the three men who had broken into the jail, and the leader—identified by newspapers as "the man with the Panama hat"—would urge the crowd to go home. (The newspapermen certainly knew who the man with the Panama hat was, but never said. Probably the Panama hat was a code that let the readers in on the secret, without forcing authorities to file charges.) He was good to his word; he urged the crowd to disperse, and they began to comply. It was about ten o'clock at night.

But, in the words of John Charles McNeill, "The dangerous men had not yet arrived." The crowd wandered off down side streets, where they gathered and regrouped.

At this moment the Rowan Rifles, ordered onto the scene an hour earlier, reported to the jail. The Rowan Rifles either had not been issued bullets or had been ordered not to fire them, but to fire blank cartridges. They fired their blank cartridges into the air. This made the crowd even angrier. Two men in the crowd were injured by shots fired from other rioters. The mob settled down again. After ten o'clock the *Charlotte Observer* reported the situation under control, and the mob dispersing.

And then they weren't. About 10:30, the leader of the Rowan Rifles ordered the militia to abandon their posts. They were being overwhelmed. At 11:00, the governor's office ordered the state militia in Greensville, Charlotte, and Statesboro to load special trains and get to the scene. Moments later, the order was rescinded. It was too late. The mob was in control of the jail, and in control of the prisoners.

Surprisingly—and here again we get to the issue of good faith—surprisingly, the mob did not murder all of the accused. Nine black persons were being held—six accused, two juvenile dependents, and a material witness. The women held in connection with the crime, Fannie Gillespie and Della (Young) Dillingham, were roughed up a little bit and left in their cells, as were the juveniles, Henry Mayhew and Della's baby, whom she had with her. The lynch mob arranged an impromptu "trial" for the five men still at their mercy, a trial which—more surprisingly—acquitted two of the accused. At first the leaders of the mob set these two free, and then, fearing that they would be murdered on the streets, returned them to the sheriff. Left in the control of the mob were Nease Gillespie, his fifteen-year-old son, John, and Jack Dillingham. These three were marched about a mile through the streets of Salisbury to a city park, to an old oak tree where, it is said, a good many men had been hung before.

The mob tried to force the three men to confess. They were battered with fists and wood, whipped with small tree branches, and cut with small knives. Forced to kneel at the foot of the oak and ordered to confess, all three men loudly insisted that they had nothing to do with the murders of the Lyerly family, and knew nothing about the crime. Between 11:00 and 11:30 on the sixth day of August 1906, twenty-four days after the murders of the Lyerly family, the three men were hung from the oak tree in Worth Park. Bullets from the crowd were fired into the dead and dying bodies. No one was prosecuted in connection with the lynchings.

The remaining defendants were held in custody until the following January, as were the material witnesses Fannie Gillespie and Henry Mayhew. Their trial was moved to Statesville, which was twenty-six miles to the west of Salisbury and fifteen miles west of Barber Junction. The prosecution tried to present a case against them, but Henry Mayhew, the eleven-year-old boy who had been bullied into betraying his family, was not allowed to testify, since what he had to say would have been hearsay. The prosecution quietly dropped the case in the middle of the trial. The accused were each given a small amount of money and allowed to leave the area.

\*　　\*　　\*

As I have stated repeatedly, most of the information in this chapter comes from *A Game Called Salisbury*, by Susan Barringer Wells. It is Wells's conclusion, and mine, that there is no real evidence against the men who were murdered on August 6. In my view, there is every reason to believe that these murders were committed by The Man from the Train.

There are two anomalies in this case, if it is considered as a part of our series. The first is that three girls who were in the house at the time of the murders survived the incident. This is the only time in The Man from the Train's career that he missed people who were in the house at the time of the murders, although there are one or two other crimes in which he fled the house with his work half-done.

The other anomaly is that the front door of the house was wide open after the murders, whereas our murderer normally locked the house up as tightly as he could, and jammed something into the doorframe. These two anomalies have a common explanation. Think about it for a minute; you can figure it out.

You got it?

He heard a train coming. There weren't a *lot* of trains on the east-west line, probably two or three trains a night, maybe fewer. If he missed a train, it might be hours before there was another one.

Out in the country you can hear a train coming from miles away. As he was nearing the completion of his business in Isaac Lyerly's bedroom, he heard the distant bleating of a train whistle. He had maybe eight minutes to catch the train, maybe ten; the train would stop briefly at the crossroads with the north-south line. Hurriedly, he dumped the bureau drawer on the victims' bed and set fire to it, without taking the time to search the rest of the house, as he normally would have done, for more victims. He left the door open as he ran for the train.

Despite those anomalies, there is more than enough reason to conclude that this is our guy. The extreme proximity to the railroad tracks, the motiveless murder, without any warning, of a peaceful family asleep in their beds at the time they were attacked, the use of the family's own axe, taken from their yard and dropped at the scene, the money left in the house and money left in plain view, the use of the blunt side of the axe, the moving of a lamp or lamps, the placing of a pillow over the body of one of the victims, setting the house on fire at the end of the crime or attempting to do so, breaking into the house through a window . . . it's him. The case merges geographically with his previous crimes, with the exception of the Nova Scotia murders.

Many of the murders, like the murders of the Lyerly family, occurred not merely right next to a railroad line, but also at places where a train would have to stop or slow down, which would facilitate a nonpaying customer—a freighter tramp—jumping on or getting off. These multiple rail lines, of course, also multiplied the opportunities for The Man from the Train to hop a ride and escape before being seen in the area after the murders.

\* \* \*

This description of Fannie, from the *Charlotte Observer* of July 21, 1906, is worth reprinting for its own merit, despite the racism embedded in it; this is edited for size and scope, but essentially the same as it originally appeared, and this is describing a courtroom appearance:

> If the blackest old hag in darkest Africa were brought here and put side by side with Fannie Gillespie, the wife of Nease, it would require an expert student of negro faces to tell which was the native of America. I have never, in all my experience with negroes, seen Fannie Gillespie's equal. She is black, dirty, mean and stubborn. For two inches back the hair has been clipped from her forehead, and the remaining kinks are done in thread. For several inches around her eyes the skin of her face is dark colored, as if she had applied tar to her face until it had come to be a part of her. She wore a filthy, short dress and nothing more. Her feet were naked, wrinkled and scaly.

"Fannie Gillespie," she said, "is my name." This is an instance where the man took the name of his wife. Nease, who had been known as Mich Graham, became a Gillespie when he married Fannie. The children in neighborhoods where Fannie has lived, fear her. They say that she is crazy and likes to run people.

She is not formidable looking, but when her foot falls it does so without making a sound or making a track. She glides swiftly, but silently. One thinks of the missing link as she approaches him.

"What is the matter with your face and head old woman?" asked a lawyer.

"Nease put pitch on me and cut my hair while I was asleep. He has been doing that for a long time. I guess he does it for it happens while I am asleep. He has whipped me many a time." . . .

Fannie Gillespie is a wonderful woman. She looks like a savage, but she thinks well. It was plain to one and all that she lied yesterday, but there was no way to correct her. . . . Old Fannie is cunning. She knows what to say and what not to say. She has a certain sort of nerve. Although she was coaxed here, the effect would have been the same had she been threatened. Half a savage and half a wizard, she is an interesting character. One moment, those who watched her as she fenced with Mr. Hammer, Mr. Kluttz or Mr. Linn were almost sorry for her, but the next they felt for the lawyers.

Although the author of this passage is not identified, there is no doubt that it was John Charles McNeill. Two months after the lynchings, McNeill was presented the Paterson Cup, a North Carolina literary prize; the cup was presented to him by Teddy Roosevelt, the sitting president of the United States, and was given to him for a book of poetry entitled *Songs Merry and Sad*. He died the following year of what was described as pernicious anemia; he was thirty-three. McNeill was known as the poet laureate of North Carolina, and the home in which he was born and died was restored and is maintained as a memorial to him. A historical marker in his hometown directs people to his burial site, and a bronze bust of him created in 1913 is in the Charlotte public library.

After being released from prison on or about January 31, 1907, Fannie moved to Statesville, where she continued to raise and care for her grandson, Henry Mayhew.

\* \* \*

William Sydney Porter, better known as O. Henry, was a native of Greensboro, fifty miles from Salisbury. In 1906 he published his most famous story, "The Gift of the Magi." The falsely accused woman in this story was named Della (Young) Dillingham. The name of the young woman in "The Gift of the Magi," the young woman who sells her hair to buy a gift for her husband, is Della Dillingham Young.

"The Gift of the Magi," however, was originally published on April 10, 1906—three months *before* the murders of the Lyerly family. This means that either:

• O. Henry knew Della Dillingham was somehow unconnected to this famous crime (which is certainly possible, since they were from the same area), or

• The use of her name or the elements of her name is just a weird coincidence.

In this section of the book, Section III, there have been twelve crimes, resulting in the murders of forty-nine people. This brings the total for all three sections to twenty-seven crimes involving 110 victims. The total of 110 victims does not include the 7 people (so far) who were murdered by lynch mobs as a result of these crimes, nor does it include the 3 or 4 people who were lawfully executed for crimes that seem similar to those committed by The Man from the Train.

| SECTION III | | | | |
|---|---|---|---|---|
| *Where* | *Who* | *No.* | *Date* | *Year* |
| Trenton Corners, New Jersey | Van Lieu family | 2 | November 17 | 1900 |
| Shirley, Maine | Allen family | 3 | May 12 | 1901 |
| Cottondale, Florida | Kelly or Caffey | 5 | October 31 | 1903 |
| Statesboro, Georgia | Hodges family | 5 | July 28 | 1904 |
| Trenton, South Carolina | Hughes family | 4 | December 8 | 1904 |
| Radford, Virginia | Linkous family | 2 | December 25 | 1904 |
| Marion, Arkansas | Boylan family | 3 | February 7 | 1905 |
| Jacksonville, Florida | Wise family | 5 | September 21 | 1905 |
| Cottonwood, Alabama | Christmas family | 3 | February 7 | 1906 |
| Dominion, Nova Scotia | Stetka family | 4 | February 16 | 1906 |
| Allentown, Florida | Ackerman family | 9 | May 13 | 1906 |
| Barber Junction, NC | Lyerly family | 4 | July 13 | 1906 |

# SECTION IV

## CHAPTER XXXII

# Hiatus

Between July 13, 1906, and March 6, 1908, a space of twenty months, there are no reports of crimes that seem related to our criminal. There are essentially three possibilities to explain this hiatus:

    1. The Man from the Train was in jail.

    2. He had left North America, and was killing people somewhere else.

    3. There was something going on in his life that prevented him from being active. He could have been injured, for example, or perhaps the outrages occurred when he was drunk, and perhaps he had stopped drinking. Sometimes a serial murderer is inactive because he is involved in a relationship that limits his outside activities, but we believe it is unlikely that The Man from the Train was capable of forming a relationship, and also that it is unlikely that he committed his crimes under the influence of alcohol.

While it is difficult to speculate on what someone was doing based merely on the fact that he wasn't killing people, the most likely explanation is that he was in jail. Let us take advantage of this break in the story to ask ourselves a few questions about the murderer, starting with:

    1. Did he stalk his victims?

2. Is it fair, accurate, and instructive to say that The Man from the Train was a coward?

On the "stalking" issue, it is our opinion that, prior to 1906, The Man from the Train generally did do some advance research on the families that he intended to kill, but that after he got out of jail in 1908, and sometimes before, he did little research and was, for the most part, just finding a house and going in. I don't think he had identified in advance the Lyerly house; I think he just got off the train, saw the house across the road from the railroad track, and thought that looked perfect.

Let's say, for the sake of argument:

1. The seminal event in 1898, which we have not yet told you about, was the first time that he had killed anybody.

2. The murder of the Van Lieu family in 1900 is an unrelated event that merely happens to give a similar appearance to The Man from the Train's crimes.

3. The murder of the Allen family in Maine in 1901 *is* him, but that this was an unplanned event that resulted from an eruption of anger on the murderer's part, when Mr. Allen insulted the murderer and drove him forcefully away from his door.

4. After the murders of the Allen family, The Man from the Train gave himself over to his murderous impulses, and that from that point on—beginning with the murders of the Kelly family on or about Halloween, 1903—he was an organized serial murderer acting out an increasingly sophisticated program.

We don't know for certain that any of this is true, but I would guess that each of these statements is true, 51 percent chance or higher.

Sometime between May 12, 1901, and October 31, 1903, The Man from the Train made the decision to commit himself to a life of recreational murder. However, I think it is unlikely that, when he made that decision, he immediately went out and murdered the Kelly family. I think it is much more likely that he began thinking through the problem of how he could commit these crimes without getting caught.

One of the things that we can say with confidence about The Man from the Train is that he was *not* a hobo, not a person who just rode the rails for long periods of time without direction. He settled in to an area, got a job, usually as a lumberjack or working in a sawmill, and lived in that area for several months, as a rule. We know this because (1) the predominance of these crimes in areas economically centered on the lumber industry is beyond chance, and (2) if he had not settled in an area for several months at a time, the crimes would be much, much more spread out than they are. If The Man from the Train was truly a hobo, the crimes would have no obvious geographic pattern; a crime in Virginia would be followed by one in Utah. But, with just a couple of exceptions, the crimes have obvious geographic patterns—as if he had remained in essentially the same area for months at a time. He lived in an area for three to six months, almost certainly was employed, and then he moved on, but not a thousand miles on; normally he just moved one hundred to four hundred miles to get outside the sphere of his last murders.

Well, did he commit his atrocities just as he arrived in an area, or while he was settled in an area, or did he commit his crimes when he was leaving an area? Obviously the more likely explanation is that he committed a crime as he was ready to depart the area.

I think it is likely that, between 1901 and 1903, The Man from the Train lived and worked in or around Marianna, Florida, and thought endlessly about how he could get by with killing people. He realized right away that his chance of getting away with the crime(s) was better when he killed people of low social standing, poor and black people. He picked houses that were isolated so that he wouldn't be seen coming or going.

He set the houses on fire when he was done, perhaps to hide evidence or perhaps because he derived pleasure from the fires, as he did from the murders. I believe that the former explanation—that he set the houses on fire to hide evidence—is more likely, but not certain. I prefer that explanation for two reasons. First, as he transitioned gradually to committing his crimes *in* small towns, rather than *near* small towns, he stopped setting the houses on fire. That's rational. If you set fire to a house with neighbors on all sides, the neighbors will come running. It's too risky to set the house on fire in that situation, so he stopped doing it—which means that it was rational behavior, given the murderous premise.

Also, I rather think that, while The Man from the Train was probably perversely proud of his murders, he may have been ashamed of his perversion. I think he was ashamed of what he did with the bodies of young girls, and that he set fires to cover it up. This is speculation.

A similar question arises with respect to the midnight entries, and here we get to the issue of cowardice. Did The Man from the Train enter houses after the family was asleep as a rational approach to avoid being arrested, or did he do it because he was a coward who was afraid to confront a living victim?

Any way you look at it, murdering people in their sleep as a form of recreation is a cowardly thing to do, whether it results from fear or from a rational avoidance of negative consequence. It is cowardly behavior.

It is *fair* to describe The Man from the Train as a coward, but is it accurate and instructive? I hang up on that issue for this reason: that what The Man from the Train did required something that was not courage, but was very much like courage. It required composure under stress. It required that he act calmly, deliberately, and aggressively under conditions of substantial risk to himself, even though he had minimized that risk.

Could you break into a stranger's house with an axe, and beat the entire family to death, and then go on about your life the same as before? No, of course you could not, and I could not. I would be terrified. I would shake in my boots; I would pee in my pants. I couldn't do it; not that I would *want* to, but I could not. It required a self-possession, a clarity of purpose, and a suppression of fear that is beyond anything normal. Is it accurate to say that the man who could do this was a coward?

It is accurate to say that he was a practical coward. He was risk averse at an extremely high level. He wasn't taking *any* chances that he didn't need to take in order to accomplish his purpose—and this is quite unusual for a serial murderer, to be *that* risk averse. Some serial murderers *like* risk; sometimes they seem to be inviting the police to come question them. The Man from the Train had a quite extraordinary degree of focus on avoiding the natural negative consequences of his actions. He thought it through. He was not merely ahead of the police and the sheriffs and the private detectives who made efforts to catch him; he was absurdly far ahead of them. The things that were being done to catch him—sending for bloodhounds, raising reward money, luring private detectives into the investigation—were pathetically far behind the curve. It may be fair to say that he was decades ahead of the police.

What he did evolved over time, and in this hiatus, this period when he was inactive, there was a transition. He was not quite the same murderer when he got out of prison. When he got out of prison he started killing people *in* small towns, rather than near small towns.

And, as a part of that, I think that he mostly stopped researching the families that he was going to kill. I think that in 1903, 1904, and 1905 he would live in an area and work in that area for several months, and during those months he would travel around the area on weekends probably, and he would look for the family that he wanted to target. He was looking for certain things. A house with a barn. A woodpile with an axe. Children's toys on the front lawn or on the porch. A house that was secluded enough that the neighbors would not see someone creeping around the back of the house after dark. A dog; he didn't want a dog, and he didn't want to be more than a five-minute walk from the railroad track. An area where there was no regular police patrol. There was one house in hundreds, one house in a thousand that had exactly the combination that he was looking for. When it was time for him to pack up and leave town, he knew where he was headed.

But by 1909 he was a very experienced murderer. He didn't *need* that preparation and research anymore; he was able to fly by the seat of his pants. This led him, on two occasions, to break into the houses of young married couples who had no children (the Cobles, in Rainier, Washington, and the Hudsons, in Paola, Kansas). That happened because he hadn't done his research; he just got off the train and looked around and found a house that looked right. This led him to commit a crime in San Antonio, a town large enough to have a police force. He did that because he hadn't done his research. The train came into San Antonio from the northeast, just clipping the edge of the town, and he did not see the city hidden behind the trees and the hills and didn't know it was there. He thought he was in a small town.

This led him or permitted him, in Colorado Springs, to break into one house and then another, right next to it; that he did this suggests he was not researching his houses in advance. In Ellsworth, Kansas, he started to break into one house, discovered that the occupant of that house was awake, and moved on a half-block away to break into another house. This is evidence that he was just improvising.

By 1910, 1911, he was a hit-and-run axe murderer, blowing into town, committing a murder, and leaving the town immediately. This, too, was clever. Working inside a town gave him a variety of targets to choose from, which made it easier for him—but staying in towns too small to have a police force reduced the chance that there would be a problem. What he realized, over time, was that he didn't need to pick isolated houses *near* a small town so long as he never established any presence in the town before the crime and was never seen in the town after the crime. Before the crime he was just a faceless stranger, giving no one his name, giving no one any reason to remember him. After the crime he was a ghost in the wind. He was safe.

In Ellsworth there is reason to believe that he dropped a bundle of clean clothing down near the railroad track, clothes to change into after the crime. He may also have done this in Villisca; clothes were found floating in the river near the place where the dogs led the pursuers. Probably he was not doing this in 1903. He realized, at some point, that being seen fleeing a crime scene in bloody clothes could be very bad for him. As he became more organized over time, he took steps to avoid this.

Once he became an organized murderer he never took anything from a scene of the crime—*nothing*—because he knew that if he was caught with something in his possession from the scene of a crime, that would be the end of him. In many crime stories from this era, a man is executed because he is found with an item from a murder scene. This man worked; he had money. He may well have stolen money at other times and probably did, but never from a murder scene.

Early on, he left bloody fingerprints on the axe. Later on he would wash the axe handle before he left. This suggests that he read newspapers, that he knew what was happening in the world. His method evolved.

It took me some time before I realized that he was committing his murders not merely near to one railroad track, but usually at the intersection of two or more, which would have maximized his opportunities to catch a train quickly. I began to wonder when he started doing that and how he figured it out, but actually, that one goes back to the beginning of the series of crimes. From 1903 on, he was working almost always near the intersection of multiple tracks.

I suspect—I don't know—but I suspect that this trick may have been common knowledge in the hobo community. The Man from the Train was not a true hobo, but he lived and traveled among them periodically. Many of them were petty thieves, sometimes more than petty thieves, and they talked among themselves about how to avoid getting caught. I'll bet they all knew that trick about committing a crime at the intersection of multiple railroad lines, so that you wouldn't be stranded on a lonely track waiting for a train. It may have been something that was obvious from experience if you lived the way they lived.

I recognize the rank improbability of what I am about to tell you, but I'm going to mention it. I think it is possible that The Man from the Train actually left money at the scene of his crimes. I don't mean left the money that was there; I mean took money out of his pocket and put it on the mantel.

I know you are going to think that is crazy, to leave money at the scene of a crime and then set the house on fire, but then, The Man from the Train was crazy—tremendously rational in terms of risk avoidance, but driven by uncontrollable anger metastasized to general hatred. It seems to me that I see the phrase "money left in the room in plain sight" too often, as if it was more often than it should be. He could have dumped money in the murder room as a way of showing contempt for money, and thus, contempt for society in general. I know it is unlikely.

We don't know when he started moving lamps around, but my guess would be that he always did that. If it was rational risk-avoidance behavior, then it may have developed over time. If it was impulse-driven, psychologically rooted behavior, then it was proba-bly always a part of his routine. This was something he did because he liked to do it; he liked the ghoulish half-light of a dark, strange house, and knowing what he was about to do. He did that in 1898.

The covering of windows with cloth, pulling the blinds shut tight, putting cloth over the windows; that was rational risk avoidance, but it was also psychologically comforting to him. Covering the windows enabled him to carry a lamp around the house after the crime, studying what he had done, dragging dead bodies around and enjoying what he had done, without the curious moving light being detected from outside the house.

I believe that The Man from the Train was driven by a combination of six factors, which changed somewhat as the series of crimes went on.

First, he was driven by intense anger and hatred. He had been abused as a child, and he had been imprisoned and rejected and not treated well as an adult. He was a small, ugly, miserable little bastard who lived a very unpleasant life, although he was a quite intelligent man who had other positive qualities such as a willingness to work and a capacity to plan.

Second, he was sexually attracted to young girls, and there were no outlets to him for sexual satisfaction, and I think he was ashamed of this attraction.

Third, as he committed the crimes, he became an adrenaline junkie. He loved the adrenaline rush, provoked by fear, of committing the crimes. Every nerve was awake for him; every fiber of his being stood on edge as the adrenaline surged through him. Nothing else gave him that feeling; nothing else was anything like it. When he thought about the next crime it excited him; when he was done with a crime he relived it over and over in his mind, relishing it. Some events were probably disappointing to him, like Paola, and others were probably special to his memory. But for this reason, I don't believe that he committed his crimes under the influence of alcohol, because I think alcohol would have dulled his senses and interfered with that sense that every nerve was on fire. Also, alcohol would have caused him to make mistakes, and he did not make many mistakes.

Fourth, I think that the crimes were his way of proving to himself that he was smarter than other people. This allegation—the criminal thought he was smarter than everybody else—is a policeman's trope;

it is something that police and prosecutors say in every case, whether there is any evidence that it is true or not, and many times I think that it is nonsense, but I do believe it is true in this case. He had been put down, all of his life—denied credit, denied opportunity, denied the good things in life; this is how he saw the world, and there was truth in it. He was an intelligent man, and I believe that this was his way of showing himself that he was smarter than others, that he could commit these crimes and no one could catch him.

Fifth, the possession of dead bodies became a major motivator for him. He loved to have possession of a body of a dead young girl, of course, but this element went beyond that. We have seen many, many stories in this book in which bodies were moved after death—bodies stacked on top of one another, persons killed in one room (leaving huge bloodstains) but their bodies found in another, bodies posed, babies killed in one bed and placed in another after death, persons killed outside and their bodies inside for no sensible or coherent reason. He loved to possess dead bodies. He loved to touch them and pick them up and move them around.

And finally, committing these crimes became his self-identity. It was who he was; it was how he thought about himself. He was the man with the secret that nobody could ever get to. You guys look at me and you see nothing—this is how he thought; you see a small and dirty man who doesn't amount to anything, but I know that I can do things and I have done things that you cannot imagine. I am the very Monster of whom you live in terror—and you have no idea that it is Me. He was a tiny man who cast a huge and terrible shadow, and he knew that, and in his mind he was the size of his shadow.

# CHAPTER XXXIII

# The Crimes of 1908

M r. and Mrs. Warren Hart lived in Frazier, Georgia. You can find Frazier on a map, but it's not easy. Frazier is not a place on the map, it is a point on the map. Frazier is eight-tenths of a mile north of Empire on the Macon & Brunswick Railroad Line. Empire itself is an unincorporated settlement of around three hundred people, about three miles south of Cochrane, which is a legitimate small town. Why Georgia felt that it needed three little towns in three miles I have no idea; it seems rather unusual. I suspect that Frazier may not have been a settlement but merely a rural railroad stop.

Anyway, Mr. and Mrs. Hart were murdered with an axe on March 4, 1908; you have probably guessed that by now, it is getting rather late in the book to surprise you with these things. The murder of the Harts is a low-information event; in fact, the murders of Mr. and Mrs. Hart seem to have made the newspapers at all only because, in the manner of the South a hundred years ago, two black men were lynched and set on fire to expiate the crimes. Perhaps the easiest way to tell this story is to start with a verbatim account of the crime from a contemporary newspaper:

## Lynch Two Negroes

### Confess the Foul Crime

### For Purpose of Robbery, Blacks Armed with Axes Brutally Slew White Couple

HAWKINSVILLE, GA—March 6. Two negroes, Curry Roberts and John Henry, were lynched near here today and their bodies burned. They were accused of the murder of Mr. and Mrs. Warren Hart. One of the negroes confessed to the crime and said the motive was robbery. Roberts and Henry were arrested Wednesday, following the discovery of the body of Warren Hart. The body of his wife was lying nearby in a dying condition. The murder took place at Frazier, near the Hart home. Mr. Hart died as a result of a blow on the head, apparently from an ax. Mrs. Hart was seriously beaten and was found unconscious. She died Wednesday without having regained consciousness. Today the negroes confessed their guilt, were taken from the county jail and carried some distance from town and hanged to a tree. The lynching party consisted of a number of men who concealed their identity with masks.

After the hanging the bodies were cut down and incinerated. There is no excitement in the county as the result of the hanging.

The crime for which the negroes were hanged was committed just at daylight Wednesday, when someone attacked Hart just as he left the house to feed his stock. The murderers went into the house and attacked Mrs. Hart with the ax, leaving her for dead. The purpose of the assault is believed to have been robbery. The murderers did not get any money, although the Harts are known to have about $1,000 in the house.

News of the murders spread rapidly throughout the section and in the village of Empire, near the scene of the murder, there was most intense excitement. Over 1,000 persons gathered, among them many friends of the aged couple, who formed a posse, procured dogs and began a search. Within a short time the two negroes were arrested and brought here for safe keeping. During the night a mob gathered near the jail, demanded Roberts and Henry, and then took them to an isolated place near the scene of the horrible murder, and lynched them.

Mr. and Mrs. Hart were 65 years old.

—*Abilene Daily Reporter*, March 7, 1908

This article is reprinted here exactly as it first appeared, complete with odd use of prepositions, the variant spelling of "axe," and the stunning lack of irony in reporting that the Negroes were taken to Hawkinsville "for safe keeping." The only thing we changed was that this particular article (in the original) referred to Curry Roberts as "Cherry" Roberts. Every newspaper article about this crime that we could find contains the same general information as this one except for the Curry/Cherry thing. We think "Curry" was more likely the name.

The two authors of this book disagree as to the likelihood that this crime was a part of the series. Rachel points out:

1. The Man from the Train never attacked anyone at dawn.

2. He rarely attacked anyone who was awake.

3. There are no children among the victims.

4. We lack sufficient information about the crime to include it on the list.

Also, at least one of the lynching victims "confessed" to the crime, although obviously under great duress, and neither of us places any weight on this alleged confession. Lynch mobs almost always say that their victim confessed; it keeps at bay the nasty questions about the actual guilt of those who are lynched.

The other side of the argument is:

1. Multiple people were murdered.

2. With an axe.

3. In the very heart of The Man from the Train's favorite killing zone, near the Florida/Georgia border.

It is clear from the reports that the Harts were *bludgeoned* with the axe, and we can lose track of how unusual this is on its own terms; people murdered with an axe are normally struck with the cutting edge of the axe. Almost the only thing we can tell about the location of the house is that it must have been virtually on top of the railroad track, since "Frazier" existed only as a railroad stop, and not as a population center.

The Man from the Train never attacked anyone at dawn, true, but I don't see how the report of the attack happening at dawn can be anything other than supposition, since obviously the murderer(s) had departed well before the crime was discovered on the morning of March 4. It must be that Mr. Hart was found dressed, and, we might assume, Mrs. Hart in her nightclothes. Nothing is reported to the effect that she was fixing breakfast when attacked or anything like that. It seems equally plausible to me that The Man from the Train may have been lurking outside the house about midnight when, for example, a dog may have begun to bark ferociously, or some other noise may have alerted Mr. Hart. Mr. Hart may have pulled on his clothes to go investigate, and may have been attacked as soon as he was outside the door.

A course of justice which ends in two executions within twenty-four hours of the crime is, it seems to us, much more likely to identify the wrong men than to identify the right ones. The "culprits" were seized without the help of such niceties as judges, hearings, or even the police or the sheriff. A mob formed, and they got some bloodhounds, the bloodhounds led them for a mile or two until they came across a couple of black men, and one of the black men was terrorized into a confession, or maybe he didn't confess; maybe that was just what his murderers said to make the narrative fit. Were they found with blood on their clothes? Were they found in possession of incriminating items? Did they leave visible tracks at the scene?

No mention of that. We are not impressed either by the bloodhounds or the alleged confession. The "confession" says that it was a robbery, but every newspaper account says that the Harts had $1,000 in the house, and that the robbers did not get the money. So it's not a robbery; the robbery, again, is merely supposition and narrative. It's a non-robbery, a crime without apparent motive, like almost all the others in this series.

This is all we really know about this crime: that four people died, not two, that the story came and went in twenty-four hours, and that the story was over before the system of justice could pull its boots on.

\*　　\*　　\*

Two railroad lines met in Watauga, Texas, and still do today. Watauga is nine miles north and slightly east of Fort Worth, north and west of Dallas. The Texas and Pacific Railroad was built through Watauga in 1876 and 1877, heading south to Fort Worth, putting what had been a settlement of a dozen or fewer people on the map. 1876 was the cattle drive era; the trains were built to (and did) replace the cattle drives, providing a more efficient way to get the cows to market. The people of Watauga wanted a railroad depot, to make the trains stop there, so they offered to rename the town "Edwards," after a railroad foreman named Edwards; the railroad built the depot but then kept using the name "Watauga," which was a Cherokee word meaning "village of many springs." In the 1880s Jay Gould's KATY railroad—the Missouri, Kansas, and Texas—built another line that crossed the Texas and Pacific Railroad at the south edge of Watauga, headed into Dallas.

The population of Watauga in 1908 appears to have been between seventy and a hundred people, although there are no published census figures. The number one nonfarm industry in the Dallas/Fort Worth area in 1910 was—again, this may not come as a surprise to you—logging.

Like a man named Longmeyer, whose house was broken into in chapter XIII of this book, M. F. Gerrell was a foreman on the KATY railroad. His wife was named Dora. A wire service story dated April 13, 1908, reports that "the people of the village of Watauga . . . are much agitated by the discovery this morning of the bodies of the entire Gerrell family." Note the words that are used: *the entire* Gerrell family, the husband, wife, and a baby girl, and also *the discovery this morning*. Other newspaper stories . . . well, one other newspaper story . . . will say that it is not the entire family, and this is a significant issue. Since this was Texas and not Georgia, the murders were immediately blamed not on "Negroes," but on "Mexicans," although the *San Antonio Light* opined on the day of the murders that "the crime is believed to have been committed by negroes for the purpose of robbery or by some members of Gerrell's gang of 35 Mexicans." So it could have been the blacks or the Mexicans; it is so hard to tell which it was when there is no evidence against either one.

April 13 was a Monday morning, April 12 a Sunday night, so we now have five ticks suggesting the possibility that this was a related case: the motiveless murder of a peaceful family (1) in a small, unincorporated settlement (2) where two railroad lines crossed (3) in a logging area (4) on a Sunday night (5). The murders were committed between midnight and 1:00 a.m., so there's six.

But how do we know it was that time of the night? Another newspaper report says that there were two other children in the house who were sleeping in an adjoining room. In that report, the children heard the baby crying a little before 1:00 a.m., went to investigate, and found *two men with clubs* murdering their parents. Also, that report says that Mr. Gerrell was both stabbed and beaten.

So here we have two significant discrepancies from the pattern: (1) that the murder weapon may have been a club, and (2) that what appears to be the best and most specific report of the crime says that there were multiple assailants.

It's a little hard to figure, isn't it? If two adult men armed with clubs and knives are in the process of beating people to death and are interrupted by two small children, would you expect the murderers to flee the scene? Also, how is it that the murders were not discovered until morning, if the criminals were interrupted *in flagrante* at 1:00 a.m.? (By the way, the term *in flagrante delicto* originally meant "caught committing a crime," or "caught blazing." The use of the term to indicate sexual misconduct is a colloquial derivative, and not the original meaning of the phrase.)

At this point, rabbit trails abound. Did The Man from the Train meet up with a partner, while he was in prison, and did the two of them work together for a while after he got out of prison? For that matter, how do we know that there weren't two men doing this all along; how do we know that The Man from the Train wasn't The Men from the Train?

We don't know, for sure—but it is one newspaper report that says that there were two men involved in Watauga, and newspapers in this era are not so reliable that it would seem to me wise to chase the rabbit any farther.

\*   \*   \*

Woodland Mills, Alabama, has every possible characteristic of the place The Man from the Train would probably go next, except the most important one. Northeastern Alabama has what could be called mountains or large hills, and the railroads prefer flatlands. The closest the railroad came to Woodland Mills was over by Hobbs Island, which is about ten miles east of Woodland Mills, but in effect farther than that, because the Tennessee River curls between the two, and you have to go about three miles out of your way to find a bridge.

We believe that it is unlikely that the Woodland Mills murders were committed by The Man from the Train; unlikely, but we cannot be certain. Tom Edmondson and his family lived in a log house, a log cabin, in rural Morgan County, Alabama, about twenty miles south of Huntsville. November 26, 1908, was Thanksgiving Day. On November 25, the Edmondson family was murdered, and their house and barn were set on fire. There were six victims: Edmondson, his wife, his mother, and three children.

All the first reports say three children. Later, months after the crime, all of the newspaper reports say two children, so . . . figure that one out. We believe there were three children. The fire consumed the house, leaving little in terms of recognizable remains. Searchers found the remains of five victims, but there were six people unaccounted for. A grand jury or a coroner's jury was impaneled, and the following week, the grand jury returned an indictment against Tom Edmondson. Their conclusion was that he had murdered his family, burned his house, and fled the area.

Edmondson had a white tenant farmer named Bob Clements; Clements rented a house and land on Edmondson's property. Clements moved out of that house some weeks after the murders, and a family named Luker moved in. The story I am about to tell you is illogical. People often do illogical things, and we cannot conclude that this didn't really happen because it is so illogical, but this is such a feast of illogical behavior that scratching one's head seems hardly sufficient. In late January 1909, Mr. Luker confronted Clements, claiming that he had found partially burned bloody rags in the fireplace, the remnants of a bloody shirt and bloody overalls. Clements threatened to kill Luker if he told anyone about finding the bloody clothing, and Clements was arrested for threatening to kill Luker.

Do you spot a couple of problems here? First, why would you

move out of a rental house, in the wake of six murders, and leave *partially burned* bloody clothing in the fireplace? The fact that you put the bloody clothing in the fireplace clearly means that you recognize that this is damaging evidence—yet you leave the bloody clothing partially burned in the fireplace, and walk out the front door?

And second, if you are the new tenant, and you find the partially burned bloody clothing in the fireplace, why do you tell the previous tenant about that, rather than the sheriff? Hey, Bob, I think you may have murdered the Edmondson family; let's talk about it? Apparently Luker felt comfortable going to the sheriff, because as soon as Clements threatened him, he went to the sheriff and had Clements arrested, but what exactly was the point of talking to Clements about it in the first place?

In any case, when Clements was arrested, his wife immediately burst into tears, and assumed (incorrectly) that he was being arrested for the Edmondson murders, and she then told what came to be accepted as the true story of the Edmondson murders. Clements was involved with Edmondson's wife. On the day of the murders Clements was talking with Edmondson's wife in the barn, or perhaps they were interrupted *in flagrante*, when Edmondson found them and confronted them. Clements killed Edmondson, and then killed the rest of the family to cover up the crime. He had returned to the Edmondson house the next day, according to his wife, to set fire to the house and barn.

There is no evidence less reliable than the allegations of an angry spouse. The story told by Mrs. Clements seemed like it might be true, however, and Clements was arrested, tried, and convicted of the murders.

Actually, he was convicted of only one of the murders, the murder of a daughter named Nettie. He was held on warrants charging him with involvement in all six murders—including that of Tom Edmondson, whose body was never found and who had himself been indicted for the murders—but was prosecuted for only one of the murders as a hedge against the prohibition of double jeopardy, a common practice in this era.

But did Mrs. Clements actually testify against her husband? We don't know. The *Atlanta Constitution* reported on February 26, 1909, at the start of the trial, that "Clements' aged father, his wife and seven small children sat around him. In his lap he held his little son." This suggests that Mrs. Clements was supporting her husband at the time of the trial, and also, it is unlikely that a wife could testify against her husband in 1909. But it does not appear that any reporter actually attended more than a few minutes of the trial, and we do not know what evidence was produced that led to Clements's conviction.

The authors accept in a general way that Clements was probably guilty of these murders, and also, if Clements wasn't, then it could have been Edmondson himself. However, we will point out the following:

1. Clements never confessed to the crime.

2. The fact that Clements (in the story told by his wife) left the house and returned the next day to set fire to the house and barn strongly suggests that the Edmondson house was sufficiently isolated that the crime was not discovered for some time, which means that we don't really know (other than by Mrs. Clements's story) when the crimes occurred. For all we know, the crimes could have occurred in the middle of the night, as most of "our" crimes did, or they could have begun, as several of the other crimes did, with a late-evening attack on the man of the family in the barn, followed by an attack on the remainder of the family in the house.

3. No account of the murders says what the murder weapon(s) was or were, on which basis we cannot and do not assume that it was an axe, but also cannot assume that it was not.

4. It does appear that there were young females among the victims.

5. As noted above, Woodland Mills has every possible characteristic

consistent with the established patterns, other than the fact that the railroad didn't go there, and

6. What would you suppose is the chief industry in a settlement called Woodland Mills?

Thus, based on what we know, Clements could possibly have been an innocent man convicted of a crime committed by the Crazy Tramp, as several other men almost certainly were.

The *Atlanta Constitution* on March 11, 1909, "reported" that "on a lonely island in the Tennessee River, several miles below Decatur, there lives a strange and mysterious white man with a negro family, according to stories told by Tennessee River steamboat men.

> By some this strange man is thought to be Tom Edmondson, who was supposed to have been murdered and his body cremated with other members of his family at Woodland Mills, this county, on November 25, 1908. Those who have seen this man and who have read descriptions of Tom Edmondson say the descriptions of the two men are one and the same.

This story, which goes on to throw the conviction of Robert Clements into doubt, was almost certainly planted in the newspaper by Clements's attorney in an effort to help his appeal. Note the spectacularly vague sourcing of the information about the man on the island, and the rank implausibility of establishing identity by comparing descriptions—not to mention the implausibility of the story itself.

\*     \*     \*

Looking at the three suspicious crimes of 1908, there is no convincing evidence that The Man from the Train was involved in any of the three. The murder of the Hart family is a low-information event. The murder of the Gerrells may have been committed by two men, who may have been using clubs, rather than axes, and the murder of the Edmondsons is more probably than not unrelated.

The Man from the Train was probably in prison in 1907, and we cannot say with real confidence that he was not still in prison, or still inactive for some other reason, in 1908. However, the fact that there are three crimes in 1908 that are more or less consistent with the pattern suggests the possibility that he was active. If he was in prison in 1908, there could well be one "incidental similarity" case that looks like it might be his, but it is not likely that there would be three.

At this point there are 121 murders that have been discussed in this book, including eleven in this section:

| SECTION IV | | | | |
|---|---|---|---|---|
| *Where* | *Who* | *No.* | *Date* | *Year* |
| Frazier, Georgia | Hart family | 2 | March 4 | 1908 |
| Watauga, Texas | Gerrell family | 3 | April 12 | 1908 |
| Woodland Mills, Alabama | Edmondson family | 6 | November 25 | 1908 |

For the sake of clarity, the authors do not believe that *all* of these 121 murders were committed by the same man. We believe that a substantial number of the murders were committed by the same man, and that any of the murders on this list might possibly have been his work.

# SECTION V

CHAPTER XXXIV

# Conversation with the Reader

We have circled back now to the point at which we began. The next murders in the series are the murders in Hurley, Virginia, which were the first story in the book. I have more to say about that crime and those that followed it, but that begins in the next chapter.

Let's assume that some of you are resisting the notion that this was in fact a series of related crimes, rather than a series of unrelated crimes. I would suppose that many of you were skeptical about this thesis when you began the book, and I would hope that most of you are not as skeptical now that you have heard most of the facts. Still, the time has come to address the nagging concerns of the unconverted. Let me make the argument that I think a skeptical reader might make, were she here to speak for herself.

What real evidence is there, that reader might argue, that these murders were all committed by the same man?

In a country the size of the United States there must be a good many families murdered each year. Many, many people lived close to the railroad track. Many of those who are murdered were no doubt murdered with axes. I am not questioning your sincerity, Bill and Rachel (the reader says politely), but how do I know, from my position, that you have not merely chosen certain crimes that accidentally happen to have these few critical characteristics in common, and then built upon that by pointing out whatever other coincidental similarities might appear?

In response to that, let me point out, first, that it was widely recognized at the time, beginning in October 1911, that this axe murderer was at work; that is, it was recognized that a limited number of these crimes were connected. The newspaper attention that came immediately to Villisca was drawn there in large part because the moment that the crime was discovered, it was suspected that this was the latest crime committed by the unknown man who had murdered several other families.

And second, let me point out that there are no fantastic or highly improbable elements of the story that we have told you or will tell you, stretching from 1898 to 1912. What element of this story would you find fantastic? Do you not believe that a man could be so evil as to do this? Do you not believe that that man could be clever enough to develop this simple scenario, by which he could escape detection (towns too small to have a police force, access to multiple railroad lines, strike late at night, be gone before dawn)? What, really, is improbable about it?

What *seems* improbable is that the series of crimes could have gone on for so long without anyone realizing what was happening. But turn that around and look at it from the other end. If you look at the first "recognized" crimes of the 1911 to 1912 era, which were the Colorado Springs murders, is it easy to believe that this is where the series of crimes begins?

To a modern reader it should be obvious that this is *not* where the series begins. A sophisticated serial murderer gets to that stage one step at a time—the same way that an athlete becomes an athlete, the same way that a writer becomes a writer, the same way that a musician becomes a musician. A serial murderer normally commits lesser crimes such as arson or molestation, graduates to murder in an isolated event, and then, more often than not, hunkers down for a time to blend into the walls. Eventually he resumes acting out his fantasies and, with the passage of the time, becomes bolder and more active.

The Man from the Train murdered two families in Colorado on one night in 1911, murdered another family two weeks later, and murdered another family two weeks after that. That is not a young, inexperienced offender. That is a serial murderer who has reached a mature phase.

Newspaper writers and ordinary citizens, at that time, *did* attempt to make connections between the Colorado Springs murders and earlier crimes in the Portland/Washington area. They lacked sufficient information to go very far with it. There simply was no way, in 1911, to connect the dots among events stretching over a period of years and occurring in different places. There was no place where information could be gathered, sifted, and systematically reviewed to look for patterns. There was no technology to compile the information or to sort through it.

Contemporary newspapers and others realized that a *Subsection* of the crimes were related, the Subsection beginning in Colorado Springs. But if you go back just weeks before Colorado Springs, to Ardenwald, Oregon, there is another little girl laid out in the middle of the room, covered with bloody fingerprints, her family murdered with an axe, with the blunt side of an axe, the axe taken from a neighbor's yard and left in the room, her family murdered in the middle of the night. And if you go back a couple months before that, to San Antonio and the Casaways, there is another one. Why would we *not* believe that these crimes are part of the same series?

Actually, the main reason that the crimes have not been connected by other writers is irrational skepticism. I'll get back to that point, irrational skepticism, but let me proceed toward it in an orderly way. I had points one and two in response to the rational skeptic above.

The third point is that, of course, we *don't* know in many cases which crimes he committed. There are perhaps fourteen crimes about which we have enough information to be certain they were committed by the same man, and then there are also many other similar crimes, and we believe that The Man from the Train was responsible for some of them or many of them, but not all of them. I have about six more arguments that I need to make here, and let me try to organize them.

*   *   *

(1) *Visualize a target, with bullet holes spread around the surface of the target.*

If the bullet holes are randomly distributed across the target, then there is no reason to believe that anyone was aiming *at* the target; it is more likely merely that the target was there, and there were a bunch of bullets flying around, and some of the bullets hit the target.

If, on the other hand, you have a cluster of bullet holes around the center of the target, and many fewer bullet holes on the outer edges of the target, then you have to conclude that someone was actually *aiming* at the target.

We have a large group of tight clusters here. If we had as many murders ten miles from a railroad track as we do a five-minute walk from a railroad track, that would be a random pattern. But when we have many, many murders within a five-minute walk of a railroad track and two or three crimes that are a few miles from a track, that's a cluster.

If we had as many murders committed at 4:00 a.m. as at midnight, some at 6:00 a.m., some in the afternoon, some at dusk, we could conclude that this was a random pattern. But all of the murders which are central to this story—all of the murders that you *have* to believe are related or you're off the reservation—all of them were committed within ninety minutes of midnight. That's a cluster.

If we had murders committed in big cities and small towns and all sizes of towns in between, we could view those as random events.

But, in fact, we have no crimes at all (relevant to this series) that were committed in a large city, one crime committed in what was then a small city (San Antonio), and the vast majority of our crimes committed in towns and settlements that were too small to have a police force. That's a cluster. That's a pattern.

If we had murders committed with an axe, and some with a knife, and some with a gun, and some with a baseball bat, then of course we could view those as random events. If we have a series of murders committed with an axe or similar instrument, that's a cluster.

Except that, in approaching this problem in this way, I have tremendously understated the implausibility of these being random, unrelated events. They were not merely near railroad tracks, they were *extremely* near to railroad tracks, and they were predominantly near the intersections of *multiple* railroad tracks, and they were almost all at places where railroad trains would have to stop, and the bloodhounds in several cases tracked the scent directly to the railroad line, at which point it was lost.

And these crimes were not merely committed with an axe, they were committed with the blunt side of the axe, and they were not merely committed with an axe, they were committed with an axe that was taken from the family's yard or from a neighbor's yard or, in two cases, the coal shed. And the axe was (generally) left in the room. And after fingerprints were developed, the handle of the axe was washed off in a bucket of water. You think it just happened that way?

*And I haven't even mentioned the idiosyncratic behavior of the criminal.* I haven't even mentioned the moving of lamps, or the removal of the chimneys from the lamps, or the placing of cloth over the windows, or the covers over the heads of the victims, or the practice of locking up the house tight as he left, or the special attention to the young female victims.

There are thirty-three elements that help identify a crime which may be connected to this series, not thirty-three distinctly different elements, but thirty-three elements with some overlap and some redundancy. I will list the thirty-three elements at the end of this chapter. But it is preposterous to suggest that there is *not* a cluster of events that surrounds a small target—and it is clear that this cluster of events describes events other than just The Subsection which has previously been connected by other writers. There is a target there, and there is somebody aiming at the target.

\*     \*     \*

(2) *There are nowhere near enough murders of families in the relevant years for these to be random clusters of events.*

The murder of an entire family is a relatively rare event. It was relatively rare in 1911, and it is relatively rare now. How rare?

We tried to document every family murder in the United States in the years 1890 to 1920. I can't tell you absolutely that we have found every single event, but we made a serious and determined effort to find every single event, and we certainly found most of them. This is the count, by years:

| 1890 | 1891 | 1892 | 1893 | 1894 | 1895 | 1896 | 1897 | 1898 | 1899 | 1900 |
|------|------|------|------|------|------|------|------|------|------|------|
| 7    | 6    | 8    | 9    | 6    | 7    | 11   | 10   | 2    | 7    | 4    |

| 1901 | 1902 | 1903 | 1904 | 1905 | 1906 | 1907 | 1908 | 1909 | 1910 | 1911 |
|------|------|------|------|------|------|------|------|------|------|------|
| 8    | 14   | 10   | 10   | 9    | 9    | 4    | 11   | 9    | 10   | 19   |

| 1912 | 1913 | 1914 | 1915 | 1916 | 1917 | 1918 | 1919 | 1920 |
|------|------|------|------|------|------|------|------|------|
| 14   | 9    | 6    | 5    | 6    | 5    | 1    | 7    | 5    |

That averages exactly eight families murdered per year, 248 in thirty-one years. In the years when The Man from the Train was most active, there would be about ten families murdered per year in the United States. (The number jumped in 1911 because there were at least two other persons murdering families that year, in addition to

The Man from the Train—the New Orleans Axeman, and Clementine Barnabet. Story to come.)

After The Man from the Train was no longer active, the number of families murdered per year dropped sharply. It could be that the number dropped sharply simply because our man was no longer active; that could be true and probably is true, but we are not making that argument.

The argument we are making is this: that there are nowhere near enough crimes here to form random clusters of identifying characteristics. The crimes that we have described for you in this book represent a very significant portion of all the family murders that occurred in the United States in those years.

Another thing that unites these murders is simply that they are so horrible. Almost every crime in this book was described in the newspapers as "the most horrible crime ever committed in this region" or "one of the most terrible crimes ever in this state" or by some similar phrase. We have quoted those phrases periodically throughout the book, and we did that to make a point: that these are not common events. *There simply are not many crimes like this.*

Further, family murders in general—what could be called unremarkable family murders—almost always have certain characteristics in common. Unremarkable family murders usually occur in daylight or in the early-evening hours (because they usually occur in the context of a heated family dispute). Unremarkable family murders almost always are committed by a family member or by a person close to the family such as a rejected suitor, a servant, or an overfriendly neighbor, often followed by the culprit's suicide. It is usually immediately obvious who has committed the crime. Often that person has a history of mental illness, alcoholism, or drug abuse, although in some cases the crime is committed due to greed. Unremarkable family murders are normally committed with a gun, a knife, or a sharp instrument such as a scythe.

339

In the years other than the years that The Man from the Train was active, unremarkable family murders will account for almost all of the total. There is the other serial murderer in 1911, and there were a few Italian immigrant families murdered by The Black Hand in the very early part of the century. The 1914 murders at the Wisconsin home of Frank Lloyd Wright, although they cannot be labeled unremarkable, actually meet all of the "normal" conditions that I outlined above. But here's my point: we are not talking about a large number of crimes that could be sifted and sorted to "find" the murders that fit the pattern; it's just not that way, at all. We're actually drawing from a very small pool of family murders. If you remove the unremarkable events, then the cluster of characteristics identifying The Man from the Train dominates the remaining events.

\* \* \*

(3) *Let us approach this as a mathematical query*, understanding that some of you are not comfortable with story problems and will want to skip ahead a couple of paragraphs. We can begin by distinguishing between the fundamental conditions of the crime, the idiosyncratic behavior of the criminal, and the fetish behavior. The fundamental conditions of the crime are:

- A family is murdered in their beds.
- The family lives within walking distance of the railroad track.
- The crime occurs near the hour of midnight.
- The crime is committed with the blunt side of an axe.
- The crime occurs in or near a small town, usually unincorporated, with little or no regular police presence.
- The crime occurs without any warning, without a robbery, and without any apparent motive.
- It is in no way clear or obvious who has committed the crime.

The second-level stuff . . . breaking into the house through a back window, removing a screen and leaving it propped up against the house, removing the chimney from a lamp and carrying the lamp around the house, picking up the axe from the family's yard or a neighbor's yard, leaving the axe at the scene of the crime, washing the axe handle in a bucket of water, committing the crimes on weekends . . . these are idiosyncratic behaviors, as opposed to fundamental conditions of the crime. And the third-level stuff, such as covering mirrors with cloth and paying special attention to the prepubescent female, that's fetish behavior.

We're just dealing now with the fundamental conditions of the crime, ignoring the idiosyncratic behavior and the fetishes.

Mathematical query: Given that there are about ten family murders per year in the United States in this era, given that most family murders will occur in daytime, given that most family murders will obviously have been committed by family members or persons close to the family, given that most of those will be committed with a gun or a sharp instrument other than an axe, how many murders would you expect there to be in the United States, per year, in which:

- A family is murdered,
- Without any warning,
- With the blunt side of an axe,
- With no robbery,
- At or near midnight,
- In or near a small town with no police force or very little police protection,
- Within a few hundred feet of a railroad track,
- Without any real evidence as to who has committed the crime?

The mathematical answer is: zero. As a random set of facts, you wouldn't expect *any* murders to meet all of those conditions, in a typical year or in a typical five-year period.

You wouldn't expect to find any murders that meet all of these conditions, at random, if there were a hundred families murdered a year. If there were a hundred families murdered a year in this period, it might happen (at random) that thirty of those would be murdered with an axe, and (let us say, very generously) twenty of them with the blunt side of an axe. Ten of those twenty crimes might occur in small towns with no police presence; three or four of those ten might occur within an hour or two of midnight. One or two of those might occur within a half-mile of a railroad; one might occur near the intersection of multiple railroad lines. That one crime might occur without any warning and without any real indication as to who was responsible, but most likely not. Given that one crime, there might or might not be valuables left in plain sight.

Realistically, there would probably not be a "random match" for this basic set of facts, even if there were a hundred family murders a year in the United States. And, in fact, if you choose a five-year period outside this period we are discussing, let's say 1922 to 1926, or 1931 to 1935, whatever . . . in that five-year period there probably will not be a single family murder in the United States that matches these fundamental conditions. There might be one or two. The odds against there being a *random cluster* of such events, with no one criminal causing the cluster, would be astronomical.

*But that's just based on the fundamental facts of the case*—not the idiosyncratic or fetishistic behavior. If you factor in the long list of idiosyncratic behaviors, it's not thousands to one against there being a random cluster of such events; it's billions to one. That is my argument, in a nutshell: it is simply not reasonable or logical to suppose that these could be random, unconnected events.

In February 1902, six members of the Earl family were murdered with an axe near Welsh, Louisiana; a man named Albert Batson was convicted of the crime and executed for it. The house was right next to the railroad track. But in that case it is obvious that the crime was *not* committed by The Man from the Train:

1. The crime was committed in daylight.
2. The crime was committed with the sharp side of the axe.
3. A note was left on the door to divert attention from the crime.
4. A team of mules was stolen from the property.
5. An effort was made to sell the mules.

Very obviously not The Man from the Train, and there are other crimes like that. My point is that when it is not him, it tends (most often) to be obvious that it is not him, because a set of facts at random will not match up with the set of facts that identifies our particular nutcase. It might match up at random on a couple of points, such as the railroad track and the axe, but it won't match up on the longer list of identifying points.

\* \* \*

(4) *The crimes are also united by obvious geographic and chronological patterns that could not reasonably be explained as random outcomes.*

June 5, 1910; Marshalltown, Iowa
November 20, 1910; Guilford, Missouri
December 7, 1910; Johnson County, Kansas (near Martin City, Missouri)
March 21, 1911; San Antonio, Texas

Take a map, put pushpins in the map 1-2-3-4, and you will see that these four crimes form an obvious geographic unit, with a clear and consistent pattern of movement. The geographic sequence lines up perfectly with the chronological sequence; not only that, but the time gaps are almost perfectly proportional to the spatial gaps.

Almost all of The Man from the Train's career is geographically and chronologically coherent in this way. Occasionally, such as after the murders in San Antonio, he will take a longer than normal train ride and surface in an entirely different part of the country two or three months later. But then there will be a cluster in the next place, and then a little gap, and then a cluster in the next place. He kills a family in Georgia, then one in Florida, then another one in Florida, then one in South Carolina. The only time in the entire series when the geography doesn't make sense is the crime in Nova Scotia.

If the crimes were not connected, why would that be true?

\*　　\*　　\*

(5) *The crimes are united by many different things, other than the broad outlines of the facts and the idiosyncratic/fetishistic behavior of the criminal.* To name one of those things: the lumber business.

The majority of The Man from the Train's crimes were committed in places where the primary industry or one of the two primary industries was logging. Sometimes it's not logging; sometimes it's mining. Think about it. What do you use in the logging business? An axe. What do you use in the mining business? A pickaxe.

Hurley, Virginia, where we started the book. Logging town.
Ardenwald, Oregon. Logging town.
Rainier, Washington. Logging town.
Colorado Springs, Colorado. Logging town.
Ellsworth, Kansas. Mining town.

Occasionally it isn't a mining or logging town; Villisca wasn't, and San Antonio wasn't. Sometimes he is just passing through town.

Anyway, let's take these three facts:

1. That most of the murders occurred in logging towns,

2. That most of the crimes occurred on the weekend, and

3. That the murderer left money and valuables in plain sight in almost every case, or else the crime was committed against persons who had nothing worth stealing.

When you put facts together and they make a sensible, coherent package, that is an indication that those facts may belong together. If you put those three above facts together, they make a sensible, coherent pattern: The Man from the Train worked for a living. He went to logging and mining towns, because logging and mining camps were always hiring workers. He committed his crimes on the weekend, because he worked during the week. And he didn't steal things from the murder scenes, because (1) he knew very well that stealing things from the scene of a murder would get you hanged, and (2) he wasn't desperate for money. Because he worked.

*   *   *

(6) *Another thing that ties these cases together is the sheer, astonishing competence of the murderer.* He is so good at what he does that you almost don't see it; you almost take for granted that this is the way it goes.

In many of the newspaper reports on these crimes, reporters are baffled by how the murderer is able to overcome the entire family so rapidly. In Villisca, for example, tests showed that the staircase creaked loudly, and that it was entirely impossible to climb the stairs to where the first murders were committed without making a loud noise. For a hundred years, people have been puzzled by how the murderer in Villisca was able to get up those stairs without waking the victims—and in San Antonio there is the exact same scenario. The stairs creak, and the police cannot understand how the criminal was able to get up the stairs without waking anybody up.

Well, I understand how he was able to do this. One minute after his first foot hit the staircase, everybody upstairs was dead. Two minutes, tops. They simply did not have time to react.

What The Man from the Train did was not easy. It was enormously difficult. If you believe that the murders were committed in one case by a jealous ex-boyfriend, in another case by a business rival, in another case by a deranged racist, then you will be very puzzled by how exactly he was able to do this without the family waking up. But if you realize that it is one person committing many of these crimes, then it makes perfect sense: he is able to do this because he knows what he is doing. He has done it dozens of times. He's not tiptoeing timidly up that staircase like a normal person would; he's charging up the staircase like the breath of Hell.

The astonishing competence of the murderer goes beyond that. He is able to slink into town, commit his murders, spend an hour or two in the house after the crime without being discovered, and get out of the house and out of town before anybody knows he is there—again, and again, and again.

One of the ways that we know that these crimes are a package is that *it is not reasonable to believe that a large number of different people possessed the skill and the self-possession necessary to have committed these crimes without getting caught and without letting potential victims get away from them.*

\*     \*     \*

But the main reason that The Man from the Train's murderous skein went undetected for more than a decade—and a primary reason why the series of crimes went unsolved—is *the irrational resistance to believing that the crimes were related*, even when there were sufficient facts to allow a clear-thinking person to see that the crimes had to be related. I have to make three arguments at once here, but they tie together. The Man from the Train was shielded from detection by three factors:

1. The fact that the public had no way to connect the dots until the newspaper wire services reached a certain point of maturity.

2. Very unusual things flabbergast us; that is, they stun us into disbelief. This is different from rational skepticism. Certain experiences and certain ideas seem unreal, and we resist believing them because they are so far outside our experience that we cannot process them as being a part of what seems like real life.

3. In many ways, experience is the worst teacher. In many ways experience is the only real teacher, yes, but in certain situations experience will teach us to believe something that is not true. Experience teaches people to believe that the earth is flat. Experience teaches people to believe that their house will not flood because the house has been there for 120 years and has never flooded before.

Experience teaches people to believe, sometimes, that what is *usually* true must always be true. Experience teaches detectives to believe that people are usually murdered by someone they know, someone in their life.

Unfortunately, the police for a hundred years "knew" this to be true even when it wasn't true. When police encountered a serial murderer, prior to 1975, they almost always insisted that they were dealing with a series of unrelated crimes. When the Manson family committed one gruesome set of murders one night and another the next, police insisted that the two crime scenes were not related, assigned different investigators to the two crimes, and refused to "join" the two investigations—even though it is difficult to see how the connections between the two crime scenes could have been any more obvious. According to Jeff Guinn in *Manson* (p. 273):

> From the outset, the Tate and LaBianca cases were hampered by the unwillingness of the investigative teams to share information. . . . They often operated out of the same long squad room, but never

effectively cooperated. LAPD administration was unconcerned—after all, the cases really had nothing to do with each other.

When the murderer known as BTK committed obviously similar crimes in Wichita, Kansas, in the 1970s, junior police officers were specifically forbidden from speculating that the crimes might be linked—even after BTK wrote to the newspapers to claim credit for the crimes.

That was *irrational skepticism*, driven by experience. Irrational skepticism of this nature survives and pollutes this discussion to the present day. JD Chandler, in the book *Murder & Mayhem in Portland, Oregon* (page 87), makes the following quite incredible statement about the links between the murders of the Hill family in Ardenwald and the murders 365 days later of the Moore family in Villisca:

> The shocking similarities between the two crimes were probably in the reporter's imagination because no charges were ever brought against anyone except Nathan Harvey.

That's it? That's all it takes to convince you that two crimes are unrelated—no charges are filed?

By that standard, all unsolved crimes are by definition unrelated to one another. The crimes of Jack the Ripper . . . all unrelated. No charges were ever filed, so obviously, there was nothing linking those crimes except the imagination of the reporters. That's irrational skepticism.

Raymond Hardy was suspected of murdering his family on a farm in Iowa on June 5, 1910. The county sheriff thought Hardy had committed the crime and blackened his name in the newspapers, but he was never prosecuted because there wasn't a scintilla of evidence to support the sheriff's slanders. Hardy wasn't a bad person or a troubled person, and he had no motive; he was just a nice farm boy, supposed to be married a few days later. After he was exonerated he lived a long, normal life, living almost sixty years after the murders. To my eyes, it is as clear as could be that Raymond Hardy was entirely innocent.

But modern articles about that case—and there are several of them on the Web—almost all insinuate that Hardy was guilty, because, well, you know, otherwise we would have to believe the family was a victim of a roving monster, and we can't believe *that*.

After Hardy was cleared, a man stepped forward to claim that he had seen a suspicious person, covered in blood, on a train leaving town on the morning after the murders. All or almost all of the modern accounts of the crime will say:

- Hardy was set free in part because of the story about the stranger on the train.
- The local people were anxious to have some alternative explanation for the crime.

Both parts of that are bass-ackwards. The story about the stranger on the train surfaced only *after* Hardy had been legally exonerated and released. And the entire history of crime screams that people prefer to believe that they *know* who committed a crime, rather than accepting that the crime may have been committed by some unknown person for some unknown reason. *Skepticism in favor of a presumption of guilt when the facts do not support a finding of guilt is irrational skepticism.* And irrational skepticism is the smoke screen behind which these murders have been hidden for a hundred years.

\* \* \*

I promised you earlier my list of thirty-three elements that we used to identify crimes that may have been committed by The Man from the Train; they are not thirty-three unique elements, but thirty-three elements with some overlap and redundancy. Here is the list:

1. Extreme proximity to the railroad tracks (usually within a quarter of a mile).

2. Crimes usually occurring near the intersection of *two* railroad lines.

3. The use of an axe.

4. The use of the blunt side of the axe, using the axe as a bludgeon rather than as a cutting instrument.

5. The taking of the axe from the family's woodpile or from a neighbor's woodpile.

6. Leaving the axe at or near the scene of the last murder.

7. Hitting each victim in the head, rather than on any other part of the body.

8. The murder of an entire family in one incident.

9. The presence among the victims of a prepubescent female.

10. Special attention being paid to the body of the prepubescent female (staging or posing of the prepubescent female, while other victims are simply left as they were when they were killed).

11. Masturbation near the body of the prepubescent female.

12. The crimes occurring in the middle of the night, usually between midnight and 2:00 a.m. or very near to that time frame.

13. Pulling a blanket over the victim's head(s) moments before the attack, presumably to minimize blood spatter.

14. Covering the victims postmortem with some item of cloth.

15. Covering other items with cloth (such as windows, mirrors, or, in one case, a telephone).

16. Attacks occurring on farms or in isolated places (up to 1908, and occasionally after) and in towns too small to have a regular police force (after 1908).

17. Setting fire to the house after the murders (up to 1906, and sometimes after 1906).

18. The crimes moving north and south along the eastern seaboard

states, up until 1909, and moving from east to west across the country after 1909.

19. The crimes tending to occur on the weekend, and particularly on Sundays.

20. The crimes tending to occur in areas in which the primary industries are logging and mining.

21. The moving of a lamp, the lamp left burning, without its glass chimney, at the scene of the crime.

22. The "timing" or spacing of the crimes, normally a few weeks between attacks, and normally at a distance one from another of one hundred to four hundred miles.

23. The clear and obvious geographical patterns formed by each set of murders.

24. The extraordinary competence of the murderer in accomplishing his grisly purpose.

25. Doors often locked or jammed shut after the crime to delay entry into the house.

26. Window shades pulled/windows and doors covered on the morning after the murders.

27. Crimes committed with extreme suddenness and with no warning of any kind.

28. Victims attacked while soundly asleep (killer may flee from the scene if anyone is awake).

29. Money and other valuables left in plain sight at the scene of the crime.

30. All or almost all of the murders in this sequence were committed in houses that burned wood for heat. Somewhere between 25 percent and 50 percent of homes in this era burned wood as their primary heat source. All or almost all of the crimes occurred in those houses.

31. Enters the house through the rear.

32. Commonly removes a window screen, enters the house through an unlocked window.

33. All or almost all crimes occur in warm weather.

There is a thirty-fourth element which could have been listed here, which is the moving of bodies postmortem or stacking of bodies atop one another. This was done in at least six cases in this series and probably more, although I decided it was better not to list it as an identifying trait.

# CHAPTER XXXV

# Hurley

My Dear Friend Tom—I arrived home last Wednesday evening. I stopped on my way home at the scene of the Hurley tragedy. It is one of the most horrible crimes ever committed. Eye or tongue or pen cannot describe it.

—W. L. Dennis, county clerk of Buchanan County

The murders of the Meadows family, which occurred in Hurley, Virginia, on September 21, 1909, are the beginning of the pivot in the series. The Man from the Train's crimes can be divided into three main groups: the early or tentative crimes; the "southern" crime series, which begins in 1903; and the "cross-country" murders. The Meadows family murders and the murders in Beckley, West Virginia, which are very close to the Meadows murders both in place and time, represent the end of the southern incidents and the beginning of the cross-country crime spree.

It has been several hundred pages since I told you the story of the Meadows family murders, so I will take two paragraphs here to summarize. A family of six was murdered near a mountain village, murdered in the manner that defines our book . . . axe, middle of the night, railroad stop, lumbering community, the whole nine yards.

The house was set on fire. The next day the *Bluefield Daily Telegraph* described it as "one of the most horrible crimes . . . in the history of this section of the country." Those who rushed to the crime scene found some footprints and got bloodhounds. The bloodhounds tracked the scent up and down mountains and through thick, brushy forests for several miles, perhaps into Kentucky, where they gang-rushed a family of three farmers who were digging their potatoes.

The farmers fled into their house and defended themselves with firearms until the militia arrived and cooler heads prevailed. Those men turned out to be not involved in the crime. A man named Howard Little, previously convicted of another murder years earlier in Kentucky, was breaking up with his wife, preparing to leave her for another woman, or at least this is what he had told the other woman. The scorned wife accused her husband, Howard, of committing the Meadows murders. He was convicted of the crime and was executed early in 1910.

There are three things that distinguish the "southern" murders, 1903 to 1909, from the "cross-country" murders of 1910 to 1912.

1. The southern murders are concentrated in the South and along the eastern seaboard. The cross-country murders run east and west across the country.

2. The southern murders occurred not *in* small towns, but (most often) right next to them, within a twenty-minute walk of a small town, usually an unincorporated town. The cross-country murders occurred (most often) actually *in* a town, and the towns are a little bit bigger, usually large enough that there is a small police presence in the town.

3. In the southern murders the house is set on fire at the conclusion of the crime. In the cross-country murders the house (usually) is not set on fire but is locked up tight when the murderer flees.

Of those three, only the first is a bright-line separation. After the Meadows family and Logan's Turnpike murders, no murders linked to the series happened in the Deep South or in a state touching the eastern seaboard, whereas in the years 1903 to 1909 almost all of the murders occurred in the South and in states touching the eastern seaboard. The other two distinctions are gradual and progressive. In the early part of the run he mostly attacked isolated farms near unincorporated settlements; at the end of the run he was committing crimes mostly *in* small cities of three to ten thousand residents, but he shifted gradually from one to the other. At the beginning of the run he mostly set fire to the houses as a part of the crime; at the end of the run he mostly locked up the house tight and pulled the blinds shut, but did not set the house on fire. But again, that was a gradual and inconsistent shift.

I believe that our criminal left the South after 1909 because he had spent 1907 and possibly 1908 as well in a prison, most probably in Florida, Georgia, or Alabama. There is a good chance that he spent that time on a chain gang. Those states in that era would round up transients and sentence them to hard labor, often based on little evidence. I think The Man from the Train got caught committing some petty crime (perhaps breaking into the home of a prospective victim), spent perhaps eighteen months on a chain gang, and decided that he had had enough of the South.

Of the thirty-three things that identify a crime committed or possibly committed by The Man from the Train, at least twenty-five can be seen in both the South and in the cross-country crime series. But perhaps the largest and most notable change that occurred at this time was not in what the vile little man did, but in what is known about the crimes.

When The Man from the Train committed murders in isolated areas of the South, little information about the crime permeated the nation's consciousness. Beginning with the murder of the Meadows family, this no longer was true. The North was very different from the South in terms of newspaper coverage and literacy, and 1911 was

355

very different from 1903 in terms of the organization of the wire services and newspaper syndicates. The combination of these two factors shined a bright light onto incidents post-1909 which were objectively similar to events that had gone almost entirely unreported pre-1909. Hurley was a rugged, isolated, inaccessible mountain enclave with no telephone. (The nearest telephone was in Grundy, Virginia, sixteen miles south.) But while the newspapers wrote about how difficult it was to get information about Hurley or to get information out of Hurley, the fact is that hundreds of newspaper stories about the murders in Hurley were published and can be found online today. With the exception of Byers, Pennsylvania (the Zoos family), and, to a lesser extent, with the exception of Rainier, Washington (the Cobles), that was always true from 1909 on.

Let me tell you what I think happened in Hurley. This involves speculation, but . . . nobody knows; you can have a speculative explanation, or you can have no explanation; it's up to you. First, I absolutely believe that The Man from the Train committed this crime. It is too good a match for the other southern crimes for that not to be true, in my opinion, and also (b) the case against Howard Little seems to me to be flimsy, and (c) the case seems to be almost certainly connected to the murders of the Hood family, six weeks later and eighty miles away.

I believe that the fiend was hiding out in an outbuilding or in the cornfield next to the Meadows house. He had been there since dusk. As he approached the house the dogs began to bark. No source says so, but the Meadows family had to have hunting dogs; I just can't see a family like this *not* having hunting dogs. It wasn't reported because it was taken for granted.

When the dogs wouldn't stop barking, George Meadows stumbled outside half dressed, probably carrying a pistol in his right hand and a lantern in his left. (I didn't spell this out in the opening chapter on this case, but Meadows came out of the house with one shoe on and one shoe off, wearing overalls with one suspender fastened and one not.) It was an overcast night, as dark as the inside of a closet. The lantern in Meadows's hand gave The Man from the Train a tremendous advantage; it illuminated his target. He attacked Meadows from behind, hit him in the head with the axe, and took the pistol and the lantern. (The fact of Meadows being hit from behind with the axe is not supposition. That was reported.)

The dogs barked furiously. The Man from the Train waited quietly for perhaps fifteen or twenty minutes, waiting to see whether another light would come on inside the house, waiting to see whether anyone was stirring around in the night. After a few minutes the dogs went quiet, more terrified than on sentry duty. The women and children in the house, hearing nothing except the dogs, drifted back to sleep, except for the two-year old. The body of the two-year-old boy was found in the doorway, leading to all manner of interpretation as to how he came to be there.

After the crime was over inside the house, The Man from the Train returned to Meadows's body and discovered to his surprise that Meadows was not quite dead. Dying but not dead, Meadows had pulled a pencil out of his pocket in a futile effort to leave a message about his attacker. (Meadows's body was found with a pencil in his hand. I grew up among farmers who wore overalls 365 days a year. They almost always carried a pencil in the breast pocket of their overalls.) The murderer put two bullets into Meadows's torso, hit him in the throat with the axe, picked up the lantern, jammed the pistol in his pocket, and headed down the road toward the railroad station. The fire was first seen by neighbors a little after 1:00 a.m.—100 percent consistent with the normal time frame of The Man from the Train. For reasons that are not clear the neighbors were slow to raise an alarm, and there was no real effort to extinguish the flames until the house had burned out.

If you have ever walked on a mountain road in pitch blackness you know how treacherous that can be, so The Man from the Train carried the lantern with him until he got back to the railroad line, then set it down on the roadway and abandoned it, still burning. Howard Little had been with his lover, Mrs. Mary Stacy, or perhaps with some other woman, never identified. Now it's 2:00 a.m., later, maybe; he is walking home in the dark, and . . . here's a lantern burning in the middle of the road. Weird. He picks up the lantern, looks around for its owner, perhaps calls out "Anybody there?" No one answers. He is not the most honest man in the county; he decides to take the lantern and goes on home. He does not know it, but the moment he picks up that lantern, he is a dead man. He has put into motion the sequence of events that will lead to his execution. He stumbles into his house and sleeps the rest of the night on the couch (a fact testified to at his trial).

By the time he wakes up and stirs around in the morning, the town is buzzing with the news of the Meadows family murders. He is expecting to go to work, but the Ritter Lumber Mill has shut down to allow the workers to participate in the manhunt. He begins to worry about the lantern, so oddly left burning in the middle of the road, and he looks it over. He sees blood on the lantern. Now he is *really* worried. He tries to clean the blood off the lantern. He does some yard work, puts the lantern in the barn where he hopes and expects that no one will find it.

Just my opinion, but I don't believe that Howard Little had any intention of leaving his wife and running away with Mary Stacy. He *told* Mrs. Stacy that he was going to do that, yes, but men like Howard Little say things like that. It is reported everywhere in connection with this crime that Little had given Mrs. Stacy $20 to buy a new dress, just days (or the day) before the murders. But he had been giving her money regularly for four years. He was just stringing Mrs. Stacy along. It could have gone on that way indefinitely had not fate intervened, but now there was this crisis; there were these horrible murders, and Howard Little had blundered into the middle of them. All of the tensions inherent in deceit came suddenly to a boil. His wife has reached that moment that happens at the end of a marriage, at which she believes to be true of her husband every evil and wicked thing that you can say about a person, that there is no terrible act which is beyond him. His mistress knows, as soon as he is arrested, that it is all over between them, and that it has not ended the way she had been promised that it would end, and now she is as angry as the wife.

The murders happened on a Tuesday night. Mr. and Mrs. Little spent Wednesday night in their bedroom together but without sleeping, having the longest and most terrible argument of their lives (this also was testified to in the trial). Hurley is in that triangle in far western Virginia where, if you go five miles west you are in Kentucky, but if you go a few miles east you are in West Virginia. After another bad night and a drop-by visit from private investigators, Howard Little decides that it might be in his best interests to leave town, but he is too late. As he heads east into West Virginia his wife is talking to investigators. A telegraph passes over his head, and Little is arrested by a group of five armed men as soon as he hits town.

When it becomes known that Little has been arrested in connection with the murders, rumors begin to swirl around Hurley. People begin to say things about Howard Little, damaging things. It's just talk. Most of the testimony that will be introduced against him at trial is rumors and gossip, but by picking up the lantern he has created actual evidence against himself. He has a cut on his leg, which the prosecutors will insist must have occurred during the murders.

I mentioned that the private detectives who arrested Little were headquartered in Bluefield, West Virginia. The *Bluefield Times* on September 28, 1909, reported or alleged:

Little is a man of unsavory reputation, having killed a man in Pike County, Kentucky, for which he served four years and was pardoned by the governor. It is said that he is seldom engaged in any honest employment, and that he has been implicated in countless bootlegging transactions. He vibrates among the three states, Kentucky, West Virginia and Virginia, as the exigencies of the law demand.

You can see how fairly Little was being treated? "It is said" that he is seldom engaged in any honest employment; in fact he had been regularly employed for many years, and was the shift foreman of the town's largest employer. Bootlegging, really? Every male in that county had been involved in countless bootlegging transactions, including the ministers; I exaggerate, but not by much. The people of that area *then and now* distill their own alcohol, and deeply resent the efforts of outsiders to regulate the sale and distribution. They'll buy their beer from the store, sure, maybe their whiskey, too—but moonshine is a tradition, not a commodity. Rachel was married in the mountains in Virginia in 2011, and moonshine was passed around at the wedding dance. And as to the claim that Little bounced from state to state "as the exigencies of the law demand": it's five miles from Hurley into Kentucky on one side, West Virginia on the other. Everybody in the area crossed state lines routinely, going to church or the store or visiting relatives.

We know that Little had substantial real property. We know that he had cows; we know that only because Ms. Lee alleged that on the morning after the murders he went out and did yard work first, whereas he normally milked the cows first thing in the morning. The lumber mill was closed for the day, giving him space to do things a little differently than he normally would. We know that he had sheep; we know that only because the private investigators who came to his house on the day before he was arrested used a pretext that they wanted to talk to him about buying some sheep. We know that he had or had control of some land, because his explanation for the cut on his leg was that he had cut it days earlier while chopping down a pine tree on his property. This is why I am skeptical that Little was actually going to run away with Mary Stacy; he would have been giving up a lot. He would be giving up a wife, four kids, cows, sheep, and a good job, to run away with a woman that he had been involved with for four years. It doesn't seem likely.

It is said to be evidence against Little that his jacket was damp on the morning after the murders, as if he had washed it and hung it up to dry. Did these people have any idea a) how much blood you would have on your jacket if you wore the jacket while murdering six people with an axe, or b) how difficult it is to wash blood out of a wool jacket?

No, they didn't. I am not putting them down for not understanding those things; they had never been involved in anything like this before. They didn't have any concept of how much blood would fly if you hit somebody in the head with an axe. The Baldwin-Felts Agency manufactured a case against Howard Little, not intentionally, not maliciously, but they had to convict somebody in order to claim the reward. Their first step was to check out the known criminals in the area, and they had a hit. Howard Little's alibi was weak, and he had stumbled home with a lantern that might have come from the crime scene.

His angry wife jumped feet-first into the case against him, making allegation after allegation. From then on, everything became evidence against him. Perhaps his mistress could have testified that he was with her, but she was a married woman. Is she really going to testify that he was with her at the time of the crime? Almost certainly the investigators told her that he had plenty of time to have committed the crime after he left her bed. The case against Little comes down to five things:

1. The earlier murder conviction,

2. The lantern, which may or may not have come from the Meadows house; when the prosecution puts on more than twenty witnesses to testify that they recognize a lantern, that rather seems like too many,

3. The cut on his leg, which may or may not be related to the crime; 99.99 percent of people who have cuts on their leg did not incur them while committing murder,

4. The fact that he was away from his house on the night in question, and no one would provide an alibi for him, and

5. The angry allegations of his wife, which were repeated endlessly in the newspapers, although she did not testify in court.

Howard Little was a man of substance, but not a man of character. He had been a United States marshal earlier in his life, and he was the shift foreman at the lumber mill. He was the boss; not the big boss back in the office, but the guy out on the floor that you didn't give any crap to. But, given his character flaws, why should we reject the notion that he might actually have committed this crime?

Little's earlier murder happened when he was a young man, almost a boy, and it was essentially a fight over a woman. I am not suggesting that it doesn't count against him; when you are convicted of one murder, certainly that counts against you when we are considering another. But young people in love are crazy or half-crazy anyway, most of them, and that was a violent time and place, the mountains of eastern Kentucky in 1892. The earlier murder happened in the same time and place as the feud between the Hatfields and McCoys. A lot of people got killed over there, and many of the murders were never prosecuted, or even really investigated. It was backcountry, mountain country, an area too rugged for the trains to get to, in the years before electricity or telephones or automobiles. People settled their business without recourse to the law, although sometimes the law interfered.

This place, Hurley, is somewhat different, much the same, and this time period, 1909, is somewhat different. But this crime is really, really different. This crime is the work of a person who is truly depraved. If you hit small children in the head with an axe, you don't have "character flaws": you are a depraved degenerate sociopath. Howard Little, for all of his flaws, was not a depraved degenerate sociopath. And he has no motive that we know of to have committed such a crime. His wife claimed that he had stolen money in the crime and that she could lead the sheriff to the money, but she failed to deliver. There is no money; there is no motive. In order to believe that he committed this crime, we have to believe that this man who had a nice house and a good job and a wife and four kids and a girlfriend on the side, we have to believe that he suddenly decided, for no known reason, to commit this despicable crime. I don't believe it. I'll leave it up to you to decide what you believe, but I don't believe it.

He was not the first person executed for a crime committed by The Man from the Train. And he may not have been the last.

CHAPTER XXXVI

# Beckley and Beyond

The offer of a $1,000 reward by the county court served to redouble the efforts of those gentlemen with Sherlock Holmes propensities, but all of their time and talents have been used to no purpose.

—*Raleigh Register*, November 25, 1909

From Hurley, Virginia, to Beckley, West Virginia, is eighty-two miles of mountains. After the murders in Hurley, The Man from the Train would have jumped the first train that came through, whether heading north or south. It seems obvious that it was headed south. If he went south, he could have reached Beckley in a fairly short loop; in fact, if you google driving directions from Hurley to Beckley today, the quickest way is to head south to get out of the mountains, drive east fifteen to twenty miles on level ground, and then head back north. If he headed north out of Hurley, on the other hand, then it requires a much longer, wider loop to get over to Beckley.

The murders of the Hood family took place on Halloween night, 1909, a month and ten days after the murders of the Meadowses. At this point we have to consider the possible significance of the calendar. The association of Halloween with criminal mischief, sometimes dark criminal mischief, did not begin with Michael Myers and the

1978 film. They've been connected for hundreds of years. It is more accurate to say that the modern Halloween is a sanitized, child-friendly version of the traditional Halloween than it is to suggest the opposite. It is possible that the first real "pattern" crime committed by The Man from the Train, the murder of the Kelly or Caffey family in 1903, was committed on Halloween; if not on Halloween, it was within a day or two of Halloween. For whatever that is worth, he also committed a crime on Friday the thirteenth.

In general, we do not think it likely that The Man from the Train was calendar-focused or calendar-driven. He was a drifter; not a hobo, but he did not live a settled life. To be directed by the calendar is characteristic of an orderly life.

Still, you have to wonder. We can be fairly certain that he was focused on Sundays; the number of attacks occurring on Sundays is obviously high. That's the calendar.

Let's say that there were thirty crimes. We would expect, at random, that there would be one date that would repeat in the thirty crimes—one. In fact, there are several. Two events occurred on September 21: September 21, 1905, and September 21, 1909. Two murders were committed on February 7 (February 7, 1905, and February 7, 1906), and the Villisca murders were committed on the first anniversary of the Hill family murders, near Portland, Oregon. The murders in Paola, Kansas, were committed on the second anniversary of the murders of the Hardy family in Marshalltown, Iowa. This is a suggestion, not a statement, but it is possible that these dates had some significance to him.

The Man from the Train committed or may have committed crimes in Texas and along the KATY railroad in April of 1908, March of 1910, and March of 1911. That was his time of year to be in Texas; that was where his seasonal work patterns took him.

Halloween, of course, is sometimes called the Night of Shadows. Shade and shadow, as concepts, have tremendously pliable metaphorical value. The transitory dimensions of darkness can be cast on anything just for being near another object, and then it's gone and it was never there.

Today to "shade" means to insult someone by phrasing it as an innocent observation *or* by not directly mentioning the subject of the insult. In the first decade of the twentieth century, it often referred to what we'd call ghosts. Ghosts haunt all stories of murders, following up the facts with their apparitions in oral narratives around the campfire, cable television con jobs, and horror tourism.

A few chapters ago, you read a ridiculous story about a man believing a mule spoke to him. In a few more chapters, there will be stories of voodoo for the purpose of covering up crimes. If you've heard of this series of crimes before, it may be because of cable channel ghost investigations of the former Moore home in Villisca. But you will find no night-vision camera ghost stories in this narrative. This is about real people who died violently, and a man whose life mission was to eliminate those lives.

In 1909 black people were also called "shades"; that was a relatively benign derogatory term for black people, Shades. The apparently not-too-whippy detectives from Beckley, after a few weeks, consulted a psychic to help them solve the crime. Who did she blame for the murders of the Hood family? Black people, of course.

We mentioned that fact in chapter II of this book, but it didn't mean to you then what it means now. Black people were lynched—murdered—for crimes almost certainly committed by The Man from the Train in Statesboro, Georgia, in 1904, in Salisbury, North Carolina, in 1906, and possibly, although less definitively, in Frazier, Georgia, in 1908. Unidentified black men were assumed to be responsible for the murders in probably a dozen other cases. This was a potentially deadly charge.

We mentioned in passing that Beckley investigators consulted a psychic named Elizabeth Blake. That's actually a rather remarkable story. In 1907 a businessman from Oklahoma, David Abbott, wrote a best-selling book called *Behind the Scenes with the Mediums*. The point of the book was to expose the tricks and deceptions used by psychics to bamboozle people.

In 1908 he wrote a follow-up book, *The History of a Strange Case*, and for this one he visited Elizabeth Blake, intending to expose her as well—and she beat him. He wound up concluding—and writing—that she was a genuine psychic. Abbott claimed that he asked her nineteen questions to which she could not possibly know the answers, and voices in the room answered all nineteen questions correctly—in daylight, and in multiple places.

But when it came to revealing the murderers, who did George Hood's ghost reveal? Nameless black men. Real useful, Elizabeth.

\*    \*    \*

After the Logan's Turnpike murders the next crime in the series is the murders of the Schultz family in Houston Heights, Texas. To refresh your memory, this is the case in which a twenty-one-year-old married woman, Alice Schultz, had been juggling a couple of extra men. Alice, her husband, her two children, and one of her side pieces were found murdered in a three-room shack by the railroad track in Houston Heights, Texas; see chapter III. The sheriff who investigated the Schultz murders, Archie Anderson, realized early in the investigation that the crime had to have been committed by a maniac from the railroad; nothing else made sense. Later, though, he got so distracted by the stories of Alice Schultz's interesting love life that he ginned up an obviously bogus prosecution of Sandy Sheffield, one of the men who was involved with her.

Early in the book, I wrote the story of the Schultz murders in understated terms, because I was afraid that what happened to Sheriff Anderson would happen to the readers: you would get so distracted by the stories about who Alice was screwing that you'd lose focus on the real evidence. But as long as you don't do that, it's actually obvious that this crime is a part of the series, rather than having had anything to do with Alice's amours.

Both the Schultz and Hood family murders hit all of the major checkmarks:

- A family was murdered
- Late at night
- With an axe
- Very near to a railroad
- With no evidence of a robbery
- Entirely without context in the sense of any rational explanation for the crime
- In both cases a prepubescent female was among the victims.

The victims were struck with the *blunt* side of the axe (or some other bludgeon), and neither crime was ever solved. In addition to those facts, the Hood family murders are tied to the series by their close connection in time and place to the Meadows family murders, and the Schultz family murders show the characteristic traits of the house being locked up tight and with all of the window shades pulled so tightly shut that it was entirely impossible to peek in the windows, and also of the heads of the victims being covered with cloth.

In both the Hood and Schultz cases, the bodies were "stacked" in one room, although at least some of the murders were committed in a different room, and in both cases the murder weapon was *not* left exactly at the scene of the crime. In both cases the victims were white but were living very near to black neighborhoods.

However, there is a meaningful "pattern break" between these two crimes. The Meadows and Hood murders are a transition out of the "southern" crime series, but are still connected to that series.

The houses were rural or semirural. The houses were set on fire after the crime was committed.

Although Texas is still sort of a southern state, and Houston is as far south as Jacksonville, the Hood murders in West Virginia represent the absolute end of the "southern" crime series, and the Schultz murders in Houston Heights represent the beginning of the cross-country crime spree. After Houston Heights, the crimes are generally *in* small towns, rather than just outside small towns. The houses are locked up tight and the windows completely covered, but the houses are not (usually) set on fire. The pace of the murders quickens dramatically; he goes from one or two crimes a year to a crime every few weeks. The victims are not as carefully selected as they were in the past. His routines become more obvious. Probably they become more obvious because he is not burning up the houses anymore, so we have more ability to study the crime scenes after the fact.

Beginning with the Hood family murders, we see a new pattern emerging. The victims are almost always entertaining guests on the night they are murdered. This is true of the Hoods and Schultzes; it is also true of the Casaways, the Moores (Villisca), the Hudsons (Paola), the Burnhams (Colorado Springs), and probably in other cases as well.

We believe that early in his run The Man from the Train was researching and preselecting his victims, but that by late 1909 he was just hopping off the train and picking a house. Probably he went skulking around the neighborhood for a couple of hours in the darkness or near-darkness, and when he saw a door open and people coming and going, lights on, that gave him a sense of who was in that house. That was a targeting mechanism.

By 1910 The Man from the Train was forty-five to fifty years old. He was getting careless, yes, but he was also a very *experienced* murderer. He could be more aggressive. Probably by this time he was dropping clean clothes where he could get to them after the event. At least sometimes he carried a gun that he could use if he had to use it, although he preferred not to. The connection of the crimes to lumber regions becomes less obvious, although several of the crimes are still committed in lumbering areas.

It doesn't look like he is putting down shallow roots anymore; it looks like he is just blowing into town, committing the murders, and getting back on the train. Still, the pattern of the crimes being committed on weekends and particularly on Sunday nights—while that pattern stretches back to the beginning of the series—becomes more obvious and more consistent beginning with the Hood family, and that fact suggests that he was still working during the week, although he must have been changing jobs more frequently than he had before.

*　*　*

While we feel that the Hood and Schultz murders were clearly committed by this villain, we could not say the same about the next two crimes in the series, the Hardy family murders near Marshalltown, Iowa, on June 5, 1910, and the Hubbell family murders, in Barnard, Missouri. Both murders could be a part of the series but might not be (and we are passing over here the Zoos family murders, which we believe were not him).

We feel strongly that Raymond Hardy did not murder his family near Marshalltown, but was falsely accused by a sheriff who was using a hammer to make the puzzle pieces fit together. However, the Hardy family murders deviate from the patterns of The Man from the Train in several important respects. The Hardy family murders are farther from the railroad track than any other murders discussed in this book, other than the Pfanschmidt murders and the murders in Woodland Mills, Alabama. The murder weapon was not actually an axe, and the murders did not take place in the middle of the night. The family was attacked while they were up and active, which would be atypical for The Man from the Train. There are no children among the victims.

None of that proves absolutely that it isn't him. He was certainly capable of wandering three or four miles away from the railroad track, and might have done so. The murder weapon was not an axe, but it was a heavy bludgeon of about the same size, and it was a weapon of opportunity, as The Man from the Train always used. They didn't happen to have an axe around, so he used something else; it's not a big deal. The manner of the attacks, each victim being hit in the top of the head from behind, is the same as the other cases. By 1910 The Man from the Train had a well-established pattern of attacking in the middle of the night, but there were other cases in which farmers were attacked while going about their evening chores.

But there is evidence of "taunting" or "warning" behavior here. It is believed that someone saddled and bridled the Hardy family's horse, without their knowledge, on the day before the crime. The Man from the Train never, ever gave any other family a warning shot like that. He always struck out of the blue, with no warning whatsoever.

Again, doesn't absolutely mean it isn't him. There are also numerous elements of the Hardy murders that are consistent with the series of crimes. There are two other possibilities. First, this may have been The Man from the Train, but it may have been an unplanned and unexpected event from his standpoint—almost an accident, as he would see it. He may have been hiding out in the Hardy family barn, just waiting out the weekend, perhaps planning to steal their horse, when he may have been discovered and confronted by Mr. Hardy, and then he murdered the family just more or less on autopilot. And second, it may have been The Man from the Train, but he may have had a partner in that crime. Several crimes in 1910 to 1911 have the appearance of being *almost* The Man from the Train but not quite. Something is going on there that we don't quite understand.

Whoever murdered the Hardy family in June of 1910 almost certainly also murdered the Bernhardt family in December of 1910. Those two crimes seem to be definitively linked together. However, whether those crimes were committed by The Man from the Train or some other nefarious actor, or by The Man from the Train in combination with some other nefarious actor, we do not know.

# CHAPTER XXXVII

# The Zoos and the Hubbells

Between the murders of the Hardy family and the Bernhardt family are the murders of the Zoos and Hubbell families, stories that I mentioned, but did not detail, during our first chronological pass through this time period.

The Zoos family was murdered with an axe on September 20, 1910, near Byers, Pennsylvania. Byers was a little railroad village west of Philadelphia and a mining town, much like many of our other crime scenes. John Zoos, a Polish immigrant, worked in a plumbago mine, got home about dusk, found his family murdered. (The word *plumbago* is now used only for a flowering plant. A hundred years ago, however, it was primarily used for graphite.) There is a low probability that the crime is related because it occurred in daylight and may have been a robbery. The crime, which involved the deaths of three people, appears never to have been seriously investigated and was absolutely and completely forgotten within a year.

\* \* \*

The family of Oda (Odell) Hubbell was murdered exactly two months later, on Sunday night, November 20, 1910. On February 9, 1911, a man named Hez Rasco was convicted of murdering Oda Hubbell.

As was the custom of the time, Rasco was charged with only one of the murders as a hedge against double jeopardy; had he been acquitted of that murder, he could still have been charged with any of the other three, as was done to Ray Pfanschmidt. Rasco was convicted, sentenced to death, and appealed his conviction to the circuit court.

The circuit court, in their ruling, did a marvelous job of summarizing the case, and I am going to quote from their ruling at length here, not only so you get to hear a voice other than mine telling you about this crime, but also because there are discrepancies between the court's summary of the facts and what is in the newspapers, and we can assume the court's opinion to be accurate:

The deceased, Oda Hubbell, 30 years old, lived with his wife and two small children in a cottage about two miles distant from the town of Guilford, in Nodaway County. On Sunday evening, November 20, 1910, this cottage was burned, and with it the bodies of the deceased, his wife and two children. The children were nearly consumed; nothing being found save some of their bones. The deceased and wife were partly burned. He had been shot in the head, and the wife's head had been crushed by a blow.

The state gave in evidence tending to prove the following facts: During Saturday night, November 19th, preceding the homicide, the deceased, the defendant, and one Wallace were playing poker for money in a box car in Guilford. Wallace went home at midnight. Deceased and defendant continued the game until 6:30 Sunday morning, soon after which they separated; deceased going to his home. On this occasion deceased exhibited to defendant a large roll of bills, amounting to $300 or $400. Deceased spent a portion of Sunday visiting his father, who lived nearby, exhibiting there the roll of bills and also a handful of silver money. That evening, at about 6:30 or 7:00, two gunshots, in quick succession, were heard in the vicinity of the home of the deceased, followed shortly by two more, muffled in sound. Later, about 10 o'clock that Sunday night, neighbors saw the cottage in flames. Those first on the ground saw, through the window, the body of deceased lying on the floor, burning fiercely. Later, an empty coal oil jug was found near it. Outside, at one corner of the house, was a pool of blood, and indications showing that a body had been dragged from thence into the house. Near the pool was found an empty shotgun shell. In the ruins of the house were found the remains of Mrs. Hubbell and the two children. The hands of Mrs. Hubbell were burned off. Around one arm was the telephone wire, and lying near, the telephone receiver. Her head had been crushed in by a blow from a blunt instrument. The back bones and some rib bones only of the children were found. A charge of shot had entered the head of the deceased, and some of the shot and the wadding of the shell were extracted therefrom. No silver money was found.

The defendant, on the morning of that day, borrowed a gun from one Cayton, also some cartridges which corresponded exactly with the one found at the pool of blood. The gun was found a few days later in the hayloft at defendant's home, with some foreign substance dried upon the stock, which substance contained blood, but not shown to be human blood. On Sunday afternoon defendant was seen near the Hubbell home, and seeking to avoid observation. At the edge of the pool of blood alluded to was observed a heel print in the mud, made by the right heel of a shoe. The heel print faced away from the house, was sunk in the mud, and indicated, it was thought, that it was made by a person who was braced and pulling toward the house. The mark indicated that the heel had three tacks or nails on each side and one in the middle, also that the inside corner of the heel was worn down, and that it was the heel of the right shoe. The next day, Monday, about noon, two bloodhounds, in charge of their master, arrived, and were put upon the scent from this heel track. Proceeding from this heel mark the trail, although broken at one point, led the dogs to the home of defendant and into his bedroom, where were found a pair of his shoes. The heel of the right shoe corresponded to the heel mark described above, being worn down at the corner, and showing the seven nails arranged as shown in the track. There was also found in the room a pair of overalls, which the defendant admitted to the sheriff, as the latter testified, were worn by him on Sunday night. A chemical examination showed that certain spots on the overalls were human blood.

The defendant, testifying in his own behalf, admitted the card playing in the box car. His story is that on Sunday morning he borrowed the shotgun and shells from Cayton, went hunting, returned about 11 o'clock in the forenoon, attempted to return the gun, knocked at Cayton's door, and, no one responding, he left the gun on the porch. The Caytons testify that they were at home at the time defendant claimed to have called, but heard no knock and saw no one, although the upper part of the door was of glass, and that they could have both seen and heard defendant had he been there. Defendant says that after this he went by train, about noon, to Ravenwood, a town 12 or 15 miles distant, and returned home about 3 o'clock on Monday morning, spending the interval in Ravenwood. He produced no substantial evidence to corroborate this story, and was contradicted in several particulars by witnesses for the state. He claimed that he went to Ravenwood to collect a poker debt from a man whom he failed to find, and waited about the station until he took the return train. He said that the blood found on the overalls came from his nose during the card game. He admitted former convictions for murder in the second degree and grand larceny. Other facts will appear in the opinion.

OK, that's a pretty solid case against Hez Rasco, real name Hezekiah, right? It is. Sometimes prosecutors become convinced that they know what happened when they don't, but I don't fundamentally question that Rasco murdered the Hubbell family. But there are nine things about this case that bug me, and I've got to tell you about them. The big one is number nine, so stay with me a moment.

First, the image of two men and only two sitting for six and a half hours in an empty box car on a side rail in the middle of the night in November playing poker for money seems to be so out of the ordinary that I find it difficult to give it complete credence. I've been involved in a lot of poker games; I've never known two guys who would do that, I don't think. Four guys or five guys, maybe, but not two.

Second, accepting that this happened, I can't get out of my head the image of The Man from the Train, watching them unseen from a dark box car nearby, and following them at dawn when they go back to their houses.

Third, Hez Rasco was Oda Hubbell's best friend. He had been to the Hubbell house many times; thus, the bloodhounds finding a trail from Hubbell's house to Rasco's is not (in itself) evidence.

Fourth, while I accept that this is an unrelated crime, for an unrelated crime it sure has a lot of odd similarities to our cases—the crime happening on a Sunday night, the house being set on fire at the conclusion of the crime, the use of coal oil (kerosene) to build the fire, the dragging of the man's body *into* the house for no obvious reason. There are other crimes in our series in which the man of the house was shot, while the women and children were bludgeoned to death, as seems to have happened here. One of the victims in this crime was an eight-year-old girl named Jessie Hubbell.

Fifth, less than three weeks later and about 115 miles due south of Guilford, the Bernhardt family was murdered. The Man from the Train at this time of the year would be heading south.

Sixth—acknowledging that points five and six overlap and are not entirely separate—there are a set of four crimes that form a perfect hand-in-glove, tongue-and-groove chronological and geographic pattern: the Hardy family murders, the Hubbells, the Bernhardts, and the Casaways. If you take the dates of those murders and put pushpins in a map representing where the crimes occurred, it could not possibly fit together any better.

The murder of an entire family is a rare crime. It just seems odd to me that this family murder (a) happened so close in time and place to an unsolved crime, and (b) fits so perfectly into the time-and-space pattern formed by the other three crimes.

Seventh, this crime is often described as occurring in Maryville, Missouri, where Rasco was tried and convicted; the crime actually happened near another small town.

Maryville, Missouri, is closely connected to Villisca. From Maryville to Villisca is fifty miles almost straight north. The bloodhounds who followed a trail to Rasco's house were the very same bloodhounds who were called to Villisca, the Nofzinger bloodhounds of Beatrice, Nebraska. The river that runs through Villisca, Iowa, is the Nodaway River; this crime happened in Nodaway County, Missouri. A railroad line ran from Maryville to Villisca. I don't mean that it ran *through* Maryville and Villisca; I mean that it started in Maryville and ended in Villisca, or started in Villisca and ended in Maryville, whichever way you want to look at it. To the people of Villisca it was known as the Maryville train; to the people of Maryville it was known as the Iowa train or the Villisca train. I find that an odd coincidence under the circumstances.

Eighth, in what was described as an irony, but might alternatively be described as a conflict of interest, the judge who presided at Rasco's trial was the lawyer who had defended him when he was on trial for the earlier murder.

Ninth, the sheriff who investigated the Hubbell family murders was a man named W. R. Tilson, who would lose his campaign for reelection as sheriff. He then ran for and won election as Nodaway County treasurer.

And who would you guess should turn up in the middle of the fraudulent prosecution of William Mansfield, in Villisca, but W. R. Tilson, county treasurer of Nodaway County, Missouri? Tilson popped up in 1916 in Villisca, telling a story that was so weird and convoluted that nobody believed it. His story was that someone, whom he believed to be William Mansfield, had come to the county treasurer's office in Maryville, unannounced, asking if someone from Villisca had left an envelope of money for him with the county treasurer. Villisca in 1916 was a weird and confusing place, and lots of people believed lots of weird and confusing stories, but nobody believed *that one*.

Tilson had become one of J. N. Wilkerson's stooges. But if Tilson was willing to participate in the fraudulent prosecution of Mansfield and Jones in Villisca, don't we have to worry about the integrity of the case that he created against Hezekiah Rasco? Isn't it possible that what happened here was the same thing that happened to Howard Little, that the investigation focused on him immediately because of his prior murder conviction, and that the rest of the case against him was manufactured?

In order to believe that Hez Rasco was innocent, one has to believe that he was deliberately framed by the police. There is sufficient evidence to convince us that Rasco is guilty, *unless that evidence was manufactured and planted by the police.* While police often make damaging mistakes, I think we can generally reject the notion that a small-town sheriff has deliberately manufactured evidence—but Tilson's participation in J. N. Wilkerson's Villisca fraud makes that more believable than it otherwise would be. But in the end, I think we have to accept that the murder of the Hubbells is an unrelated case.

The appeals court rejected Rasco's motion for a new trial, and he was executed by the state of Missouri on March 26, 1912. Winifred Bonfils (Winifred Black), a famous reporter for the Hearst newspapers, interviewed Rasco in his jail cell and wrote the following:

Young, slim, erect, square shouldered, sleek haired, as well
groomed apparently as any club man, his hands carefully
manicured . . . as vibrant with life as an electric engine, and
as full of subtle, quick agility and grace as a cat.

Where in the world did he, a farmer's boy, born almost
in the cornfields and brought up almost at the tail of a
plow, ever get the quick, springing tread of an Indian and
the square shoulders and set of the head of a West Pointer?

Rasco was a voracious reader; he explained his educated appearance
by the fact that he had read so many books. His favorite book was
Victor Hugo's *Les Misérables*, which he said that he had read many
times. Rasco insisted until the moment he was executed that he was
innocent. He was baptized the day before his execution. The minister
wanted to bring a water tank into the prison for the baptism, but
the sheriff, fearing that Rasco would drown himself in the tank, refused to allow it, so Rasco was baptized in a bathtub in the women's
section of the prison at Maryville, where he was to be hanged. As he
completed the baptism, Rasco said he forgave those who had falsely
accused him of the murder.

Rasco left a letter, to be opened by his minister after his death. It
was widely expected that this would include a posthumous confession,
but it did not; instead, Rasco thanked the minister and others for
their comfort to him as a condemned man, and warned young men
to stay away from gambling and liquor.

*   *   *

On June 10, 1913, Arthur Kellar and his daughter, Margaret, were
murdered, probably with an axe, in Harrisonville, Missouri. The
authors are satisfied that this murder had nothing to do with our case.

# CHAPTER XXXVIII

# Clementine Barnabet

Eleven black families were murdered in Texas, Louisiana, and Mississippi in 1911 and 1912, mostly—or entirely—with an axe. We are not going to tell you about all of those crimes in any detail, because the last few are not relevant to our story, but it is a remarkable number. In this era there were about eight families (or substantial portions of families) murdered per year in the United States. Prorate that to three states and two years, it comes out to one expected event.

These murders are known as the Clementine Barnabet Murders or the Church of Sacrifice Murders. We wrote earlier (chapter V) about the New Orleans Axeman—also in Louisiana, also active in 1911 and 1912. But it is easy to see that the murders committed by The Man from the Train and the New Orleans Axeman are different and not related. With the Clementine Barnabet Murders, it is not as easy to dismiss the possibility of some confusion between the two. It is our opinion that at least two and possibly as many as four of the Texas/ Louisiana murders were actually committed by The Man from the Train, although most of the crimes were committed by other persons.

November 12, 1909, was a Friday. About 1:00 a.m. on November 13, neighbors heard screams coming from the house of Edna

Opelousas in Rayne, Louisiana. Running to her defense, they found Ms. Opelousas dead from a blow by an axe. Her three children (aged four to nine) were still alive, but all had been mortally wounded. The murderer(s) had escaped.

(Edna's actual name may have been Edmee. Census records show an Edmee Opelousas, born in Louisiana in April 1882, who had three younger sisters. If this is she, then she had probably never been married. We're going to call her Edmee going forward.)

A man named George Washington was arrested on the morning of the murders on suspicion of having some connection to the crime, and, later on, his wife and daughter were arrested as well. His release was not noted by as many newspapers, although he must have been released. The Rayne city marshal told the press that

- The victims had been stabbed with a knife as well as hit in the head with an axe,
- He (the marshal) was in possession of the knife, and
- He was headed to Crowley, where he believed the knife had come from, to try to identify the knife's owner.

Ho—Kay. Not sure how you can tell where a knife came from like that. The main point there is the multiple weapons. Multiple weapons almost certainly indicate multiple murderers.

Crowley and Rayne were just a few miles apart, almost walking distance. In the 1880s the towns were about the same size and had been rivals in pursuit of the position of the parish seat of Acadia Parish. Crowley won the battle, and since then had grown to be the larger town. A man named Houston Goodwill was arrested the following week. Goodwill was married to one of Edmee's younger sisters and had been kicked out of the house a couple of weeks before in a domestic dispute.

A chilling fact for you. The Man from the Train's previous murder, on Halloween 1909, was in Beckley, West Virginia. His next murder, in March of 1910, was in Houston Heights, Texas. If you go on a mapping service today and ask for directions from Beckley, West Virginia, to Houston Heights, Texas, the route will send you directly through Rayne, Louisiana. Look at it this way: the mapping service will *not* send you through 99.9 percent of the little towns in America. It *will* send you through Rayne, Louisiana, as well as Crowley, Lafayette, and Lake Charles. Do the math—and the time frame is about right. The murders in Rayne were committed twelve days after the crime in West Virginia.

In spite of this, the indications that this was *not* The Man from the Train seem to outweigh the indications that it was. If there are multiple murderers here, then it isn't him. No one ever heard any of The Man from the Train's victims scream, in part because he preferred isolated houses, but mostly because he didn't stab people with knives before he hit them in the head with an axe. If you stab someone with a knife, they will scream; if you hit them in the head with an axe while they are asleep, they won't. Clementine Barnabet would later claim this crime as her own, but we will get to that later.

A year passes after the murders in Rayne.

On January 27, 1911, the *Galveston Daily News* reported in a front-page story that Walter Byers, his wife, and their child had been murdered in Crowley, Louisiana, it was believed, on January 24. The bodies were found on January 26, after the odor began to reach the neighbors. The Byerses were well-liked people and are not believed to have had any enemies.

Not a lot is known about this case. However, the facts that are clearly known are:

1.The Byers home was very close to a railroad switchyard used by at least six different railroad lines.

2. Someone broke into the Byers home through a back window,

3. And "brained" the family with an axe, according to the *Galves-*

*ton Daily News*. We assume from the use of the term "brained" that (a) they were hit in the head, and (b) the murderer used the blunt side of the axe.

4. The crime occurred while the family was asleep.

Why, then, isn't this a Man from the Train case?

Actually, it may be, and let me point out a few other things. According to Donna Fricker ("The Louisiana Lumber Boom, c. 1880–1925"), in 1910 Louisiana was the second-largest lumber-producing state in the United States. The lumber business swept through Louisiana at the end of the nineteenth century, cut down millions of acres of old trees, and had pretty much busted out by 1925.

Also, we know that The Man from the Train always went south in the winter, and this is January and thirty miles from the Gulf of Mexico. Crowley sets up from the Gulf of Mexico in exactly the same way as Marianna, Florida, and also Cottondale, Florida, and Milton, Florida. And I'm not done. The Man from the Train's next murder, the Casaway family, occurred two months later and in the next state over—The Man from the Train's normal time-and-distance gap.

OK, then, why *the hell* isn't this a Man from the Train case?

Because people have been writing for a hundred years that it's a Clementine Barnabet case; Clementine did confess to committing these murders, and we don't want to argue about it. However, if you back away from the assumption that this is a Clementine Barnabet case and just look logically at the question "Is this more like a Clementine Barnabet case or more like a Man from the Train case?" it is actually more like a Man from the Train case than a Clementine Barnabet case.

But in order for you to see that for yourself, we'll have to explain about Clementine. The region in which these murders occurred was populated by a mix of African American, creole, and Cajun peoples. All of the victims in this chapter are black except for Elizabeth Casaway. The black community was deeply shaken by the murder of this young family, the Byerses. The *Galveston Daily News* reported in a February 1 follow-up story that "leading negro citizens have held a mass meeting and adopted resolutions declaring that they will give every assistance in their power to help the officers in finding the guilty persons." Dozens of people were arrested and questioned by police, but the investigation ultimately went nowhere.

Just one month passes now.

On February 24, 1911, a family of four was murdered in Lafayette, Louisiana. From Crowley to Lafayette is just twenty-five miles. Although Lafayette is no longer in Acadia Parish, it's basically the same area. The Lafayette victims were Alexandre Andrus, his wife, Meme (or Mimi), and their two children, Joachin and Agnes. Joachin was three years old; Agnes was a baby, sleeping in a crib. The Andrus family lived in a cabin on Doucet Street in Lafayette, "isolated by its proximity to the river" and "just beyond the railroad-track where it crosses Vermilion street," according to the *Lafayette Advertiser*.

A man named "Dillon" wrote a book as a WPA project entitled *Conjure Ways: Louisiana Voodoo Outside New Orleans*. That book—like many other sources—*assumes* that these murders were somehow connected to voodoo, although there is basically no evidence for that proposition. Dillon records that the Andrus family was "quiet and respected." On the night of Thursday, February 23, 1911, the quiet and respected family was tucked in. Alexandre, Mimi, and Joachin shared a bed, with Agnes in a cradle nearby. Sometime well after midnight the family was murdered with the blade of an axe. Mimi's brother Lezime Felix was first to find the family. He brought the sheriff and coroner to their bodies, which were still warm. The discovery was recounted in court records by Mana Martin, Meme's mother:

I am the mother of Meme Andrus, and this morning about seven o'clock, I was told by my son, Lezime Felix, that my daughter Meme was murdered. I then came over to their house. I found all doors locked save the kitchen door. I found Alexandre Andrus, my daughter Meme, and their two children, all dead in bed in the positions found by the jury, and a bloody axe lying on the floor at the foot of the bed.

The positions referred to in her statement are surpassingly peculiar, and are the first indication that these murders had religious overtones. According to an article in the *Lafayette Advertiser* published several days later, "The man and woman were taken up by the murderer and placed on their knees beside the bed, the woman's arm over the man's shoulder, as if in the attitude of prayer. The baby was then placed beside the mother on the bed."

We have here several indications that this crime was not committed by The Man from the Train:

1. The crime occurred late in the night, apparently near morning (based on the fact that the bodies were still warm when they were found).

2. The murders were committed with the blade of the axe, rather than the blunt side of the axe.

3. A door was left open.

4. The bodies were posed as if praying or were murdered while they were actually praying, which is not something The Man from the Train ever did that we know of.

5. There is no other case in which The Man from the Train committed two crimes three weeks and twenty-five miles apart. It's too close for comfort.

None of that is 100 percent convincing, but it appears to be more of a copycat crime than an act of the same person or persons.

The first person to be held responsible for the murder of the Andrus family was Raymond Barnabet, father of Clementine. Raymond Barnabet was arrested, put on trial, and temporarily convicted of the crime. Raymond Barnabet lived near the Andrus family with his girlfriend, Dina Porter, and two of his children, Clementine, aged eighteen, and Zepherin, a younger teenaged boy who was called Ferran. Raymond had another daughter, Pauline, who was grown up and lived with her own family (actually, she lived in Rayne), and a son named Tatite, who was in jail. We believe, although we are not 100 percent certain of this, that Tatite was in jail for homosexual activity. It is likely that the sheriff focused on the Barnabet family because of his knowledge of them through the prosecution of Tatite.

At Raymond's trial, Dina, Clementine, and Ferran all told slightly different stories about the night of the crime. Dina said that Raymond left at 7:00 p.m. the night of the murders, saying he was taking the train to nearby Broussard, and returned in the early hours of the morning, complaining because his supper hadn't been saved for him and he'd lost his pipe on the train. She also told the court that Raymond had previously tried to kill her with an axe in a jealous rage.

Clementine and Ferran agreed that Raymond was gone that evening and came home bitching loudly about his evening meal. According to Clementine, her father arrived home at dawn, smoking a pipe, covered in blood and brains. Clementine said that Raymond was yelling about killing the Andrus family and threatened to do the same to his own family. There are several critical differences here: Dina had Raymond returning home in the early hours of the morning, perhaps before the murders were committed, and insisted that his clothes were clean. Ferran basically supported Clementine but added that Raymond did not have his pipe. We don't know what all the noise about the pipe is; it seems as if the newspapers failed to mention that a pipe had been found near the scene of the murder or something. We don't know.

Anyway, the Barnabets shared a dwelling with a family named Stevens; the Stevenses occupied the main part of the building, and the Barnabets a portion of it. Clementine claimed that Raymond had a bloodstained blue shirt, and that she had given Mrs. Stevens this shirt to wash on the morning of the crime.

The WPA account of the case, collected twenty-five years later, describes the Barnabets as "filthy, shifty, degenerate examples of the lowest of the African type." The Stevenses were people of a much better reputation, and were described by the WPA account as "clean, modest, direct and uncontradictory in their statements." Let's hope that by now we all understand that cleanliness and honesty don't have anything to do with race, and the race should have been left out of that.

Anyway, Mrs. Stevens and her daughter Adelle contradicted all of Clementine's and Ferran's inflammatory claims. Mrs. Stevens testified that she rose with the sun and heard no commotion of the kind described by the Barnabets. Adelle testified that their side of the house was all quiet until late in the morning, and that Clementine never brought over any wash, let alone a shirt covered in brains and blood; you would remember a thing like that. Adelle further testified that they knocked on the Barnabets' door and informed them of the Andrus murder, and that the members of the household responded to the shocking news with appropriate solemnity. Mrs. Stevens volunteered that Clementine and Ferran were persons of bad reputation, implying that their testimony against their father should not be believed.

Perhaps one witness should not testify as to the reliability of another witness, but there is little or no doubt that Clementine was lying. The crucial parts of Clementine's testimony were contradicted by Dina Porter, who lived with her and had been witness to all of the things Clementine claimed to have seen, as well as by the Stevens family, who lived in another part of the house, and by Raymond Barnabet. Also, a month after the trial, Clementine would begin to say that she herself had committed the crime, or had led those who committed it. Also, Clementine was just a terrible liar, although frankly we kind of like her anyway.

But while Clementine's story wasn't true, she was charismatic and a good storyteller, and the jury believed her. Raymond Barnabet denied any involvement in the murder of the Andrus family, but in October 1911, he was convicted of the crime. Temporarily.

What happens in many of these cases is that, in the absence of evidence, the crime is pinned on *a person of low social standing who is known to be in the vicinity of the crime.* We have seen this repeatedly. There was no evidence at all that Henry Lambert murdered the Allen family, but he was a person of low social status who was near the scene of the crime, and the state of Maine convicted him and locked him up for twenty years before admitting they had made a mistake. There is no real reason to believe that George Wilson murdered Archie and Nettie Coble in Rainier, Washington, but he was a person of low social standing who lived near the scene of the crime. He was bullied into a probably bogus confession and convicted of the crime. There is no evidence, really, that Reed and Cato murdered the Hodges family, but one of the two was bullied into a false confession, and then they were killed by a lynch mob.

There are others like that in this book, but you get my point. The murder of the Andrus family was probably not a Man from the Train case, but Raymond Barnabet is that kind of ancillary victim: he was a person of low social standing who lived near the scene of the crime. Police and prosecutors, not knowing who had committed the crime, succeeded (for a time) in pinning it on him. But just weeks later, Raymond was granted a new trial because he was drunk at his first trial. It seems that the second day of his first trial, he convinced another prisoner to get him some cheap port called "spartan wine," which he drank all of on an empty stomach.

This is a fairly unique reason to get a new trial. Sometimes the lawyers are drunk on the job, and that leads to a new trial, but an intoxicated defendant? The court's eagerness to grant him a new trial (which occurred before Clementine's confession to the crimes) is a sign that, despite the racism of the time and place, someone in the justice system was trying to give Raymond something resembling due process.

We have hardly begun the story of Clementine Barnabet, but other events are running forward, and we're going to put the Barnabets aside for a moment and catch up.

On March 21, 1911, the Casaway family was murdered in San Antonio. We told you their story in chapter VIII of this book. At the time, no one or very few people connected this to the events in Louisiana, although later on many people did. Some sources—many sources, actually—have made the Casaways an after-the-fact part of the Clementine Barnabet story. From our standpoint there is no doubt that the Casaways were murdered by The Man from the Train. There is a lot of information about the Casaways, and it is clear that that crime was committed by the same murderer who went on to commit the crimes in Ardenwald, Oregon, Colorado Springs, and Villisca.

So the March murder is unconnected, but there had been murders in January and February 1911, and there are three if you count the Casaways. In October 1911, Raymond Barnabet was convicted of the crime from February, but in November 1911, with Raymond still in jail, there was a fourth crime, oddly enough with another baby named Agnes.

There is an area in Lafayette known as the Mills Addition. The family of Norbert and Azema Randall lived on Madison Street in Mills Addition, less than a quarter-mile from the railroad tracks. The Randalls were young people of good standing in their community. On the evening of November 26, 1911, Norbert and Azema were at home with three of their children: Rene, aged six, Norbert Junior, aged five, and Agnes, aged two. Their oldest daughter was staying with a relative that evening, but they had a little neighbor boy named Albert Scyth (sometimes written Sise) with them. It was a Sunday night, and it rained that night.

Before seven the next morning the other daughter arrived home.

We know she was about ten and had been at her uncle's, but we don't know her name or if she had a key to unlock the back door, or if the murderer had left it open. The view into the home was lit by an arc lamp behind her. Once she saw what was inside, she ran down the street screaming.

Watching her run away, from the porch of a neighbor's house, was Clementine Barnabet.

*   *   *

The police arrived, according to the newspapers, a half hour after sunrise. A half hour after sunrise on November 11 in Louisiana would be 6:52 a.m., or eight minutes before the bodies were reported discovered, so that was a really good police response time. Norbert, Azema, and Agnes lay in the bed near the door, covered by a mosquito net torn in half from the blows of the axe. Norbert was shot once in the head, and then he, his wife, and his baby had all been bludgeoned with the blunt side of the axe. Not far away were the three other children, tangled in a lifeless pile in the bed where they had slept. One of them had woken for a moment before death, judging from the single, tiny, bloody footprint on the floor. Of the murder weapon, the *Biloxi Daily Herald* wrote:

> Sheriff Lacoste found the axe with which the crime had been
> committed leaning against the wall near the foot of the bed,
> and it had been carefully washed of all bloodstains, showing
> the remarkable coolness and deliberation of the fiend.

Let's take a moment to make the argument that this is the work of The Man from the Train. The Randalls lived a very short distance from the train, not far from Houston Heights and San Antonio, not long after the death of the Casaways. Their murder was sudden and without apparent motive. The murder weapon was the blunt side of the axe, left in the room. The victim's heads were covered—with a mosquito net rather than bedclothes, but covered nonetheless. There was a guest in the home that night, and a young girl was among the victims. There wasn't a lamp without its chimney, the windows weren't covered, and the door wasn't locked—as far as we know—but these are still too many of the key elements for it to be a random cluster, in my view. This looks like the work of a cool, deliberate, and above all experienced fiend—not an eighteen-year-old woman.

Clementine Barnabet was now employed as a domestic by a family named Guidry. (Ron Guidry, the greatest Cajun baseball player of all time, was born in Lafayette forty years after these events.) The Guidrys lived just down the block from the Randalls. Clementine watched from the Guidrys' porch as the little girl ran screaming from the Randall house, and she laughed.

Police turned their attention to Clementine. A latch to the Guidrys' home was caked in blood, and inside Clementine's room police found a dress, apron, and underwear covered in blood and brains. At first, Clementine denied it, but soon after she was bragging. Hours after her arrest, she laughed at a judge on the witness stand, laughed and laughed and laughed at all of them, and told everyone that she had killed the Randalls, the Andruses, and the family in Rayne, whose name she did not know.

Clementine was eighteen years old at the time of these murders, probably fifteen or sixteen when the Opelousas family was murdered in 1909. She had large doe eyes, a slender figure, and smooth skin. Clementine had what one could describe as a pixie face. The lower half of her face was round but small and delicate. The word to describe her, honestly, is *cute*—cute being usually nonthreatening, like a child or a puppy. Many of the drawings that are attached to articles about her make her look mature and exotic, but that isn't at all what she looked like. If, in fact, she had done everything she said she had done, she would be a figure without equal in the history of crime.

Also present near the scene was King Harrison. Clementine Barnabet and Azema Randall were members of King Harrison's church. He was the Johnny Appleseed of the Christ Sanctified Holy Church, having established several branches of the church along the Southern Pacific Railroad. Clementine was supposed to be a "deaconess" in the Christ Sanctified Holy Church, whatever that means; the term "deaconess" is not commonly used by religious denominations, and when it is used, it almost always applies to more mature women.

Certainly neither King Harrison nor Christ Sanctified Holy Church approved of murder, but Clementine claimed she was the leader of a group within the Christ Sanctified Holy Church known as the Church of Sacrifice. She said she had murdered the Randalls because they disobeyed the church's orders. She also claimed she had a charm from a local voodoo doctor that would prevent her from being punished.

Well, that's a hell of a story, and as you can imagine, the newspapers had a field day. Her race was always noted, usually in the headline, often alongside the claim that she was light-skinned. Usually the observation of how white she might be was followed by a tribute to her beauty and cunning. Many stories about her claim that she was only one-eighth black, which cannot be true. The reports reached newspapers on both coasts, and like a story retold by a six-year-old, the basic facts of the case were retained while the details were embellished or made up. Stories featured dialogue written in insulting dialect and tales of voodoo churches and unsubstantiated sacrifices. These accounts, as far as we know, were carried only in white newspapers. All accounts agree that Clementine was "being examined for her sanity."

For two months, Clementine sat in jail while the authorities figured out what to do. According to the WPA account, she curtailed her confessions and spoke to no one, "like a sphinx," but occasionally she asked for her mother.

On Saturday, January 20, 1912, Harriet Crane stopped by her daughter Merle Warner's house, a small home near the railroad tracks on the west side of Crowley. She stopped by to see Merle and her three children, Pearl (aged nine), Harriet (eight) and Garry (seven). Mrs. Crane found the house to be eerily silent, sensed that something was wrong, and could not stand to go inside. The *Galveston Daily News* doesn't record whether the door was locked or the windows covered. What it does say is that she was "afraid to enter and willed a colored man to go for her."

You can probably guess what had happened to the Warners, and this will save me the awkwardness of putting it in words. The bodies had been moved to lie together in bed after death, and the axe was dropped at the scene, though it was bloody and not cleaned.

Well, Raymond Barnabet was in jail, and Clementine was in jail, so what now? Sheriff Lacoste arrested Zepherin (Ferran) Barnabet. He had an alibi, but Lacoste figured he was acting on the orders of his incarcerated father and sister.

But on the very night that Ferran was arrested, January 20, there was another crime about fifty miles from Crowley (seventy-five miles from Lafayette) in Lake Charles, Louisiana. In 1912 the city was still recovering from a huge fire that had wiped out most of downtown in 1910. The Broussards lived not far from downtown at 331 Rock Street, "the last one on the street towards the river and within a few rods of the Kansas City Southern switch track," according to the *Galveston Daily News*. Felix Broussard was an older man, around the age of fifty. He worked at the rice mill, where he got along well with his coworkers and employers, and lived with his wife, who we believe was his second wife. We are told that she was pretty but know nothing else about her, not even a name. They had three children: Margaret, aged eight, Alberta, aged six, and Louis, aged three. Felix also had two adult children living in Texas.

In the newspapers, Felix Broussard got the same "good sort of negro" treatment that Walter Byers, Alexandre Andrus, Louis Casaway, and Norbert Russell had received after their deaths. Acknowledging the humanity of these victims provided some journalists an excuse to bite off a little more racism and take liberties with the details of their life and death, especially the superstitious gossip such as that published in a special report on the crimes by the *Los Angeles Times* on January 30, 1912:

> The day before the tragedies, [Felix] told some friends he was "going home to glory and going mighty soon." Although Saturday is not the usual negro wash day, his wife washed all the clothes for every member of the family. From this it has been argued that the victims must have knew, in advance, their fate.

This is gossip, or possibly just straight-up fiction. You have to understand: newspapers in this era would just make stuff up—not all of them, but some of them. This article was reprinted in the *El Paso Herald* on March 14, 1912. In its different iterations, it is the most colorfully and emphatically racist article that we have come across in researching this book.

If you're counting murdered families in this chapter we are now up to seven—the Opelousas, Byers, Casaway, Andrus, Randall, Warner, and Broussard families; however, we said that there were eleven in 1911 and 1912, and the Opelousas family doesn't count in that total because that crime happened in 1909.

The Broussards' murderer had broken into the house through a back window. An excellent account of the crime published in the *Galveston Daily News* of January 22 speculated as to whether the killer had cased the home beforehand:

> The belief is that the murderer doubtless spotted out the place some time in advance, and thus learned of the family's

size and the arrangement of things in the house, as no bun-
gling was done by the fiend. The negro woman who lived
next door was up at 1:30 o'clock Sunday morning cooking
for the next day, and said that she heard nothing at that time.

At ten o'clock the next morning, a neighbor found them. The parents
were alone in bed, heads crushed by the blunt end of an axe, but not
Felix's axe, which was still in the kitchen. In the next room were
the children, still in the positions of sleep, apparently unmoved. The
axe was beneath their bed, the blood patterns showing that only the
blunt side of the axe had been used. A bucket was placed under their
heads to catch the blood.

This crime shows the competence of The Man from the Train—
which few crimes do that aren't his—but this one clearly isn't. Putting
the axe under the bed and using a bucket to catch the blood would
be departures from pattern for him, but moderate ones. But someone
had written on the inside of the kitchen door the following words:

"When he maketh inquisition for blood, he forgetteth not the cry
of the humble."

And then, to the side, the words "HUMAN FIVE," sometimes
written as "HUMAN, FIVE." We believe that these words were
written with a pencil, although we can't be certain of that.

The quote, repeated in papers from the *Galveston Daily News*
to the *Washington Post*, is always described as a biblical quotation,
although it actually isn't. It's actually a quotation from *Uncle Tom's
Cabin*, misquoted in *Uncle Tom's Cabin* from Psalm 9:12. The actual
quotation from the King James Bible reads:

"When he maketh inquisition for blood, *he remembereth them*: he
forgetteth not the cry of the humble." [emphasis added]

This was not an obvious reference to that most "cussed and discussed" novel, as Langston Hughes described *Uncle Tom's Cabin*. Every newspaper account from the time took the phrase to be direct from the Bible. This was not a commonly written version of the psalm, which appeared in many publications of the day. So far as we know, Rachel McCarthy James was the first person to realize that the quotation did not actually come from the Bible, but from *Uncle Tom's Cabin*.

Clementine confessed to murdering the Broussards, although she had been in jail at the time. (Probably Clementine was confused about the calendar of events, and did not realize that the Broussards had been murdered after her arrest.) Newspapers from as far away as India were enthralled with the religious and racial aspects of Clementine's confession. Many newspapers claimed that she targeted families with five people because of the magic number five, which they claimed to have had some significance in voodoo. This is simply not true. The Opelousas family contained four people, the Byerses were only three, and the Andrus family four, while the Randall family numbered six.

The gruesome murders of the Broussard family set off a flurry of police activity. Clementine's brother Ferran was released from jail. King Harrison, the preacher of the Sanctification Church, which had branches in each of the towns mentioned here, was arrested not long after the bodies were found, and released shortly after that. Eliza Richards, a friend of Clementine's, was arrested and released, as were other people.

By early 1912 the police had lost the trust of the black community. Many black lodges, churches, and organizations volunteered information, help, and funding to catch the killers of the Byerses and the Casaways, but after the Broussard murders they were focused on protecting themselves or packing up and leaving. The *Los Angeles Times* noted the shift in sentiment, but attributed it to the popularity of voodoo.

The *El Paso Herald* report based on the racist *Los Angeles Times* piece recorded the death of a family named Wexford in the early months of the year 1912. This report spends a lot of time trying to explain why the killer would be satisfied now that they had killed five families of five, despite the fact that of the families they cite, only the Broussards actually numbered five. During their summary of the murders, they wrote the following:

> Two months ago six members of the Wexford family perished at the hand of the fanatics but one was an infant born only the day before the tragedy and in all probability had not been taken into consideration when the plans for the human sacrifice were consummated.

We can't find any other evidence of a "Wexford" family being murdered in this area and are not inclined to believe that this ever happened. Perhaps by "Wexford" they meant "Warner," but since the Warners didn't have a day-old baby, either, that wouldn't help all that much. But we could be missing something.

In any case, the murderous rampage was not over, but was crossing state lines and entering a new phase. If you get on the train in Lafayette, Louisiana, and head west, in eighteen miles you will hit Rayne. Get back on the train and go another seven miles, and you come to Crowley. Get back on the train and go another fifty miles west, you're in Lake Charles. Get back on the train in Lake Charles and go another sixty miles, you're in Beaumont, Texas.

The family of Hattie Dove lived at 1428 Cable Street in Beaumont, Texas, right next to a Baptist church and a third of a mile from the railroad track. Hattie and her family are going to meet an unfortunate end in just a moment here, but at some point these crimes cease to be part of the original series and become copycat crimes. The authors of this book believe that someone or someones, perhaps motivated by racism and perhaps by some other sickness, took the template of the Louisiana/Acadia Parish murders, which were all over the newspapers at that time, and used it as the basis for a series of unrelated crimes, committed not by Clementine or her friends or by The Man from the Train, but by some third actor, probably two men acting together. We don't believe that any of the Texas crimes in this series were actually committed by the same people who committed the Louisiana crimes, except that The Man from the Train probably committed crimes in both states. Other people who have written about these crimes have put them together as one series, and you can believe what you want to believe.

But let's go back and tie up the story of Clementine a little bit, before we go on into Texas and Mississippi. Clementine is in jail by this time, and her conviction is beginning to look ever more certain, because by now she is filling up notebooks with her confessions. The Lafayette prosecutor, District Attorney Bruner, began preparing a grand jury investigation. In January 1912, a chemist named Metz had tested the bloody skirt and shirtwaist found in Clementine's closet to see if the blood was menstrual or not; he found it was blood "which flowed from wounds of a living body," as the *Thibodaux Sentinel* of January 27, 1912, put it. There is certainly a difference between period blood and regular old circulating blood; period blood is partially the shedding of the uterine lining. We'd like to know more about his 1912 methodology, but OK.

Metz also tested and found that some blood on a pillow in the Randall house matched the blood on Clementine's clothes. This is clearly BS designed to help the prosecution. Blood typing had just been developed a few years earlier by Karl Landsteiner in Austria. There was little knowledge or understanding of it, even in the scientific community, at that time. The public in 1912 knew that blood typing was possible, because it had been used in some high-profile paternity cases, but knew almost nothing about it. Metz took advantage of this to make a claim which seems to the authors to be well beyond the scientific envelope of 1912. Since there were six victims from three unrelated genetic backgrounds in the Randall murders, all of whom had shed blood, there would almost certainly be blood from multiple blood types (A, B, O, and AB). It is likely that Clementine had the same blood type as at least one of the six victims, which would render this "match" meaningless by any methods available into the 1970s. It is our opinion that Dr. Metz was taking advantage of the gullibility of the public to make a claim that would have seemed reasonable at the time but which lacks credibility in retrospect.

But Clementine was also helping the prosecution. Clementine now claimed that her first murders had occurred in Rayne. Her sister Pauline lived in Rayne, and she now claimed that she had traveled to Rayne to visit her sister and, while there, had murdered a woman and her four children:

> I went to my sister, who lived at Rayne, near the O. G. railroad depot, and later during the night went up town, disguised as a man, and securing an ax in a yard near the cabin where I killed the mother and four children. . . .
>
> Upon entering the house, I struck the woman on the right temple and killed her instantly. One of the children was awakened by the noise, and before he could raise his head from the pillow I struck him a blow somewhere near the left ear, then I struck the other two. I left the man's clothes which I wore in the house and left the house in woman's clothes, returned to my sister's house and later during the same night I boarded a night train for Lafayette arriving here about midnight. It was about nine when I killed them.

The police in Rayne now arrested Pauline, alleging that she was acting "suspicious." Back in Lafayette, Sheriff Lacoste arrested Valena Mabry, whom Clementine called Irene and claimed had been her assistant in the murder of the Randalls. Mabry vigorously denied any connection to the crime, and was eventually released without being prosecuted.

When Clementine met the grand jury in April 1912, she had more than just laughter for them. She made a full confession not just to the officers of the court but to a reporter named RH Broussard from the *New Orleans Item* (and yes, there are a lot of Broussards in this story). RH Broussard's version of her story began in New Iberia, a town south of Lafayette. Clementine and four friends met an "old negro who told us that he could sell us 'candjas.'" (The spelling of that last word seems to be unique, to the best of Google's ability, at least. In the WPA account, this item was referred to as a "conjure bag.") In her confession, Clementine stated that the conjure bag was promised to allow her and her friends to "do as we pleased and we would never be detected and would be protected from the hands of the law by the mere fact of these 'candjas' being in our possession."

This fact about the candjas is the entire basis for the belief that these crimes are related to voodoo. Thousands and thousands of newspaper articles and many subsequent books and articles link these crimes to voodoo, but as far as we know the only actual link to voodoo is just this one fact—that Clementine and a couple of her goofy teenaged friends had once bought a couple of conjure bags. The man who sold them the charms was named Joseph Thibodeaux. Thibodeaux was arrested by Sheriff Lacoste, who hoped that Thibodeaux could lead them to the killers of the rest of the victims—those who had been murdered after Clementine was already in custody. The forty-five-year-old Thibodeaux admitted to selling people papers "for various things" but denied selling charms. Sheriff Lacoste brought him in front of Clementine, and she identified him as the man who sold her the charms and described his house. "Yes, you said I wouldn't be arrested," she told him, "but look here I am in jail."

After buying the charms for three dollars, Clementine said that she and her friends returned to Lafayette and began making plans for what to get away with. She claimed that before the conjure bags, they had never thought to commit murder. They drew straws to see who would kill first, and she drew the short straw. She then went to Rayne, to visit her sister, and murdered a family while she was there. She said she chose the family because they had left a light burning inside while they slept, and she could see them sleeping. She said. Clementine returned to Lafayette and her friends, and, in her telling, they waited to see whether they would be arrested. When they were not arrested, she said they figured that the charm had worked and they were free to murder at will.

She next confessed to the murder of the Byers family in Crowley, Louisiana:

> In Crowley I entered the house with one of the women, while the other kept watch, and as I had the ax in my hand I committed the murders. I struck the man first and just as I did so the woman woke up, I struck her a blow in the face with the butt end of the ax and felled her. I then struck her once or twice to be sure that she was dead. Once this was done it was an easy matter to get rid of the two small children. We thought it was better to kill them than to leave orphans, as they would suffer.

As stated earlier, we believe it is more likely that this crime was committed by The Man from the Train, but there is no point in arguing about that now.

Back in Lafayette, Clementine claimed that she and her friends sat back and enjoyed the furor they had created. There was a semblance of a logical plan to the strategy to commit the next murder, that of the Andrus family in their hometown; she claimed to plan the event on the evening of an election, when all the police officers were busy campaigning. She said she and her friends did not preselect their victims, but again a home near the railroad was targeted. From her confession:

> When we reached the railroad crossing we saw a light burning in a cabin near Ramagosa's store. We decided that that was a good place so we went there; myself and one of the women entered the house and I struck [Alexandre Andrus] first, then his wife, and afterwards his two small children, one of whom was an infant in the cradle near the bed. We had overlooked him until he woke up and began to cry. I turned around and struck him in the forehead, killing him instantly.

Clementine then recounted watching Alexandre's brother find the bodies, and then claimed that she helped to wash and prepare them for burial, a claim that is clearly untrue.

Clementine outlined the murder of the Randalls in less detail, skimping on the bloody details. She picked up an axe from a neighbor that Sunday night after a church celebration. On the way to the Randalls, she saw cops and the preacher of the church, King Harrison; she told the latter to avoid the area that night. Taking her brother Tatite's gun, Clementine said she broke into the Randall home and shot the father in the chest. She claimed to have "caressed" all of her victims, adults and children and babies, for sexual stimulation.

She gave the names of her alleged accomplices, who appeared in her story as randomly as dropped stitches on a home-knit blanket, sometimes entering the house with her to commit a crime and then welcoming her back to safety after committing the crime. The accomplices were found, sometimes arrested, and then released once they were able to put the lie to Clementine, whose confessions always seemed to unravel at the slightest tug.

Clementine confessed to murdering eighteen people, but the grand jury charged her with only one murder, that of Azema Randall.

Standard practice at that time; prosecutors are always looking for a loophole in the constitutional prohibition against double jeopardy. Her trial began on October 21, 1912. The previous week she was examined by a team of medical professionals, who said in a court document reproduced by the WPA effort that she was "morally depraved, unusually ignorant and of a low grade of mentality, but not deficient in such a manner as to constitute her imbecile or idiot." She was eligible to stand trial.

The *Chicago Defender*, a black newspaper, covered her trial and heaped praise upon her lawyer, a man by the name of Kennedy, saying that he gave "one of the most magnificent presentations ever heard in court." He argued that her confessions were unreliable and the product of a bad childhood, that the clothes with Randall's blood on it were bundled with clothes that came from Clementine's room, and that Metz, the chemist who tested the clothes, was unreliable. Clementine was convicted of the murder of Azema Randall at 10:30 p.m. on October 25. She was sentenced the next day to life in prison.

*       *       *

Clementine confessed to murdering eighteen people, but it would seem to be impossible to believe that she actually did exactly what she said that she did. This leaves two possibilities: that Clementine was involved with a cult or sect of murderers, who continued to commit crimes after she was arrested, or that Clementine had no actual connection to the murders, but has become in history the fall guy for the crimes of others.

While either of these is certainly possible, the authors are both inclined to believe that the latter option is the more likely. We don't think Clementine actually had any involvement in the Acadia Parish murders.

The evidence for Clementine's involvement in the crimes can be summarized in five points:

1. Clementine was very close to two of the crimes at the time that they occurred,
2. She acted inappropriately,
3. She gave detailed and elaborate confessions to the crimes,
4. Blood was found on her clothing after one of the crimes, and
5. Clementine was the first person to offer an explanation of the religious symbolism which is found at a couple of the murder scenes.

Number 1 isn't anything. The coincidence of her being near two of the crime scenes triggered her arrest, but really, what does it amount to? When the Boston Strangler was murdering women in the early 1960s, police noticed a crew painting apartments near the scene of the first crime, and then noticed that a crew was painting apartments near the scene of the second crime. When they checked, it turned out to be the same painting crew. It was an odd coincidence, but it was just a coincidence. That was in a big city. The two murder scenes that Clementine was definitely known to be near were both in a small town, in the part of town near where she lived. It isn't strange that she happened to be near both scenes.

Her behavior was certainly inappropriate, but (1) she was young, superstitious, and high-strung, and (2) she had been through an extraordinary series of gut-wrenching events:

1. A family living near to her, and known to her, was murdered in a grotesque and gruesome manner.
2. Her father was accused of that crime.
3. (This is speculation, and I'll deal with that in a moment.) She

was put through the wringer by police who were investigating that crime.

4. She testified against her father, probably under great pressure from the police.

5. Another family was murdered, again close to her.

This series of traumatic events would destabilize a good many people. Another young lady in our book, about the same age (Lydia Howell in Houston Heights, chapter III) had a complete nervous breakdown and was institutionalized for months following just one of these stressors, the murder of a family that was well known to her. It seems not the least bit odd, to us, that Clementine went completely around the bend after these five events, and began to behave in a grossly inappropriate manner. For that matter, *simply to be living in that area while all of these terrible murders were occurring was no doubt very stressful.* It was a bizarre situation.

The Andrus family was murdered near her home in February 1911, and her father was accused of the crime. It is likely that she was examined by the police about this crime in a vigorous manner. It is likely that she (and her brother, separately) was taken into a small room with two large police officers who probably said to her something like: "We know what happened here and we know that you know what happened here. You are not leaving this room until you come clean."

There are many cases now, in the twenty-first century, in which, when a murder occurs, the teenaged family members are "shaken" by the police in exactly this way, to see what they know about the crimes. With white police officers dealing with black teenagers in the South a hundred years ago with no cameras rolling, it is likely that those examinations were rougher and more intense than they would be now. But the problem with this practice is that a vulnerable teenager, "interviewed" in this manner, will often give a false confession or offer false testimony in an effort to bring the terrifying and traumatic police interview to an end.

We believe that Clementine (and her brother) did in fact tell the police what they wanted to hear. Her relationship with her father was rocky anyway. Her parents had split up, and her father was alcoholic and abusive.

Clementine certainly gave false testimony against her father in his murder trial, and we assume that she did so under great pressure from the police, and we assume that this was a terrible emotional burden for her. When there was *another* horrible murder near to her, Clementine began to act in completely inappropriate ways and told stories that were not true. She was not in her right mind, which, under the circumstances, is quite understandable. But are those confessions true?

*   *   *

Clementine in her confessions told one fact that could be checked out to a certain degree. She gave information leading to the arrest of the man who had sold her the "candjas," Joseph Thibodeaux of New Iberia. Other than this one fact, nothing that Clementine said about the murders (a) can be confirmed by any other party, or (b) has the ring of truth about it. A great deal of what she said is demonstrably false.

In a modern police investigation, if Clementine told police that she had traveled to Crowley in January 1911 to murder the Byers family, the police, interviewing her just weeks later, would have asked about two hundred follow-up questions, like: Which train did you take over there? What time was it? Who sold you the ticket? Do you remember what the ticket agent looked like? Did you see anyone that you knew on the train? Was the train crowded or empty? What clothes were you wearing that day, do you remember? Did you get blood on your clothes? Who was the conductor who punched your ticket, do you remember him? When you got to Crowley, what time was it? Where was the Byers house, from the train? What do you remember about the Byers house? Did it have a porch? Did it have a porch swing? Was there anything on the porch that you remember? Did the house have a big yard? Where was the house that you took the axe from? Was the axe sticking up out of the woodpile, or was it just leaning against the woodpile? When you went in the house, what do you remember about the inside of the house? What room were you in when you broke in? Was it the kitchen or a bedroom? Did it have wallpaper? What color were the walls?

You make the person who is giving a confession answer questions like that so you can tell whether they are lying or telling the truth. If they're lying, they'll give a long string of "I don't remembers" and wrong answers, and they will fail to correct deliberate mistakes made by the interviewer. If things check out, they're telling the truth.

This was never done with Clementine; there was never any effort to check out her confessions and see whether she was telling the truth. It is unlikely that the police had any training at all, and it is unlikely that they had significant experience in murder investigation. But also, we believe that they let her confession stand because they wanted it to be true. And they wanted it to be true because they desperately wanted for this thing to be over with.

So these three points against Clementine are not convincing:

1. Clementine was very close to two of the crimes at the time they occurred,

2. She acted inappropriately,

3. She gave detailed and elaborate confessions to the crimes.

And that leaves us with these two:

1. Blood was found on her clothing after one of the crimes, and

2. Clementine was the first person to offer an explanation of the religious symbolism which is found at a couple of the murder scenes.

The blood is the best evidence against her. But Clementine's lawyer argued, at her trial, that the police had seized items from Clementine's room at the Guidrys', and had thrown them into a bundle with things taken from the crime scene. It is possible that this is true, and it is also possible (though less likely) that the police, believing Clementine to be guilty, had planted evidence to ensure her conviction.

On the religious symbolism:

1. There actually isn't all that much religious symbolism in the murders. One family was "posed" postmortem in a manner that some people thought looked as if they were praying, and a biblical passage taken actually from *Uncle Tom's Cabin* was written on the door of one house. These are the only facts we are aware of that support the theory that a religious cult was behind the murders.

2. Clementine's explanation that she had murdered the Randall family to punish them for disobeying her church appears only in her first confession. In her later and much more detailed confessions, she dropped that and told an entirely different story of why and how she and her never-identified friends committed the crimes.

Clementine knew Azema Randall through her church. When accused of murdering Azema, her first confused, crazy thought was that it had something to do with the church, because the church was the only thing that connected her to Azema.

We are not arguing absolutely that Clementine was not involved in the murders. We are arguing that, on balance, the theory that Clementine was not involved is (a) easier to believe than the arguments against her, and (b) much, much easier to believe than the theory that Clementine was the leader of a murderous religious cult.

Clementine, sentenced to life in prison, escaped for a few hours on July 31, 1913, but was recaptured the same day. She was in prison for ten years, was released on April 28, 1923, and disappeared. Presumably she left the area and assumed a different name, but no one knows where she went or what name she began using. You may have known her years ago; she could plausibly have lived into the 1970s. She would have been seventy-seven years old in 1970.

We think that, if authorities had actually believed that she was behind these terrible murders, it is unlikely that she would have been released after a few years in jail. She was turned loose so soon because the authorities didn't believe her story, either.

\* \* \*

The family of Hattie Dove lived at 1428 Cable Street in Beaumont, Texas, right next to a Baptist church and a third of a mile from the railroad track. Beaumont, as I mentioned earlier, is sixty miles west of Lake Charles, Louisiana. Hattie, still a young woman in her thirties, was separated from her children's father, who lived in Nagadoches. She lived in Beaumont with her three teenaged children, Ernest, Ethel, and Jesse. Jesse, eighteen, was married but had separated from her husband and come back home. A man named John Smith, who worked nights, boarded at the house. The Dove family had lived in Beaumont only about a year, and had not made many friends or any enemies in Beaumont.

The house on Cable Street was still active at 9:30 on the night of February 19, 1912. Around midnight, an axe was removed from the woodpile in a yard about two blocks over, and replaced with another. Probably the assailant had picked up an axe, then saw the other axe and decided it was better for his purposes. The assailant or assailants broke into the Dove home through a kitchen window. The blunt end of the axe was used to bash the head of Hattie and the sharp end to destroy Ernest, who shared a bed in the back room.

Most reports said that the victims appeared to be killed in their sleep with the back of an axe, but the *Beaumont Enterprise* described the scene of the daughter's bodies to be one of struggle, with bedclothes and blood everywhere. The axe was dropped at the scene along with the cloth that wiped it clean. With no better explanation, the Dove family murders were added to the list of the Church of Sacrifice Murders, what might better be called the Acadia Parish crimes.

At this point we need to go into quick-summary mode, although (a) some of these murders we are rushing past are actually very interesting stories, (b) I can't absolutely guarantee you that they are all unconnected to our series, and (c) many people have concluded that these other crimes are connected to the Acadia Parish murders, although they probably are not.

- The family of Ellen Monroe (five people) was murdered in Glidden, Texas, on March 27, 1912.
- The family of William Burton (four people) was murdered at 724 Center Street in San Antonio on April 11, 1912. The house at 724 Center Street is two blocks from where the Casaway family was murdered in March 1911.
- The family of Alice Marshall (three people) was murdered in Hempstead, Texas, on April 15, 1912. Several other people also survived that attack.

The last murder to be commonly tied to the Church of Sacrifice series . . .

Let's back off of that. There is no "Church of Sacrifice," OK? There never was. Clementine made it up while she was confused and panicked and out of her mind, and it gained credibility because of racist stereotypes. Some of the cops in the later cases tried to solve their crimes by chasing down rumors about the Church of Sacrifice, rather than by doing normal police work, not that that was going to work, either. But there wasn't any Church of Sacrifice.

The last murders to be commonly tied to what had begun in Acadia Parish in 1909 were the murders of the Walmsley family near Philadelphia, Mississippi, in November 1912. Philadelphia, of course, would be made famous by another three murders a half-century later, the three civil rights workers murdered in 1964. In 1912 the murdered three were William Walmsley, his wife, Sallie, and their four-year-old daughter. Their bodies were discovered on November 23.

In the spring of 1912 the Mississippi River flooded, killing hundreds of people—two hundred in Mississippi alone. Memphis was flooded, Arkansas, Louisiana; eastern Texas was flooded, although not directly by the Mississippi. In Acadia Parish, the murders became the parish's second-biggest problem, starting their long march toward the dark attic of history, where they would rest hidden behind wars, scandals, and assassinations.

Do you know what an aneurism is? An aneurism is like a balloon effect in a vein or an artery. A portion of the vein weakens so that, under pressure, it suddenly swells up much larger than it is supposed to be.

In the history of axe murderers the years 1911 and 1912 are like an aneurism. In the course of researching this book, we looked at hundreds, perhaps thousands, of murders committed between 1890 and 1920. We did not attempt to count every single murder, but we did try to record every instance in which most of a family was murdered at once, whether with an axe or by some other method. We surely missed a few, because this is not an encyclopedia, but we identified 248 familicides, comprising a thousand people. It's about eight families murdered per year. More than half of those crimes had obvious solutions, such as a murder committed by a family member or a jealous neighbor. There is usually in there one or two murders a year which have some of the earmarks of The Man from the Train— the use of an axe, the proximity to the railroad, the town too small to have a police force, the attack within an hour of midnight and utterly without warning, the use of the blunt side of the axe, etc. etc. etc.

For most of this era it is actually fewer than eight families murdered per year (with an axe or by any other method). And then you come to the 1910 to 1912 era, and . . . Jesus H. Christ, what is happening here? Axe murders start appearing like dandelions. Murdering your neighbors with an axe became the nation's fourth-largest sport.

In part this is because The Man from the Train was hyperactive in that era, and in part it is because of the Acadia Parish murders, and in part it is because of the New Orleans Axeman, but there is more to it than that. There are things happening here, in these two years, that we cannot and do not understand.

Those who investigated the crimes in Villisca and other places in 1911 and 1912 frequently attributed them to religious cults. The sheriff of Montgomery County, Iowa, thought that the Villisca crime had been committed by a negro religious cult (using his terminology). This explanation makes no sense to people who don't know the story of Clementine Barnabet. If you know the story the explanation is still wrong, but at least it makes sense.

Ideas spread from one person to another. It would be nice if only good ideas spread, but unfortunately bad ideas get spread around, too—really, really horrible ideas. There are trends and fashions in crime as much as in any other area. In the 1870s there were gunfights and gunfighters. In the 1880s there were train robbers. In the 1930s there were a bunch of roving criminal gangs like the Dillinger gang, Bonnie and Clyde, Ma Barker and her boys, and Pretty Boy Floyd. You didn't have those gangs in 1923 and you didn't have them in 1943, but in 1933 they were all over the nation. There was an era when kidnapping was the *crime du jour*. For many years no one ever heard of a drive-by shooting, and then, all of sudden, there were drive-by shootings every night. The 1960s were the era of the political assassination. In 1975 nobody had ever heard of a school shooting, and then there were school shootings.

The period from 1910 to 1912 was the era of the axe murderer. It is not a silly argument to say that this era came about *because of* The Man from the Train, that he was the man who spread the idea across the country. He was the Typhoid Mary of the Axe Murder Epidemic.

Violence follows violence. One murder leads to another, even when there is no apparent connection. In this book we have seen small town after small town in which, after The Man from the Train was there,

there was another murder the next month—and we didn't always tell you when that happened. These were in small towns where there should have been one murder every fifty years or something. Murder leaves the idea of murder hanging in the air.

So what happened in this era, and who killed all of those families in Texas in 1912? We don't know. We're not sociologists or psychologists or criminologists or detectives. We're not even real historians. We're just writers. These are just the facts as best we can tell.

# CHAPTER XXXIX

# Harry Ryan

Continuing now the "second circuit" of these crimes, the next crimes we discussed were the murders of the Bernhardt family along the Kansas-Missouri border, near Martin City, Missouri, probably on the evening of December 7, 1910. On December 17, 1910, a small man walked into a pool hall in Iola, Kansas, ninety-four miles south of the crime scene, and asked the proprietor if he had any newspaper stories about the Bernhardt murders. The man was a stranger, badly dressed, and his enthusiastic enjoyment of the newspaper articles gave the pool hall manager the creeps. The proprietor engaged the little tramp in conversation and secretly sent someone running for the cops. The stranger tried to leave after a little while but was detained by patrons until the Iola chief of police, Chief Coffield, arrived.

Coffield took the man into custody and questioned him at length. He gave his name as Harry Ryan. He carried no identification, but in 1910 this was not unusual; most people carried no official ID at that time, but his answers as to who he was and where he was from seemed evasive. He offered no information that could be checked out. And, in this context, Harry Ryan said something that, when I read it a hundred years later, would send chills surging up my spine.

He said that he had done some work the previous summer up in Marshalltown, Iowa.

From Iola, Kansas, to Marshalltown, Iowa, is 350 miles. If you draw a circle around Iola with a 350-mile radius, that circle will encompass about 6,500 small towns. When he was questioned about a family murder in Johnson County, Kansas, Harry Ryan had offered the one other little town where there had been an extremely similar family murder as the one other place where he had been. What are the odds?

Not only the place, but the time as well; Ryan told the sheriff that he had "done some work *last summer*" in Marshalltown, Iowa. The Hardy family had been murdered near Marshalltown on June 5, 1910. Harry Ryan insisted that he knew nothing about the Bernhardt murders, but did acknowledge that he had been in the area of the Bernhardt farm at about the time the family was murdered. He said that he had been in Olathe about ten days earlier, he didn't know when exactly; the Bernhardt farm was a few miles from Olathe, and the crime had occurred ten days earlier. And, by his own voluntary statement, he had placed himself at or near the scene of a similar crime six months earlier.

Pass the palm of your hand over the top of your head and say, "Whoosh." It went right past them. "Marshalltown" and "last summer" didn't mean a thing to Chief Coffield, nor to the newspapermen who reported on the case. To the best of my knowledge, no person ever realized that the Hardy and Bernhardt murders (a) were similar and (b) might be connected, until the authors realized that in early 2012. Marshalltown is mentioned in the Harry Ryan stories only because that was the most notable of the places where Harry Ryan volunteered that he had been.

Sheriff Coffield took a photograph of Harry Ryan and sent it by courier service to the sheriff of Marshall County, Iowa, Sheriff A. A. Nicholson. Nicholson carried the photograph around town and reported back that he could find no one in his town who had ever seen Harry Ryan or heard of him. No bells went off. There is no evidence in the record that either the Allen County or the Marshall County authorities made any connection to the Hardy family murders. Nicholson, in any case, was convinced that Raymond Hardy had murdered the Hardy family; in his mind that was a closed case, although the grand jury had refused to indict.

After the Hardy murders, it was reported briefly that a man was being held in connection with the case in Sioux City, Iowa, which is about two hundred miles west of Marshalltown. Asked if he had ever been arrested before, Harry Ryan said that yes, he had been arrested once before. Where were you arrested? Sioux City, Iowa.

Before Marshalltown was mentioned, Police Chief Coffield called the Johnson County sheriff, Sheriff Stead, and told him that he was holding someone who should be questioned about the Bernhardt family murders. Sheriff Stead took the train down to Iola, talked to Harry Ryan for a little less than an hour, decided that he had no connection to the Bernhardt murders, and took the next train back to Olathe.

In 1910 (and until 1972) police could hold a person who had no address and no employment on a charge of "vagrancy." While he was in custody, Harry Ryan was interviewed several times by several different small-town reporters, and long or at least substantial interviews with him were printed in several different small-town Kansas newspapers. Ryan seems to have been quite intelligent and generally polite, and enjoyed being interviewed, although he never did tell anyone who he was or where he was from. But obviously, it is quite unusual for several different small-town newspapers to take that much interest in a tramp who is being held on a charge of vagrancy. How do we explain this?

It is our opinion that Chief Coffield believed, deep in his gut, that Harry Ryan had something to do with the Bernhardt family murders. Coffield called Sheriff Stead and said something like, "I've got this guy in custody who had something to do with the Bernhardt family; you'd better get down here and question him." Sheriff Stead went down, but Sheriff Stead had it in his head that if Harry Ryan didn't know the Bernhardts, didn't have any connection to them and had never worked as a farmhand for them, then he couldn't have had anything to do with their murders. That was conventional thinking at the time. Sheriff Stead thought that Chief Coffield was just wasting his time.

What is Coffield to do? The Bernhardt murder isn't his case. He has no jurisdiction; he has no authority. If Sheriff Stead says that Harry Ryan isn't involved, that's the end of that rope. Also, at some risk of getting lost in the weeds, Sheriff Stead's successor had been elected several weeks before the Bernhardts were murdered. Stead was leaving office on January 1, within two weeks, and was barely on speaking terms with his successor, a man named Cave; Cave suggested to reporters that he had been locked out of the investigation, and would have to start fresh when he took office in January.

Coffield still thinks that Harry Ryan is involved, and he is not going to let Ryan go without a fight, so what is he going to do? He starts talking to the newspaper guys. He tells the reporters to come over and talk to this guy. He is trying to keep the investigation alive.

But there is something going on here, with these 1910 family murders, that we do not understand. Both the Hardy and Bernhardt family murders start in the barn and about nightfall, which is different from our most dominant pattern. In neither case is there a prepubescent female among the victims, and in neither case is there clear evidence of signature behaviors such as moving lamps or covering the victims' heads with cloth (although victims in both cases were covered with hay, which could serve the same function). Also, in both of these cases there is a handprint in blood on the wall next to one of the victims, pointing downward, as if the murderer had braced himself against the wall while raining blows on the victim. We are not aware of any other case in this series in which this feature was found. In addition, the Hardy family murders (a) show evidence of taunting behavior, and (b) are not near the railroad track. So in some ways these two crimes (and the Hubbell family murders, which are between them both in place and time) do look like related crimes, and in some ways they do not. Something is happening here, and we don't know what it is.

*Was* Harry Ryan taunting the police when he said that he had "done some work last summer" in Marshalltown, Iowa, gambling that the police would not connect the dots, or else gambling that if they did connect the dots they could not use his words against him?

We do not believe that Harry Ryan was The Man from the Train, for three reasons or four. First, he seems, based on the newspaper reports, to have been too young. The Man from the Train was very small, and Harry Ryan was very small, but we believe The Man from the Train was near fifty by this time. Harry Ryan was in his late twenties. Second, we do not believe that The Man from the Train would have engaged in any kind of taunting behavior, because he was tremendously risk averse, and taunting involved risk. Third, The Man from the Train would never have been stupid enough to wander into a pool hall a hundred miles from the scene of one of his crimes and start asking complete strangers about the murders. The Man from the Train, after he committed a crime, got on the train and got out of the area *immediately*, before the crimes were discovered in most cases.

But there is a fourth reason we are fairly sure that Harry Ryan, while he may have been involved in some of the crimes, was not our principal culprit. We actually believe that we know who The Man from the Train was.

And the time has come for us to tell you.

CHAPTER XL

# The First Crime

I found the First Crime on a cold January night in 2013. I was not yet an author of this book, just a research assistant. Bill had sent me working backward through the years, trying to figure out where this series of crimes began. He told me that eventually I would find the First Crime, and that when the murderer committed the First Crime he would make mistakes that would reveal who he was. I didn't really believe it, and Bill told me later that he didn't really believe it, either, but it was a working premise. *Maybe* you can find the First Crime; *maybe* he'll leave the door open to tell us who he was.

When I began my search for these murders, Bill asked me to focus on the years around the crime in Hurley, in 1909, 1908. When I asked about looking earlier in the decade, he told me that "for our purposes, a crime in 1899 would be pretty far afield . . . even if you found a case, it would be hard to believe he was active that far back." But my gut told me that he was already well practiced by 1909, so Bill let me follow my hunch. I used 1900 as my beginning point and started combing through newspapers in those years for reports of families murdered in the night. Soon enough I found the Lyerlys, the Hugheses, the Hodgeses, the Kellys (or Caffeys), the Allens. I knew his crimes went back to nearly 1900. But I hadn't found the blueprint.

I had just moved from Virginia back to Kansas, living in a little house that sits closer to the train than most of the houses in this story; it is not fifteen feet from the house to the railroad track at the closest point. I'm at home there now, but at the time it was a bit creepy. The north wind rattled the windows. My husband had left me alone with our cats and unpacked boxes to go see a Michael Jackson cover band. Chasing a lead from a story in a Boston newspaper about an unrelated crime from 1901, I found a 1904 book entitled *History of the Department of Police Service of Worcester, Mass., from 1674 to 1900* on Google Books. That night, I tried to contact Bill six different ways to tell him what I found, because the second I read this, I knew who he was:

> The Worcester police worked for over a year in connection with the state police to cause the arrest of Paul Mueller for the murder of the Newton family in West Brookfield. Mueller murdered Francis D. Newton, wife, and daughter Elsie with an axe on the night of Jan. [7, 1898], and was seen walking in the direction of the Boston & Albany railroad, where he took a train leaving at 1 o'clock in the morning. Not a trace of him has been found since.

*    *    *

The dog wouldn't stop barking from inside the Newton house. It was Sunday, January 9, 1898, and no one had seen Francis Newton since that Friday around five o'clock when a neighbor, Joseph Upham, visited to collect a single dollar Francis owed to him. Upham recalled Newton's ten-year-old daughter, Elsie, playing on the floor with her mother, Sarah, as the men took care of business. "All was cheerful," the *Boston Globe* said of the homey scene in Rice's Corner, just south of Brookfield, Massachusetts. During his visit, Francis took Upham to the barn to show off some new equipment. The Newtons' farmhand,

Paul Mueller, was working in the barn. Upham detected no tension or discomfort between Newton and Mueller.

But on Sunday afternoon, Francis's fifteen cows were lowing loud and desperate, unfed and strained by two days' worth of milk. Elmer Newcomb, the closest neighbor a quarter-mile away, was confused by the apparent neglect. A prosperous if not wealthy farmer, Newton was "careful of his possessions, but not stingy [and he] had the faculty of applying business principles to a farm."

Elmer, followed by William Bemis and William Eaton, became concerned and came over to feed and water Newton's cows. They figured the family had gone away for the weekend without letting them know (but why didn't he ask someone to look after the cattle?). After they fed and milked the livestock, they left without any snooping.

Once off the deserted property, the farmers engaged in a little of what the *New York World* called "thinking it over," which I interpret as the kind of self-consciously serious gossip that grown men don't like to admit that they enjoy. Newton was prosperous enough to make neighbors jealous, and he was not warm, and those two qualities could have led to some comments that they regretted later, when they found out. After talking, though, they did agree it was odd "that the Newtons should go away without making arrangements for feeding the cattle." William Eaton in particular was urging a return visit. It takes considerable confidence that something is amiss to overcome the resistance to breaking into your neighbors' house. William Bemis wasn't there yet, and he begged off, but Elmer and Eaton assembled three more neighbors, Arthur Rice, George Pike, and Herbert Duane.

The rescue party ventured over to the white two-story farmhouse on Sunday night around 10:00 p.m. The front and back doors were locked, and the curtains tightly drawn. No one answered their knocks and calls and kicks to the door except the dog, still barking. The men shuffled uncomfortably around the wraparound porch but eventually they found their way in through an unlocked window with a broken pane leading into the parlor. The house was chilly and desolate, trashed like a college dorm room after finals—clothes everywhere, bureau drawers pulled out, papers scattered because they don't matter anymore.

Finding a lamp and lighting it, the men crept farther into the house, to Elsie and Sarah's room in the "L" of the house on the first floor. They found the mother and daughter in beds soaked in blood, covers piled over their heads.

* * *

Brookfield, Massachusetts, was and is a peaceful town. At the start of 1898, the *Boston Globe* wrote, "it was 30 years since anything resembling a murder [had] last occurred within the borders of the town," the most recent being the killing of a man named Deveger near the railroad tracks a little while after the Civil War.

Francis Newton wasn't originally from Brookfield. Born in New Braintree around 1853, he came to Brookfield as a young man, first keeping up a milk route and later running a bakery in Hartford, Connecticut, fifty miles to the south. At some point he married his wife, Sarah, and around 1888 they adopted a baby from Sweden. They named her Ethel and called her Elsie. They lived in Hartford while Newton ran the West Side bakery.

In 1896 the family had moved into a dilapidated and isolated home on a back road between Brookfield and Sturbridge. It was called the Sturbridge Road by locals, although we should note that this is not the Sturbridge Road that you will know if you live in that area now, the road that runs from Sturbridge down into Connecticut. Though Francis was middle-aged by the time he bought the farm, he worked hard on improving the barn and house until it was "a very fair farm."

Now the powerfully built Newton lay in his bed, his head bashed beyond recognition. His body remained in his nightclothes with blankets piled to tightly cover his body and face. He was struck four times over the left temple, driving the steel into his brain each time, and once in the cheek. The wall behind him and the lamp on his bedside table were marked with dried blood. There were no signs of struggle, indicating that Newton had been asleep when attacked. His drawers were rifled through, as was his pocketbook, "the lining of which had been pulled out by the nervous fingers of the man who was in such a hurry to possess himself of the contents," as the *Globe* noted.

Downstairs his wife and daughter's heads were in a similar state, hit five times over the right temple; the medical examiner judged from the blood spattered on the head of the bed and the walls that the attack had been more vigorous than that against the man of the house. The *Globe* said that the murderer surely must be "freely sprinkled" with blood, as if he hadn't thought to wash his face in the forty-eight hours between the murders and their discovery. Sarah and Elsie's nightgowns were thrown up and their bodies had been attacked as well as their faces. They were not robbed; their trinkets were untouched, and a gold watch worn by Mrs. Newton remained on her wrist. Nor was there evidence of rape; in the euphemistic parlance of the day, the *Globe* said they "had not been outraged," as if being bludgeoned beyond recognition was not an outrage.

Death was instantaneous for all victims; the medical examiner, identified as "Baker," believed that they had not even woken up before death and stated that "he was positive that none of the wounds were inflicted with the edge of the blade of the ax" (*Boston Globe*, January 11, 1898). The following Friday, after five consecutive days of heavy daily coverage, the *Globe* would conclude, probably erroneously, that the family had been drugged. An empty bottle of laudanum was found in the spare room and a local veterinarian had twice treated Newton's horses for laudanum poisoning. The axe lay on the floor of the bedroom where the women had been killed, next to Elsie's bed.

The murderer had exited the house by crawling out a window, leaving the doors locked from the inside. A ten-gallon can of kerosene was open, and kerosene soaked a pile of wood. The murderer had flung a kerosene lamp, lighted, at the woodpile, but the arson attempt had failed; after "charring a few sticks the flame went out, as it did not catch on the oil which was flowing from the can and had not enough strength to ignite the hard oak wood."

Police initially assumed that the motive for the murder was robbery, the conventional first explanation. The top headline in the *Globe*'s first account of the event was KILLED FOR $40. It was not, in fact, a robbery, although the murderer had taken a few dollars. Newton did not keep large amounts of money on his person and had not withdrawn any recently from the bank. Newton's gold watch was still on its chain, in its vest, hung neatly over a chair in his desecrated bedroom.

Missing from the scene was the farmhand, Paul Mueller. He was last seen the night of the murder, heading toward the nearest train.

\* \* \*

North of Sturbridge, Massachusetts, there is a body of water which is now usually described as Quacumquasit Pond, but which in 1898 was referred to as Quacumquasit Lake. There was a resort at Quacumquasit Lake, with stables, boats, a picnic area, a dance hall (also described as a roadhouse), and a small hotel. In early summer, 1897, Paul Mueller stopped by the Point of Pines resort, penniless, looking for work. The man who ran the resort, Captain H. D. Hodgson, offered Mueller a place to stay in exchange for work. Mueller, who apparently had some pretty solid carpentry skills, did carpentry and repair work at the Point of Pines in exchange for room and board but was never paid money by Hodgson, who was operating the resort on a shoestring.

More remarkably, there was a horse with what was thought to be a broken leg. A horse with a broken leg was normally put down, in 1898 and often still today, because a broken leg pitches a horse into a painful death spiral. Mueller asked for an opportunity to save the horse, built a brace for the horse's leg, and saved the horse's life. This created something of a sensation around the neighborhood. Mueller said that he had learned how to do that in the German army.

Probably in October 1897, Mueller and Hodgson were hauling a load of wood when a dispute erupted between them. Mueller got out of the wagon and stormed away. This happened on the road in front of the Newton farmhouse, which was three to four miles from the Point of Pines resort. Mueller walked up the driveway to the Newton house on Sturbridge Road, and asked Francis Newton if he could work for him.

Newton hired Mueller, and Mueller later filed suit against Hodgson, claiming that he should have been paid for his work. Records of that lawsuit may still exist in some old box in the attic of a courthouse, but it is reported that Mueller collected nothing. Hodgson closed the Point of Pines, sold off his furniture, and went back to Gloucester to work on the sea—and, in an odd note, in mid-January, when the search for Paul Mueller was the biggest story in the Boston newspapers, one "Captain Hodgson of Gloucester" pops up on the front page of the *Boston Globe* in an unrelated story. His fishing schooner had lost a man at sea.

After the tragedy at the Newton farm an unidentified newspaper editorialist blamed the victims for allowing the murderer to move into their house:

The moral of this crime, like that of the murders of Mehitable White at Braintree, Mary Emerson at West Dedham and Bertha

Manchester at Fall River, is that it is extremely unsafe for lonely farmers to employ any man who happens along without any knowledge of his character.

—*Boston Globe*, January 11, 1898

Newton probably had heard about Mueller saving the horse. Certainly Mueller gave off what we would now call bad vibes, but Newton needed help on the farm, and Mueller was good help at a good price. Mueller slept in a room just off Newton's own bedroom, a room so close it was "but a step from one to the other." The only way in to Mueller's room was through Francis Newton's. This would make Mr. Newton the first to die that January night.

Multiple sources stated to the newspapers that Newton was happy with Mueller's work. Newton's brother-in-law described Mueller to the *Globe* as "efficient and agreeable," although he said that Mueller could be "cranky." By all accounts, Mueller was a hardworking farmhand and an efficient woodchopper. Farmers used horse-drawn sleds to haul loads in the winter. Applying his carpentry skills, Mueller built a sled for Newton. The *Boston Globe* on January 13 reported that Mueller "was never known to be drunk, although he would take an occasional glass of liquor or beer." The same article also notes specifically that Mueller *was* left-handed; not speculation, not theory: he *was* left-handed.

The *Globe* noted that Newton had a reputation as a strict man, "in the habit of speaking sharply to his hired men and making them toe the mark. He had been heard to do so to Mueller and to tell him if he did not do the work better he would have to get out." Newton was a hard man, and Mueller, too, was decidedly not interested in getting people to like him. He was often described as "sullen." But sometimes two sour personalities can complement one another.

Mueller may have been cheap labor because he did not look or sound quite right. He was notably Other. He was very short and stout (somewhere between five four and five five, weighing about 155 pounds), with long greasy dark hair, a poorly trimmed mustache and occasional beard. He was believed to be thirty-five years old in 1898. His English was recently acquired and sometimes hard to understand. The *Boston Globe* on January 14 states explicitly that he was German, although other sources speculate that he could have been Polish or Bulgarian. His most striking feature was tiny, widely spaced teeth; later on numerous men would be arrested for having tiny, widely spaced teeth and a German accent. His feet were size six. He had a scar running from his wrist to his little finger and another above his right eye, and he walked with a "sailor's gait." He was an "experienced tramp" who dressed like he didn't have a place to sleep even when he did. He didn't look like the rest of Brookfield's community of affluent farmers.

Now Mueller had disappeared. At 11:30 that Friday, a neighbor named Welch walked by the darkened house, thinking nothing of it except that it was almost midnight so they were probably asleep. Less than a half hour later, several people saw Mueller walking away from the farm, in the direction of the Brookfield train depot. According to the January 11, 1898, *Portsmouth Herald*, William Eaton on his way home from a grange meeting saw Mueller about a mile from the farm, just before midnight. Fifteen minutes or so later, George Pike and Arthur Rice saw him walking quickly along what is described as the plank walk. They had both said, "Hello, Paul!" but he did not reply and did not look in their direction.

After that sighting, the account of Mueller's actions dissolves into a pool of uncertain identifications and a bizarre fixation on his clothing, so easy to discard and replace with his new fortune of $40. Some claimed that Mueller wasn't headed for the train that night, and relied on the kindness of strangers instead. An East Brookfield resident claimed that Mueller showed up at his house on Saturday night at 8:15, about twenty-one hours after the murders. A short dark man, drunk and hungry, asked for food and lodgings, saying, "I have got to get down east as quick as I can as they will murder me if I stay round here." He offered card tricks as compensation. No one else in East Brookfield remembered this man, and the police apparently ignored the report.

More probably Mueller went right to the train. The New York express on the Boston and Albany railroad left the West Brookfield depot at 1:29 that morning. It was six miles by road from the scene of the crime to the West Brookfield depot, but the distance could be cut by almost two miles by walking the railroad track from Brookfield to West Brookfield. Mueller walked quickly, covering four miles or more in an hour or so. In the first *Globe* report, the all-night ticket agent was sure that no one bought a ticket that night, and the yard watchman didn't recall anyone jumping on the train from the station side that night, either. Then in the late edition, they remembered a short, poorly dressed stranger who bought a ticket for Springfield, Massachusetts, at 1:05 a.m. that morning, and then quietly waited in the shadows for the train to come.

He paid for the ticket with a half dollar coin from 1836. Arthur Rice, one of the neighbors who discovered the bodies and saw Mueller—we imagine that Mr. Rice was all up in the police's face about this case—said the coin belonged to Newton, who had a coin collection that Rice had admired. The story of Newton's coin collection survived in newspaper accounts of the crime for years, and was mentioned as late as 1902 as one of the key facts establishing Mueller's guilt. It seems odd that a ticket agent would not at first remember selling a ticket at 1:05 a.m. to a shabbily dressed troll who paid for the ticket with an antique coin, but police relied on the ticket agent's revised memory and followed Mueller's trail to Springfield.

The brakeman on the Springfield express night train, Arthur Cooley, remembered a small stout "laboring" man with long dark hair acting shifty, first on the Springfield platform (presumably while buying another ticket) and then in the smoking cab. "He kept eyeing me, and everywhere I went about the car I could see that he was watching. When I entered the door back of him he looked around, and that made me eye him closely. He would lie down in the seat every few minutes and try to sleep, then he would start up, look about the cab for a few minutes, and then try it again." The man got off, or at least off the smoking car, in New Haven, Connecticut, but not before the brakeman noted his dress in some detail: "He wore dark clothes and his coat was a rusty color. He wore a light checked cap and had no bags."

Like the Brookfield ticket taker, New Haven ticket agent Harold Brotherton had a delayed realization about a man of Mueller's description in the wake of attention from *Globe* reporters. He, too, sold Mueller a ticket, at 4:00 a.m. on Saturday, about five hours after the murders. The ticket was again for a short distance, only to Bridgeport, Connecticut. Though Mueller disappeared onto the train immediately thereafter, the agent also noted Mueller's golf cap, of checked design, with a red thread.

A baggage handler named Tracey saw the short, capped man get off the smoking train at New Haven and did not see him get back on. The apparently fashionable and observant man said: "We see a good many men wearing those caps, but they are all students, and so I was somewhat surprised to see a man of his appearance with this style of cap." Brotherton seemed amused by the golf cap, calling it "singular" in contrast with his poor clothing. Tracey watched the man leave his area, and he did not return.

The *Globe* was convinced that Mueller would have visited a lunch counter; they devoted considerable column inches to speculating on Mueller's possible lunch counter activities. On January 11, the *Globe* reported that someone might have seen Mueller at a lunch counter in Palmer, maybe. Palmer was a small town halfway between Brookfield and Springfield. They were confident of no facts, and it's not apparent why they reported it, but then, this is still what happens when reporters run out of facts.

The *Globe*'s weird focus on the lunch counter reflects the clever function of Mueller's contrivance to change trains as often as possible. Since there were no security cameras or photographs of any kind to confirm his appearance, police had to rely on fuzzy eyewitness accounts, degraded by time and distraction. Mueller's frequent stops meant that no one saw or talked to him for very long. Each person who did notice him had a different perception of where he was going. Police tracking him had to chase those reports down, from station to station, two days behind a train, comparing and contrasting different accounts. Instead of clarifying, these reports did more to confuse than help the police, and Mueller's trail vanished near the coast in southern Connecticut. Mueller had received mail from a sister living in Paterson, New Jersey, and it was suspected that he might be headed to Paterson to seek shelter with his sister. From New Haven to Paterson is eighty-eight miles.

Running away is a skill. Like an athlete, the ones who are best at it make it look easy. His method seems simple, and it is. His method seems obvious, and it is. The Man from the Train makes it seem absurdly easy to evade capture, because he was good at it. The *Boston Globe* reported on February 13, 1898, that Brookfield authorities were losing hope about finding Mueller, and were planning to raise a $5,000 reward fund for his arrest. "This amount would set some professional detectives to work on the case," said the *Globe*, "for it would be sufficient to pay for the time spent if Mueller was caught." But Robert Pinkerton, interviewed on the subject, said that Mueller's trail was too cold, that the money would do no good, and that if Mueller was ever caught it would just be a matter of luck.

The *Boston Globe* (and other newspapers) explored the possibility that Mueller had done this before. In July 1897, a sixty-five-year-old widow named Hattie Woodward was found dead in her isolated farmhouse, her feet under a stove, her large and able body showing signs of a struggle. The culprit was thought to be another short dark foreign man named Joseph Borres, who had been hired at a neighboring farm for the previous two months and then promptly disappeared. The newspapers discussed the possibility that Borres and Mueller were one and the same. It seems clear to the authors that they were not.

It's not $5,000, but the Brookfield community raised a fund of $500 as a reward for Mueller's capture, and detectives tracked him north and south to Connecticut and New York. At one point they thought he took a boat from New York to Europe. Detective Tarbell, one of the lead investigators on the case, brought back from New Haven "a pair of trousers that were left by a man in that city" with stains on them that might or might not have been human blood. A worker at Point of Pines was unable to positively identify this random pair of pants as belonging to Mueller. The mysterious trousers were the last physical evidence connected with Mueller.

The most puzzling omission in the chase for Paul Mueller was the failure to make a drawing of him. There were dozens of people in Brookfield who knew what Paul Mueller looked like. While it was not Standard Operating Procedure for police in 1898 to make a drawing based on witness reports, it had certainly been done in many other cases. Wanted posters from the Wild West era routinely included a drawing of the suspect. It would seem that one would have been useful in this case. The *Boston Globe* printed line drawings of Arthur Rice, the last man to see Mueller on the road, and of Tarbell, the policeman in charge of the case, as well as many other items, such as a drawing of the kerosene can, but we located no published drawings of Mueller.

The story of Paul Mueller lived on in New England newspapers for several years. Gradually the newspapers began to conflate his story with that of others. They would refer to him as Mueller, Muller, or

Miller; the spelling of names was much less fixed in 1900 than it is now. Many people were marginally literate; they might spell their name one way one time, another way another time . . . what did it matter? Most of the people in this book had their names spelled different ways by different newspapers. New England newspapers began increasingly to bring into the Paul Mueller story reports about a man named Ed Gigner, Gignor, Gignon, or Gognon, who spent some time in Athol, New York, in the summer of 1896, and who once received a letter from a sister addressed to him as "Ed Miller." It seems obvious to us that Gigner, whoever the hell he was, was *not* Paul Mueller, and that talking about him just confused the issue and contributed to Mueller's eluding justice.

But the Mueller/Newton/Brookfield crime was not invisible or underreported. It was as widely reported in its day as the Villisca murders. Enough information exists that a short book could be written about the case. The New York newspapers published long stories about the Brookfield murders and the search for Paul Mueller. Reports of Mueller in one prison or another poured in across the country. In the first month after the event, seven different men, mostly transients, as close as Worcester and as far away as Nebraska, were arrested and held on suspicion of being Mueller. Another five were arrested in the year after. The mistaken arrests were made until 1905, with a total of sixteen or more men arrested for being short and poorly dressed in the presence of an officer who couldn't forget about the Newtons.

Chapter XXIX of this book was about the murders of the Stetka family near Sydney, Nova Scotia, in February 1906. In late February 1898, a man was arrested in rural Sydney, within fifteen miles of where the Stetkas would be murdered, after talking a lot about the crime in Brookfield. Somebody noticed that he answered the description of Paul Mueller: German, short, stout, long dark hair, and poorly trimmed facial hair.

The arrest of these ersatz Muellers always made the papers; their release did not always make it and apparently did not in this case. But while we assume that this man must have been cleared of suspicion of being Mueller, the fact that this happened so close to the place where the Stetkas would be murdered eight years later, in an isolated, thinly populated area hundreds of miles from anything else connected with this story, seems worthy of note.

But none of those sixteen men was Mueller. He fled successfully; no one ever recognized him as the farmhand who had killed his employer's family. Mueller was last seen headed for the train forevermore, and seven years after the crime happened, it disappeared almost entirely from record and memory, replaced by other victims and other towns.

# CHAPTER XLI

# Brookfield and Villisca

On the morning of January 7, 1898, Paul Mueller did not truly believe that he would murder Frank Newton and his family. In his two months of working on the Newton farm Mueller had grown to intensely hate Newton. Newton was a big, strong man who insulted him, ordered him around, and treated him without much respect, although Mueller knew that he worked hard and that he did good work. He hated Newton and he fantasized about hitting him in the head with an axe, yes, but he had fantasized about killing people for many years, all of his life, really, and he had never done it. He did not truly expect that this Friday would be any different.

Something happened that day, though, that would make it different. Friday is usually payday, and Newton was close with a dollar. It is possible that there was a disagreement about money. Perhaps Mueller broke something on the farm or in the house, and Newton was going to hold the cost of it out of his pay, or maybe Newton and Mueller had gone somewhere on an errand and had lunch, and Newton had paid for the lunch but now was going to charge Mueller for it.

One newspaper report says that Newton was last seen alive when he took a neighbor out to the barn to show him a new piece of equipment, and a different report, published on a different day, says that Mueller had built a sled for Newton. One wonders if the "new piece of equipment" that Newton was showing off was not, in fact, the sled that Mueller had built. It makes sense; Mueller had only been working there a few weeks, so the sled had to be almost new, and farmers do not rapidly accumulate new pieces of equipment, or their barns would fill up with junk. This is speculation, but perhaps Mueller had expected to be paid a bonus for building the sled.

Mueller had limited command of the English language, and almost certainly did not self-advocate effectively even in his native tongue, and probably he accepted whatever Newton said or did, but seethed about it. But it may not have been money; it may have been that Newton tried to get an extra hour's work out of Mueller too late in the day, or that there was a misunderstanding about how some task was to be performed, or it is possible that Mueller, living in the Newton house, may have happened to catch a glimpse of Elsie Newton in a naked or vulnerable position, and this fired his perverted lust. Something happened that day, and we will never know what it was, but the volcano in Paul Mueller's horrible heart could no longer be contained.

Mueller cut firewood every day, and probably carried firewood into the house every day. On this day, he snuck the axe into the house, up to his room, and hid it there under his bed. The die was cast. He was waiting for the family to fall asleep.

Paul Mueller was The Man from the Train, and Paul Mueller committed the murders in Villisca as well as many other crimes.

A serial murderer must, of course, have a first crime, and it is common for the first crime to reveal information about him that in later crimes he will conceal. A serial murderer's first crime is often poorly planned or completely unplanned. Often, in his first crime, he kills a person or persons with whom he has known ties, making him the obvious suspect in the crime.

Let us begin by noting the following characteristics of the Brookfield and Villisca crimes:

*Brookfield Murders*: All Doors Locked or Jammed Shut
    *Villisca*: All Doors Locked or Jammed Shut

*Brookfield Murders*: All Window Shades and Blinds completely
    closed
    *Villisca*: All Window Shades and Blinds completely
    closed

*Brookfield Murders*: Murder Weapon: Axe
    *Villisca*: Murder Weapon: Axe

*Brookfield Murders*: Blunt Side of Axe or Sharp: Blunt
    *Villisca*: Blunt Side of Axe or Sharp: Blunt

*Brookfield Murders*: Family attacked after they had gone to sleep
    *Villisca*: Family attacked after they had gone to sleep

*Brookfield Murders*: All victims hit repeatedly in the head, some
    in the body
    *Villisca*: All victims hit repeatedly in the head, one
    also in the body

*Brookfield Murders*: Victims' heads covered with cloth
    *Villisca*: Victims' heads covered with cloth

*Brookfield Murders*: 10-year-old girl (and mother) sexually exposed
    in death
    *Villisca*: 12-year-old girl sexually exposed in death

*Brookfield Murders*: Axe left on the floor next to little girl's bed
*Villisca*: Axe left on the floor next to little girl's bed

*Brookfield Murders*: Jewelry and valuables left in plain sight; some coins stolen
*Villisca*: Jewelry and other valuables left in plain sight, nothing stolen

*Brookfield Murders*: Paul Mueller was left-handed
*Villisca*: Investigators believed that the murderer was left-handed. The fact that Lyn Kelly was left-handed was used against him when he was put on trial for the Villisca murders.

In addition to these eleven points, many other elements tie Paul Mueller to the Villisca murders or to the series of murders. The articles written about Paul Mueller at the time of the Brookfield murders specifically note that he would travel around on trains, as a tramp, but that after doing this for a while he would settle down in one location and work—as it seems obvious that The Man from the Train must also have done.

The articles written about Mueller specifically note that he was an efficient woodchopper, and that he had many other job skills. Two articles that we found say that Mueller had worked as a woodcutter.

The articles written about Mueller specifically note that he was a competent person and a competent worker, as The Man from the Train had to have been.

It is generally believed that the Villisca murderer was very short. This is generally believed to be true because the upstairs ceiling in the Moore house was not very high. When the murderer swung the axe over his head, he just grazed the ceiling, whereas if he had been of average height or taller, the axe would have hit the ceiling when he swung it over his head.

Paul Mueller was very short.

Paul Mueller attempted unsuccessfully to set the Newtons' house on fire, and this was not done in Villisca, but we know why that was. The Newtons' house was rural. It would take time for neighbors to respond to a fire. The Moore house was in a small city, and people would have responded immediately to a fire, thus endangering the criminal's ability to make a clean getaway.

Other than that and the body count, there is no significant difference between the Brookfield and Villisca murder scenes.

Paul Mueller had size six feet, very small feet. The first time that two murders in this series were linked by investigators was when private detectives noted the similarity of the crime scenes in Ardenwald, Oregon (near Portland), and Rainier, Washington. Among the things the detectives noticed was that the shoe prints in blood at the two scenes appeared to be the same size. They were size six.

When the Allen family was murdered in Maine in 1901 there were shoe prints in the mud. They were size six.

When the Casaways were murdered in San Antonio in 1911, there were shoe prints found outside the house. The reports do not tell us what the size of these prints was, but a man was arrested because (a) he had had a fight some years earlier with Louis Casaway, and (b) he was of the right size to have left the shoe prints. This suggests, not necessarily that the shoe prints were small, but that they were of an unusual size for a man's foot.

Authorities investigating the Brookfield murders believed that the man of the house, Francis Newton, was the first to die. The Man from the Train almost always killed the man of the house first.

Criminal profiler Robert Ressler, interviewed for *Villisca: Living with a Mystery*, speculates that the murderer there was over thirty-five years old, because he was very organized and very much in control of the crime scene. Although his exact age is unknown, Paul Mueller would have been near fifty by that time.

After murdering the Newtons, Paul Mueller crawled out a window to leave the house. This was how The Man from the Train most often entered and left the houses he attacked.

Of course, on a certain level it is not an answer to say that The Man from the Train was Paul Mueller, because we know so little about this Paul Mueller. We know much more about Lyn Kelly or Frank Jones than we do about Paul Mueller; hell, we know more about Hez Rasco and James Linkous and Nease Gillespie than we do about Paul Mueller. We don't know where he was born or where he was educated or where he died. The name "Paul Mueller" is too common to be easily researched. Research for articles on him is complicated because there was an optometrist in San Antonio named Paul Mueller who advertised heavily in Texas, yielding hundreds of "bad hits" on the name. Mueller was not born in the United States, had probably only been in the United States for a few years before the murders, and presumably stopped using the name "Paul Mueller" once he had ruined that name. He's hard to get background information about—not that someone could not do that, if he or she had the right research skills, but it would not be easy.

After Mueller murdered the Newton family he was both thrilled and horrified by what he had done. He was a careful man, a cautious man, and he had put himself in great danger. More than that, I believe that Paul Mueller, up until that day, had tried to live by the rules. He wasn't a thief; he wasn't lazy. He was a poor man who had no advantages in life, but he had tried to do the things a young man is told to do: get out and see the world, yes, but work hard and develop your job skills. He had hoped, somehow, to find where it was that he belonged, and who it was that he belonged to.

But playing by the rules had never worked for Paul Mueller. He was an ugly little man with no social skills. He dressed badly, had bad teeth, and he did not smile. People did not like him. They didn't give him any breaks. They didn't give him any respect. Affection? What was that? Who would ever love him, or kiss him, or hug him? Acceptance was a ship that was disappearing beneath the horizon.

And so, the hatred grew. Resentment. Loneliness. Anger. Lust. He was a repressed man; following the rules was repression, until the point was reached at which he could be repressed no more.

Mueller was not a smiling, deferential, Caspar Milquetoast of a man in his outward aspect. He was a man who showed a lot of anger. The *Boston Globe* on January 13 said that "it was known that Muller was allowed to do pretty much as he wanted to while at the Point of Pines on Quacumquasit Lake, as his employer, Capt Hodgson, was afraid of his treacherous and revengeful temper." Newton's brother-in-law described him as "cranky," which is a little bit like describing John D. Rockefeller as "affluent." One sentence from a *Globe* article that I can't get out of my head says that among the duties Mueller was assigned at the Point of Pines was to act as a bouncer at the dance hall and the hotel dining room. I was surprised, first, to learn that the word *bouncer* was used in 1898, but more particularly, bouncers are almost always big, strong men. Bouncers are guys you don't mess with. I've never seen a five-foot-four-inch bouncer. Certainly this reflects the fact that Hodgson, strapped for cash, was stretching his employees to cover roles that were not natural to them, but it also tells us something about Paul Mueller: that the chip on his shoulder was not difficult for others to notice.

Most probably, Paul Mueller had no sexual experience before the murders began, other than masturbation. He was a disgusting-looking little man, not clean, and he was living in a sexually repressive time. He had not developed normally from a sexual standpoint. He was fixated on young girls, but not completely; all sex was an abstraction to him, and it is easy for an abstraction to change shape.

That night in the lamp-lit house, when he had possession of the bodies of Sarah and Elsie Newton and there was blood all over them but they were *his*, was the most exciting moment of his life. Although he was quite old for his sexual appetites to be formed, I believe that his sexuality took shape on that terrible night, and when he relived the event later in his mind. Blood was perfume to him.

When he fled that night he put on a golf cap, a brightly colored, checked hat. It was a fashion among college kids. Perhaps he did that because he had figured out that the hat would distract people, that all they would remember of his appearance was that silly-looking hat, so that when he took the hat off he would be invisible. Perhaps, but I prefer a different explanation. I see the hat as emblematic of his naïveté and of his lack of an accurate self-image. It is difficult for a man to *accept* that he is a sexual zero. A desperate man will cling to anything that gives him the illusion that he has something. Mueller didn't see or understand the difference between him wearing a golf hat, and a college kid wearing a golf hat. He had not come to terms with who he was, what his place in life was, and he had not come to terms with that because the terms that were being dictated to him were so harsh. You're a nothing. You're a nobody. You're a loser. He just couldn't deal with it anymore.

He was appalled by what he had done, but at the same time it was the thrill of his life. He derived great satisfaction from having done it. It was the one bright secret in his dreadful little closet.

We cannot be certain that Mueller did not murder the Van Lieu family in New Jersey in 1900, but I am going to assume that he did not. I will note that Mueller had a sister living in Paterson, New Jersey, about seventy-five miles from the scene of the Van Lieu murders, that he was last seen near there and heading in that direction, and that after his disappearance police believed that he might try to seek shelter with that sister.

In either case, after the Newtons, Paul Mueller did not murder anyone for almost three years. If Mueller had been comfortable immediately with what he had done there would have been another murder sixty days later, but there wasn't. He still fantasized about killing people, as he always had, but didn't follow through on it for more than two years.

And then one summer day he was walking down a lonely road in Maine, hot and tired, and he knocked on the door of the house of Wesley Allen, asking for a drink of water. What was that, a drink of water—but Allen emerged from the house in a bad temper and yelled at him to get his lazy butt on down the road.

Wesley Allen was about the same age and about the same size as Francis Newton, both big men about fifty years of age, and the Allen house sat near the road in a manner similar to the Newtons' house. Mueller caught a glimpse of Carrie Allen. Father, mother, daughter: it was the same setup as the Newton house! The beast inside him exploded once again. The second time was easier than the first, and after the second time that was who he was.

Paul Mueller was The Man from the Train. I am not here to argue with you, and you can believe what you want to believe. I believe that Paul Mueller was The Man from the Train.

# CHAPTER XLII

# Where the Evening Is
# Spread Out Against the Sky

The people who lived in small towns a hundred years ago lived lives every bit as rich and varied as your life or my life. Everything meaningful that has ever happened in your life happened just as often to people in small towns a hundred years ago as it does to people in New York or LA in the twenty-first century. People who lived in small towns a hundred years ago fell in love, fell out of love, got married, got divorced, and had affairs inside and outside of marriage. They got jobs, got promoted, and got fired. They started their own businesses, sometimes got rich, more often went bankrupt or just gave it up and closed the doors.

They formed lifetime friendships; they fell into bitter rivalries with people they could not avoid. They joined groups of people who had interests like their own. They played sports; they got fat, got determined to get back into shape, sometimes succeeded and more often failed. They had children and raised their children. They suffered through their children's failings, and sometimes those were terrible failings. They took vacations; they traveled far from home and brought back souvenirs. They bought a new house or, down on their luck, moved into a dumpy house and hoped to get into someplace better.

They rooted for faraway sports teams. They buried their parents and buried their brothers and sisters and sometimes buried their children. They got cancer and had heart attacks and contracted diseases that they had never heard of. Most of them were honest people, but there were thieves among them and thugs and con men. They bought new things, new toys, new inventions, and they were as excited by these new things as you are by yours. They suffered through fires, floods, and other natural disasters. They drank, and some of them became alcoholics, and some of them became drug addicts.

Amusements? I lived in a town of three hundred people in the 1950s. If we had wanted to, we could have gone to some type of organized event 365 days a year—football games, or basketball, or baseball, church, church picnics, church pageants, school plays, school programs, political rallies, parades, band concerts, VFW meetings, Knights of Columbus events, holiday celebrations, fund-raisers, community meetings, store openings, private parties, public parties. On average, these events were exactly as interesting as the events that you go to now.

If you read about a crime in a small town, you will encounter frequently the comment that these people lived in the kind of quiet place where nothing very interesting ever happened. This is a despicable thing to say. It is a form of bigotry directed at the past, and bigotry directed at people who live in small towns—and worse yet, it's ignorant. Pardon my French, but it's an ignorant asshole comment, and if you ever say anything like that, you are revealing yourself to be an ignorant asshole.

This book is almost entirely about people who lived in small towns a hundred years ago—as much about how they died as about how they lived, but the flash of death illuminates the lives that the victims had lived. The Man from the Train murdered these people, placing no value on their lives. But when you say that they lived lives in which nothing very interesting ever happened, you are also devaluing their lives.

Small-town people are different from city people in some ways, and people a hundred years ago were different from twenty-first-century urban people in some ways; I'm not saying that those people were exactly like us. In many ways our lives are better than theirs were; in many ways their lives were better than ours are. I'm not saying that everything was the same; I am saying that it is ignorant to suggest that they lived boring lives in which nothing ever happened.

\*     \*     \*

At this point there are three questions that we need to address before we go our separate ways. Those three are:

1. What could have been done to stop him?
2. How many people did he kill? and
3. What happened to him?

We don't absolutely *know* the answers to any of those questions, but we have thought about them a lot more than you have or will, so we'll share our thoughts with you; take them for whatever you think they're worth.

Four things needed to be done, to give authorities some chance to catch the roving axe murderer of 1911 and 1912, Paul Mueller. It is no help to say that they should have called state police forces or the federal government; the state police forces did not exist at the time in most of these states, and the federal government regarded crime as a local problem. That's saying that they should have invented the future.

The first thing that needed to be done was: stop denying that this was happening. Take off the blinders. Let go of the irrational skepticism.

In Houston Heights, Texas, in 1910, the county sheriff told the newspapers a few days after the murders of the Schultz family that the crime had probably been committed by a madman from the railroad that ran right by the house, and that he had probably just got back on the train and left town. Having said that, he then spent three years trying to prosecute an obviously innocent young man who was involved with the woman who had been killed.

In this book we have seen this several times—that the police or prosecutors would *say* that they thought the crime was committed by a person just passing through town, but wouldn't follow through on that. All of the real detectives who investigated the murders in Villisca said at one time or another that the crime had to be committed by persons just passing through town. But if the crime was committed by a local person, they could arrest him and prosecute him. If it was committed by a person just passing through town, they were helpless; they couldn't do anything. Because they desperately wanted to solve the crime, they bought into the theory that it had to be a local person.

In Georgia and South Carolina in 1904, authorities could have realized that the Hodges and Hughes family murders had to be related. Had they not committed themselves prematurely to the silly notion that the crimes were committed by a gang of black assassins known as the "Before Day Club," they would have been the first people to realize what was happening. They probably wouldn't have found Paul Mueller, but perhaps they could have prevented the lynching of innocent men.

When one family was murdered just west of Bluefield, West Virginia, in 1909, and another family just north of Bluefield six weeks later, officials could have seen that the Meadows and Hood family murders had to be connected. Unfortunately, private detectives had "solved" the Meadows murders by hanging the crime around the neck of Howard Little. In their minds, this severed the two crime scenes; they couldn't be connected, because Howard Little was in jail when the Hood family was killed.

The first thing that needed to be done was: open your eyes and see what is happening. Don't make up reasons why this can't be happening; it is happening.

The second thing that needed to be done was to coordinate the bits and pieces of information from many different crime scenes, rather than investigating each crime as if it had occurred in isolation. In researching this book, we found an astonishing number of times when suspicious persons were spotted near the crime scene before the crime occurred—but no description of that person, however vague, was ever published.

Detectives in Ardenwald, Oregon, and Rainier, Washington, had shoe prints and possibly fingerprints in blood; detectives in Colorado Springs had fingerprints or partial prints in ink from a spilled ink jar. A little girl in Paola, Kansas, woke up and found a man in her room, and lived to tell about it.

As much as we can tell, no effort was ever made to bring these bits and pieces of information together. I am not saying that this *would* have solved the crimes and ended the murders; probably it wouldn't have. Probably the mysterious man seen in Villisca and the stranger seen near the Bernhardt farm in Kansas would have turned out to be two different people, neither of whom had anything to do with either crime, probably. I am not saying that this would have solved the crime by itself; I am saying that it should have been done as a logical step toward a solution, and that it probably would have been done if authorities had not irrationally insisted until late in the series that the crimes were not linked.

The third thing that should have been done is: use the railroad detectives. The irony of this case is that at the time that The Man from the Train was traveling around murdering people, the railroads had the best police forces in the country, other than perhaps the large private detective agencies with which they worked hand in glove. In 1910 every major railroad had its own police force. In 1910 a lot of policing was private. There were bank dicks (bank detectives), and hotel dicks, and detectives routinely hired in other lines of work—factories hired "company dicks" to keep the employees from stealing from the factory—but the best of these were the railroad dicks.

If you look at the list of people who were incarcerated in your state in 1910, what you will probably find is that many of them were not arrested by the sheriff of one county or another or by city police; they were arrested by the railroads. In my state, *most* of the people who were in the state prison in 1910 had actually been arrested by the railroad detectives, for crimes committed on the railroads.

This relationship had started with private detectives hired to fight union efforts back in the 1860s. Mine owners and railroads, in the 1860s, hired private detectives to infiltrate and destroy the unions—with some justification, in that a substantial number of people were being killed in union-related violence. I'm not on the railroads' side here, but I'm just saying. The railroads became the biggest customers of the Pinkertons, the Burns Agency, and the other private detective agencies. When those agencies expanded their businesses to offer other security services, they went to their biggest customers.

By 1910 the battles against the unions were far from over, but the railroads had large and sophisticated police operations, supported by the private detective agencies. The two main tasks of the railroad detectives were (1) to stop tramps and other people from jumping onto trains for free rides, and (2) to suppress criminal activity on the railroads.

In this era there were lunch counters in many thousands of little towns set up to feed people from the trains. The train would stop for twenty minutes in a small town; a person making a long train journey would hop off the train and grab a bite to eat, then get back on the train. It became a common crime for someone to steal the passengers' hand luggage when the passenger hopped off to get something to eat. There were criminals who made a living doing that—lots of them, at one point. The railroad dicks' job was to catch them and put them out of business.

I mentioned the 1962 movie *The Music Man*, set in Iowa in 1912, which centers on a con man who came to town, and in Villisca there were actual con men who came to town after the murders to try to take advantage of the situation. You may remember the movie *The Sting,* which is set in about the same era, or the movie *Paper Moon,* again set in the same era, again about con men.

There are con men in all eras, of course, but in this era there were a particular type of con men, guys who went from small town to small town, trying to take advantage of the gullible local yokels—and of customers on the trains. It was the railroad dicks' job to put the con men out of business. These were large, aggressive police operations, and they knew what they were doing.

The third thing that should have been done is that state authorities should have gone to the railroads and asked for their assistance in catching this murderer. A point was reached at which everybody knew there was going to be another murder like this in some small town sometime in the next few weeks. That point *should* have been reached years earlier, but eventually they got there. They should have been prepared, then, to jump on the next crime as soon as it happened.

What should have been done was to shut down the railroad system in a 150-mile circle around the crime and move the railroad dicks in in force to take inventory of what they had. Again, I am not saying that this *would* have solved the crime, and I know that you can't shut down the nation's transportation system for an extended period of time, but you can freeze a portion of it for a few hours while you gather information. You might find bloody clothes; you might find a tramp who has seen somebody hop on or hop off the train at 4:00 a.m. near the scene of the latest murder.

And the fourth thing they needed to do was: work with the hobo communities. There were hobo villages in this era, places where the trains slowed down and tramps jumped on and off the trains and formed little villages usually populated by eight people or less.

450

There are still villages like that today, of course, people living in boxes under bridges or camping out in wooded areas in the middle of cities; we don't think of it the same way, but it's the same thing.

The police, when they talked to these people at all, almost always went after them in a hostile manner—rousting the tramps, tearing up their stuff, driving them out of town. What needed to be done was to work *with* those communities—in the same way that police now, trying to find a serial murderer who is killing prostitutes, recognize the need to work with the prostitutes.

Who do you think might have had information about Paul Mueller while he was active? Nobody, because he didn't talk to anybody about what he was doing, but *if* anybody had any information about these crimes, if anybody had seen anything or heard anything suspicious, it would have been the hobos. It would have been the bums. That's who the police should have been talking to.

*     *     *

So how many people did Paul Mueller kill? We will never know for sure, of course, but we can divide the crimes into four buckets, a "100 percent bucket," a "70 percent group," a "40 percent group," and a "10 percent group." The number we are going to give you in a moment is kind of astonishing, but we swear to you that we have tried to be conservative in making this estimate. If we felt that the likelihood of the crime having been committed by Paul Mueller was 40 to 70 percent, we would place that in the "40 percent" bucket. If it was 10 percent to 40 percent, that would go in the 10 percent bucket.

There are fourteen crimes that we feel certain were committed by The Man from the Train. Those are, chronologically, the Newtons, the Lyerlys, the Hugheses, the Meadowses, Hoods, Schultzes, Casaways, Hills, Burnhams, Waynes, Dawsons, Showmans, Hudsons, and Moores (Villisca). About all of those cases there is a good deal of information available, and about all of those cases there is sufficient reason to conclude that these were committed by the same man. There were a total of fifty-nine persons murdered in those fourteen incidents.

In the 70 percent bucket are (generally) crimes about which we have a little bit less information or (sometimes) a little bit of contradictory information. There are seven crimes in this group, which are the Allens, Kellys (or Caffeys), Hodgeses, Linkouses, Ackermans, Cobles, and Pfanschmidts. These crimes we believe were committed by The Man from the Train, although we are less than certain. In these incidents a total of thirty persons were murdered.

In the 40 percent bucket are crimes that are more or less a toss-up; in some ways it looks like him, doesn't look like him . . . we don't know. In this group there are eight more crimes: the Van Lieu, Boylan, Christmas, Gerrell, Byers, Hardy, Bernhardt, and Hinterkaifeck murders. A total of twenty-seven persons perished in these crimes.

In the 10 percent bucket are another nine crimes: the Wise, Stetka, Hart, Edmondson, Zoos, Hubbell, Opelousas, Randall, and Warner families. In these nine crimes another thirty-seven lives were taken.

If we assume that The Man from the Train is responsible for 100 percent of the first group, 70 percent of the second group, etc., that produces an estimate of ninety-five murder victims. (There are also five to seven possibly related crimes, some not covered in this book, that we are going to completely ignore in this accounting.) This estimate, however, does not include those persons who were legally executed for crimes actually committed by Paul Mueller, or those who were murdered by lynch mobs. Four persons were legally executed for crimes that either were or might possibly have been committed by Paul Mueller (Bob Hensen, James Linkous, Howard Little, and Hez Rasco). In addition to those, at least seven persons were murdered by lynch mobs because they were believed to have committed crimes that they probably had not committed. Those seven were Paul Reed and Will Cato (Georgia, 1904), Nease Gillespie, John Gillespie, and

Jack Dillingham (North Carolina, 1906), and Curry Roberts and John Henry (Georgia, 1908). If we assign proportional responsibility for these deaths in the same way as for the murders themselves, that would increase our best estimate to 101 victims.

In addition to these 101, at least four other persons were convicted of murders probably committed by The Man from the Train and were held in prison for years, but were not executed; those four were Henry Lambert, John Knight, George Wilson, and Ray Pfanschmidt. Robert Clements in Alabama was convicted of a murder that could possibly be part of the series. In addition to these persons, many others were publicly accused of one of the crimes, most of whom were taken into custody and held for some time. It is impossible to know how many of these persons there were, but the number certainly would be over a hundred. About ten of these were brought to trial and were acquitted or had the prosecution dropped in the middle of the trial.

\*     \*     \*

The third question that I wanted to address in closing is: What happened to Paul Mueller after the Pfanschmidt murders in September 1912?

There are four apparent possibilities:

1. He died soon after that.
2. He was arrested for some other crime and sent to jail. He could have been caught breaking into someone's house and sent away, for example, without anyone realizing who he was.
3. He lived on but stopped killing people for some reason.
4. He went back to Europe and continued to murder people.

Any of those four is a consistent and logical continuation of his story; however, if you want to know what I *think*, I think he probably went back to Europe and continued to murder people.

Mueller's first murders, the Newton family, attracted substantial newspaper coverage, and probably the police came closer to catching Mueller than they ever realized they had. But after the Newtons, his next several crimes—his next ten or fifteen—attracted relatively little newspaper coverage, and there is no reason to believe that the police were ever within a hundred miles of catching him. But gradually, over the years, this had changed. By 1912 the public was very much aware that a crazy axe murderer was on the loose, and they had a pretty good general idea of where he was.

Paul Mueller was a smart man, and he had to see where this was heading. They were a hundred miles behind him, and then they were ten miles behind him, and now they're right behind him. Pretty soon now, they're going to be one step ahead of him, and then that's the end of the road for him. I think that he had to see that coming, so he got out.

If Mueller had been gradually slowing down, as a murderer, then I might believe that he just stopped killing people. But, in fact, he had been murdering families at a frantic pace in 1911 and 1912. Something sudden had to happen to put him out of business in this country.

The Pfanschmidt family was murdered in September, so he would have headed south soon after that, since he always went south in the winter. I think he got to New Orleans, probably, found work on a freighter heading to Europe, and went back to Europe.

If he did go back to Europe at that time, he would soon have found himself enveloped in World War I. Although Mueller had been in the German army twenty years earlier, I do not think that he would have rejoined the army during the war; in fact, I think that, if conscripted into the army, he would probably have gone AWOL at the first opportunity.

1. Mueller was in his fifties by that time, old enough to be excused from military service.

2. He was tremendously averse to personal risk.

3. He was exceptionally good at avoiding capture. If he went AWOL, once he was in the wind, they weren't going to find him.

And the chaos of wartime would have been perfect for him—as it was, for example, for Marcel Petiot, a French doctor and serial killer during World War II. People fighting the war didn't have the time to chase down criminals like they normally would have.

And then, there is Hinterkaifeck . . .

# CHAPTER XLIII

# Hinterkaifeck

The word *Hinterkaifeck* applies only to the scene of the murders; it has no other meaning. Kaifeck was a small village forty-five miles north of Munich, a flea speck, really, and Hinterkaifeck, meaning "behind Kaifeck," was a farm in the hills near Kaifeck.

Several months before the murders at Hinterkaifeck, the maid quit her job. The farm's descent into true strangeness started when the maid suddenly quit her job and wished to leave immediately. When asked why she had so suddenly decided to abruptly leave, Maria explained that she had been hearing strange voices and other noises in and around the house, as well as the sound of disembodied footsteps emanating from the attic. The terror stricken maid had become convinced that the house was haunted and wished to stay there not a moment longer. She was reportedly white faced and emaciated when she said her final goodbyes. After her departure, the Gruebers chalked it up to the poor woman being simply mentally disturbed.

OK, cut the crap. All that happened was that the maid quit, and then later, after the murders, she told reporters, "Oooh, I knewewew

456

there was something spookeee going on out there." They had a critter living in the attic; so what? It doesn't have a damned thing to do with the murders.

The murders at Hinterkaifeck are often described as the most notorious unsolved crime in the history of Germany. All famous crime stories come to be encrusted with mythology, but I've never run into a crime more encrusted with mythology than this one. There is no way to tell the story without Vili or Thor bursting in a side door to interrupt you.

Andreas Grueber was a nasty old bastard who lived on a prosperous farm with his wife, Cazilia, who was nine years older than he was, his daughter Viktoria, and his grandchildren, Cazilia and Josef. Josef was two years old. Viktoria, thirty-five, had been widowed by the Great War, and had been living with her father for several years before Josef was born. It was believed by the neighbors that Andreas was not only Josef's grandfather, but also his father.

Again, this is part of the mythology of the crime, but (a) nobody knows whether this is true, and (b) even if it is true, it almost certainly doesn't have anything to do with the murders. Grueber was a wife beater, and it is written everywhere that he had forbidden Viktoria from pursuing any other relationships after her husband had died.

In mid-March of 1922, Grueber found footprints in the snow, leading out of the woods behind his house and up to his door—but there were no footprints leading away from the house. Alarmed by this, Grueber searched the house, the grounds, and the outbuildings, but found nothing.

Now here, are we dealing with fact or mythology, and, if it is fact, is it relevant fact or irrelevant? We don't know. This is the essence of the problem: every family has twenty-five neighbors, more or less, and when there is an event that commands the attention of the nation there will be two or five immature, irresponsible, attention-seeking neighbors who will tell stories that will become a part of the narrative of the crime. Obviously it wasn't Grueber who told reporters about these mysterious footprints in the snow, so who was it? The footprints in the snow may have been real, but that may have happened two months earlier rather than two weeks, and may have been moved into the narrative by a neighbor who wanted to be part of the action.

In the days before the murders, Grueber told another neighbor—or did he?—about a series of mysterious events around the farm. The family heard noises in the attic but searched the attic and could find no explanation. The next morning they found a newspaper on their porch that no member of the family could explain. On March 30, 1922, "a set of keys to the house mysteriously disappeared and could not be found anywhere. In his search for the keys Andreas came upon the disturbing discovery of scratches on the lock to the toolshed, as if someone had tried to pick it."

OK, we've got a squirrel in the attic, we lost our house keys, and some drifter tried to break into the toolshed; it sounds like a normal week at my house. Whether there was anything out of the ordinary going on at the Gruebers' in the last week of their lives is debatable, but most probably not.

On Saturday, March 31, a new maid arrived at Hinterkaifeck. Maria Baumgartner, forty-four. On Sunday, April 1, Viktoria Grueber did not show up at church, which was unusual for her; she had a beautiful singing voice and was always in the choir. On Monday, nine-year-old Cazilia Grueber did not show up for school—nor on Tuesday, nor Wednesday. At some point neighbors . . .

The bodies, except for one, were all in the barn. They had been killed with a mattock, which is a type of pickaxe. They had all been hit in the heads, most of them decapitated or nearly decapitated. The body of Maria Baumgartner was found in the house, murdered in her sleep in the room she had just moved into.

The bodies had been stacked on top of one another in two or three stacks, and each stack had been covered with hay—but for the body of little Cazilia, who had apparently survived the first blow, and had pulled out some of her hair in her agony.

The murderer had apparently remained at the farm for some time after the crime, and here again we hit the mythology of the crime. Food had been taken from the kitchen and eaten, although how anybody knows that this was done by the criminal, rather than by the family, is beyond me. Smoke had been seen rising from the chimney days after the murders are believed to have been committed, and, most chillingly, the livestock had been cared for, and the dog had been let off his chain. Again, there are normal explanations for these events. One of the neighbors may have tended to the livestock as soon as the crimes were discovered, without the others being aware that he had done so, or the crime may have occurred a day later than people believe that it did, and Viktoria may have had some entirely unrelated reason for skipping church on Sunday morning.

The murders at Hinterkaifeck were never solved, although hundreds of people were questioned in connection with them, the last of those in 1986. The house and outbuildings on the farm were burned down in 1923, no one knows by whom. The crime was the subject of a German-language horror movie released in 2009.

Let's just look at the facts here: Paul Mueller was German—maybe Austrian—and it is entirely reasonable to suppose that he might have returned to Germany when the clock ran out on him in the United States. The use of the axe, hitting people in the heads, the stacking of bodies, covering the bodies with hay, and the special attention to the body of the nine-year-old girl are all elements familiar to us from The Man from the Train. To the best of my knowledge, the crime did occur within one mile of the railroad, although I am unable to locate the farm precisely.

It is ten years between Villisca and Hinterkaifeck; to include this crime in the series changes a fourteen-year odyssey into a twenty-four-year odyssey, and I know how I react, as a reader, when someone attempts to connect two famous crimes. Paul Mueller would have been close to sixty years old by 1922, and I will let you decide how improbable you think it is that he could have crossed the ocean and continued to murder people. Only don't indulge yourself in irrational skepticism. There's no real reason to believe that it's not him.

# Rachel's Acknowledgments

We could not have written this book without the research of Beth Klingensmith, who wrote a long and insightful academic paper on the topic at Emporia State University in 2006. Librarians are great, and several of them assisted in collecting and locating important information, including Dagmar Weschke at the Radford Public Library; Pati Threatt at the Frazar Memorial Library in Lake Charles, Louisiana; and Nolan Eller at the Northwestern State University of Louisiana. I also spoke to a couple of ladies at the Beckley public library who helped me figure out where to find the site of a crime. NewspaperArchive.com is super frustrating to work with, but it offered a very broad range of historical newspapers without which we would not have been able to complete this book. My father-in-law, Barry Graham, helpfully shared his perspective of Hurley geography, gleaned through years of work as an electrician with AEP. Many of my good friends offered advice and support and enthusiasm, including Carmen Sambuco, Allison McCarthy, Casey Bridgers, Emily Compton, Rachel Emery, Melissa Eastlake, and Miranda Dennis. I also want to give a shout-out to Hollins University, where I learned how to research. The team at Scribner, including Taylor Noel, Brant Rumble, John Glynn, Emily Greenwald, and Rick Horgan, were patient and helpful throughout the process. My husband, Jason, is terrific and took care of a lot of dog walks while I was wrapped up in research. Lastly, my parents, Bill and Susan, have never failed to give me as much support as possible. This was especially true in the writing of this book.

# Bill's Acknowledgments

My first acknowledgment, as always, is to the patience of my wife, Susan McCarthy, which, I should tell you, was worked especially thin by the fact that I wrote this book while I was supposed to be working on a different book, cowritten with her. I would also like to thank my first editor at Scribner, Brant Rumble, and my second editor, John Glynn, and my third editor, Rick Horgan; apparently I am hell on editors. Others at Simon and Schuster who were vital include Mia Crowley-Hald, who served as the production editor, and Taylor Noel, our publicist; thank you, Taylor. Nan Graham was supportive from above; thank you, Ms. Graham.

I would like to thank my daughter and coauthor, Rachel, whom I hired to do research on the book when I thought I might be missing a corner of the story, but who discovered that I was missing most of the story. Chuck Verrill and Liz Darhansoff have represented my interests in the publishing business for uninterrupted decades. Thirty-six years, I guess. I try in each book to acknowledge my debt to Dan Okrent, whose interest in my work helped my writing career get off the ground some forty years ago.

My personal friends Cal Karlin and Joe Posnanski read the book before it was published; thank you, Joe and Cal, and also Matthew

Namee. I would like to thank some very nice lady at the Kansas State Historical Society, who may have been Susan Forbes, Sara Keckleson or Sarah Garten. I am sorry, I have lost the slip of paper that had your name on it.

The primary indebtedness of this book is to those who have written about these crimes before, or who have written before about the places and times which are critical to the book. It is my belief that it is inadequate to acknowledge in a footnote those whose work you use, and that sources should be directly acknowledged in the text. I have tried to do this throughout this book. Literally thousands of people have written about one of these crimes or another, although (a) none of those people had a full view of the series of crimes, and (b) most of those people are now dead and would get little pleasure from being acknowledged by me. But a short summary of the living and more recently deceased: Frederick Brogdon, JD Chandler, Susan Cronk, Dr. Edgar Epperly, Donna Fricker, Alan G. Gauthreaux, Beth Klingensmith, Gary Krist, Beth Lane, John Nova Lomax, Roy Marshall, Dr. Charlton Moseley, Keven McQueen, Kelly and Tammy Rundle, Troy Taylor, Mike Vance and Susan Barringer Wells. Out of that list, I would especially like to thank Dr. Moseley for allowing me to quote from his work.

Thank you all, and my apologies to whomever I have forgotten to thank, and also to anyone whose name I have misspelled or whose well-earned title I have omitted.